A TIME FOR TEACHING

Exploration Series in Education

UNDER THE ADVISORY EDITORSHIP

OF *John Guy Fowlkes*

A Time for Teaching

Willard Abraham PROFESSOR OF
EDUCATION AND CHAIRMAN, DEPART-
MENT OF EDUCATIONAL SERVICES;
ARIZONA STATE UNIVERSITY, TEMPE

Harper & Row PUBLISHERS
NEW YORK, EVANSTON, AND LONDON

For Eddie, Andy, and Amy Rebecca

Contents

Editor's Introduction

This volume is a different kind of introduction to education from those traditionally presented for those who wish "to look at Education as a possible career." It opens, appropriately, with a sweeping view of schools and education—not only at home in the United States but also in Europe and Russia. A description of the structure of educational institutions is presented along with a telling commentary on what some people term the "basics" or "foundation fields": social studies and humanities, English, foreign languages, and science and mathematics. Teaching machines, programmed learning, educational television, and other newfangled important educational developments are reported. To no degree does Dr. Abraham accept the old saying that "Them who can't do anything else teach." Indeed, the imperative need for truly professional teachers including men as well as women teachers is emphasized. Some basic needs in the program of teacher education are stressed including the importance of continuing self-education, both by utilizing good reading material and taking advantage of varied opportunities open to "professional teachers."

Lest it be assumed that this volume is a saga of sweetness and brightness, attention is called to an extensive treatment of what the author terms "controversial issues," classified under the headings "Some of the Big Ones" and "Some of the Smaller Ones." Among the issues discussed are the education of Negro children, religion and the schools, teaching about communism, homework, reading, and report cards. Plainly the author is not cowardly.

Although a persuasive plea is made for effective educational opportunity the urgent need for recognizing and encouraging the gifted is reported. The concluding chapter, "A Time for Public Relations and Parents," is a significant and up-to-the-minute discussion.

Intriguing as the very topics treated made this work, it has another quality which makes it even more compelling in its power of attention getting. This book is not only well written but the author's style is spicy and at times will probably be not only stimulating but provoking to its readers.

A Time For Teaching is indeed an excellent introduction to education. Hence it is indeed valuable for those who are trying to answer the question, "Should I Teach?"

A Time For Teaching can also be profitably perused by those who have had considerable educational experience as a review of some of the critical elements in the development of educational programs and staffs essential for the welfare of the world.

JOHN GUY FOWLKES

Preface

Early in the spring of 1958, soon after the publication of *Common Sense About Gifted Children* by Harper & Row, they suggested that its author write an introductory text for future teachers. "Use the writing style of your gifted-child book," they said. "Write the book you would want to use . . . keep it readable . . . provocative." Now, almost six years later, that book has been completed.

An effort has been made to keep some educational objectives consistently in mind. During these six years of controversy, name-calling, and bitterness in what is generally considered a fairly placid profession, even a beginning student of the educational scene can recognize the difficulty of writing, revising, and adjusting one's ideas. After all, these were the years when education could not insulate itself from a world on the brink of final disaster, from a total environment dominated by what in the past might have seemed remote activities. The caves of Cuba and the battle for Katanga became backdrops for a first-grader learning to read, a sixth-grader studying latitude and longitude, and a high school graduate deciding on a career.

These were also the years of Rickover, Rafferty, and Conant; of federal aid, phonics, and integration; of team teaching, programmed instruction, and educational television. An era that gave lip service to the "knowledge explosion"; that began to *act* in meeting the challenge of the neglected gifted child; that started to recognize the tragedy of starvation, illiteracy, and infant mortality which permeated most of the earth's surface. That era could not possibly limit the preparation of new teachers to the *status quo*.

We need a different approach to our future teachers, a difference that must begin with their own early education, their selection for and attraction to this profession on which the future of all of us depends, and their preparation before and after they start to teach.

Something more critical than more classrooms and higher teachers' salaries is involved. It is, as the *Saturday Evening Post* said (October 20, 1962), "our capacity to produce the men who will be qualified to lead the free world."

Any one book that future teachers read during their first formal course in preparing for their profession cannot possibly do the entire job of informing, inspiring, and altering attitudes. But it can help to open the door a little bit; it can be part of the wedge. Thus, the major objective of this book has been based on several clear-cut hypotheses:

1. The main problems of the profession can be disclosed right at the outset of one's preparation for it. The excitement of educational controversies is a stimulant—not a deterrent—to attracting the additional strong teachers so sorely needed in our schools. Let them see that here there are people with ideas and vitality.

2. Our future teachers, in their second and third years of college, are generally more mature than many of us were at their age. They do, and *should,* resent having the provocative issues of their chosen life work hidden from them, disclosed in a censored form, or delayed until the graduate level. They deserve to know them early in their preparation and in a truthful, practical, and realistic manner. If some subjects seem beyond their depth, at least the first glimmer of understanding can come —and then a skillful college or university instructor can help them avoid forming rigid conclusions too early. Let's encourage these young people to face the realities of their profession and their world, and to stretch for concepts.

3. Selectivity is a personal business on the part of the author. A deliberate effort has therefore been made to leave to others the *details* related to the various educational subjects and to introduce—hit the highlights—without getting bogged down in the verbiage. Elements of curriculum and of historical, philosophical, and psychological foundations of education, which are more than adequately covered in many other publications, are not duplicated here. Emphasis is on developments and trends not readily available elsewhere, on basic understandings of which too many future (and present) teachers are deprived.

4. Worthwhile and exciting discussions and further reading can be provoked by a revelation of "off-beat" as well as of more conservative ideas, plentifully supplemented by footnote and bibliographical references. Such teaching aids can provide sources for additional study, can stimulate the student who is eager to approach this profession *as* a profession, and can help the college or university instructor round out the foundation he is trying to provide. Whether or not he agrees with the ideas as ex-

pressed in this book is not important; in fact, the less agreement the better from the point of view of young students whose interest and enthusiasm can be tickled by controversy.

5. Sometimes it is necessary to overstate an issue in order to provoke a reaction and action. An author has to be on guard against his biases, but he has to be just as careful *not* to eliminate them completely. Watered-down opinions in textbooks have frequently resulted in a lack of vitality and stimulation necessary for learning.

In the preparation of much of this manuscript the idea in the following statement by Myron Lieberman has been kept in mind: "Public education constitutes one of the important occupational frontiers in American life. This frontier requires pioneers, every bit as resourceful as those who conquered geographical frontiers in an earlier day. It is a frontier on which many roles are wandering in search of leaders who understand the problems and the potentialities of public education . . . a handful of such leaders can bring about a revolution in education, a revolution such that the practice of free public education in the United States will stand as its major contribution to the human community of the future."*

In closing, a word of sincere thanks is essential, for no manuscript is the product of just one individual and help and inspiration come from many directions.

I am grateful for the local typing and proofreading talent of Barbara Stickler, an undergraduate student whose competence and maturity were a constant delight; Bruce Ingmire, a graduate assistant whose potentialities for brilliance in college teaching are vividly apparent; Judy Wilson, Kathy Ralston, and Janet Henry for their friendly and understanding helpfulness.

I also wish to thank Frances Unger Meade, Director of Programming of Learning Incorporated, for sharing her creative thinking in the area of programmed instruction which became the basis for many of the ideas expressed here on that subject; Dean G. D. McGrath for his encouragement and support; and the inspiration, faith, and patience of those closest of all—Dale, Eddie, Andy, and Amy Rebecca.

WILLARD ABRAHAM

Tempe, Arizona
Spring, 1964

* Myron Lieberman, *The Future of Public Education*. Chicago, The University of Chicago Press, 1960, p. 288.

A TIME FOR TEACHING

Prologue

You have decided, at least tentatively, that teaching is the career for you. No decision will ever be more important—except, perhaps, whom you will marry. And there is even some question about the relative importance of that one! Theodor Reik, the psychiatrist, said that women love men but men love their work, so if you are a man, your job may have little competition for top spot.

Perhaps you have given the decision a great deal of thought, or some, or very little. Maybe you have talked to people, read some articles, or based your choice on the willowy foundation of "the thing to do," "it runs in the family," or "what else *can* I do?" Or teaching may have been your goal as far back as you can remember, based on a desire to do something of substance, of value.

The pages that follow will dig deep below superficial approaches. They will encourage you to come along on a journey that puts teaching where it belongs—in the middle of the stupendous events in the world around us, on the pedestal of importance rivaled by no other profession or occupation. No one must be more aware of the state of education than a future teacher. Walter Lippmann once said:

> We are entering upon an era which will test to the utmost the capacity of our democracy to cope with the gravest problems of modern times. . . . We are entering upon this difficult and dangerous period with what I believe we must call a growing deficit in the quantity and the quality of American education. . . . We have to make a breakthrough to a radically higher and broader conception of what is needed and of what can be done. Our educational effort today . . . is still in approximately the same position as was the military effort of this country before Pearl Harbor.[1]

[1] Walter Lippmann in The Fund for the Advancement of Education, *Decade of Experiment*, New York, The Fund, 1961, p. 10.

1

A fear of some people as they view the exciting growth of the past few years is that there are, and will be, no new frontiers. Are not Alaska and Hawaii now among the states? Have we not pierced the heavens and gained comparatively thorough insight into the secrets within the earth itself? Some of us are, no doubt, ready to join with Alexander, who wept because he felt that he had conquered the entire world and there was nothing left to conquer. Teachers, more than anyone, must view tomorrow with hope, but a hope based on realism, work, and desire. The children they teach are the major ingredients in that wave of the future, the link with what will happen when we are no longer around to view the product of our efforts. A new era demands a new kind of teacher, prepared in new ways, for children who have never been here before. Those children do not know yet that adults do things a certain way because they have always been done that way. It isn't our job to impose limitations in advance on a child's future, which to him extends far beyond that place on the horizon where sky and road meet. Despite the frequent "going-to-the-dogs" attitude of newspapers and magazines toward youth on the verge of maturity, thoughtful adults see far more hope. This hope is evident in pleas such as the following:

I think I may appeal confidently to American youth, because for a long time I have loved them as well as their great country. I should like to say to them: the world, which hungers not only for bread but for the freeing word of truth, the world needs you, it asks you to be as courageous in the field of intellect and reason as in the battles of land and sea and air.[2]

This need requires a generation whose eye is on the big problem of our era—the basic one of survival—rather than limited to what course to take, how large a class should be, and how to grade a student's paper. It is easy to get bogged down in details and lose the war on the broad tapestry of the world scene. "All that is necessary for the triumph of evil is that good men do nothing," wrote Edmund Burke, and maybe this includes the good men and women teachers who use much of their time in counting lunch money, drilling gifted children on what they already know, or meeting in endless committees, hour after month after year—for a lifetime of delay and waste.

[2] Jacques Maritain, *Education at the Crossroads*, New Haven, Yale University Press, 1943, p. 117.

Our current sharp curve in man's history has perhaps brought more change in the past 25 years than in the preceding 2000! Not only change, itself, but also the rate at which it is taking place is vital in our thinking. We are forced to question those who still feel that what once was still is and must be; these people are bound to be wrong. These times are, perhaps, the most turbulent ever; maybe we will have to wait for history to explain the details. Yet each of you considering entry into the teaching profession has a chance to take a key role in this period, to share in its skepticism, conflict, curiosity, and insecurity. The time needs its rightful leaders, persons who are willing and able to grab the wheel and head toward the future. This is what our children need; this is what they deserve, and what their parents must demand. We cannot limit our children to the atmosphere of our own childhood.

As we shall see, the field of education is setting at least one significant trend—a trend that a limited number of professional pioneers have attempted to establish since the early 1900s; it is experimenting, starting down new roads, and questioning the "tried and true." But so far the efforts toward change and newness are spotty, as you may well know on the basis of your own recent or current classroom frustrations. We experiment in little ways, with movable desks placed in neat rows "because the room looks too messed up otherwise." In big ways, we experiment with discussions about the values and problems of the United Nations, running for cover when a vitriolic lady questions our loyalty. We hear criticism of "modern" methods of instruction, and suddenly we realize that teaching techniques have not significantly changed in thousands of communities.

No one should occupy a place of greater prominence in taking a fresh look at the major world, national, and technical educational problems of today than the teacher. If this means a complete denial or rejection of the old public caricature of the teacher as a shy, withdrawn, and sheltered being, let that be so. If it means establishing a substitute image of daring, creativity, knowledge, vigor, pioneering, and determination, let us applaud the change and join the procession.

If education gets some of the blame for our shortcomings, it should also take credit for our strengths. Is the advertising man or education responsible for our brushing our teeth twice a day? Is the statesman or education the driving force behind any relaxation we may have in

international conflict? Is the scientist or education in the forefront
of our conquest of space? Is the medical research man or education
the reason why polio is on its way out? Stop for a moment to think
seriously about each of these achievements; could any of them have
been accomplished without a whole corps of teachers somewhere in
the background? Has anything of value in agriculture, health, labor
relations, politics, or peaceful living ever been accomplished without the teaching factor prominently in the picture?

But gain does not come easily. Occupying a continent, creating a
nation, building the biggest and strongest collective mechanization
the world has ever known, and bringing human dignity to the individual all demand tremendous effort. The way stations of war,
economic depression, and political accusation and name-calling have
been deeply ingrained in the fabric of our past years.

The teacher can contribute more to the strengths of the future
than anyone else by welcoming intelligence, stimulating ideas, and
discarding worry over an intellectual elite. This is a time for teachers who know their subject, their children, and themselves; a time
for attracting the best people to teach and sending the others to less
vital arenas for their income. It is time to say:

> You can come out now, all you
> Starry-eyed dreamers, intellectuals, bleeding hearts,
> Screwball untouchables. Put on clean shirts,
> Brush the unruly hair, and apply for work.
> The nation needs you, has granted amnesty
> For crimes of intelligence, so do not shirk
> The clarion call for brains. The practical men,
> The hard-headed realists concede your use,
> Are profferring support, and not abuse—
> So throw those shoulders back. You've stooped so long
> In the outdated posture of being wrong,
> You blink now in the light
> Of being, and being acknowledged to be,
> Right.[3]

Now, as we see today and tomorrow melt together, we must demand of all who want the best for our children, our country, and
our world, that which is true, necessary, and kind. And we who have
preceded you into teaching must question you directly:

[3] "The Cave Men," *The Reporter*, November 28, 1957, p. 5.

Are you willing to make clear-cut choices, sometimes avoid tradition, ask "Why?" and demand an answer? Are you willing to prepare for and exert leadership, to experiment for an era that has already shown its pattern to be one of swift and relentless change? Are you willing to sidestep the haggling over old objectives, goals, and other wordy philosophizing and dig into the job of educating *every* child with whom you have contact right up to the hilt of his capacity, perhaps establishing new goals?

Are you willing to discuss the fallacies George S. Counts saw in our society more than 30 years ago and decide whether they are fallacies today:

Man is born free.

The child is good by nature.

The child lives in a world of his own.

Education is a pure essence that remains unchanged, and must therefore be divorced from politics and live apart from social forces.

No bias shall be given in instruction.

Education develops a person who sees all sides of every issue.

Education is primarily intellectualistic in its processes and goals.

The school is an all-powerful educational agency.

Ignorance, not knowledge, is the way to wisdom; control and planning have no place.

The main responsibility of the school is to prepare the individual to adjust himself to social change.[4]

On the subject of change Counts' own bias came through clearly when he said that hesitation and complete neutrality are signs of weakness. This was true more than a generation ago; it is true today; and it certainly will be in the generation to come.

THE WORLD OF TOMORROW

Before World War II when we talked about television, most of us thought in terms of "some day." It was the same before automobiles, electric lights, and central plumbing. But now we know that miracles can take place and anticipated developments may become realities. Expectations must also be viewed realistically: Do they

[4] George S. Counts, *Dare the School Build a New Social Order?* New York, The John Day Company, Inc., 1932.

make any sense on the basis of what we already know? Mark Twain held projections up to a beautiful bit of ridicule when he wrote these words in *Life on the Mississippi:*

> In the space of one hundred and seventy-six years the Lower Mississippi has shortened itself two hundred and forty-two miles. That is an average of a trifle over one mile and a third per year. Therefore, any calm person, who is not blind or idiotic, can see that in the Old Oolitic Silurian Period, just a million years ago next November, the Lower Mississippi River was upward of one million three hundred thousand miles long, and stuck out over the Gulf of Mexico like a fishing-rod. And by the same token any person can see that seven hundred and forty-two years from now the Lower Mississippi will be only a mile and three-quarters long, and Cairo and New Orleans will have joined their streets together, and be plodding along under a single mayor and mutual board of aldermen. There is something fascinating about science. One gets such wholesale returns of conjecture out of such a tri-fling investment of fact.[5]

And yet, we must recognize a forecast or projection for what it is, realize the limitations of even a scientific approach, and still look at our immediate past and recognize that startling changes for the days and years ahead are totally in the realm of probability. If the developments listed below, for example, were to take place before next Saturday night, what changes would they bring in your life and your studies the following Monday morning? What meaning would they have for you as a new teacher next fall or the fall after? Would everything be the same in spite of these developments? Try them out, one by one, and seek implications for you as a college student and future teacher; for the children who would live with them; for their parents.

One continuous city, from 50 miles north of Boston to Norfolk, Virginia, 700 miles south, cutting across state boundaries and making them obsolete; or maybe even from Portland, Maine to Atlanta, Georgia, a metropolitan area of 50 million people

New sources of water which will bring 50 million people to the desert regions of the Southwest

A tripling in the number of retired persons over 65 years old; life spans

[5] Mark Twain, *Life on the Mississippi*, New York, Harper & Row, Publishers, Inc. (edition published by P. E. Collier and Son Co., 1917), p. 156.

of 80 years common, with some extending up to 125 or 150 years; dozens
of years of leisure for our working force

Superliners for travel to Europe carrying 6000 passengers and charging
each only $50

An earth satellite which by means of electronics will receive and deliver a
letter to any part of the world in a matter of seconds

Projection of thoughts electronically, making speech less necessary

A work week of 24 hours, perhaps requiring missionaries from other countries to teach us how to use leisure with satisfaction

Suburban areas stretching out almost endlessly, shapelessly, and without
plan or design, with the probability of becoming our slums of tomorrow

The death rate from natural causes, between the ages of 1 month and 40
years, approaching zero

A vastly expanding population and a greatly reduced number of unskilled
jobs

Industries employing millions making products that do not exist today

Automated production lines and office procedures, requiring less manpower;
better pay and working conditions; an unwritten law in business and
industry that in order to survive commercially we "automate or die"

New terminology that will become everyday language: *thermoelectric power*
as a source of electricity; *solar energy* as generating power for our homes,
stores, and offices; *ultrasonic sound waves* for many purposes, including
cleaning our clothes

Such developments, and items you could add from the newspapers
and current magazines, mean that tomorrow demands changes in the
people who teach, the teaching they do, and the total purpose, complexion, and content of our schools. In adjusting to this world of
tomorrow, we will expect much of our teachers; we need every new
idea we can get. Somehow the thought arises that maybe persons
without ideas should head in directions where unimaginative people
can be happy and productive. The classroom can no longer be that
kind of place.

We need conservation and encouragement of intelligence wherever
it is being throttled or overlooked. We need a breakdown of the
educational lock step whenever intelligence is not respected. We need
a clear recognition that intelligence is the basic commodity that has
led us to the threshold of this world of tomorrow and to the heights
of the present. And we certainly must recognize immediately that
cosmic survival depends on the fullest development of intelligence.

Respect for unorthodox thoughts must be elevated to top priority in an era where commonness and mediocrity threaten our total existence. It is difficult to be patient with those who want to take the slow road of indifference. Education is already overloaded with pleasant but ineffectual workers, including teachers and administrators. We need the kind of person who is eager to share the excitement expressed in the following statement:

> No other age in history has had the same potential. About no earlier period in history could it be said that the earth could be made sufficient for the needs of all its people. The conquest of disease and poverty is clearly within reach. Hunger and thirst can be made technologically obsolete; the control of solar energy for utilizing photosynthesis is a specific and attainable prospect. Man has the potential sources of energy that can give him time to fulfill himself and develop his creative resources on a scale and with an intensity that have never before been possible.[6]

SOME CURRENT BASIC ISSUES

International

Absorbed as each of us is with personal crises, we may lose perspective toward problems around us. Perhaps we ignore them because they are of such tremendous proportions, almost incomprehensible in their immensity. Or else our own little world is so selfishly satisfying that we want to restrict the scope of our concern. Or we may just not know that there is anything else. But teachers cannot restrict their thoughts and activities to the pleasure of their own company. They are forced to be aware of the world outside and to lead their children into it with understanding, sensitivity, and a basic concern for the problems of others. Such concern is far from being entirely unselfish for, as John Donne wrote, "No man is an island, entire of itself; every man is a piece of the continent, a part of the main." Albert Schweitzer put us in the picture by admonishing us that "we must all carry our share of the misery which lies upon the world." And Theodore Brameld recently wrote:

[6] Norman Cousins, *In Place of Folly*, New York, Harper & Row, Publishers, Inc., 1961, pp. 195–196.

In the depression years of the 1930s America was chiefly absorbed in its internal problems of poverty, unemployment, and insecurity; in the years we are now experiencing the indignation and vision of the "social frontier" educators need to be recaptured but also redirected—redirected not so much toward ourselves any longer as toward the desperate plight, growing power, and emerging goals of the underdeveloped areas of the world, inhabited by the bulk of the world's population.[7]

We need help in seeing that the smallness of our share of the eons of time, although significant to each of us, fits into a broad pattern of which we may not be aware. And if with our relative maturity and years, we fail to see our setting accurately, how can we expect more of children? It is difficult for our young people to understand extreme deprivation when their own lives never touch it. An environment of abundance is hardly an appropriate viewing point for accepting the world's squalor, sickness, and struggle for food, a place to sleep, and warmth of a minimal kind. We are a very small island in this morass of restlessness and misery. Being a citizen of a nation is vital, of course; but being a citizen of all mankind is important in helping us perpetuate the luxury of our own particular niche.

The freedom explosion in dozens of countries and among millions of people since World War II had a good reason for taking place: At least 50 percent of the people of the world are in a situation of extreme poverty and can see no way out. They eat far less than the minimum needed for sustenance, live short lives, and bury (or dispose of) babies under a year old by the thousands. The high diet standard of the United States is shared by only 9 percent of the world's population. Elsewhere, disease is as constant as the sun's rising and setting and the basic rudiments of sanitation and housing are completely unknown. At least two-fifths of the world's people are illiterate.

Those who are well fed may try to guard their possessions jealously, but they can do so securely only if a greater majority gets at least a little of the better things. The underprivileged provoke tensions because they know that at exactly the same time that hopelessness, violence, and starvation are their own constant companions, somewhere parents assume that their children will live to adulthood,

[7] Theodore Brameld, *Education for the Emerging Age,* New York, Harper & Row, Publishers, Inc., 1961, pp. 14–15.

and hope, peace, and a full stomach are taken for granted. If we were in their position, would we be any less ready to shift our restlessness into active revolt against the ties that were binding us and our children? Would we be concerned with how soon we have color television—or would our question more probably be, "How can I get a handful of food for my child so his stomach doesn't continue to swell and bloat because of malnutrition?"

Can we dismiss the subject with the naïve, Pollyanna approach that has so antagonized the deprived multitudes, the attitude exemplified by comments like, "They enjoy it that way"; "Where there's a will there's a way"; "We did it, so can they"; "They can improve things if they *really* want to." Others may continue to dismiss these massive human problems in that way, but not teachers. Teachers must be the aware ones, the active ones, the ones who provide the direction so that children can understand a world that is more on the move than it has ever been before.

Related to poverty is the problem of overpopulation: too many people for the available food, housing, medical aid, natural resources, and other necessary and desirable commodities of our everyday life. The following passage tells us how tremendous and immediate the issue is:

> At the present time the annual increase in world population runs to about forty-three millions. This means that every four years mankind adds to its numbers the equivalent of the present population of the United States, every eight and a half years the equivalent of the present population of India. At the rate of increase prevailing between the birth of Christ and the death of Queen Elizabeth I, it took sixteen centuries for the population of the earth to double. At the present rate it will double in less than half a century. And this fantastically rapid doubling of our numbers will be taking place on a planet whose most desirable and productive areas are already densely populated, whose soils are being eroded by the frantic efforts of bad farmers to raise more food, and whose easily available mineral capital is being squandered with the reckless extravagance of a drunken sailor getting rid of his accumulated pay.[8]

According to the United Nations statistical yearbook (released in May, 1963) the population of Asia is greater than the rest of the

[8] Aldous Huxley, *Brave New World Revisited,* New York, Harper & Row, Publishers, Inc., 1958, pp. 9–10.

world put together, and Communist China which has the largest population also has the fastest annual growth rate of any of the major countries of the world.

How aware are we of the cost of the greatest armaments race the world has ever known? Admittedly this problem evades full solution at the moment; but as well-educated persons we should at least be aware of such startling facts as the following, which were collected not long ago:

The world is now spending $14 million an *hour* on arms and armies.

The United States and the Soviet Union together spend about 73 percent of the total (or $88 billion each year); we are the biggest spender of all in this field—$46 billion a year.

The cost is about $40 a year for each man, woman and child now living.

If pooled, this money could be used for one or a combination of the following peaceful purposes: more than double the average annual cash income of 1.2 billion persons who now make less than $100 a year; pay for adequate housing for 240 million families in underdeveloped nations; provide food for 3 billion who wake up hungry every day of their lives, a hunger that has seldom if ever been satisfied; furnish medical care for the millions who are sick with no chance of cure in their poor environments. The constructive energies of 15 million men could be released for creative purposes rather than the destructive ones to which they are now dedicated. The 60 million men in the lines behind them, keeping them armed, fed, and supplied could then also be transferred to peaceful goals. There would be an accompanying transfer of some of our greatest scientific brains to the secrets of the earth, heavens, or life itself.[9]

These are the basic world problems of tomorrow, and ignoring them will not make them vanish. They constitute the framework of the setting in which our children will grow up—a setting that has an inherent dishonesty if we avoid thoughts of the unpleasant and make our children avoid them too. Like it or not, our present world is a fertile place for demagogues who capitalize periodically on deprivation, desire for a scapegoat, human frailties, and man's too-frequent inhumanity to his fellow man.

As the twentieth century edges to a close, with its issues of poverty and population, it has yet to face up to a future that is even more overwhelming; one that will require all of our teaching leadership,

[9] Facts from the *New York Times*, February 26, 1961, p. 1.

intellectual brilliance, and patient and persistent attention. Already some of the greatest minds have searched for solutions and found them consistently evasive.

The race between education and catastrophe that H. G. Wells foresaw more than 25 years ago is now at its height. Here are a few of the steps in the drama which could have all of us playing a star role in the last act much sooner than we permit ourselves to believe:

Early in 1958 a declaration was handed to the Secretary-General of the United Nations. It was signed by 9235 of the world's leading scientists and declared that radioactivity gradually created by nuclear tests represents a serious and increasing danger to all of us. The probability was pointed out of expanding numbers of deformed children in the future, as was the possibility of generation after generation with a higher incidence of mentally and physically handicapped children.

Japanese protests have been made to both Moscow and Washington regarding the radioactive clouds from northeast Siberia and from Pacific islands. Winds carry them over Japan, with resultant rainfall poisoning soil and vegetation and especially the dietary staples of rice and fish.

Still ailing as atom bomb victims, traced back to Hiroshima and Nagasaki, are 230,000 persons, some with burns, others with cancer. Suicides, abnormal babies, and permanent hospitalization (of 4500) are all in the picture presented by the United States Atomic Bomb Casualty Commission.

The importance of the problem urged Dr. Albert Schweitzer to make a radio plea directly to all the people of the world, rather than to their governments. His remarks, "A Declaration of Conscience," were read in full over Radio Oslo under the auspices of the Nobel Prize committee and broadcast in their entirety to all major nations except the United States, the U.S.S.R., and Communist China.

Norman Cousins, editor of the *Saturday Review,* went to Lambarene, French Equatorial Africa, to talk with Dr. Schweitzer about the problem, and he reported their conversation:

Only a few years ago, he [Dr. Schweitzer] added, the statement that this planet could be made unfit for life seemed absurdly melodramatic. But there was no longer any question that such power now existed. And even without a war, the atmosphere could become dangerously contaminated.

"After our talk yesterday," he said, "I reflected that danger of this magnitude is not easily grasped by the human mind. As day after day passes, and as the sun continues to rise and set, the sheer regularity of nature seems to rule out such terrible thoughts. But what we seem to forget is that, yes, the sun will continue to rise and set and the moon will continue to move across the skies, but mankind can create a situation in which the sun and moon can look down upon an earth that has been stripped of life. . . . It is a serious thing that the governments have supplied so little information to their peoples on this subject. . . . Nothing that a government knows about the nature of this new force is improper for its people to know." [10]

What are the points raised by some of the world's greatest intellects on this issue and ignored to a large extent by the remaining millions? Should discussion of these issues be limited to a Saturday night movie showing of *On the Beach*—or should every teacher know the implications and be willing to share them? How many teachers have read, or even know about, books like *No More War!* by Linus Pauling, 1962 Nobel Peace Prize winner, *May Man Prevail?* by Erich Fromm, and *In Place of Folly* by Norman Cousins? Does their realism get even a small part of the attention given to the escapism of a book like James Michener's *Hawaii?* We can concede that the latter deserves all the attention it receives, but do the ideas of the former warrant any less?

Some of the items related to this problem demand our intensive attention and understanding; they must have a priority somewhere in teacher education commensurate with their importance. The following are worthy of full discussion, debate, and the broadest distribution, despite the 1963 Test Ban Treaty.

At least a dozen additional nations will have atomic bombs (or the equivalent) within 5 or 6 years; and governmental responsibility runs the gamut from caution to extreme irresponsibility.

The greater the spread of their knowledge, the more certain the possibility of nuclear explosions through accident, foolishness, or political idiocy.

There is apparently no safe amount of radiation; it is impossible to visualize the panic that will take place among all of us if we discover *too late* that the "safety limits" have already been passed with no method available to us for washing the skies clean of its deadly contamination.

Children have a lower tolerance to radioactive strontium than adults do.

A study of radiologists exposed to X-ray apparatus showed that they had a greater percentage of stillbirths and children with congenital defects in their descendents than did other physicians, and a higher incidence of leukemia than did the population as a whole.

The poisonous qualities of uranium, hydrogen, and cobalt from the testing

[10] Norman Cousins, "The Schweitzer Declaration," *Saturday Review*, May 18, 1957, p. 14.

of bombs are permanently stored up in an uneven distribution in each of us, never to be disposed of; and *never* is about as permanent as a matter can be!

Bertrand Russell declared that 90 percent of the human race would rather be dead than sensible. Charles P. Snow, scientist and novelist, pointed out the statistical truth that the more countries we have producing the deadly weapons the nearer comes the inevitable explosion—if enforceable agreement on their banning is not reached. Incidents, accidents, and mistakes can and already have happened, but fortunately on a somewhat limited scale. What assurance is there that a nuclear bomb, despite its unarmed condition and other safeguards, will not be involved in an explosion—or that a trigger-happy pilot, submarine commander, or other person with the highest of all motives (as misguided as they would be) might not set off the spark? Even if we assume that there is full control in the United States, U.S.S.R., Great Britain, and France, how about men and women in key posts in any one of a number of other countries? Could they not have the key to these explosive powers in the next few years, before our children have even reached adulthood and while we ourselves are still on the scene?

An attack of 20,000 megatons could kill 95 percent of the total population in the United States, and a combined total of 50,000 are already available in this country and Russia. An estimated 25,000 to 100,000 persons have died or will die of leukemia by 1978 as the result of nuclear tests conducted before 1960. Percentages of population, like 1/100 of 1 percent, sound small, but not when they mean thousands of people—or include a member of one's own family. A philosophic approach to the subject puts it this way:

In the past, folly and wickedness had limited consequences; today they draw all mankind to perdition. Now, unless all of us live with and for one another, we shall all be destroyed together. This new situation demands a corresponding answer. It is not enough to find new institutions; we must change ourselves, our characters, our moral-political wills. What used to distinguish individuals, to be effective in small groups but impotent in society at large, has now become a condition for the continued existence of mankind.

I do not think I am exaggerating. Whoever goes on living as before has not grasped the menace. . . . Man must change if he wants to go on living.

If he thinks only of today, a day will come when the outbreak of nuclear war is apt to finish everything.

The change can come only in every man's manner of living. Every little act, every word, every attitude in millions and billions of people matter. What happens on a large scale is but a symptom of what is done in the privacy of many lives. The man who cannot live in peace with his neighbor, the mischief-maker or secret ill-wisher or slanderer or liar, the adulterer or undutiful son or negligent parent or lawbreaker—by his conduct, which even behind locked doors is never wholly private—keeps peace from the world. He does, in miniature, what on a larger scale makes mankind destroy itself. Nothing that man is and does is quite without political significance.[11]

Whether or not he agrees with the implied or stated analyses and solutions of Schweitzer, Cousins, and Jaspers, the teacher who is indifferent to the problem and who deprives children of the knowledge that is the keynote of their entire existence may be a failure. Teaching long division, the officers of the President's cabinet, and the parts of a sentence is important, but it is not enough.

The United States

The international problems related to poverty, population, and radiation provide a framework for an understanding of some of our national concerns. That the former affect our lives every day should be obvious to all of us, especially to our teachers. That the latter, which are itemized below, are an integral part of what we are and will be should be even more apparent to all who read the newspapers, listen to political and statesmanlike speeches, and dig for real meanings behind both. Again, their importance for teachers is even greater than for the population as a whole. And teachers who ignore, overlook, or discount their need to know, absorb, transmit, and explain do the unforgiveable; they fail themselves and their responsibility toward society and the future.

Do we recognize, for example, that in a deprived world we (with only 6 percent of the world's land and 7 percent of its population) drive 76 percent of its automobiles, talk on 58 percent of its telephones, produce 40 percent of its electric power, watch or listen to 31 percent of its radios and television sets, and read 27 percent of its newspapers? We use 9 tons of steel per person (India uses a few

[11] Karl Jaspers, *The Future of Mankind*, University of Chicago Press, 1961.

pounds per person) and have one physician for every 750 persons (India has one for about 6000). With our relatively small population we are capable of consuming 50 percent of the world's production of goods, and in the past 40 years we have used more of the world's resources than *all* the people of the *entire* world had used in the 4000 years up to 1914.

We see ourselves as hard working and frugal, but each of us consumes twice as much in goods as we did in 1940, and two-fifths of our possessions are not essential. Although we have abundance and material wealth, we have not learned to live with them. Credit cards incongruously clutter our bulging wallets for country clubs, gasoline, meals, motels, food, clothing, discount houses, and all kinds of household and personal essentials and nonessentials that make us feel better, act more pleasantly, and smell more sweetly. John W. Gardner stated the dangers related to this problem quite well when he reminded us that our dedication to the goals of our country needs constant renewal:

> It is hard for Americans to realize that the survival of the idea for which the nation stands is not inevitable. It may survive if enough Americ care enough.
>
> It would be easier for us to grasp this truth if we weren't so blessedly comfortable. Part of our problem is how to stay awake on a full stomach. And the fateful question remains open: Can we as a people, despite the narcotic of easy living and the endless distractions of a well-heeled society, respond with vigor and courage and dedication to the demands that history has placed upon us?
>
> All of the signs are not encouraging. At just this moment in history when we need all of our vitality and drive and capacity for sustained effort, we are in danger of losing our bearings, in danger of surrendering to a "cult of easiness." It does not require a carping critic to detect the slackness, slovenliness and bad workmanship in our national life.[12]

The era of abundance is not universally here; even in our own country the elements of inadequate housing, food, and clothing are very much with us. Visit the not-very-well-hidden dirt and degradation of any of our big cities, choose any state of the 50, and you can easily find poverty that will shock and embarrass. The contrasts of

[12] John W. Gardner, *Excellence*, New York, Harper & Row, Publishers, Inc., 1961, p. 147.

opulence and deprivation naggingly accompany each other as we view the metropolitan gold coast and neighboring slum, the wealthy farmer and subsistence tenant farmer. We consume with a speed that production cannot always match, use strategic resources that we must sometimes depend on obtaining from other countries, and ignore the warnings that wealth is not necessarily endless and bottomless.

Our material heights are accompanied by some less pleasurable accomplishments: traffic deaths, disease, mental illness, financial and emotional anxieties, delinquency of juveniles and their parents, and corrupt leadership in business, labor, and politics. Our houses, subways, freeways, daily schedules, and neighbors squeeze us into more tightly compressed areas of space and time each day. And as we become aware of all this, we must realize that our neighbors in other countries have always had these pressures, and many assume they always will have.

Problems by the dozens emerge for all of us in the prognostications of skilled economic and political prophets. In the next decade production of goods and services will go 50 percent higher accompanied by a 25 percent increase in our standard of living, a national population increase to substantially over 200 million, and the largest 10-year increase of workers in our history. The number of women in the labor market will increase at a rate nearly two times that of men; increases in demands for professional and technical workers will be sensational; and our mobility will increase to where half the male workers live in a different state every year.

Does this sound like something with which the complacent teacher who liked the way things "used to be" can manage to live? Or must he shake himself loose from the *status quo* and search in all of this bigness for the elements of compassion and understanding, and the potentials of lasting world greatness to match our productivity? Our too-frequent satisfaction with mediocrity has been a persistent stumbling block. Recognizing, rewarding, and developing excellence is a prime objective; we must respect excellence in art, music, business, law, medicine, science laboratories, human relations, and in the semiskilled and unskilled occupations. Such excellence is observed through actual performance, but it requires a backdrop of ability, character, and motivation. We make the mistake of not always inspiring or expecting high performance. Does each of us perform at the top level of which he is capable? Do we have such expectations of our own children and the ones in our classrooms? Disturbing in its simplicity is the idea that a society only produces great men in those fields in which it understands greatness. Where are we as a nation if we fear the kind of greatness for which we have most admiration? The one century and place that produced Cortez and Pizarro could hardly bring forth a Jefferson or Mozart; a Franklin, Monroe, and John Adams. Is that thought comfortable to you in the era of our most demanding challenge? Perhaps we are too close to it to note the intellectual and other skills developing all around us; or perhaps they are failing to materialize in the quantity and quality needed.

Our respect for goodness and greatness emerges in less than the most desirable proportions when we restrict the "pursuit of happiness" to having a good time, worshiping frivolity, or being completely satisfied with the unexciting goal of security. Such objectives show the lack of understanding some of us have of the demands of the times. Perhaps in the temporary years of childhood "the spirit of the good time" is satisfactory; but it loses some of its appeal as the boy becomes the man and it is seen with all its flimsiness in an adult society. There is a place for it, of course, but should it dominate our goals, our beliefs, our thoughts of the future? Can we be satisfied if our plans for tomorrow are dictated by what gives us the most laughs? Or is survival made of stronger stuff?

If we assume that even in what some dramatically refer to as "the moment of truth" our citizens always know where they are headed, know what they want, recognize their basic likes and dislikes, and behave in a rational manner, we assume what never was and perhaps never will be. Of teachers we should expect the clearest goals of all, the best self-analysis, and the most rational behavior; but our disappointment is sometimes overwhelming. In his convincing indictment of our gullibility, Vance Packard has analyzed the weaknesses of the great American public in being easily persuaded to buy and do what basically may have little appeal for us. The human qualities that make us fear banks, enjoy certain cars, be enticed into buying homes that are too expensive for us, smoke a well-advertised cigar or cigarette, patronize a particular supermarket, and feed the snappiest, poppingest, and crackingest cereals to our children every morning are all part of this basic gullibility. The thoughtful voters, rugged individualists, and hardheaded consumers that some of us *think* we are, are not what the "symbol manipulator" visualizes as he plans his sales campaigns. Our misty yearnings, daydreams, irrational emotions, and compulsive actions are what come to the fore.

It is expecting too much to hope that teachers are immune to all these human frailties, but perhaps not too much to expect them to be at least slightly more rational than the population as a whole. And the hope is ever burning that they will help guide children out of an emotional marsh and into the air of reason, intuition, and insight. But honestly, if they themselves lack these attributes, can we expect that they will lead others toward them?

It is the old story of the missing dessert for dinner tonight being more important than a million Chinese going without full meals yesterday, today, and tomorrow. Our concern is with what touches us most intimately. Packard states the case through the words of an account executive, whose client, a political candidate, timidly suggests that he ought to make a foreign policy speech on the crisis in the atomic age. "Look," the adviser replies, "if you want to impress the longhairs, intellectuals, and Columbia students, do it on your own time, not on my TV time. Consider your market, man! . . . Your market is forty, fifty million slobs sitting at home catching your stuff on TV and radio. Are those slobs worried about the atomic age? Nuts. They're worried about next Friday's grocery bill."[13]

That is not exactly an elegant way to make the point, but it is fairly close to reality. The manipulation of our thinking and buying, the invasion of our privacy of thought and action are part of the temper of the times. It would be no fun if we were always coldly logical and rational, but it is not an either-or proposition. Those with an education ought to have some semblance of rationality; they should be expected to help the young who follow their guidance stay on the road of logic at least once in a while. If teachers do not set that pace occasionally, who will or can?

The globe is beset by problems. So is our country, whether it is the "Negro issue" going into high gear or the unemployment of

[13] Vance Packard, *The Hidden Persuaders*, New York, David McKay Company, Inc., 1957, p. 233.

unskilled young people. Perhaps we cannot solve these problems directly as teachers, but we can at least convey the concept of *change* to our students. We can try to understand ourselves. We can work to help each child understand his world and realize his abilities more fully.

As we continue to face national problems, understanding and maybe even leadership can come from the teaching profession. Of increasing intensity are the problems of loneliness, sickness, and emotional strife of the aged. These people have a desire for continued independence, a hunger to be part of the stream of life, and a need for useful productivity and involvement, all goals not so easily prepared for or attained. The "golden age" has the highest suicide rate of any age group; it is of great concern in the medical-care issue; it needs understanding even more than money. Is it unreasonable to expect teachers to provide leadership in preparing for the problem years of advanced age, and by intelligent planning help set a pattern based on more hope, respect, and fertile activity than we now have for most of our older people?

Another crucial issue on the national scene concerns our periodic binges of anticommunism based on emotion rather than reason. All loyal citizens agree on the communist menace. All agree that we should stand up to it, fight it if necessary. The difference is in the "how," and teachers and other educated people must lead the way. An extremely vocal group, differing in size from year to year, spreads suspicion and attacks our neighbors by name-calling, accusation, and guilt by association. "All who disagree with me in any way are dupes," they say, "tools of the Communists, worse than those who carry party cards." So they make up lists, conduct whispering campaigns, write accusing letters to the suspects and to the editors of local newspapers. Another group, not nearly so well organized or zealously involved, feels that the enemy is elsewhere rather than in the neighboring house. They believe that communism spreads where new nations are aided economically by the U.S.S.R.; where migrants of our own country are uneducated, starved, and pressured; when children are badgered by ignorance or not educated to their capacity; and when teachers are carelessly selected and prepared. And they think that we have to fear another force too: the always smoldering threat of fascism and its disastrous possibilities. The teacher must be in the forefront of a level-headed unemotional approach to our dangers and our strengths.

All these, and many more, constitute the picture, the challenge, and the need for thought and understanding by every teacher, regardless of level of instruction or location. To sidestep them through ignorance or oversight can no longer be condoned. As leaders representing only one segment of our society, teachers may find it difficult to work with others whom they may read about but fail to interpret accurately. Although studies of teachers' backgrounds show they come most frequently from the "middle class," that term does not mean the same thing to all people; nor does one of its members necessarily understand the problems of all. It is difficult for any of us to be representative or "average."

Teachers must know about the past, current, changing, and future social structure, and how it affects their students and themselves. Just a superficial approach to it, a recognition of the glossy surface differences in it, is not enough. Both the facts and feeling must be much deeper than that, and generalizations will not do either. Teachers must ask themselves: What are the ambitions, problems, past difficulties of *this* family? How do they live, what do they need, where have they been? Who is this particular child, what are his conflicts and frustrations, how capable is he, how much is he being challenged, neglected, misunderstood? And how about me as a teacher? Do I favor the children from the "upper" levels of our social ladder just because they have rich parents? Or do I honestly allocate my time to students on the basis of their needs (needs that can ultimately be met)? Am I aware that talent and intellectual potential can thrive in all groups, among all parts of our society, even though they are much easier to see as we go up the social line? The public school teacher must recognize ability and decide what to do about it, and this is quite a responsibility. James B. Conant refers to these accumulated problems, especially in underprivileged areas, as "social dynamite."[14] He has pointed out the startling differences between slum and suburban public schools.

The teacher should be sensitive to how "frozen" or "liquid" the social pattern is in his particular teaching community, and what

[14] James B. Conant, *Slums and Suburbs,* New York, McGraw-Hill Book Company, Inc., 1961.

effect it has on the individual child. It made a big difference to Stella Dallas' daughter (in the old version of that story) that her mother was rejected by the society of which she wanted to be a part; that rejection rubbed off on the little girl for a long time; other parents would not even permit their children to go to her birthday party. Many other aspects of the social structure affect the child early in his development: Is it assumed that he will go to college, regardless of his aptitude for it? Or is an incomplete elementary or high school education the expectation level?

Although the schools are the greatest vehicle we have for equalizing opportunity on the basis of need and ability, the amount of social mobility it can encourage is still too limited. The upward road remains one of less than frequent travel, despite the sudden fortunes and startling individual successes in business, acting, and writing. Most people stay near their birth level, a fact that is too often true in our country and almost always true elsewhere. But life in the various classes has been brought closer together in recent years. There is a kind of aristocracy of the masses as a result of television, paperback books, mushrooming numbers of country clubs, magazine subscriptions reaching almost astronomical proportions, symphony orchestras and art museums in most cities and many smaller towns, concerts, recordings, painting by the public, musical instruments for most people's children, and amateur theatricals. What does this commitment to progress and learning mean to the teacher? He must certainly know what these children and their families want and need, and he must help satisfy them to the extent of his ability. The teacher who is not well informed about what sociology, anthropology, psychology, and economics can tell us about people and their problems is a person deficient in some of the basic understandings of his work. Without the tools the job cannot be done.

CONCLUDING REMARKS

To be proficient in teaching means to be part of the world around us. Being separate from it reduces the contribution a teacher can make and increases the danger of perpetuating a narrow viewpoint and a routinized spirit and outlook. Teachers must know this world as it enters into a new one tomorrow. Its problems as we stand ready to slip into an atomic eternity, its music and art already introduced into most homes, its world-wide issues of poverty and population, its automation and mechanical genius, and the national setting of growth, materialism, and waste—from all these the teacher will construct guidelines for children. Without knowledge of them, a teacher cannot teach.

Perhaps this is asking a great deal of one entering an occupation; but considering the seriousness of the times, can we expect any less? Can we condone mediocrity among those who provide the leadership our youth need or close our eyes to narrow-mindedness, inaccuracy, and intellectual obstacles as we have been prone to do up to this time? We have had enough of the limited viewpoint, and in this time of change it is no longer appropriate or even possible. Experimental attitudes are more in line with these years. So is a desire to reject what has not worked. So is the search for new ways of teaching, new persons to do it, and new objectives for the entire process.

In this era when creativity is essential, the future teacher must face the problems of our nation and world, analyze them, and help in their solution. Each is immense in scope, challenging in complexity. The teacher in this time of change must answer the daily call to avoid impending disaster. Your energy, knowledge, and will to do battle are urgently needed in the immediate struggle that faces all of us and our children.

CHAPTER 1

A TIME FOR *Taking Stock in Education*

What is having the greatest influence on education today? Is it what the Russians are doing? Is it the fear of the tidal wave of enrollments already started on all levels? Is it the sudden concern —expressed in thousands of words and pages—of those who say they represent "public indignation"? Is it the gradual realization that the schools really *do* belong to the people, and just saying so in the past without thinking and acting so was shrugging off responsibility?

After viewing some of the basic national and international issues of our time, we can move into problems even more pertinently related to the field of education. Not only in this country are they being viewed with thoroughness. One report states that 40 nations of the world have a teacher shortage and are engaged in school reform. That figure must be far too low. If every country that fails to educate all children to their capacities were to admit that failure, it would be difficult to find even *one* country denying its educational limitations.

In this chapter our emphasis will be primarily on the educational issues and problems this country faces—or neglects to face. There will be some that the future teacher may not have encountered up to this point. If he doesn't think or know about them, his outlook and understanding will be too naïve and self-satisfied. After we go through some of our own issues and concerns, we will touch on a few in the world scene and specific ones of the U.S.S.R. These areas are important because of the shrinking earth (not because we are afraid of the progress or competition of others) and all must at least be considered so that the picture will be reasonably complete. We must not fall into smug self-sufficiency as we frequently do when we equate the United States with the world or the universe; when we

refer to ourselves as "Americans" and forget the citizens of many
other countries who also are Americans; when we assume that what
we have is inevitably best—until we drive a small foreign car or use
a foreign camera.

As we move through these problems, perhaps logic, reason, and
doubt can replace the unquestioned beliefs which we have because
of habit. "I've made up my mind so don't confuse me with facts" is
the kind of thinking you should lay to rest *before* you begin to teach.
Trying to do it later may not accomplish the task at all.

EDUCATIONAL GOALS

The keenest minds looking at education in the United States today
generally agree that a touch here, a recommendation there, and a
now-and-then feeling about the whole thing will contribute little to
meeting the basic needs of our schools. Waiting around for others to
tell us what to do or for committees to organize, debate, and water
down their recommendations so that "consensus" can be arrived at
will leave us far behind in the timetable that this profession's leadership must set up.

You are arriving just in time for the speed-up, and if you move
fast enough you can grab the ring on the merry-go-round and join
the riders. You may even be able to help convert the melancholy
chariots and animals that have been going around in circles to a
route based on an unimpeded ten-lane highway toward new educational thought. You will be in plenty of time to convert the vivid
recommendations of thoughtful men and women into action. The
administrators and teachers long in the saddle need your enthusiasm,
strength, and ideals to help them split with the past of which they
have been an integral part. Just as a fish never knows he has been in
water until he is out of it, so some of the present occupants of the
drivers' seats within our schools may not realize they are in a new
time until you help them see they are already part of an era of
change.

John W. Gardner, president of the Carnegie Corporation of New
York, is the spokesman for the section on education of the President's Commission on National Goals. He provides an example of

the new and unfettered look at the years ahead with statements like these:

The teaching of every subject in the elementary grades through high school should be re-appraised intensively; the inflexible tradition of the one-teacher classroom must be evaluated; the rigid division into grades needs experimentation; unused school buildings late in the day, week ends and summers are luxuries we cannot afford; innovations like educational television and teaching machines deserve a fair trial, based on realistic enthusiasm.[1]

This report of national significance refuses to be tied to the past. But the goals it outlines are not dreams, not in the richest country in the world in its richest years. It says our expenditures for education must double by 1970 (to $40 billion rather than the $20 billion of 1960), inefficient school districts should be consolidated, each state ought to have a high-level board of education, and teachers' salaries should be raised and made competitive with those on other jobs involving comparable ability and preparation (a little difficult to accomplish, Gardner implies, in communities where marching bands and winning basketball teams are more important as issues than what teachers are paid!) We must give our immediate attention to accelerated desegregation, the best of all educational programs in underprivileged neighborhoods, the critical need for more efficiency on all levels of education, encouragement for experimentation from first grade through college, and using highly paid and qualified university professors for purposes other than drill.

The report offers no panaceas, no promise of immediate success, and no priority list for action. As good as we think we are, educationally speaking, we are not good enough, it says, and the soft spots are both numerous and serious. Complacency has no room in the picture, nor does a piecemeal, spotty, catch-as-catch-can approach. The federal government, the states, and local communities are all deeply involved in the problems and must be just as deeply involved in the solutions. Some of our educational accomplishments have been "majestic," it says, but many states are far from the educational level of the best ones. To penalize a child just because he lives in one place rather than another is hardly fair.

[1] President's Commission on National Goals, *Goals for Americans*, Englewood Cliffs, N. J., Prentice-Hall, Inc., 1960, pp. 6–7, 82–99.

In early 1961 the President's Task Force on Education had some pertinent things to say about educational goals and how to reach them. It identified some overriding problems which should be brought into bold relief more often for every future teacher and potential educational leader. Such needs, the Task Force said, include the wealthier states with their pockets of distress; the low income states, where people make proportionately greater financial sacrifices for education; the many states which still have teachers with little or no college education; and the overburdened, overpopulated cities. Its priority recommendations for legislation were for federal support for the public school system and higher education and a strengthening of the National Defense Education Act. It felt that education has to be of permanent interest to the federal government and of personal concern to the President for the problems to be solved.

These designs for tomorrow spring from ideas expressed by others through the ages. Although agreement has always been far from a sure thing, we have always had goals. The ability to read, universal schooling, qualified teachers, appropriate materials and methods, surroundings conducive to learning, and sound administration that provides creative leadership would be on most people's lists. Of what would your list of goals consist? If you had a chance or would take the time to brainstorm, let yourself go, think freely about the educational scene, what would you see as its objectives in our country's crucial years? In specific terms, what should the schools do? What should you help them do? Discuss these questions with your classes, your instructor, or your friends. You will rarely find agreement. What are the schools for, anyway?

Jane Addams said they should give a child's experience social value, teach him to direct his own activities and adjust them to those of other people. Mark Van Doren insists that education is to make people happier than they would have been without it; but he does not define happiness as having a good time; he means freedom to use one's mind, expand one's interests. John Fischer of Columbia University said that the real purpose behind our educational programs is not political, social, or economic; it is moral, based on giving each child the respect and acceptance due a human personality. Do you agree with any of them?

How would you have registered your opinion if you had been asked by the National Opinion Research Center what the most important thing is that children should get from their education? The five most frequent replies of the public responding were under these headings, but *not* necessarily in this order: regular school subjects; character education; vocational training; citizenship education; social adjustment. College graduates put character education way in the lead. High school graduates agreed, but gave regular school subjects equal importance. Those who had completed grade school or less placed regular school subjects on top, with vocational training right behind it.

Opinions concerning the purposes of education vary depending on experience and the importance attached to education. They may be stated in glowing terms of vague ideals or in bedrock specifics of the needs of *this* child in *his* lifetime. At an International Conference on Public Education in Geneva, Switzerland, in July, 1959, the U.S. Office of Education said: "Education in the United States of America is based on two fundamental principles: Every person has an equal right to educational opportunities and an educated citizenry is essential to freedom and human welfare."

After you try your hand at a list of goals, check it against the consolidated one offered below. Which would you eliminate? Is there any kind of priority you think appropriate for the list?

Maximum development of individual potentialities at all levels for all children

Quantity *and* quality: no choice between the two available, whether those terms are used or the alternate ones of "mass" and "elite"

". . . to liberate, to abolish kingcraft, priestcraft, castle monopoly, to pull down the gallows, to burn up the bloody statute-book, to take in the immigrant, to open the doors of the sea and the fields of the earth"[2]

The creation of a full community in which children cannot help growing up to be democratic, dedicated to freedom, intelligent in choices, reverent toward the good life, and eager to share the tasks of the age

Preparation of the individual to make wise decisions (according to Paul Woodring, the major aim of education, and all else is but contributory[3])

[2] Ralph Waldo Emerson, quoted in *The National Purpose*, New York, Holt, Rinehart and Winston, Inc., 1960, p. 8.

[3] Paul Woodring, *A Fourth of a Nation*, New York, McGraw-Hill Book Company, Inc., 1957, p. 111.

A composite purpose based on unsettling minds, widening horizons, inflaming intellects, teaching men to think straight and for themselves—rather than the teaching of facts, theories, and laws; reforming, amusing, or creating technicians, expert or otherwise

Learning that is tied in with and will lead to the establishment of a just and peaceful world order, based on the skills and techniques necessary to run a modern industrial society—but learning that is also related to the generous heart, the bold imagination, and the liberal ideals of a truly democratic philosophy

Ability to read, write, spell, add, subtract, multiply, divide, and know basic facts of geography, science, history and the difference between aimless mental activity and orderly thought

Development of intellectual facilities to the fullest and preparation for becoming a contributing member of our society—both based on learning basic skills and cultivation of reasoning and creativity

These are big ideas, sometimes wordy, frequently debatable. You could quibble easily over the meanings of the terms, and many educators and others have carried on lengthy and heated arguments over them. "Basic skills," "basic knowledge," "maximum development," "excellence," "democracy," "standards"—pick your words and your weapons and you will be in the company of thoughtful men and women who have preceded you in the battle.

But perhaps the picture can be simplified. Maybe each teacher and school administrator should say, ". . . accept our aims; be wary of our methods; give us time."[4] Each of us can develop our own aims and methods in time, if they are not complicated by considering the needs of everyone, bringing everyone into educational planning, and burying the child in an avalanche of words, ideas, and discussion. The decision is yours. What kinds of goals are workable and have meaning for you? What are the basic purposes of education as you see them?

SOME MAJOR PROBLEMS IN EDUCATION

If you think the *goals* of education present a complex subject, start giving some thought to the problems and issues of what's wrong

---

[4] Robert M. Hutchins, *Some Observations on American Education*, New York, Cambridge University Press, 1956, p. 23.

with education. And as you enter the teaching profession you ought to know what some of these involve. Within the next 2 or 3 years you will be seeking, and will be asked for, answers, so it is time to make a start.

Again, your own list *could* be a place to begin, but it would be much too incomplete and subjective, based on your own limited educational experiences. "Limited?" you ask, "with 12 years plus behind me? With the kinds of teachers I've been exposed to? If you want to know about educational problems, I can tell you from bitter, first-hand experience. Just give me a chance to tell you about . . ." And you would be right, of course—but only partly. Your list might include the English teacher who could not spell and did not know grammar, the fifth-grade teacher who apparently decided the first day in class that she did not like you and lost no opportunity to show her antipathy through sarcasm and insults, and the administrator who knew a great deal more about athletics and making a budget balance than he did about making the curriculum come out "right" for the students.

Unfortunately the list of problems is much longer than any individual could assemble on the basis of his own schooling. The fact that they seem overwhelming is compensated for only by the fact that we really *do* have the personnel, creativity, and funds in this country to cope with them. There is also consolation in the large numbers of teachers and future teachers, administrators and future administrators, college professors, parents, political leaders and others who are ready to "do battle" with their ideas, words, money, and deeds to solve these problems. Of course, they are counterbalanced by persons who represent a tragic attitude of lethargy, stubbornness, and ineptitude when it comes to the difficulties that our schools and our entire educational program face. There are far too many instructors in teacher preparation, who should represent the very best in teaching skills and instead are satisfied to rest on the laurels of an aging doctorate and yellowing lecture notes. There are teachers and administrators who show no interest or inclination in keeping up with the plentiful research in their field; future teachers who have selected this profession as a kind of last resort, and whose qualifications are sadly lacking for the most demanding job on the scene today and tomorrow; parents who are chronic complainers but absentee helpers; politicians who get into the act only to feather their own nest, with moves based only on expediency.

So if you would like to, you can (1) start your list with the problems you vividly recall from your earlier years of elementary and secondary school, (2) add to it from the deficiencies you may see around you in the educational setting today, (3) supplement it with the people in all the groups listed above who constitute one of the reasons why progress is far slower than it should be, and (4) go on with an evaluation of the composite list below which has been accumulated from many writers, thinkers, and speakers in the field. And if after you give this crucial subject the thought and discussion it deserves you do not feel it needs the pioneering spirit, the hard work, and the creative approach that you can help bring to it, then maybe this is the time to look elsewhere for your life's work. That is a safe challenge to toss at you, however, for the need is so apparent that it fairly shrieks for your aid, your youth, your vitality, and your intelligence. Without them, the big job to which these add up can never be done.

Can you set up any kind of priority for the items on the list to follow? Are there some you think do not belong on it? Are there others you want to add? (Hardly seems possible, but there could be; even the authorities and so-called authorities could have omitted a big one.) Do you have solutions in mind now, or would you rather read on before proposing them? Obviously every problem does not exist everywhere, but its presence in *any* locality or for *any* child puts it on the list.

The teacher shortage
Substandard teachers on all levels of instruction
Teacher turnover; the temporary noncareer teacher
Low salaries in education
Inequalities of educational opportunity—rural versus urban; race versus race; community versus community; state versus state
Overcrowded schools on all levels: double sessions, big classes
More limited percentage of national income spent for education in the United States than in some other countries
Teacher morale, overloads, and concern with unnecessary and nonteaching activities
Parent morale regarding the schools

Gaps and chasms between academicians and professional educators; between high school and college; between administrators and teachers; between parents and schools

Inadequacies of some local school boards, state boards of education, college and university boards of trustees

Teacher recruitment, attraction of the best as well as elimination of the obviously unqualified, both before they enter and after they are on the job

In-service activities for teachers and administrators to up-date their preparation, alert them to the increasingly serious issues that have entered the world and that therefore are now part of the learning children must receive

Public attitudes toward and understanding of the teaching profession

The one-teacher school and the small, inadequate school district

The absence in many communities of programs for handicapped children: the mentally retarded, the blind, the deaf, and the orthopedically handicapped

The "big talk" about the gifted versus the relatively limited amount of action

Lag between research and practice all through the profession on issues like delinquency, discipline, and education of the underprivileged and migrants

The verbiage about creativity, but the continuing drive toward conformity

Rigidity in the following: school organization; school year, day, and periods; school entry in kindergarten or first grade; student acceleration and subjects for study (are we *sure* that foreign languages should be taught beginning in high school, that algebra should come before geometry, that physics should precede chemistry?)

Persistent pockets and patterns of illiteracy

Shortage in facilities and classrooms, old schools, inflexible rooms

National honors to teachers, scientists, literary leaders

The quality and limited offering at both educational ends: nursery schools and adult education

The drop-outs: the lower socioeconomic groups, the culturally deprived, racial groups, the bright, the larger percentage of girls, and the loss in human resources represented by all of these

Experimentation in the schools, examination of new ideas: where? how much?

Guidance: the qualifications of those who do it; the limited numbers of those who are qualified; the lack of recognition of the need; the error of basing it on the past and the *status quo* (an approach bound to be wrong when the future has always evolved through change)

Students who coast through school, unconcerned about the future and un-
motivated to take advantage of their opportunities

Selection of what to teach from the rapidly growing body of human knowledge

Indifference of our young people to the political and philosophical origins
and nature of the world's most powerful country; evidence of such indifference in the weaknesses displayed through Korean War crack-ups of
our young soldiers

Seeing the classroom, rather than our military might and industry, as the
front line of defense

The problems of academic freedom and subversion, real and imagined

Replacing the mere provision of the opportunity to learn by the insistence
that all *shall* learn to their capacity

The maintenance of high standards in schools located in communities where
status seeking, preoccupation with consumption, other forms of materialism, television watching, and divorce rates are all problems of social
concern (schools do not exist in a vacuum)

A network television program when school began in the fall of
1959 singled out three top educational problems in the United States:
integration, overcrowdedness, education of the gifted. A five-part
series in *Life* in the spring of 1958, called "Crisis in Education,"
chose these as the key concerns: overcrowdedness, underpaid teachers, elective courses, bright children, no general agreement on what
school should teach and low standards. A more recent listing of
issues appeared in Fred M. Hechinger's education column in the
New York Times on January 1, 1961. He selected federal aid, the
broadening of the National Defense Education Act beyond its major
emphasis on science and foreign language, the crisis in numbers and
content of medical education, educational assistance of the United
States to foreign countries, and national patterns of education as they
relate to our national goals. The year of 1963 obviously placed integration right at the top of the list as a problem area.

The conclusions that can be drawn may be obvious to you. Only
a big enterprise could have so many difficulties. Only a sturdy profession could show the progress ours has with this oppressive collec-
tion of burdens to carry. We can meet the challenge only with top
talent, full energy, drastic breaks with approaches of the past, vastly
increased allocations of funds from many sources, and a recognition
that time is limited and almost used up for getting the job accom-

plished. Any less is an admission that we really are not equal to the task—and this country has never admitted that when faced with and made alert to any problem. We have had dramatic evidence of that in wars and depressions. We need this spirit now more than ever.

Two Special Problems: Illiteracy and Dropouts

If you were asked to select a few problems for special attention or discussion, your choice might be based on what has affected you most closely of late. You might skip over two problems that affect people by the thousands and have a direct influence on all of us: the *illiterate* and the *school dropout*.

Is there really a problem of illiteracy in the United States? Is it significant? Just look through these data and draw your own conclusions.

During World War II, 700,000 young men were rejected from military service because of illiteracy; 500,000 were taken in, and many of them were assigned to special training units to be taught to read and write. Another 700,000 had the barest of educations. Add them up, and you find that almost 2 million men out of the 18 million screened—or 1 in 9—were total or borderline illiterates.

Enough men for more than 40 military divisions were rejected during World War II as "mentally deficient." (At the peak of mobilization the United States had 89 divisions.) Although some may truly have been mentally deficient, many more were educationally deprived, and their limitations could be traced to their educational rather than their mental limitations. Almost half were rejected on the same grounds during the Korean War.

As recently as 1940, 12 percent of the employed males in the United States had less than 5 years of schooling, many of them either none or very little, not a very happy figure in a nation that prides itself on the universality of its educational program. The figures can convert into a brighter picture if viewed in another way: 6.3 million illiterates in 1890 (or 1 in 7); 2.5 million in 1950 (or 1 in 50).

Varying figures have been used to describe our incidence of illiteracy. In the summer of 1957, 10 million adult Americans were labeled "functional illiterates," a technical term used to cover those who do not command a knowledge of reading, writing, and arithmetic equal to that of the average fifth-grade child. At that time a representative group from industry, labor, education, religion, social welfare, and government met in Washington for the purpose of establishing a National Commission on Adult Literacy.

Looking at the problem from the direction of military needs gives a slanted view. Numbers of men would not be the decisive factor if another war were to come, but neither would we have the time to educate illiterates as we did in the early 1940s. (The Herman Kahn book, *On Thermonuclear War,* says it could possibly all be settled within an hour anyway!) The U.S.S.R. has exploited this social blight of ours on numerous occasions for propaganda purposes, comparing their rapid increase in literacy with our slower progress (of course, they had much farther to climb). But it is an effective propaganda device in the beginning-to-stir and educationally backward new countries of Asia and Africa. They have a hard time understanding the fact that we have any illiteracy at all, and the Russian figures make a deep impression on them.

The seriousness of the problem of illiteracy becomes clear when we realize that the children who are "logical candidates" for adult illiteracy need our best schools and teachers, and frequently get the poorest; that their neighborhoods, which should provide the richest environments to help bring these children out of the educational doldrums, are instead crowded, drab, dirty, and without human or material inspiration; that these are the children whose school day and school year may be among the shortest in the country. The conclusion is obvious: those with the greatest educational need continue, in most parts of the country, to have that need unsatisfied and perpetuated through inadequate facilities and personnel. Outstanding exceptions, of course, are the Higher Horizons Project (New York City) and related types of programs which we will discuss later.

The place of the illiterate in our economy becomes more desperate every year. Higher skills are needed, in industry and even in domestic service (getting a telephone message accurately is both a business and a social necessity). Farming is demanding the development of higher abilities too. So competition for the lessening number of jobs becomes a serious business affecting something as basic as how the very next meal will be paid for.

In addition to the plans in New York City and several other large population areas, many teachers and school administrators all over the country have gone far beyond the basic duties of their jobs to encourage, motivate, even cajole and coax parents and children into continuing educations for children who obviously need and can profit from them. The classic case of Billie Davis reported in the National Education Association's film, "A Desk for Billie," includes several examples of the dedicated professional person's aid to the migrant child. The Conservation of Human Resources Project, with which Eli Ginzberg has been associated, has attempted to tackle the giant task of finding out more about the factors which contribute to or retard the full development of the human potential. Waste and underutilization of human resources in our era of survival is tragic, and illiteracy is part of the tragedy.

The problem of the school dropout is revealed in some startling data not usually known, even among our school people. Although there have been follow-up programs which identify numbers and reasons for school leaving, most schools just have no idea at all of the reasons for this school loss, or more specifically, of their own contribution toward the nearly 1 million who leave each year.

With half of the top high school graduates in many communities either not starting or not finishing college, with 90 percent (or more) of the children in many "less chance" neighborhoods not even completing high school, with the dropout rate significantly high in every state and nearly every major city in the country, with more than 2 million 14- to 17-year-olds not in school right now, with about 175,000 girls leaving school each year to marry, the significance of the problem begins to emerge. In the 1960s 7½ million young people will enter the labor force without having completed high school, and 2½ million of these will not have even a grade-school education. Those figures mean that every third young worker entering the labor force during the 1960s will lack a high school education, although most have at least average intelligence, and many are bright enough to do college work.

Children go on in school for many overlapping reasons. Studies agree that college entry depends far less on intelligence than it does on class position and family income. For certain cultural levels and lower socioeconomic levels, high school completion is a dream and college is for other people's children. Although they may not verbalize their thoughts, the basic idea may be, "I went to school 4 years, and if my child goes 8 years, isn't that 100 percent improvement?" A "yes" answer hardly justifies the loss to all of us if the youngster is capable of far more.

There is a fallacy that public education is free. Hidden annual high school costs of $50 or more, plus the loss in the total family income of $40 or $50 a week because one adolescent is in school instead of on the job, mean that the family is $2000 in the red each year. Perhaps a compensating item is the figure sometimes used of $100,000 or more as the average difference in life earnings of college over high school graduates. Most of the reasons why children leave school can be found among the following:

Low parental and/or community levels of aspiration

Inability to afford keeping a child in school

Poor teachers and teaching; the accumulation of major and trivial antagonisms toward school over the years; boredom with school subjects; an active dislike of teachers

Early maturity; the eagerness to "move on" or get married; the attraction of relatively large starting salaries

Absence of motivation from any source; the numbing effect of repeated failure to be challenged

Less positive attitudes in some communities and families toward the continued education of girls

Dropout rates higher among rural and low-intelligence children and closely related to where the father is on the occupational ladder

Ridicule by peer group members who have already dropped out and who have begun to accumulate salary seniority at the one industry in town

Inability to study, fear of failure, illness, fuzzy personal goals and ambitions, an unclear picture of their own image in the years ahead

A need for more individualized instruction to foster greater academic success

Discriminatory practices in some schools and in some parts of industry; the awareness of young people of such practices and a resultant attitude of "what's the use?"

Lack of knowledge of one's own skills, interests, and capabilities

Lack of information about career possibilities and educational requirements

Broken and problem homes

The solution is sometimes inherent in the situation, sometimes completely elusive. Better teachers, better and earlier guidance, "exit" interviews, information for parents, early identification of potential dropouts, knowledge among all of us of the effect continued failure has on a person, basic belief in the values of education, identification of the personal needs of young people and educational programs adapted to them—all of these are part of the solution. The following estimate has been made about a specific element of the issue: If every Negro child received an education equivalent to that of the average white child in the northern part of the country, the annual increase in Negro high school and college graduates would more than double.[5]

It cannot be argued that children of families in lower socioeconomic levels do not want more education. The facts indicate exactly the opposite. The increased school enrollment that followed the establishment of the National Youth Administration in the 1930s and the frequency of "lack of money" as a reason for leaving school indicate that finances play a big part. Quitting early frequently contributes to ultimate frustration when the child, grown older, realizes what might have been; and it contributes to serious social and economic waste when he settles into a vocation far beneath his capabilities or is unemployed. (The recent unemployment rate among out-of-school teenagers is 20 percent, compared to 7 percent for the population as a whole.)

The adult who left school early but had the ability to become a skilled surgeon, the one who might have brought the creative tendencies of children to fruition in the classroom, and the one who could have developed to capacity in engineering are losses to the community as school dropouts are ignored and permitted to continue at a high rate. This problem, as is true of illiteracy, has attracted greater attention in recent years. Among the most valuable products of that attention is *School and Early Employment Experience of Youth* (Bulletin no. 1277 of the U.S. Department of Labor, 1960), a 5-year report of seven communities. It concludes that young people who drop out of high school earn less than graduates, have to take less skilled jobs, and have higher rates of unemployment. Other sources have indicated that they contribute to an incidence of juvenile delinquency that is ten times higher than among high school

[5] Eli Ginzberg, *Human Resources: The Wealth of a Nation*, New York, Simon and Schuster, Inc., 1958, p. 58.

graduates. By 1970, fewer than 5 percent of all available jobs will be of the unskilled variety, and where will the uneducated be then?

The reasons given for leaving school may not be the real ones at all. For example, lack of money may hide the distaste for some teacher. The boy or girl may not even know the *real* reason for dropping out. The significant thing is that he leaves, that he and/or his family feel it is the proper thing to do, and that the labor force of the United States is deprived of one more hand operating to full capacity in the cause of freedom and security.

HOW PEOPLE FEEL ABOUT THE SCHOOLS

From the magnitude of education's goals and the size of its problems one would think that the teaching profession is highly respected, encouraged, and recognized for its real worth. But is that true? Or is the public attitude based more on apathy and misunderstanding, related more to William James' plaintive comment that "plenty of people wish well to any good cause, but very few care to exert themselves to help it, and still fewer will risk anything in its support"? As candidates for political office frequently say, let us look at the record, or at least part of it. This look may make you cringe a bit, but you are entitled to a preview of your chosen work and to some insight into what people think about it.

Because we too often view the schools in isolation, perhaps a good starting place is an Elmo Roper report which tapped a broader set of attitudes by asking this question: "In every community, the schools, the newspapers, the local government, the television stations, [all have] a different job to do. Would you say that the local schools are doing an excellent, good, fair, or poor job?" The same question was asked for each of the others, and the results came out this way:

	Excellent	Good	Fair	Poor	Don't Know
Schools	20%	44%	21%	5%	10%
Newspapers	14	50	25	5	6
Local government	6	38	32	11	13
TV stations	11	48	26	6	9

SOURCE: Reported in *Phi Delta Kappan*, June, 1960, p. 410.

Another effort at summarizing public attitudes toward the schools was made in a compilation of the reports of all major polls from 1950 to 1958. It indicated five significant opinion areas:

A strong endorsement of the goals of American education—to create an enlightened electorate and to provide all children with an education appropriate to them as individuals.

A general lack of agreement on what should be done to remedy curricular deficiencies.

A conviction that the value of practical training is greater than liberal education.

Evidence that educators are more demanding of American education than is the general public.

An overwhelming opinion in favor of federal financial support.[6]

Although there is evidence that both parents and school administrators feel the schools demand too little of children, the administrators are nearly twice as strong in this opinion. Parents generally favor automatic promotions, and pressures are from outside the school for nonacademic courses. The schools themselves may often become the public whipping boy for reasons that are not often recognized. One can control the tax money that goes for teachers' salaries, while that designated for moon shots, highways, foreign aid, and fish hatcheries cannot be controlled. One may vote against school bond issues; but is it because the schools are too costly, or because a disproportionate share of school expenses are carried by the property owner? One hears that Johnny cannot read or spell, but are we all clear on what education equal to our times really is?

The attitudes of parents and the community transfer easily to the attitudes of children. If the former take schools lightly and question their value as a whole, we can hardly expect the opinions of children to be on a higher level. If in the home the futility of study is stressed or the example set by parental "homework" of writing letters, mending clothes, or keeping the house clean and orderly is taken with a grain of salt, the child's attitude toward school work and conduct can hardly be conducive to academic accomplishment. If the family encourages subjective criticism of individual teachers, school regulations, and courses of study, the child would be less than human if

6 "Public Opinion on Education," *NEA Research Bulletin*, October 1958, p. 74.

those adult discussions did not deflate any affirmative attitudes he might have had toward school.

Today's teachers unfortunately must struggle against ideas that hardly fit in with the profession on which we depend for the preservation of our culture. A book that stresses our tendency to ignore excellence in all phases of our society puts the point this way:

Despite all the bromides about the crucial importance of individual teachers, the paucity of provisions for their recognition (not to mention their compensation) suggests the existence of some fundamental ambiguities in American attitudes. Charles Howard of the University of Oregon tells of going with a delegation to intercede with the then Governor about teachers' salaries, and being told that the best teacher the Governor ever had was Old Aunt Het, who never got but forty dollars a month, and never needed more.

Old Aunt Het is still very much with us, and I suspect she will remain with us until the image of the American school teacher is drastically changed.[7]

That the image is changing very slowly was demonstrated in 199 New York communities a few years ago where four out of ten children and almost half the parents said they had no respect for their teachers' knowledge. In 79 of the communities more than half the male teachers held jobs after hours to make ends meet, and most communities took it for granted that teachers should perform after-school duties for no extra pay. When asked whether they would like their sons to go into teaching, a strong group answered, "No."

On the other hand, a similar survey in New London, Connecticut, revealed that most of the people had no teachers among their friends, most would like very much to have them as friends, more than eight out of ten favored the employment of teachers from minority groups, and the overwhelming majority felt that standards of conduct should be the same for teachers as for others in the community. They thought teachers were justified in unionizing, should be active politically, and definitely felt that teaching should be classified as a profession.

So, choose your groups to poll, ask your questions, and the answers run the gamut from respect to ridicule, from support to opposition. An occupation that some people feel requires no special expertness, that can attract applicants despite the low salaries, that includes thousands of women passing their time until a husband or family comes along, that is viewed sometimes with a patronizing, often with an unfriendly eye, that some segments of the public assume is filled with persons who cannot earn a good living elsewhere, such an occupation has an uphill battle toward respectability. Despite the many well-loved teachers it includes, the total effect is far from the top level of social status and group values.

If we look at the results of public indifference, rather than the causes for it, we get some thought-provoking help from an astute observer of the educational scene.

The reality is that public education is not in the mainstream of American life. For example, one cannot think of a person working in the field of public education who is a nationally known personality. The field of labor brings to mind names like John L. Lewis, Walter Reuther, or George Meany. In medicine, one thinks of Dr. Jonas Salk, of Dr. Paul Dudley White. Similarly, in the arts, government, law, theology, industry, and many other major fields, one can quickly name several persons whose names are known all over the country. Not all are known for desirable reasons, but they are people who make national and even international news. It is a measure of the public indifference to our schools that there are no such names in the field of public education. Even in the segregation crises, educators are secondary figures. Politicians, journalists, NAACP leaders, and some students are more important personalities than the professional school people, who are more or less puppets in the whole situation.[8]

The salary factor is considered to be the key one by some writers on educational subjects. Their comments may appear to be sharp and bitter, but the element of truth manages to squeeze through just the same.

In American society there is a distressing tendency for most of our quickest, brightest minds to chase the quick, fast buck. The greatest number of our most competent youth do not exactly batter down the doors of the academy, clamoring for a place on the faculty. They never did, from the days of Ichabod Crane to date. If we were to assign enormous social prestige and a salary of $50,000 a year, tax free, to the job of teaching second grade, this deplorable situation would doubtless change within the hour. We

[8] Myron Lieberman, *The Future of Public Education*, The University of Chicago Press, 1960, p. 284.

would see an incredible jump in the number and quality of those applying for the job. As long as a canary might expect malnutrition on the kind of salary we most often offer our teachers, however, we must face the fact that the teaching profession will remain exactly what it is—too small, and limited to the dedicated and the incompetent.[9]

Problems related to professional respect are not all related to you personally, but they may be part of your entry into an area that is often undervalued in our culture, where both inspiration and dedication may go largely unnoticed, and where the results of good or great teaching may mature at a much later date and distant point. It is a profession that is sometimes fairly, sometimes unfairly, caricatured, and in which occasional eccentricities and poor human relations are viewed as the usual thing by those for whom the caricature has become real.

You will have to become accustomed to such faulty generalizations, and perhaps when the products of the education you impart reach adulthood in your community, the attitudes toward teachers and teaching will be less distorted. But that is asking for a great deal of patience and time on your part. And yet, changes in human feelings *do* emerge, though slowly, certainly more slowly than the startling changes in the scientific world around us.

Perhaps consistency in society's attitudes toward teachers is too much to expect. But its inconsistencies are too apparent to go unnoticed. Society wants and expects an elementary teacher to be an expert in mathematics, history, geography, science (both biological and physical), reading and the other language arts, music, dramatics, art, and a whole list of other subjects, to keep up with each field and its research, and to know intimately each child's abilities, aptitudes, interests, and idiosyncrasies. "But what's in it for me?" the alert future teacher sometimes asks, and not so meekly either. "How do I buy bread, shoes, and perhaps a small bottle of wine for my spaghetti now and then? How well am I paid for being an expert in so many fields?" The questions are fair, and the answers stated in nonmonetary terms like "satisfaction," "inspiration," and "enjoyment" are becoming less and less appropriate each year as young people's realistic looks at life increase.

A social position below most professions and business and the

[9] John Keats, *Schools Without Scholars*, Boston, Houghton Mifflin Company, 1958, pp. 133–134.

economic need for holding a second job will have to be on their way out, and fast too. But prestige cannot be legislated, dragging a higher pay scale along with it. It will have to be earned by a series of actions that all have to be accomplished at the same time. These include strengthening teacher preparation programs on every campus, more selectivity of future teachers in every school, college, and department of education, electing responsible and intelligent school boards in every community, eliciting the cooperation of every parent toward solving the almost insurmountable problems of schools, and many others that involve the *entire* public in bringing new vigor into our most vital profession. No one person can accomplish these tasks; nor can they be accomplished with only a piecemeal effort.

An encouraging angle to education's current status is that it is being talked about and written about, from nursery school through the university and adult levels, as never before. Perhaps that in itself is recognition of its importance. Of course, the comments are not always pleasant, but at least they are evidence that teachers and teaching are on the public's tongues and minds. If we were ignored, we would have to be pessimistic about changes in attitudes; but no teacher can look through the daily papers and popular magazines and feel isolated and unknown. You are going into a profession that is like a goldfish bowl.

Some changes have already taken place, though perhaps not of the most important type. This little verse illustrates one of them:

> The other day
> Our lady Vice-Principal
> Got onto the street car.
> She was wearing a brand-new dress.
> I heard a woman in the seat back of me
> Remark to her friend:
> "Ain't it awful the way these women dress?
> You can't tell school teachers from ladies now-a-days."[10]

If the greater changes related to total respect, better salaries, and a full understanding of the job of education were also to come, you would be entering a profession well on its way toward the status it deserves. Your years in it may see them materialize.

[10] Virginia Church, "Almost Human," in *Teachers are People*, Santa Barbara, Wallace Hebberd, 1945; quoted in Emma Reinhardt, *American Education*, New York, Harper & Row, Publishers, Inc., 1960, p. 7.

THE POWER STRUCTURE OF EDUCATION

One of the first things a person who is serious about entering the teaching field should do is to shed any notions that are accepted because they sound good, because everyone knows they are true, or because it is just comfortable to adopt them without thinking. Your days of being a yes-man to what appears in print, whether in a textbook or the daily newspaper, and to what is uttered in deep or pompous tones over television and radio, should be either gone or rapidly on their way out. But you must ask questions because you really want to know; question because you are tired of accepting without proof, fact, or full understanding; challenge because time is short and it demands full exposure of all points of view.

When the statement is made, for example, that the schools belong to the people, it is easy to agree. Of course they do. But the question immediately arises concerning *which* people we are talking about. Parents? taxpayers? All who live in a particular community, city, state, part of the country—or the entire country? And the schools belong to them for what purpose? To set policies? To select textbooks? To hire and fire teachers? To vote on bond issues? To designate curricular content?

If one community cannot afford, or refuses, to educate its children up to their capacities, should their inability or refusal go unnoticed? A child is a child, you say, and he is entitled to a full education no matter who he is, how much his parents earn, where he was born, or what the color of his skin or his religion is. He should not be penalized because of where he lives. The accident of birth or home locality should not be the deciding factor about his education, either its caliber or length. The real problem—and one you must continue to ask about all through your professional career—is who makes the decision for what? Just because Johnny's family is almost always on the move and he is in each school for less than a month (if at all), does that absolve all local communities, each state, and the federal government of its responsibility to educate him? Tom's school does not offer chemistry (and he wants to be a chemist), Mary's school board feels one year of high school mathematics is plenty (and she likes nothing better than the advanced intricacies of math), and

Jim's is incapable of offering more than 2 years of a foreign language, restricting it to Spanish when he knows Latin will be more useful to him (and 4 years of it at that).

You have to encourage the gadfly of doubt in your thinking, based on down-to-earth questions like these:

Do all states and communities have the same amount of taxable wealth to support their schools? What does that fact mean?

What can be done about *interstate* problems in education, whether they pertain to migrant children and our increasingly mobile and interdependent total population, research that can benefit all of us (our current expenditure is about $25 *million* in a $20 *billion* enterprise), or inequalities that penalize children who were apparently unwise in selecting the families into which they were born? Who should do something about these problems?

Should we discuss—or continue to ignore—the fact that it is only in education that the board members who set up licensing standards are practically never from within the occupation, a fact that would be ridiculed in law, medicine, dentistry, and the other professions?

For a highly vocal minority in our country their hair begins to bristle on their necks as soon as the federal government is brought into the power-structure discussion. One well-known senator even went so far as to maintain on a widely seen television debate that we have far more to fear from Washington than from Moscow! Words like "interference," "control," and "domination" are tossed in to straighten out the "misinformed." But statements like the one that follows are seldom used or listened to (italics are mine):

Many persons believe that public education was not made a federal responsibility in the Constitution because the founding fathers feared the potentialities for dictatorship in a federal school system. Actually, education was not included as a federal function in the Constitution because the idea of free public education had not even occurred to the founding fathers. At the time of the American Revolution, the concept of universal public education was receiving attention for the first time and then only from a few frontier thinkers. *Our decentralized school system was not an inspired stroke of genius but a historical accident,* resulting from the fact that the ideal of free public education for all became widely accepted only long after the American Revolution.[11]

Perhaps we are wary of Soviet Russia's centralized educational

[11] Lieberman, *op. cit.,* pp. 39–40.

system; but on the other hand, in England and other European countries there is *less* pressure and interference than our teachers and administrators feel. The influences of national pressure groups are frequently felt in our local communities when an essay contest is set up or scuttled, when "UNESCO" and "United Nations" suddenly become questionable terms, when "phonics" or "readiness" or "driver training" becomes the rallying cry for excited, subjective movements. "Ours is a heterogeneous country, but in most communities the predominant racial, religious, economic, or political groups are able to veto whatever in the school program displeases them."[12]

Local authority to tax for support of the schools exists in every community and state, but how long would the people stay if the taxes were raised to the point where they would sustain school systems that an enlightened few feel are absolutely necessary in the years ahead? Business and industry would hit the road to other areas less concerned about education, leaving those few still enlightened but also very lonely! And what is the role of the federal government at this point in the total complicated picture of support for public education?

Another important question is related to lay versus expert control of education. Somehow some people have the notion that the more removed a person is from the field of education the more he knows about it; and they may have an accompanying mistrust of the educator, assuming that he represents a vested interest. But what about the layman on the board: will he never represent a narrow group, a limited point of view? Of course, but the sanctity of the uninformed school board remains intact and largely unquestioned.

Local school-board elections may be important, but the number who vote in them is generally limited. The local people elected are also limited in what they can, and sometimes want to do. In the long run, the attitudes and votes of congressmen on educational issues may be vastly more important. So will be the leadership and persistence of an enlightened president in calling our attention to the place of education in national goals.

One factor related to education's power structure is whether the leadership is in the school or in the society. Many writers in the past, like George Counts and Harold Rugg, and some in the present, like

12 *Ibid.*, p. 39.

Theodore Brameld, have tried to grab a hold on this slippery subject. The problem has been stated clearly and succinctly by another current writer:

Does society determine what the school should be, and the school then simply follow the dictates of society? This is as it has always been in the development of educational systems as delegated agencies of social control. Kandel, in his comprehensive study of comparative educational systems throughout the world, was led to remark that the society *always* leads and the school *always* follows.

But a contrary viewpoint is finding increasing, if not yet widespread, expression in our own country at least. That is the view that the school ought to be a positive force for social leadership, never to be content merely to reflect social change, often with a considerable period of culture lag involved. Those who advocate that the schools should take leadership in educational matters point out patiently, but with only partially restrained annoyance, that research studies continue to show that there is a twenty-five to fifty-year lag between the time some educational innovation is proved successful and its general adoption into the life and work of the school. They suggest, therefore, that the school should become actually a leader or a "reconstructor" of society, and the educator a "social engineer" who blueprints and brings about these changes. Although the overt supporters of this view are not very many in numerical proportion to the more conservative believers in the school as a follower of society, the force and impact of their rather compelling arguments have made the question a real issue in American education.[13]

Yes, the schools belong to the people and the people hire professional personnel to operate them; and the professional persons are caught in a squeeze play of pressures and money, two facts of educational life which they are never permitted to forget. The intertwining controls are external (fraternal, parental, religious, patriotic, political, labor, industrial, governmental, and others) as well as internal (teachers, students, textbook publishers, professional organizations, accrediting agencies, the next-higher educational level and all the people in it, and many others).

A complicated picture? It certainly is—and one that requires all the intelligence, knowledge, and tact that you can bring to it. It also requires constant attention to the key question raised earlier: who

[13] Kenneth H. Hansen, *Philosophy for American Education*, Englewood Cliffs, N. J., Prentice-Hall, Inc., 1960, pp. 187–188.

makes the decisions that affect this child in his reading lesson, in his full day of educational activity, in his entire curricular setting, in his whole educational career? A related one that certainly ought to be asked is this one: Who *should* make them? Understanding the complex set of answers to those questions, and recognizing your significant role in them, are a big part of getting ready for your job.

EDUCATION ON THE WORLD STAGE

The picture of education in our own country is only part of the panorama. You cannot take stock of the total situation unless you take a complete 360-degree turn rather than a slight twist of your head to right or left. Even a tiny rural school in the broad expanse of our southwest desert, our northwest forests, or our middle west farmlands is far from being isolated in the world today. It is bound to the Haitian parents who literally sell the fillings out of their teeth so their children can get enough money to go to school, to the Sicilian farmers who after dawn-to-dusk days in their fields spend full evenings five nights a week learning to read and write, to the children in India who squat for hours and eagerly watch their teachers in flimsy schoolrooms or in no schoolroom at all. Our own children and schools are part of the tapestry which includes illiterates that outnumber our own a hundredfold, new countries by the dozens who see the education of their children as the factor on which their economic success must be based, and continents, vastly greater than our own in population and size.

You can go into many countries, old or new, and note the educational ferment. They want skilled personnel from the United States to help prepare their teachers, to assist in setting up or changing their schools and school programs, to be the catalyst toward reducing or eliminating illiteracy, starvation, and disease. And if they cannot get a boost from us, they will seek it elsewhere. More than 50,000 foreign students are on campuses in this country (in 1952, there were fewer than 30,000). In 1960, students and faculty totalling 15,000 went abroad to study, teach, do research, or assist foreign educational institutions. Nearly 70 of our universities have almost 100 contracts to help out educationally in 33 countries, and 7000 persons were brought to the United States in 1960 for specialized educational preparation. The International Teacher Exchange program in 1960 tripled the figure of a decade earlier (still under 1000) and our international teacher-development efforts included 81 countries.

As big as those figures seem, they are much too small according to some who have studied the situation closely. At the request of the Department of State a committee was set up by the Ford Foundation under Dr. J. L. Morrill, former president of the University of Minnesota, to dig into this subject. The committee recommended that there be a special assistant to the secretary of state for coordinating our many international educational and cultural functions; a special presidential assistant to be concerned with these problems; a careful look at various universities and their contracts to be certain that they are equipped for the tasks they have taken on. A big break-through must be made in these international activities, for our own benefit. That we have a long way to go in our educational relationships with other countries was indicated in a colorful way by Dr. Harlan Cleveland, dean of Syracuse University's Maxwell Graduate School, who said: "We know in our hearts that we are in the world for keeps, yet we are still tackling twenty-year problems with five-year plans staffed with two-year personnel with one-year appropriations."[14]

Again we have evidence that the dream of education does not come cheaply for either other countries or for us. It is costly in time, personnel, and money. But our commitment to it with words is not enough, and it never will be. With the new countries of Africa looking to our land-grant colleges rather than to British universities as their model, with their awareness of our economic and social successes combined with a huge educational enterprise (and the relationship is hardly coincidental to them any more than it is to us), with the knowledge they have of great needs in almost every direction, with all this we cannot fail to provide the encouragement and help they need. If factors like those do not stimulate us, the presence of our major competitor on the world scene and its eagerness to be helpful no doubt should!

In many parts of the world the student struggle is for the basics:

[14] *New York Times,* January 15, 1961.

food, shelter, books. The World University Service has national committees in 41 countries that are helping meet those needs on the college and university level by pioneering projects which then may receive further development on the local level. Among the W.U.S. 1961–1962 programs are the organization of cooperative student hostels in Greece, Burma, India, Pakistan, Indonesia, and Korea; support of student health services in Hong Kong, the Sudan, Thailand, and Vietnam; establishment of projects for community development under university sponsorship in many African countries; and assistance for student printing and publishing centers for the production of inexpensive textbooks and materials and for cooperative bookstores.

These basics of getting a shelter from sun and storm and enough to eat just to stay alive as a foundation for study and research, are somewhat different from the educational basics you have heard and read about. But they are the concerns for millions of the world's youths in countries just beginning to rise out of the starvation level. If these stark economic problems are not solved, the education will not come. They are firm in their efforts to solve them and their educational needs at the same time—and in the immediate future.

They see, for example, a problem of illiteracy much more intense than ours: 56 of 109 countries and territories covering 80 percent of the world's population have illiteracy percentages above 40, with a median of about 55 percent. That means that half the world's population cannot read or write. But the situation is even worse than that. One study[15] reveals that in 11 African countries more than 80 percent of the population is illiterate, and in 14 Asian countries more than 60 percent. Of every ten children in the world, five do not go to school at all, four are in primary school (most of them will not even reach the level of functional literacy), and only one is receiving a postprimary education. In 9 countries with more than 90 percent illiteracy the population is 93 million; and in 12 with 80–89 percent illiteracy the population is 473 million.

The children we teach (and their teachers too) take in stride the new flashy shopping center, the conveniences (and problems) of sub-

[15] Reported in William S. Gray, The Teaching of Reading and Writing, Chicago, Scott, Foresman and Company, 1956, pp. 28–29.

urban and tract housing, and the latest bulletin on a new television series. But these less pleasant facts must also be accepted, for they too are an integral part of the child and adult world in which we live.

European Style

"Is European education better than ours?" This question has been asked often, and the answers have more frequently been shouted in anger than discussed objectively.

"Better for whom?" might be an appropriate starting point. For all children? For certain age levels? For a special part of the socio-economic ladder? For specific intellectual levels? As in so many phases of the school picture, the answers are not clear-cut. You read Admiral Rickover (and some educators get red and hot under the collar at the mere mention of his name), and you have to admit that even though his dogmatism and writing style may annoy you, a few of his ideas make very good sense, particularly those related to gifted children. Likewise, as we look at various facets of education in European countries, some are black, some white, some gray. At the very moment the United States seems to be most critical of its own educational business, the people and schools in western Europe are moving closer to what they see here. While some folks at home are lauding foreign schools, Europeans are scuttling age-old ideas in favor of some of ours. Why is that? Obviously they are not fully satisfied. An editorial in the educational supplement of the *London Times* exhorted England to "look to America" for guidance in the new technology of education.[16]

One of their dissatisfactions is with a series of tests for children around the age of 11 which determine educational and vocational futures. These tests favor the wealthier groups, whose children have the enriched environments and the preparation needed to pass them. It may honestly be noted that these all-important tests are sometimes of the parents' ability to pay for supplementary boning-up more than they are of the child's capacity to learn. We worry about our waste of talent, and with good reason; but their waste is even greater, with 80 to 85 percent knowing at this early age that formal education will and must soon cease. On the surface it is academic

---

[16] Reported in the *New York Times*, March 5, 1961.

ability that decides whether a child will go on. In reality, family tradition, class, and wealth play an influential role in a majority of countries of western Europe. And the "late bloomers" from poor families do not stand a chance.

Gradually they are borrowing from our philosophy, not yet fully a practice, of universal education, both elementary and secondary, to the limit of the child's ability regardless of social or economic background. But they are developing a significant trend that we ought to note and think about. In Scotland the trend is not even new. Although it is a poor country there is a century-old policy of subsidizing the university education of every able man, even if his parents represent the very lowest socioeconomic group. At Oxford and Cambridge more than half the students receive substantial scholarships, so that some of the lower- and middle-class intelligence is not lost; the less the family income is the larger the student grant. Eton has many secondary-level students who are the sons of tradesmen and workingmen attending at practically no cost. The governments of West Germany and Denmark also make it very easy for children who are intellectually gifted to receive scholarship aid. (Too frequently our own point of view is that they will manage to muddle through.) France, too, prides itself on the uncompromising objective of enabling each student with appropriate capabilities to go to the academic top, with government financial support if necessary.

Still, most of the 16- and 17-year-olds in Europe are not in school while most of ours are. Essentially their program is to educate an elite; ours is to educate as many as possible. Both have their favorable and unfavorable points. Theirs includes greater attention to and concern for the academically able but at the same time neglects the many. Ours includes the only comprehensive secondary-school system in the world, an admirable experiment toward universal education, but frequently we sacrifice quality for quantity.

Comparisons are sometimes made between the scholastic achievement of their students and ours, and you have to be on guard against the data used in such comparisons. Are similar groups being used, our honor groups and theirs, for example? Or is the comparison between our mass educational product and their selective minority? Perhaps it is more fair to ask how our doctors, lawyers, and scientists compare with theirs. In addition, their university students are preparing for a profession, while only some of ours are.

Few of us want to develop a system of education based on class, and many Europeans are on the rampage against their own. Even fewer of us favor the European education which played at least *some* part in the start of two wars in one generation; which gave birth to Naziism and Communism; and which resulted in the brutal death of 6 million men, women, and children. This unbelievable cruelty must have been related in some way to the educational system of which the performers of these deeds were a product.

Byron S. Hollinshead, in his effort at a factual comparison between American and European education, first points out that we need plenty of improvement and then asks:

What then is the American, this new Man, who has made the deserts bloom, who has taken the peasantry out of farming, who has removed the drudgery from factories, whose productivity per worker is by far the highest there is, who is surrounded by the world's best existing systems of communication and transportation. Was this progress made by a people with an inferior educational system? If so, inferior to what? To their own ideals perhaps but to little else. . . .

"You Americans, you are always several steps ahead of us. How do you do it? In science, your equipment and techniques are better. Your society is not so stratified, giving more opportunities to the individual. In citizenship your people seem willing to make more sacrifices for the common good. Your government is so stable. How does that happen? Your system of education gives a chance to everybody. How can you afford to educate so many? How do you make Americans out of Europeans so quickly? National feelings are very strong here in Europe but emigrants to the United States settle down quickly and peacefully with formerly hated neighbors. Is there some secret about this?"[17]

Sweetness-and-light comments like these have more than one element of truth in them, but they also have a tendency to lull us more completely into a sleep of complacency regarding how good we are. When you remember some of the teachers you have had, read again his references to "citizenship," "sacrifices," and "a chance to every-

[17] Byron S. Hollinshead, "Is European Education Better?" *The Educational Record*, April, 1958.

body," observe the neglect, deficiencies, and waste in our educational programs, you may come away with something clear-cut in your thinking. It might go this way: As good as it is, our education has to be better, and quickly too; as good or bad as European programs are, we must improve on our own and on theirs, and we can; as much progress as we have made, it is essential that we make more; as many scientists, university professors, and other intellectuals as we can point to as products of our own schools, we must aim even higher.

Russian Style

In the daily newspapers, semipopular books, mass magazines, and professional literature, the discussions and descriptions of educational programs in the U.S.S.R. have been a virtual torrent. How we feel about what they are doing depends a great deal on how we feel about them in a broader vein. Is our attitude one of superiority, fear, belligerency, anger, hopefulness, hopelessness, frustration, antagonism, or tolerance? The answer we give may be an indication of what we think of their educational offerings.

Before we look at them, let us get one thing clear: The reports that come to this country about Russian education are often biased. Their schools and teachers are frequently viewed by visitors, prepared to see either the good or the bad, whose comments after they come back home indicate clearly their personal prejudices. Furthermore, articles and books may be written to startle the public rather than state the facts, and may be based on a quick 10-day or 2-week visit. How accurate would a visitor's report be of education in the United States if he visited only New York or Mississippi or one part of California? Russia is a tremendous country too; despite the apparent nationalization of their schools, the diversity because of the many varied cultures, languages, and teacher backgrounds must also be great.

Dependability of source, repetition of information, and obvious logic (or lack thereof) have been used as the criteria for including items among the eight major areas discussed below. Their net effect should give you, in brief form, some understanding of education in the U.S.S.R. This understanding is necessary in view of the recent Russian achievements in space and the figures comparing education in our country and theirs frequently published in the press. Let us look at some of the highlights of their educational growth and its current status.

MOTIVATION

During World War II, Russian losses as they affect this field reached fantastic proportions: About 20 million persons died, more than 80,000 schools and 300 institutions of higher learning were destroyed or badly damaged, more than 40,000 libraries containing 100 million books were destroyed. With a high level of illiteracy and a composite blow like that, what would you do if you were in the driver's seat? The choice is simple. You either give up or knuckle down to the job ahead. It is obvious that they chose to do the latter.

Part of their aggressiveness is a "show-'em" attitude, a feeling that this is what only Communism can do. Part of it is no doubt the tenacity of purpose of a people, a desire to follow through on something that has become vitally important in a relatively short period of time. And part of it may be a late awakening to what many parents in central and western Europe have wanted and been able to secure for their children for generations.

ATTITUDES

There is unanimity of opinion about the Russian commitment to their schools and teaching, and all who return from visits to their cities, villages, and rural areas seem to come to the same conclusions: "they have a community respect for education, almost a missionary zeal about education that is unlike anything in America";[18] "where people stand in line waiting to be served, perhaps one in five will be reading a book; so do many while they are riding a bus. Serious books are abundant and inexpensive . . . the incentives to improve one's capabilities by participating in one of the many study programs consist of various amounts of time off to study, with pay and related assistance . . . the people of Russia value education and self-improvement highly";[19] "in the organization of a planned society in

[18] Ruth Dunbar, "Russian Education Re-examined," *Current Issues in Higher Education*, Washington, D. C., NEA, 1959, p. 53.

[19] T. W. Schultz, "Human Capital: A Growing Asset," *Saturday Review*, January 21, 1961, pp. 38, 39.

the Soviet Union, education is regarded as one of the chief resources and techniques for achieving social, economic, cultural, and scientific objectives in the national interest. Tremendous responsibilities are therefore placed on Soviet schools, and comprehensive support is provided for them by all segments and agencies of Soviet society . . . everywhere we went in the U.S.S.R. we were struck by the zeal and enthusiasm which people have for education. It is a kind of grand passion with them."[20]

The "zeal and enthusiasm" may be partly related to the inferiority they feel in material possessions. One Soviet scientist said: "You Americans have a better standard of living than we have. But the American loves his car, his refrigerator, his house. He does not, as the Russians do, love his country."[21] But despite all the high-level words and big ideas, elementary education attendance is still uneven though compulsory, especially in rural areas, and less than half the youngsters of high school age are in school. Fewer than one in ten of their labor force has completed high school. All of these figures are going up every year, however.

CURRICULUM

If you have not encountered the list that follows, your recent years have certainly been sheltered. The reputed educational diet of all who are graduated from Soviet high schools is 5 years of physics, 4 years of chemistry, 1 year of astronomy, 5 years of biology, 10 years of mathematics and trigonometry, and 5 years of a foreign language. As it relates to a 10-year education, science and mathematics occupy 31.4 percent of the student's time, humanities and social studies 48 percent, polytechnic education 13.2 percent, physical education 7.4 percent. Mathematics is begun in first grade, biology in fourth, physics in sixth, chemistry in seventh. (The curriculum has gone through several revisions. For example, back in 1953 and 1954 one of the educational goals was to revise the secondary-school curriculum in order to lighten pupil load and introduce more vocational training and recreation.)

Our reactions to these statistics are varied: "They have only a

[20] U. S. Department of Health, Education, and Welfare, *Soviet Commitment to Education,* Bulletin 1959, no. 16, Government Printing Office, 1959, p. 1.

[21] Leonid I. Sedov, quoted in *Time,* October 21, 1957, p. 51.

small minority who finish high school"; "Let's do the same"; "Let's give our children more, harder, heavier"; "But they teach the subjects fewer days during the week, teach directly for examinations, call it *metallurgy* when it's really only *sheet metal*"; "That's their business, for their society." About certain phases of this subject there can be little argument, however. Their tailor-made curriculum is set up and manipulated to serve the needs of the state. It is part of a vast network of in-school, out-of-school, and summer activities that combine recreation, education, and indoctrination.

Although it is important that we examine their curriculum, we must decide what is best for *us*. Being in the same small world with them we must conclude that what they do in education, as well as in every other important segment of their culture, has deep significance for us. But if we tighten up, as we should do and are doing in a spotty way, it is because we need to for ourselves. Max Lerner said it succinctly:

> I find a curious eagerness now on the part of a number of people to say that we ought to imitate the Russian system of education, as if the Russians had found the key to a good life. They undoubtedly have very practical, concrete things that we can learn, but when it comes to the crucial question of how to bring up young men and women in a free society, they don't know anything about how to do it, because they have not been practicing it.[22]

TEACHING TECHNIQUES

The teaching keynotes seem to be attentive listening, acceptance without question of what is read or heard, strict discipline, little or no discussion of issues, lecture-recitation methods, early teaching of conformity, unimaginative instruction, and rote memory. The needs of the state supercede the needs or desires of the individual in both teaching techniques and educational content. The maximum amount of homework is fixed by the Republic Ministries of Education, with daily limits ranging from 1 to 4 hours. Techniques based on question-and-answer, memorization of facts, and full attention to the business at hand dominate the classroom.

We may be smug and say that all this is old stuff to us, old-fashioned, long gone, good riddance and all that. But perhaps we

[22] *NEA Journal*, October, 1958, p. 458.

should not be so quick to dismiss every bit of it. Are we so sure that some of our teachers and children could not profit from some of these techniques? Is there a chance that the pendulum of *laissez faire,* fear of hurting children's personalities, and eagerness for togetherness, group activity, and social acceptance has swung too far in some classrooms, and that it is time for taking special stock of that factor? We may not like the techniques they use, but are there children who can gain from a more frequent use of some of them? Again, it is the reasonable approach that makes sense, rather than the assumption that all is black (them) or white (us). By the way, their school week consists of 6 days, and just a little figuring would indicate that in 10 years the Soviet child spends the same number of days in school as ours does in 12 years. However, it is not fair to discuss this point apart from our own commitment to a 5-day working week for adults.

A few years ago a number of Soviet physicians and pediatricians charged educational authorities with endangering the health of school children by lesson and homework overloads. They called attention to chronic overexhaustion, frequent headaches, weakened vision, and proneness to infectious diseases, and demanded correction of the problem.

MONEY

Everything is relative, of course, but the evidence is that they use a higher percentage of their national income than we do on education. Argue, if you want to, that our total income is greater than theirs or that numbers are open to doubt and question. The figures sometimes used are our 3 percent of our national income with 1 percent on higher education, versus their 9 percent, with 3 percent on higher education. These figures vary greatly depending on which sources you use.

Admiral Rickover brought the money topic into focus when he said:

Most European countries, by 1957-58 figures, put about 2½ to 3½ per cent of their national income into public education; we invest 3½ per cent, or nearly the same; Russia invests more than 6 per cent, and some experts believe it may be nearer 12 per cent. When a country with a much lower living standard than ours spends a greater percentage of national income on education, it is time we pause and reflect.[23]

TEACHERS

If you want to use salary as the basis for comparison, note the statement frequently made that Russian professors and academicians earn as much in Russian values as the head of General Motors does here. The Russian professor earns 8 times as much as the average factory worker (our professors make about 1½ times the average factory worker's pay). Respect and prestige apparently go along with the pay. Their elementary- and secondary-school teachers do not do nearly as well, but salaries are far better in comparison with other occupations than ours, making it pay very well to choose teaching as a career. Salaries of beginning teachers equal, in general, those of doctors and engineers.

Their clerical duties are minimal, and extra teachers or tutors are available to work with slow learners (pushing all children through the uniform curriculum) and to assist as aides. To achieve their objective of having every student pass, there are individual tutors, incentives, awards, and restriction of student privileges. This idea is based on the Marxian view that intelligence is environmental rather than hereditary, so there is no basic recognition of individual differences. Responsibility for student failure is the teacher's. Teachers devote an average of 18 hours a week to formal classroom work, compared to our schedule of 30 or more. The average class size has been reduced from 33 (in 1927) to 28 (in 1940) to 17 (in 1957), somewhat different from many of the classes *you* may have observed in recent months! Most teachers of the early grades have only 2 years of preparation, much like our old normal-school products. Those for fifth grade and up have 5 years of preparation. Just as in our country, there is increasing emphasis on subject matter in the preparation of both elementary and secondary teachers, and perhaps we are keeping pace with them on that trend which has been long overdue.

But do you think we can match them on this one: Of five students who apply for admission to institutions of teacher education, only one is accepted. We could go a long way in that direction in order to

[23] H. G. Rickover, *Education and Freedom,* New York, E. P. Dutton & Co., Inc., 1959, p. 177.

tighten up the sloppy selection techniques in many of our liberal arts colleges, where most teachers are prepared. However, we would hardly want to imitate their absence of academic freedom, discouragement of teacher initiative, and unawareness of our concept of teacher tenure (although our full acceptance of the tenure item might be questioned a bit as we observe some of the incompetents it freezes into jobs and imposes on numerous generations of children).

HIGHER EDUCATION

In Russia all tuition is free for higher education, and it is estimated that about 80 percent of the students also receive enough to pay their living expenses. In general, the higher the grades, the larger the stipend is. We may not like being put into the spot of admiring a Soviet practice, but most reasonable men and women would hardly dispute the wisdom of salvaging the foremost intellects among our youth and making sure that they receive educations so that their professional contributions are in accordance with their abilities. To do less (as we have tended to do) is wasteful and foolhardy.

The Russian system is a far cry from the old European type of education in that women constitute 60 percent of those preparing for medicine and about 30 percent of the future engineers. Competitive entrance examinations are tough, their content depending on the field to be entered. It is a Soviet practice to approve a single standard curriculum for each basic field and specialty, and all students must complete required courses in communist philosophy.

The teaching staff of Soviet higher education is required by law to spend an average of 3 hours a day on research. If some of the other points do not disturb our college and university teachers, that one should be a real irritant for many in the profession who are in actual semiretirement at a relatively youthful age! Most of the major research in Russia is not performed in universities, despite this legal requirement, but in special research organizations usually associated with a particular industry.

THE FUTURE

Within a few years the Russians expect to have preschool facilities available for all who want them, universal and compulsory schooling for 8 years, increased emphasis on vocational schools, and evening and correspondence classes in higher education. Curricular revisions are planned to help reduce the dropout rate, as they realize that all should not take an educational program planned for those going into higher education. Work experiences will be required beginning in first grade and "practical subject matter" will be emphasized all the way through. Pioneer centers will continue to be the major out-of-school source for youth activities and for encouraging talented boys and girls. The 1958 reform law "on the strengthening of ties between school and life" puts emphasis on intensified vocational, industrial, and agricultural training. (They will also have to solve the problem of science and mathematics teachers leaving for better jobs; that has a familiar ring to it!)

Criticism is mounting against mechanical memorization and a trend is developing toward increased self-reliance, initiative, and student participation. Both home economics and driver training are becoming part of the curriculum. (Perhaps such developments will be disillusioning to those who view Soviet education as a model for us to follow in every detail.) There is a burning desire to surpass us in education as well as in productivity, standard of living, world trade, and athletics. The slogan most frequently seen in posters and films is "Reach and Overreach America." Complete literacy is their immediate goal.

So what does all of this add up to? And what does it have to do with us? Our teachers should know something about the country, the people, and the educational program of our prime adversary in the years ahead. But it is also necessary to realize that they are preparing children for their society and we for ours. Harold Taylor, former president of Sarah Lawrence College, sees the we-versus-they picture in this way: "The truth is that the world will judge the Soviet and the American system of education by the quality of human beings which each of them develops, and whether or not these two countries can give leadership in the arts and sciences to cure the problems of disease, poverty, starvation and ignorance."[24]

The sources available to you on this whole subject are many, but do a little checking on their reliability before you swallow them. You

[24] In a speech at the ninth annual conference of the Bank Street College of Education, New York, March 4, 1961.

may be interested in publications from the U.S. Office of Education, such as *Soviet Education Programs: Foundation, Curriculums, Teacher Preparation,* Bulletin 1960, no. 17, available from the Government Printing Office (price, $1.25).

CONCLUDING REMARKS

Our effort in this chapter to take stock of the educational scene has primarily emphasized the present. This is amplified by a view of the entire subject from a different vantage point in the pages coming up. A little later there is a searching look at what the years ahead promise for our schools on the basis of experimentation, research, and hints already available to us.

That the current stock-taking could have easily been expanded at least a hundred times goes almost without saying. Ask practically anyone, in or out of the profession, what he thinks educational goals are and he will bend your ear with his ideas. Ask about the illiterate or the dropout, attitudes toward schools and teachers, or education in Russia and other European countries and if you escape without dogmatic opinions—whether or not they are supported by knowledge—the episode would be a rare one. Evidence of education as everybody's business is plentiful if we are to judge by those who are free with their ideas, beliefs, and judgments, regardless of the information or lack thereof to back them up. As a future teacher it will be better to reserve yours until more of the facts are in your possession.

CHAPTER 2

A TIME FOR *Seeing the Whole Picture*

Trying to grasp the entire picture of education is not easy, and yet you have to make the effort. When we finish there will still be many loose ends, many facts, figures, and ideas you will need to fill in to understand the profession toward which you are aiming. Some things you must realize even this early. One is that education is a huge enterprise, no matter whose standards you use.

More than $22 billion have been spent on the elementary- and secondary-school plant since 1919, most of it since the end of World War II. The total value—public, private, and parochial—is $30 billion (more than 4 times the assets of General Motors) ; building costs in 1960 were estimated at $3.2 billion (more than the assets of our richest railroad line). In fact, General Motors, American Telephone and Telegraph, and the entire oil industry would have to move over to make room at the top of the list for educational investment, personnel, time, and energy. Education has more employees, more "customers," more "branches," more members on its governing boards than any single private enterprise. It affects all levels of children and adults, on either the receiving or the giving ends, or both. It includes parents and teachers, from nursery school through university, adult education, and community involvements, and students ranging from 3 years to 30, 60, and even 90 years of age as our population of older people with time on their hands skyrockets. It extends to everything that people can learn, whether in formal classroom settings or over the back hedge.

Education should be seen in a framework that shows our population in the United States doubling in a single generation, the average family moving once every 5 years (and younger families about twice

64

as often), and a total population growth predicted between 1970 and 1980 that will be greater than the expansion we have faced at any time in our history.

The 1960 White House Conference on Children and Youth revealed many facts with which future teachers should be acquainted. All of them will affect your contribution to teaching, and they may even affect your decision to enter the field. In addition, they may have a real influence on what you derive from the profession, including salary. Here are some of these facts for you to think about:

Our population patterns are changing; we have many more children and older people, both numerically and in percentages.

Families are, and will be, larger; 58 percent of the children are now in families of three or more children.

The child population is becoming concentrated in a few states; in seven of them 44 percent of the children are under 18 years of age (California, Illinois, Michigan, New York, Ohio, Pennsylvania, Texas).

About 30 percent of all mothers with children under the age of 18 are in the labor force, an 80 percent increase in just one decade.

Larger percentages of students are in the labor force, in spite of the general recognition of the importance of education and a tightening of compulsory school-attendance laws.

People are working fewer hours and have more leisure; the typical 10-hour day and 6-day week of 1900 is now on its way to becoming a 4-day week and a 6- or 7-hour day.

More children are going to school, in all age groups from 5 to 20 years of age.

Broken homes, births out of wedlock, juvenile delinquency, manpower shortages in public health and welfare, city slums, poor rural and inadequate city housing, child employment in agriculture, high unemployment of young workers and those with least schooling, child migratory workers, prematurity and congenital malformations, difficulties related to accidents, blindness, mental limitations, emotional disturbances, and poor diet—all of these are among the childhood problems to which the effective teacher must be alert.

Progress has been made toward solution of some of these problems through distribution of surplus food to needy families, casework provided by child-welfare agencies, social-agency assistance in the realm of child adoption, war against slums, extended library services to rural areas, strengthening of child-labor laws, activities of state vocational rehabilitation agencies, increased preparation of handicapped young people to earn a living, services related to maternal and child health, immunization against spread of communicable diseases, diagnosis of physical and mental deviations of children, improvement of teeth, and prevention of blindness.[1]

From these peripheral areas of the "whole picture," we now can move into the educational setting. What in brief are the facts and figures of education in the United States today? How do some of them project into tomorrow?

SOME SELECTED EDUCATIONAL DATA

No area of human endeavor has more numbers for pushing around, interpreting and filing (either in file cabinets or in a more convenient receptacle) than the field for which you are preparing. If you are unfortunate in your choice of instructors you may have to memorize many of them. If you are a little luckier, however, you may be encouraged to note a few of them and remember even fewer. Those who are allergic to numbers should be warned that the paragraphs which follow include some significant material, some of which was summarized in a widely quoted Rockefeller report as follows:

Our schools are overcrowded, understaffed, and ill-equipped. In the fall of 1957, the shortage of public school classrooms stood at 142,000. There were 1,943,000 pupils in excess of "normal" classroom capacity. Some elementary and high schools and colleges found it impossible to hire well-qualified teachers in such basic subjects as English, languages, and social sciences; some have even had to drop chemistry, physics and mathematics from their curriculum since there were no teachers to teach them.[2]

Although it was assumed by many that the classroom and teacher shortage was a temporary matter, it has been a chronic condition for more than 15 years. Shared space, shared equipment, and resulting inefficiencies are the inheritance of 418,000 school children attending curtailed sessions in 37 different states. The classroom shortage still

[1] Based on figures from *Children in a Changing World*, Washington, D. C., White House Conference on Children and Youth, U. S. Department of Health, Education, and Welfare, Children's Bureau, 1960.

[2] Rockefeller Brothers Fund, *The Pursuit of Excellence*, Garden City, N. Y., Doubleday & Company, Inc., 1958, p. 21.

remains very close to what it was a few years ago, on the basis of releases from *both* Republican and Democratic national administrations. In some ways this becomes an element of national neglect rather than the sole possession of any large group in our country.

All the attendance estimates are upward for elementary, secondary, college and university levels. The figures and percentages vary, depending on the sources you use, but of one thing you can be certain: the crowded schools of the present will be jammed to double or sometimes triple their current condition in the decade ahead. The public school problem will be concentrated mainly in about 200 large cities. Even with longer school days and years, more summer sessions, and expanded use of present facilities, there is no relief in sight. (Catholic and independent schools are growing even faster than the public schools.)

Our school-age population of 1900 doubled in 1960 and will be 50 percent higher by 1980. With the schools now having a greater holding power, those percentages become even harder to absorb than the population figures themselves indicate. In spite of these exploding enrollments, 7.5 million young people entering the labor force in the 1960s will not have completed high school (and a full one-third of them will not even have an elementary school education). More than 600,000 6- to 13-year-olds are not in school at all at the present time, and more than 2 million 14- to 17-year-olds are out of school. The highest dropout rates are in Virginia, South Carolina, Georgia, Kentucky, and Mississippi, where half the students are not graduated from high school. Although these states have smaller populations, this is a sad footnote to the pride we take in the largest public school system in the world.

More than 51 million people in the United States (more than 1 in 4) currently receive some sort of schooling, and now we have more than 90 percent of our school-age children in school (compared with less than 70 percent in 1900). Nearly universal, secondary education today is contrasted with only about 11 percent of our young people going to high school in 1900. With the annual expenditure per student growing from about $20 in 1900 to a current range of about $230 in Mississippi to $645 in New York (the average is around $432), the upkeep of this enterprise is sizable, to put it mildly. The money for public schools contributed by local sources represents 56 percent, the state, 40 percent, and the federal government 4 percent.

Although the figures are changing, until very recently more than half of each group of fifth-graders were not graduated from high school, and a third of those who entered high school did not finish. Three out of four high schools were too small to provide what is commonly considered to be a quality education, only one out of five elementary schools had a library, and most children went to schools that did not have a kindergarten.

Now let us take a close look at the 2 million teachers who were in these schools. A child had 1 chance in 4 that his teacher would not be a college graduate, 1 in 9 or 10 that during his elementary school career he would have at least one teacher who did not finish college, and 1 in 14 that he would have an "emergency" teacher at some time. Although teachers and administrators from large urban areas may question these figures, it must be remembered that this is a big country and their situations are hardly representative. Things are looking up in some ways as indicated by the fact that in 1946 only 15 states required a college degree for beginning elementary teachers while 15 years later more than 40 did. In 1946, only 45 percent of employed elementary teachers had a degree; in 1961, the figure was 75 percent. There were 123,000 emergency teaching certificates in 1946, 1 in 6, cut down to 1 in 14 only 15 years later.

The college graduating classes in 1960 produced nearly 130,000 newly eligible teachers, two-thirds for the secondary schools, one-third for the elementary schools. That is just one more of the out-of-balance factors of this profession since teaching positions on the elementary level exceed the others by eight to five. Fewer than three out of four of these graduates will actually go into teaching. These are sad figures when one notes authoritative estimates that 280,000 new teachers are needed in 1965 to take care of enrollment increases, and 810,000 are needed as replacements.

Variations around the country, by states, are great, which means that a child must choose carefully, not only his parents, but also where they are to live while he is in school. Almost all the elementary teachers in Oklahoma have completed college, but only 17.4 percent in South Dakota have (in fact, 31 percent of them have less than 2 years of college in that state). When a factor like pupil-teacher ratio is considered, however, South Dakota shines while Mississippi is at the bottom. The school enrollment as a percentage of the total school-age population varies from 97.4 percent in California to 69.2 percent in Rhode Island. Enrollment increases during the last full decade also vary: Alaska, 182.4 percent; Arkansas, 3.7 percent.

Other state ranges are these: Average length of school term: Illinois, 186.9 days; Arizona, 165.2 days. Percentage of eighth-grade enrollment that become high school graduates: Wisconsin, 94.5 percent; South Carolina, 47.0 percent. Personal income per child of school age: Connecticut, $12,607; Mississippi, $3,722. Net migration in a recent 8-year period: Nevada, plus 50.6 percent; Arkansas, minus 22 percent.

One other small group of figures should be brought to your attention, related to a subject that you may think is long buried. It is the one-teacher school, a diminishing bit of Americana but still very much with us. And if you would like the isolation and semisolitude it offers, you should know it exists. There are fewer than 25,000 of them, however, a 50 percent drop since the early 1950s, and about one-tenth the number we had in 1920. Still attending one-room schools are 400,000 children, with the largest number in Nebraska, Wisconsin, North Dakota, and South Dakota. Maybe the disadvantages are obvious to you, but there are advantages too, such as no double sessions and small classes (the average is 17). Their disappearing act is part of the over-all consolidation of school districts, the number of districts dropping 40 percent in the decade of the 1950s.

Now that we have all these figures in your hands (and it would have been little trouble to increase this limited offering 10, 20, or even 100 times), you verbal individuals who might not be "number oriented" can come back into the fold. Those of you who have stayed with it through the last few pages should know that there are a lot more where all of these came from.

THE EDUCATIONAL LADDER

Almost all that you have read so far should be of value regardless of the educational level with which you are concerned. Too often, even before that first teaching job comes along, college students state with more or less dogmatism that they intend to be a first-grade teacher or a fifth-grade teacher or a math teacher. But here is some news for you based on fact, not on guesswork or rumor: There is no such thing as a teacher of any of the kinds mentioned above. Further-more, there is no such thing as a class of the type indicated, at least not *exclusively* devoted to a particular level or subject.

If you think that such statements are unrealistic, accept them as a challenge, do some visiting, careful observing, and see what a realistic appraisal shows. Try to find a first-grade class where all abilities of every child are on that level, neither higher nor lower. See whether his reading achievement, understanding of science and arithmetic concepts, and emotional maturity are "first grade." Choose another classroom of older children and repeat your observation. Visit a high school mathematics class and see whether the teacher can and *should* ignore the varied reading abilities of the students.

Many studies have been made in many cities, and the conclusions are always the same: each grade level includes a variation of student abilities. A range of 5 years or more is not unusual. In fact, it would be an extremely rare class in which a range of at least 2 or 3 years was not present. The numerous individual differences implied in this discussion will receive more detailed treatment later.

But now, as you attempt to obtain an overview of education's domain, the facets that are part of it will be laid out for you. In this section we will note briefly the four levels where most of you will teach: nursery, elementary, junior high, and secondary. The im-portance of being aware of all of them, regardless of where your current interest seems to aim is easy to see. You have to know where children have been in order to know where they are going.

The Nursery School

Bringing the 3- and 4-year-olds into this discussion may appear strange to you. "They don't go to *school*, do they?" you might ask. "They *shouldn't* go to school!" you might say with real feeling, but perhaps not much information.

Because most people bring up their children in accordance with their reading diet of Gesell, Spock, and company, they know that the environment of children should change as they grow older. From the basic ingredients of food, warmth, and comfort in infancy, it expands outward toward other people, the community, and different activities and playthings. Their task as parents is to help that environment stretch and to filter in the materials and events that will broaden and deepen it.

Nursery schools can be good, indifferent, or poor. They can be operated professionally and competently, or they can be the fly-by-night variety, open only for profit with the children as pawns in the whole proceedings. They can help build affirmative attitudes toward later schooling, or they can be just a baby-sitting service so that mothers are free to work or play. Their personnel and equipment can be extremely appropriate, barely adequate, or downright dangerous. That there are poor nursery schools in operation, and financially successful, is a fact. That parents have checked on them (and been fooled) or have not checked at all is also a fact. But that *all* nursery schools are unnecessary, useless, or even a source of evil or injury to children is far from the truth. To think or say so is as faulty as condemning *all* parenthood or marriage because of neglectful parents or wandering husbands! A nursery school that is operated efficiently has strong advantages for most children. Among them are the following:

Greater areas for play space than in the average home

More and larger play equipment, big blocks, climbing apparatus, the harmless hulk of an old fire engine or truck for which the average family has neither the room nor the money

Opportunities to play and participate in activities, under well-qualified supervision, in twosomes, groups, or alone

A chance for varied activities based on individual needs of the child for more or less aggression, independence, and self-expression; opportunities for climbing, running, and digging and to use materials such as clay, paints, books, dolls, records, and trains

Consistent handling of the child: the release of tensions, discipline, and the recognition of control and authority

An open door to the beginnings of science, numbers, music, art, and concepts of time and space, as well as another link in the reading process, for a child *begins* to learn to read in infancy when he first discerns differences in his environment, gradually refining those differences as his experiences broaden

A setting for conversations, stories, and excursions, for persuasion and compromise, for taking turns and sticking up for one's own rights, for settling conflicts

Assistance to parents in seeing their child's personality, ability, and development in a setting with other children, and therefore more objectively and realistically

Help for parents in their follow-through on community trips, books, science concepts, and games

An opportunity to learn that groups and people exist outside the family, a wedge toward the bigger world which the child can enter gradually

This setting for 3- and 4-year-old children can enrich family life. With this additional exposure to the child's play and work, there can be a heightening of pleasure and understandings. But a cautionary note is important because some proponents of nursery schools let their enthusiasm run clear beyond the bounds of common sense. These schools are *not* the answer for all childhood problems of insecurity, speech, and slow maturing. They will *not* compensate for the rejection a child may feel when a new baby enters the home scene. They *cannot* make up for a broken home, parents who never wanted him in the first place, or a mother who puts her pleasures or luxuries ahead of him. Although they can help in all of these situations, their contribution is limited. If the child's problem is due to a neglectful, overbearing, inconsistent, or possessive mother or father, then to expect a nursery school to fix things up might be asking too much. Whether the difficulty is refusing to eat, toilet training, stubbornness, or physical or emotional immaturity, a skilled nursery school staff may be helpful, but it will not necessarily be able to remove the cause.

Another erroneous concept sometimes oversold by zealous advocates is that the nursery school will benefit *all* children, regardless of their home, neighborhood, intelligence, and maturity. A more fair point of view is this one: Most children can profit from these expanded experiences, but only if (1) the child is ready to be away from home part of the day, (2) the nursery school supplements rather than duplicates the home, and (3) the staff, equipment, and physical setting are appropriate to the child's needs.

In other words, the basic question is whether nursery school is good for *this* child. It is not true that an inadequate situation is better than none at all. Some children will definitely be better off without going to nursery school just for the sake of having more experiences. However, for a particular child it may be profitable to have the free-and-easy home life balanced by order and routine, the absence of toys and equipment compensated for by plenty of them in the nursery school, and cramped home conditions and poor relationships balanced by space, acceptance, and a mother substitute at the "home away from home."

Several other misunderstandings regarding these early childhood settings need straightening out. For example, does a child's being with other children a few hours every day really expose him to additional sicknesses? Doctors do not seem to think so. Will kindergarten present a problem, particularly if a progressive, well-planned nursery-school program is followed by a rigid school environment? If properly arranged, each step has its place and each contributes to what comes later. A child should not be deprived of good early experiences, and it is better to have him receive some sound guidance than none at all.

Questions of when the child should start, and how long he ought to attend, are individual matters which differ from child to child. However, few can begin profitably at the age of 2, and many gain relatively little from a second year unless it is especially carefully planned to meet their changing physical and emotional needs. Two years of repetitive activities can easily lead to boredom in kindergarten.

Many different kinds of nursery schools have started in recent years, with the largest increase during and since World War II in big cities and industrial centers. Well-prepared nursery-school teachers, interested and anxious mothers taking turns with play groups, public and private elementary schools, and city, neighborhood, and charitable enterprises have all sprung up, some carefully planned, some with no planning at all. Their approaches vary too, as they relate to individual and group activities, size of classes, permissive as opposed to restrictive environments, physical and mental development, bodily care, and play or formal educational activities.

Nursery schools are not a new development. Back at the White House Conference of 1930, *The Children's Charter* recommended for "younger children, nursery schools and kindergartens to supplement home care." And the intervening years have seen the trend toward a vast increase in their number all across the country.

Many teachers in the elementary schools say they can tell when a child has attended a good nursery school by his achievement and his ability to get along with others. But the caliber of the nursery school and the specific needs of the child are the decisive factors in how practical this experience will be.

The persons most sold on nursery-school experiences say that to skip them is to deprive many children of a sound educational start. They, as well as those who are most active in the kindergarten movement in this country, sometimes ask a startling question: "If one level is to be eliminated, why not one a little later on, say, fifth or sixth grade? They will miss it less than this necessary beginning." We dismiss so many questions with a shrug of our shoulders and a response something like, "It has always been this way" (as if *that* constitutes a good reason for either doing or not doing something); perhaps this one deserves discussion. It may not be so easy to be on the affirmative side of a debate in defense of the upper grades as you may think at first!

Nursery schools and the people who teach in them can make a strong contribution to a child's development. This early level, with the littlest school children of all, may be a vocational goal that you have never considered before. Perhaps now you may want to give it some thought. You may pass it by quickly if you are a member of the male sex. So another question must be asked, a brief, but needling one: Where is it decreed, where is it written, what law says that men must not teach small children? In many families the fathers are the more patient, understanding, and effective guides and teachers. So again, because "it has always been this way" we assume that it always should be. Why? Women have entered numerous all-male occupations, and in this case an occasional turnabout might be a good idea. It could very well be a sound move financially for certain men who have the teaching knack and administrative ability that are needed.

As for the worry that it leaves a man open to ridicule, suspicion of feminine tendencies, or social ostracism, this depends entirely on the individual involved. An extremely effective teacher at a well-known private school in the middle west teaches science at all levels, kindergarten through high school. He also teaches science courses to future teachers, and could very easily add one more step in his range of abilities by including 3- and 4-year-olds. He is big, husky, has a deep voice, and a seemingly gruff manner. But if you followed him into the kindergarten to the science corner you would see him enter into their environment and share the wonderful world with them. His voice, manner, and material rapidly adapt to their level. But if anyone wants to accuse him of feminine leanings, he had better have his running shoes on!

A strong influence on the education of young children will be felt in the next few years by the rebirth of interest in "The Montessori Method," which derived its name from its Italian originator, Dr. Maria Montessori. Its emphasis is on preparing the child to learn rather than on teaching him, on independent work in an ungraded setting, and on an environment prepared for the child.

The Elementary School

Earlier the expression "kindergarten movement" was mentioned. The implication of a "movement" is that something is on its way but not yet an accomplished fact. That actually is the situation of kindergartens in the United States today. If you live in certain parts of the country you may take kindergartens for granted; you may have had them for years. But they are not taken for granted in many sections of the middle and mountain states (including both the eastern and western peaks). In fact, it is more accurate to assume that there are no kindergartens, especially in rural and small-town schools. This is a fact difficult for people to absorb when they have been educated in and have lived in a community where kindergartens were an integral part of the schools since the 1920s, or even earlier. Our mistake is in believing that what we have experienced is also the experience of others—as provincial an attitude as one could harbor and an attitude that teachers, most of all, must shake out of their make-up.

The elementary-school system as a whole is big in the United States today, sometimes bursting. It is often satisfied with what it is doing, occasionally experimenting toward new horizons. No picture can be painted of *the* school because in 50 states and thousands of communities the differences are necessarily great. If you want to find new, fresh ideas, stimulating teaching, and progressive leadership, you can. If you seek ultraconservatism in both the classroom and the administrative offices, you would certainly have no difficulty at all in locating it. Our mistake is often made in generalizing on what we see and have lived through; and our conclusions are inevitably based on less than adequate information. The setting is just too broad for comfortably absorbing all its variations.

But trends, as they pertain to this educational level, are plentiful. Many of them are discussed in some detail later. They include a sharpening of teaching techniques and materials, a tightening of the preparation program that precedes the first teaching job, and a concern (too frequently verbal rather than active) for the individual differences in every class. They also include research and the persistent lag in teachers and administrators making use of findings.

Who you are, what your background is, and what you *want* to see will dictate the straws in the wind for the elementary school. "No more frills," one will conclude happily. "What *are* frills?" another will ask, and in a sincere way too. "Higher standards," may be in order. "What kind and for whom?" one may ask.

One source sees in the shifting winds of the 1960s this array:

Even more emphasis on science and a trend toward its becoming the core of the elementary-school program. A recent survey of curricula in 29 representative school districts selected at random all across the country indicated that almost twice as much content is devoted to science as to the social studies; 17 of the districts suggested techniques for correlating science with language arts, social studies, and art. There is very little evidence that this trend has let up.

Downward pressure through the grades of content material. Reading and number concepts reserved for the grades are now taught in some kindergartens, and the push is on for quick academic growth. Because children are wiser in the ways of the world than they have ever been, our ideas of what a first-grader should do or know must be flexible and subject to change.

Homogeneous grouping. This kind of grouping is mainly by mental age and brings all kinds of problems along with its hoped-for solutions. If children really are as different as we say they are, then how can we expect to "homogenize" them? Aren't they *still* individuals, still in need of the individualized approaches we so glibly state as solutions? Does this effort at bringing them together reduce the spread, or does it result in a greater spread within a short while? Whatever the answers are, the factual data include these situations: The attempt at homogeneous grouping has extended down as far as the first grade; 70 of 130 elementary schools surveyed had instituted some kind of ability grouping; divisions are made on the basis of I.Q. scores, interests, achievement scores or reading needs. The research is beginning to pour forth on this subject, and the results are just what you would expect. Are you in favor of homogeneous grouping? You can find studies that indicate higher academic achievement and other growth results accruing more plentifully to children in such settings. Do you incline in the direction of heterogeneous grouping? Indications of the advantages of the latter can also be found in current research. It all depends on who does it, where, and how. But, in any event, the subject is one you will hear debated a great deal during your years of teacher preparation and your early years of teaching.

Further departmentalization in the elementary school. The fact that one teacher cannot be expected to know everything has been made particularly clear by the vast amount of knowledge that has accumulated since World War II alone. Added to the recent history of the Depression, the New Deal, Naziism, and the war itself, have been the events related to Communism, the Cold War, the Korean War, and the Truman, Eisenhower, Kennedy, and Johnson administrations. Added to the already existing body of scientific knowledge have been major break-throughs surrounding the smashing of the atom and the explorations in space. An avalanche of materials and techniques has brought new vitality to mathematics, literature, art, and music. Such is the world of knowledge which faces the elementary-school teacher today. And frankly, it is almost enough to scare off all but the brazen, the conceited, the ultradevoted, and the ignorant. So, in a sporadic way, specialists are coming in to help, especially in areas like science, art, music, physical education, and reading. Another approach is to encourage, or require, future teachers to take more subject matter in their preparation, a trend which can be sound despite the slowness with which it is coming. Some professional educators are fearful of it, as you might expect, worried that some semblance of content specialization will somehow interfere with the goal of giving the child a method and means of solving problems. It is just another example of the educational bugaboo of either-or, instead of the thoroughly reasonable conclusion that we can have both. When we discuss teacher preparation later on, this subject will come in for a further airing.

The trend toward bigness. In this trend, we see school districts consolidating and growing larger, children traveling greater distances to school, and less direct contact between teachers and top administrators. In addition, there is a social isolation in which schools often have children of only one social class represented such as in the suburbs and in economically poor sections of large cities. Perhaps we would like to stem the tide toward larger schools and school districts, more students entering them every year, and bigger instructional and administrative staffs; but they are all part of a prolific population that is on the move in every direction—geographically, socially, occupationally, educationally. We might as well make up our minds that this is how it is and will be. The inflexible may want to close themselves into a secluded corner, but it is too late to accomplish that goal. As the dean of a certain college of education once said when he talked of inadequate salaries, inappropriate teaching loads, and almost nonexistent travel budgets, "We don't have much choice, ladies and gentlemen. It's either get happy—or get out!"[3]

These are only some of the signs of the times in elementary education. From every teacher and administrator working on this level you can obtain many more. From the overly abundant number of books in elementary-school curriculum, history, philosophy, and administration you could build up a list to fill all your hours this semester, and then some.

The Junior High School

Although there is some question of which grades (from 7 to 9) we are talking about, and although the in-again-out-again junior high school is at the mercy of the school budget and administrators, more than four out of five secondary-school pupils are now enrolled in districts that have some form of such a school.

You may very well know some of the reasons for setting 12- to 14-year-olds in a separate educational setting. Probably not very many years ago you were that age, and it may not be long before you view these ages from the other side of the desk. Although some school districts now have junior high schools and intend to keep them, others have lived through the era and vow "never again," and still others have never tried them out. Some view it as the worst possible arrangement, the poorest time to separate children, to skim off into this transitional setting the suddenly buxom girls and the boys who need another few years to grow up.

The importance of junior high schools has attracted quite a bit of foundation money and the attention of a man whose work in the past was far removed from these schools. He is James B. Conant, former president of Harvard and former ambassador to West Germany. From a somewhat superficial survey he pulled out a series of recommendations, and the fur has been flying ever since! Neither "progressive" nor "conservative" is satisfied with what he had to say. Both find plenty to be angry about, and some items with which they

[3] J. D. McAulay, "Elementary Education—Five Straws in the Wind," *Phi Delta Kappan*, June, 1960, pp. 394–396.

can agree. And yet, there are hundreds of junior high school administrators, teachers' committees, and PTA's that use his ideas as a check list to see whether or not they "pass." He did not intend that they be used in that way, but what has that to do with the uses to which schools can put a little booklet that costs only a few cents? He would probably be the first to protest the quoting, checking, and adulation, but it is too late. The lists are available and are being misused by people who find them so "helpful" in finding out whether they have a "good" school.

Despite the abuses of the publication, it remains a useful summary of what the junior high school is and perhaps should be. It gives an easy-to-handle picture of education as it relates to the preteens and early teens. Among Conant's comments are the ones that follow, in condensed form, all worth discussion but only *after* you accumulate a great deal more information. There is no reason for your saying he is right or wrong just because the words happen to hit you in a pleasant way or seem, without evidence, to "make sense."

1. All children in seventh and eighth grades should study English, social studies, mathematics, and science, and should receive instruction in art, music, and physical education, plus home economics for girls and industrial arts for boys.

2. Some should start algebra in eighth grade and the study of a modern foreign language on a conversational basis in seventh grade (with a bilingual teacher).

3. Instruction in reading and arithmetic should continue as long as the students can profit from it; superior students should read above grade level; by the end of ninth grade even the poorest readers (except the mentally retarded) should read at least at the sixth-grade level.

4. Group activities should be part of the total program, including musical and dramatic programs, assembly and homeroom activities, interest clubs, intramural athletics, and student council.

5. A smooth transition should be provided from elementary to secondary school.

6. The daily class schedule should be flexible to avoid forcing a student to make difficult choices, for example, between science and foreign language.

7. Instruction should provide intellectual challenge for the whole range of abilities.

8. A full-time guidance specialist, or equivalent, should be available for every 250 to 300 students in grades 7 and 8.

9. Meaningful homework is profitable, and it should be coordinated among the teachers so a student is not caught in a "squeeze play."

10. High standards should be maintained in academic courses because mastery is necessary; a few students might be held back, but no more than 2 years in the first eight grades.

11. Ninth grade should provide for electives and a continuation of the required courses.

12. The following facilities should be available: A well-stocked library, a gymnasium with locker rooms and showers, specially equipped home economics and industrial arts rooms, an auditorium or assembly space for at least half the student body, cafeteria space for at least one-third of the student body.

13. There should be careful coordination in every subject area from kindergarten through twelfth grade.

14. A balanced staff of 50 professionals for 1000 students is the minimum acceptable ratio for an adequately staffed school system.

15. The teacher load should be approximately the same in most subject areas; reasonable limits are five teaching periods, involving 125 to 150 students each day; physical education might be higher (up to 200) and English lower (down to 100 or fewer); the load for a professional librarian should not exceed 750 students.

16. No other duty should take precedence over classroom instruction.

17. The principal should not be bogged down with routine tasks, but should be the instructional leader.[4]

In contrast with the warm hand Conant gave to the "academic essentials" was the frigid glare he tossed toward interscholastic athletics, marching bands, and graduation ceremonies with diplomas, caps, and gowns. Those recommendations may not bother a lot of teachers, but many parents will be unhappy about them! He recommended that the development toward using teachers aides be watched with interest as part of the effort of relieving teachers of peripheral duties and giving back to them the time to teach. Subject by subject grouping on an ability basis, preferably with three groups, should be used in academic courses, he said, with the largest number in the middle group.

His ideas are not particularly startling; in fact, they are purposely conservative, and that adds to the frustration of those who see the

[4] Condensed from James B. Conant, *Recommendations for Education in the Junior High School Years: A Memorandum to School Boards,* Princeton, N. J., Educational Testing Service, 1960.

necessity of moving ahead in education with big steps. But he has little patience with the *status quo* or a "what is, is right" attitude. And that, on the other hand, offers little consolation to the stand-patters.

A publication on junior high schools where breadth and thoroughness are the keynotes is a bulletin of the National Association of Secondary-School Principals, released in February, 1962: *Junior High School Development, Practices, and Research*. Other valuable ones are *Modern Education for the Junior High School Years* by Van Til, Vars, and Lounsbury (Bobbs-Merrill) and *The Junior High School We Need* (Association for Supervision and Curriculum Development).

The Senior High School

Conant also had a great deal to say a year or so earlier about the senior high school. Although, as in his discussion of the junior high years, he was only one of many voices, his was widely heard, quoted, and argued about. He joined others who on many occasions spoke of the need for strengthening the all-inclusive comprehensive high schools, which are supposed to satisfy the needs of all children, regardless of their capacities or goals. Lawrence G. Derthick, former U.S. Commissioner of Education, was among them, stressing the flexibility of the high schools, their ability to adapt to the varying needs of different intellectual, socioeconomic, and cultural groups, their contribution toward lowering traditional class barriers, and their help in preparing more young people to adjust to a society that needs an increasingly larger number of educated men and women.

Some view these as the most crucial years in a young person's life, but how can any really be singled out for that label? Important, of course, but certainly no more so than the habit-forming years that preceded them and the career-preparing ones which follow. These years may be part of the continuum of learning and the acquisition of good study habits and pleasure from intellectual growth; or they may be a waste of time and family and community resources. Some children are self-starters, need no outside motivation, but others need stimulation in order to get going. Tragically, that stimulation never reaches thousands every year, and they drop out before, during, or soon after the high school years.

Some oversimplify this huge educational segment and the whole massive high school program: "The trouble with our high school graduates is not so much that they are ill-prepared, as that they are, at best, likely to be indifferent to learning as an intolerable labor, teachers as vengeful taskmasters, classrooms as minor prisons, books as offensive bores, and the entire educational process as tyrannical and unpleasant."[5]

The American high school, with its strengths and weaknesses, is unique in the history of world education. It is expected to provide an education for all youth, for a quantity which no other country has ever attempted to educate. With its huge numbers, it has attempted to meet the needs of individuals, a quantity-quality objective to which we all seem to subscribe just before we shoot off in many directions trying to figure out how the job can be done.

In his study, Conant lists three major objectives of this comprehensive, nonspecialized, nonselective high school to which all children are admitted: (1) to provide a general education for all future citizens; (2) to provide good elective programs for those who wish to use their acquired skills immediately on graduation; (3) to provide satisfactory programs for those whose vocations will depend on their subsequent education in a college or university.[6]

In 21 recommendations he tells what he thinks the high school should be. You may not agree with him; it is not necessary that you should. On the basis of your own recent high school years you may have some ideas and suggestions of your own that may make more sense in the setting you know best. That is entirely possible, despite his erudition and your lack of experience. Your contacts may have been intense, while his included a large number (55) of relatively short visits. Check these highlights of what he has to say against what you know and think. How many of his ideas seem practical to you?

1. Counseling should start early, in the elementary grades, and there should be close articulation between the elementary and secondary schools. It should be just as close if a junior high school is involved. The ratio of students to counselor should be 250–300 to 1.

[5] George Williams, *Some of My Best Friends are Professors*, New York, Abelard-Schuman, Limited, 1958, p. 209.

[6] From James B. Conant, *The American High School Today*, New York, McGraw-Hill Book Company, Inc., 1959.

2. Every student should have an individualized program, and students should not be classified arbitrarily as "college preparatory," "vocational," "commercial," or with other similar labels.

3. The requirements for graduation for all students should be 4 years of English, 3 or 4 years of social studies, 1 year of mathematics, and at least 1 year of science. Since all are required to take these courses, students should receive passing grades if they work up to capacity, even if a certain "desirable" level of achievement has not been reached.

4. The students should be grouped according to ability, subject by subject, in both required and elective subjects.

5. In addition to a diploma each student should receive a durable record of the courses studied and grades obtained.

6. English composition should occupy about half the total time devoted to the study of English.

7. Programs should be available for girls in areas like typing, stenography, use of clerical machines, and home economics.

8. Those who are in ninth grade but reading at a sixth-grade level or below should receive special consideration.

9. For academically talented students (approximately the top 15 percent nationally), the following minimum program is strongly recommended: 4 years of mathematics; 4 years of one foreign language; 3 years of science; 4 years of English; 3 years of social studies. This program should require at least 15 hours of homework each week.

10. For highly gifted pupils (about 3 percent nationally of the total student population), special arrangements should be made. These arrangements may include a special guidance officer, advanced placement programs (which means early study of some subjects usually pursued on the college level), and other selectively set up classes and studies.

11. To provide meaningful statistics about the education of the academically talented, the principal should prepare an academic inventory each year, summarizing the programs of these students with a follow-up of what happens to them after graduation.

12. Each school day should include at least six periods in addition to physical education and driver education. The day may be organized into seven or eight periods, each shortened to forty-five minutes.

13. Standards in advanced courses should be such that enrollees in each successive course of a sequence demonstrate the ability required to handle it.

14. Students should not be given a rank in class based on grades in all subjects. This practice sometimes encourages the brightest students to follow a human line of least resistance which leads to easy courses.

15. Lists should be published of students who had selected courses for the academically talented and had made average grades of B.

16. Developmental reading programs should be available on a voluntary basis for all students.

17. A tuition-free summer school is recommended for the ones who have to repeat a subject and the bright students who want to broaden the scope of their elective programs.

18. No matter how few students enroll, a third and fourth year of a foreign language should be offered.

19. All students should obtain some understanding of the nature of science and the scientific approach; the course in physical science or biology should be given in at least three sections grouped by ability.

20. Homerooms should represent a cross-section of ability, and students should be kept together in them for the entire high school program.

21. In twelfth grade a course in American problems or American government should be required. Each class should be a cross-section of the school.[7]

Conant concludes:

I can sum up my conclusions in a few sentences. The number of small high schools must be drastically reduced through district reorganization. Aside from this important change, I believe no radical alteration in the basic pattern of American education is necessary in order to improve our public high schools. If all the high schools were functioning as well as some I have visited, the education of all American youth would be satisfactory, except for the study of foreign languages and the guidance of the more able girls. Most of the schools which I found unsatisfactory in one or more respects could become satisfactory by relatively minor changes . . . I think one general criticism would be in order: The academically talented student, as a rule, is not being sufficiently challenged, does not work hard enough, and his program of academic subjects is not of sufficient range . . . a correction of this situation in many instances will depend upon an altered attitude of the community quite as much as upon action by a school board or the school administration.[8]

Just as with his subsequent study of the junior high school, this one has been used by some school administrators and communities as a kind of check list. They may erroneously conclude that they "pass" if they can go down the list and nod affirmatively at half or more of

[7] *Ibid.*
[8] *Ibid.,* p. 40.

his recommendations. His ideas are not to be noted with such rigidity. He never planned that they be either. The hunger of some individuals and groups for certainty and security may be satisfied, but no one can relax with a feeling of great accomplishment and complacency just because an arbitrary check-list approach is used. It could be that only *one* of his recommendations is omitted or dismally misinterpreted (it hardly matters which one), and the resulting school setup could be dreadfully deficient in meeting the needs of one group of students or perhaps one student. "Not important," you may conclude, "because after all, the majority are taken care of." Perhaps; but quite important if that minority of one happens to be you or a member of your family.

Many of Conant's recommendations are quantitative rather than qualitative and philosophical, making them both easy to understand and apply, and also limited in their continuing usefulness and meaning. Depth and richness are not present in them. Those primarily interested in the secondary school as a career could do far worse than starting with Conant's very readable pages as a kickoff to further reading. For most college students its brevity (only 140 pages) is a laudable factor. It might be followed by Edward A. Krug's *The Secondary School Curriculum* (Harper, 1960) and the many bibliographical references to which that source can lead you.

So far our climb up the educational hill has included brief views of nursery through secondary school. Now we are ready for the big jump, to the level you know best because your intimacy is current. Your attitudes about it are frequently fresh and very definite because you know what you like, what you are fed up with, and what you actively dislike.

As we move on we can try to be charitable—at least at the beginning. But that initial feeling need not interfere with the searching look that the college and university deserve in our effort to fill you in to a limited extent on its place in the whole picture to which this chapter is devoted.

Higher Education

Within the next few years every family, and almost every individual, will be personally involved in higher education—through the taxes they pay, if nothing else. That involvement will increase more than ever its influence on our daily lives. You are feeling it now in the most direct way of all, and the fact that larger numbers will attend colleges and universities in the years ahead (multiplied by the number of persons in their families, directly involved with them) magnifies the ways in which they will affect the social, economic, religious, political, educational, and moral lives of all of us.

Colleges and universities are worried about that future, too, and with the best of reasons. It can be stated very simply: We do not have enough of practically anything to satisfy future demands to be placed on higher education. Present resources, buildings and personnel, are pressed to capacity in many institutions, and the major crush is yet to come. Enrollments will double, more or less, by 1970, but the growth of institutions will be uneven. Our 18- to 24-year-old population will increase by 60–70 percent, while the total population will increase by only about 17 percent.

The shortage of qualified teachers we face on this level is both definite and dangerous. Right now we lack enough who are qualified and who in turn can help prepare the ones needed in just a few years. About 20,000 to 30,000 new teachers could easily be used each year, but only 10,000 annually are completing doctoral degrees and only half of them actually enter teaching. Subtract from them the ones who stay only temporarily (the green of something more attractive than grass has quite a pulling power), and you see the issue in a nutshell.

Cost estimates for meeting the student avalanche we face vary a great deal, and all are astronomical if we really intend to do the job. In 1970, higher education is estimated to cost around $7 billion (almost double the 1958 figure). It is equal to $34 a person, and if you are interested in some comparative figures, we annually spend $15.77 on parimutuel betting, $85 on tobacco and alcohol, $79 on recreation, and $87 on cars.

Other predictions often noted are as follows: public supported colleges are expected to grow faster than private ones; the pressure of numbers will affect a relatively few prestige institutions, mostly in the East; there will be tremendous expansion of urban and junior colleges, large classes, more instruction by television, more use of independent study, higher tuition fees, more scholarships, higher admissions standards (but not in all colleges), and a shortage of dormitory space; year-round college attendance will be the trend, as will larger graduate schools, fewer teachers' colleges, and more state-wide, regional, and national planning.

It will take more than wishful thinking to provide assistance in the midst of this expanding pressure for advanced education when the 4 million children born each year during the 1950s reach college age. If only half of them go to college, there will be 8 million students to be satisfied by 1970.

The basic purposes of higher education are little different from the purposes of education as a whole, maybe a bit more sophisticated and tending toward advancement of knowledge as well as its dis-semination, but fundamentally not much different. The price of excellence at this level is high and inevitably rising; and yet it costs the people less than the wasteful ineffectiveness of educational medi-ocrity. Waste comes from several directions, and is unfortunately very much with us in areas like these: unnecessary duplication of courses and programs among and within institutions; courses of dubious value; inept teachers and poor teaching; poorly motivated, poorly prepared students; faulty, unclear, or incomplete institu-tional goals.

The college and university today present many "faces," some of them showing real promise for the tough years ahead, some carrying old ideas into an era where youthful, vibrant, virile new thoughts are the only ones that count. Among the "faces" shown to the students, their parents, and the rest of the people who help support many of the institutions are these—and from your personal experi-ence you can no doubt add others:

Scholarly creativity: But it is concentrated in too few institutions, with scholarship restricted to a personnel base that is too narrow.

Fine professors: But through false economy too many of them are drill masters (in subjects like foreign languages) and have to perform their own secretarial and clerical duties.

Rising salaries: But there is evidence that many college graduates receive more money on their first jobs than do the teachers who taught them.

More money for higher education: But most states spend at least three times as much on their roads. Economist John Galbraith said that his major concern about the United States was "the tendency to over-invest in things and under-invest in people."

Talking democracy: But the face shown within many institutions of higher learning is that of autocracy, of an administrative hierarchy that fails to follow the democratic principles that it frequently preaches with quite a bit of eloquence.

A squeeze on many smaller colleges, forcing them to expand and lose the route of academic achievement to which they were dedicated: But on the other hand, there is St. John's College of Annapolis, Maryland, determined to maintain a limit of 300 students, and reproducing itself in separate colleges around the country, like the one in Santa Fe, New Mexico.

Experimentation with teaching aids of all types: But the use of the graduate assistant, or his equivalent, in the crucial first-year courses was found economical and satisfying to everyone except the person most concerned, the student.

Currently graduating men and women in all the professions: But whereas in 1900 nearly half of the college graduates had prepared in law, medicine, dentistry or the ministry, the figure now is only about 8 percent, with the tables turned toward education and business.

Space utilization currently a key subject of college and university discussion: But recent studies indicate classroom usage at only about 46 percent of capacity and laboratories at about 38 percent of capacity with some colleges closed for a third of the year.

Rapidly increasing course and program evaluation: But a strong instructional strain remains of what Earl McGrath, former U. S. Commissioner of Education, referred to as "the trival and transient" rather than "the significant and permanent," what Seymour Harris said is a "proliferation of courses" that "is a scandal from the viewpoint of both economics and education," and what President Grayson Kirk of Columbia University criticized when he stated that "too many colleges have become travesties on seats of learning by glorifying sports, social organizations, and recreational activities to the point of absurdity."

In spite of all this, it is rather easy to find elements in higher education that represent scholarship and forward-looking activities. The themes of recent national conferences of the Association for Higher Education are good examples: "The Race Against Time: New Perspectives and Imperatives in Higher Education" and "Platform for Higher Education: Guide Lines for the Sixties."

Another affirmative angle is that of government publications such as the following, which are all available from the United States Government Printing Office in Washington: *New Dimensions in*

Higher Education—Impact of College; New Dimensions in Higher Education—Study Abroad; New Dimensions in Higher Education—Quest for Quality. Each sells at the bargain price of 15 cents.

Adult Education

The educational ladder we have just climbed from nursery school through college is only part of the whole picture. It fails to tell the complete story because education begins earlier and lasts longer. Listen to the questions of a young child, and you will understand. Visit the downtown evening campus of any college or university, and you will get the point.

Those who assume that people learn only in a formalized classroom environment are uninformed about what the educative process really is. A mother tells a baby that this ball is red, that toy is blue, the stuffed animal is white—and learning takes place. The 2-year-old stacks a few blocks, listens to a record, looks at a book—and learning takes place. An adult attends a lecture, watches a debate on television, discusses opposing theories of government, labor relations, or educational philosophies—and learning takes place.

It is all around us all the time. A few years ago the President's Commission on Education Beyond High School released some estimated figures on enrollment in adult education that were impressive in their magnitude:

Public school adult education	3,500,000
University extension and evening college	1,500,000
Private correspondence schools	1,000,000
Educational radio and television	5,000,000
Library adult education	1,961,000
Men's and women's clubs	1,525,000
Parent-teacher associations	350,000
Religious institutions	15,500,000
Business and industry	750,000
Labor unions	850,000
Armed forces education programs	388,000
Health and welfare agencies	6,500,000
Agricultural extension	8,684,000
Others	2,000,000
	49,508,000

Admittedly, the enrollments overlap, with some people involved in two or more of these formal and informal activities, but the figures are large anyway. When you add to all of these people the many thousands who stretch their horizons in other ways, the extent of participation is even more striking. After all, many subway, bus and street-car riders read more than the daily papers and comic books. The expanding library-circulation figures, book-club memberships, magazine subscriptions, and informal study and discussion groups all give testimony to the fact that education is increasingly large in scope, with neither age nor geographic barriers.

On-the-job training in industry, vocational preparation in the armed services, and the many other educational outlets that people enter voluntarily provide breadth and depth that our schools and institutions of higher learning may sometimes fail to offer. More learning may actually take place in them. They can be compared with elective courses, which are frequently more beneficial and interesting than your required courses. A skillful teacher may stimulate your sense of inquiry in the latter, but the instructor of the elective course has a head start based on your initial motivation.

In classes, groups, as part of a job, in living rooms, over the back fence, through a well-prepared teacher, friend, or neighbor—education and learning can come. They may not be in terms of college credits, transcripts, and grades; they may be as simple as a new idea, technique, outlook, approach, word, or deed. And they may relate to writing, speaking, thinking, or doing; to music, art, cabinet work, or business machines; to specific vocational training or to the current best-seller list. The range of possibilities is tremendous, and the increasing participation in them by both adults and children indicates clearly the basic respect that we have for education. It may not rub off on our attitudes toward formalized schooling in all cases, but the belief in the values of education is demonstrated by the time and money we pump into it, collectively and individually.

Adult education varies from the Senior Center in Winnetka, Illinois, which attempts to break down the barriers between young and old, to the extension division of the University of California at Los Angeles with its 70,000 students; it may range from literacy training to the fight of skilled physicians against obsolescence in their profession. It must create its clientele which does not come ready-made.

And it must work hard to hold the students, for recapturing the art of study or capturing it so late for the first time is far from easy. But the effort pays off for those who agree with Margaret Mead's statement that "no one will live all his life in the world in which he was born."

On the basis of all of these factors, adult education can indeed become the biggest segment of the entire educational ladder.

SOME CURRICULAR COMMENTS

What teachers teach depends on many factors: the school board, the administrators, the teachers, the parents, and the children. Because words come far cheaper than action the curricular content frequently lags behind what the school says it is, and even farther behind what the educator says it *should* be. In recent years we have had a surge of adaptations in various subjects and in approaches to them through grouping, testing, pupil-teacher planning, and administrative experimentation.

Many of the current trends are based on G. K. Chesterton's notion that there is no such thing as an uninteresting subject, just disinterested people. The approach now seems to be toward making people more interested by reorganizing, revitalizing, and rebuilding subject content; by eliminating the outdated, the dull, and the unnecessary; by adapting the content to children who themselves will be forced to adapt to a future environment at which we can now only guess. The trend is to question what is taught and bring the best judgment to bear regarding change. We do not want to be accused of the stultifying action that Laura Zirbes once ridiculed when she commented, "As someone said about the curriculum, they let the Greeks move into the fourth grade and never moved them out."

Curricular content and technique have been analyzed in a most intimate way in recent years. They will continue to be searched and researched. If you assume that it will be good enough to teach as you were taught, you had better give some more thought to the whole subject. Skimming through some of the developments mentioned below will give you an idea that change is the order of the day. A relatively quick way of augmenting that idea is to refer to the publications of the Project on the Academically Talented Student of the National Education Association, headed by Charles Bish; subjects included are English, social sciences, mathematics, physical sciences, modern foreign languages, and music.

Because science and mathematics have recently been most in the forefront of awe and admiration, we will look at other areas first, for a change, to give them the recognition that they, too, deserve.

Social Sciences and Humanities

Scattered reports reveal the following: The National Science Foundation now has a Division of Social Science, on the same level as the physical and biological sciences; it includes the areas of anthropology, economics, and sociology. All Pennsylvania high school students take a world-culture course for one semester (required) or one year (encouraged); it is oriented to current situations, with emphasis on Asia, the Middle East, and Africa. Independent schools have provided some leadership toward a historical approach to Asia and Africa; the writings of David Mallery have been helpful.

The study of peoples and problems with an international flavor has rich resources and must be built on important basic principles, like the following: All people want their children to have what is good in life; all people want a sense of belonging; all people view the world on the basis of their cultural background; more people are colored than white, deprived rather than fully satisfied, illiterate rather than literate. Art and music are still on the "neglected" list, especially after eighth grade, with the 30,000 years of man's art and the products of man's sense of beauty, rhythm, and creativity largely ignored; "not basic enough," some people persist in saying.

The John Hay Fellows Program (Charles R. Keller, Director) was established in 1952 to give high school teachers an uninterrupted year or summer to read, reflect, and grow as individuals; emphasis is on the humanities; among its cooperating colleges and universities, to which about 75 teachers a year and more than 100 during summers have gone, are these: University of California at Berkeley, University of Chicago, Columbia, Harvard, Northwestern, Yale, Williams College, Bennington College, Colorado College. The John Hay program was expanded for 1963–1964 to provide awards for 85 teachers. Keller has pointedly stated that there has been little significant thinking and action in the social studies since 1916, that the term "social studies" should be replaced by "history and the social studies," that we should rid ourselves of the idea that the purpose of these subjects is to make good citizens (their rightful role, he says, is to teach facts in a logical sequence about the past, present, and future of the United States and people of other countries), and that we begin teaching history and the social studies in fifth grade and plan on a national scale through the senior year of college. He also takes potshots at the traditional theory that a child must begin with the familiar (the neighborhood) and move out; earlier civilizations can be stressed even in the primary grades, he feels.

An important balance should be established in the curriculum, without equating all studies in exclusively utilitarian terms. "So you piously praise these things while spending the tax money on the conquest of space or the defeat of disease. Vast sums are now available for improving the teaching of mathematics, physics, chemistry, biology, and modern languages. Very little cash is being appropriated for the improvement of instruction in music, history, art, or literature. Technology is enjoying both praise and subsidies; the arts must be content with serenades."[9]

Project Social Studies is a recent plan of the U.S. Office of Education, aimed at improving research, instruction, teacher education, and the dissemination of information in the field. Other organizations are helping speed up the slower developments of the past: Association of American Geographers, National Council for Geographic Education, National Council for the Social Studies, American Anthropological Association.

In June, 1963, three of the country's leading scholarly organizations announced the establishment of the Commission on the Humanities. The objective of this national group is to recommend means of improving teaching, scholarship and creativity. The Commission has made an impressive beginning ("cease to speak in platitudes . . . must specify as precisely as possible the present and future needs"). Time will tell whether they can help turn the tide of support for basic research which shows the federal government putting 71 percent of these funds into the physical sciences, only 1 percent

[9] Fred H. Stocking, "The Important Balance," *Harvard Graduate School of Education Association Bulletin*, Special Edition 1959, p. 11.

into the social sciences, and virtually nothing into the humanities.

In his recent book Martin Mayer sees the major roadblocks of social studies' reform as (1) the often intellectually unsophisticated conservatism of school administrators, (2) the lag in teacher preparation, and (3) the reluctance of major scholars to put themselves into the role of educators of children.[10]

So the retreat of the social studies and humanities seems finally to have stopped.

English

Although usually considered as part of the humanities, English is singled out for special comment here because of its importance in an era when sound, fully understood communication is essential. As in the other academic fields, many of the newer ideas are products of the professional organizations, in this case the National Council of Teachers of English. It is not the leadership that is a point of concern, however; it is the "followership," the lag between suggestion and practice, between the ideas of the prominent thinkers in a field and the performance of the teachers in classrooms.

A recent publication of the Council makes its position clear; its worries include the following: More than half of those teaching English in elementary and secondary schools are inadequately prepared; only a few state departments of education employ specialists in English (which lags far behind home economics and driver education); 59 percent of the colleges preparing teachers of high school English do not require an advanced course in composition; lack of financial support results in overloading in the high school (150 to 175 students a semester), lack of modern equipment, and inadequate libraries; the blame for inadequacies is placed clearly on the doorstep of the liberal arts colleges (not teachers' colleges) where most high school teachers are prepared; basic English is postponed, diluted, and permissively taught.

A devastating array of figures supports the Council's concern regarding the emergency situation in which it finds itself: Certified elementary teachers in 19 states currently need no specified requirement in English; certified high school English teachers in 16 states

[10] Martin Mayer, *Where, When and Why,* New York, Harper & Row, Publishers, Inc., 1963.

need only 12 semester hours in English (*or* in "related" fields); 94 percent of the colleges preparing elementary teachers do not require a systematized study of the history and structure of the English language; more than 61 percent do not require a course in grammar and usage; fewer than 200 of the 1200 colleges in the country graduate teachers informed about important advances in the field during the last 25 years; only a third of the colleges require future English teachers to study world literature; only a fifth require a study of contemporary literature or of literary criticism; 70 percent of the colleges find it necessary to offer remedial work in English; the average amount per pupil spent on library books is about half the cost of one book.

The picture is one of poor planning, preparation, and teaching; too few teachers, administrators and parents who understand the importance of English and the tragedy of its neglect; too little articulation from one level to the next; and teacher loads that are too heavy. In this first national assessment in 35 years, the Council asks for financial support from Congress or foundations, stimulation and assistance to match that received by the sciences, mathematics, and foreign languages, and upgraded collegiate programs.

The report concludes as follows:

... neither informed laymen nor leading teachers of English are satisfied with the results of present-day English teaching. Results that might have been satisfactory two decades ago are no longer acceptable, because our complex society demands levels of proficiency and accumulations of knowledge that no earlier society required. To achieve the necessary results drastic and far-reaching remedies are required. The problems in the teaching of English, as in science, mathematics, and foreign languages are of such magnitude that the attempts toward solution must be broad in scope, imaginative, thorough—and immediate.[11]

Through its Commission on English, the College Entrance Examination Board has stepped up its program to help eliminate the deterioration of high school English teaching, with emphasis on a knowledge of grammar and clear descriptive writing; formal teaching of language, composition, and literature; and fewer students per teacher. Summer programs for teachers, kinescopes of tested class-

[11] National Council of Teachers of English, *The National Interest and the Teaching of English,* Champaign, Ill., 1961.

room practices, and the development of sample curricula, book lists, and assignments will be part of the program to help improve the teaching of English (they are already part of the program in mathematics). The Commission's publication *End-of-Year Examinations in English for College-Bound Students* was made available to English teachers in May, 1963. Experimentation is progressing rapidly with various kinds of programmed exercises or self-correcting materials that students can pursue alone. At Rutgers they estimate that teachers will teach more students with far less effort with such materials. A monthly guide for students and teachers, called *Studies in Mass Media,* is now available from the National Council of Teachers of English; it includes articles on recordings, current plays, magazines, newspapers, current films, and television programs.

Project English, launched by the U.S. Office of Education, aims to help raise the quality of the English curriculum and instruction through research, experimentation, and curriculum centers, which will plan, develop, and test new instructional materials and methods. The Project defines problems and encourages both study and action. The Proceedings of its Research Conference held in May, 1962, are now available.[12] The Project also releases newsletters regularly to those interested. The National Education Association (NEA) entered the picture in the fall of 1962 with its English Composition Project; the objective of this 3- to 5-year program is to improve the quality of student writing in grades 7 to 12.

Foreign Languages

More than 1½ million students were enrolled in high school language courses in 1960. Spanish is now in the lead by quite a bit, but the list includes French, German, Italian, Japanese, Russian, Latin, Norwegian, Swedish, Portuguese, and Modern Greek; and Chinese is gaining in popularity.

They are on the move in elementary schools too (from fewer than 5,000 students studying them in 1941, to 329,071 in 1955, to well over a million now). Foreign-language teaching has become a gimmick in some schools and school districts where they want to fool the public into thinking they have a gifted-child program (they teach a lan-

[12] U. S. Department of Health, Education, and Welfare, *Needed Research in the Teaching of English,* Washington, D. C., Office of Education, 1963.

guage in one grade only, and on the record they are "challenging the gifted"). Flexible speech organs, freedom from self-consciousness, and the prospect of no accent have encouraged early foreign-language teaching, although cost, lack of qualified personnel, and the impractical aspect related to the uselessness of the knowledge are all given as reasons on the other side of the coin.

Language laboratories are becoming standard equipment in many schools. Through a process of listening, repeating, correcting, and repeating, effective simultaneous practice is possible in large groups. The student hears voices of native speakers who serve as models for him to copy. Although these laboratories can be elaborate, they can also be developed on the basis of minimal essentials: record player, tape recorder, tape and disc recordings. But all of the reports on the laboratories are not entirely affirmative. One from the Metropolitan School Study Council in New York City released in July, 1963, indicates that they have been somewhat "oversold" to the public and teachers; although they can be used effectively, many schools are doing as well, or even better, without them. The controversy over the usefulness of this equipment is likely to continue for the next few years. Three University of Michigan students recently received A's upon completion of what the University referred to as the first completely automated college spoken-language course. Taught entirely by machine, graded by a professor who never saw them, these students learned to speak Spanish like natives in less than 200 hours. In private schools, too, foreign language teaching has taken a giant step forward; 82.5 percent of the students in independent secondary schools are studying, in the following order of frequency, French, Spanish, German, and Hebrew. Russian was way down the list— which may give you something to wonder about. The oral-aural (or audio-lingual) method of teaching foreign languages is on the upswing. It results from an increasing recognition that speaking, conversation, and full communication are necessities for getting along in the world, whether with our neighbors next door or our neighbors of different races and political beliefs thousands of miles (but only an hour or two) away from us.

By June, 1963, more than 11,000 foreign-language teachers had been retrained through the language institutes created under the National Defense Education Act (NDEA), which has offered an increasing number of summer institutes each year; in the summer of 1963, 83 institutes enrolled more than 4400 teachers. The current upsurge in language teaching certainly applies to quantity, and in some cases to quality. Part of the total trend is earlier teaching of foreign languages, on the kindergarten or first-grade level. The Modern Language Association is a major force in many of these developments; so are the FLES project (Foreign Language-Elementary School), the NEA Department of Foreign Languages, and the many projects designed to improve instruction under the NDEA. (A particularly interesting series of articles on this subject appeared in the *Saturday Review* of February 16, 1963).

Science and Mathematics

Russia may have been the catalyst, but rumblings of revision have been going on for years in teaching the various sciences and mathematics. Groups not known or not in existence a few years ago are now in the forefront: the Physical Sciences Study Committee, The School Mathematics Study Group, The Chemical Bond Approach, the Chemistry Education Material Study, and the Biological Sciences Curriculum Study. Names are also new: Jerrold Zacharias, physicist, Massachusetts Institute of Technology; and Max Beberman, mathematician, the University of Illinois.

The pressure to develop new curricula has come mainly from the scholars in these fields. They are dissatisfied with the way their subjects are being taught in high schools, with the lag behind new discoveries, and with the neglect in transferring insights from one area to the total learning process. So new textbooks, monographs, and other materials for both teachers and students are now available, and there are plenty of other activities: National Science Foundation summer institutes for teachers, talent searches, science fairs, junior academies of science. A national organization, called Future Scientists of America, has been formed; it is part of the National Science Teachers Association (department of the NEA), is aimed at high school students, and publishes a quarterly newsletter, which includes articles and comments on activities of local chapters and recent scientific developments.

The National Science Teachers Association itself has conducted a nation-wide study of elementary-school science programs. It has concentrated on experimental evidence of curricular successes, points of deficiency, and needs for in-service education. The National Academy of Sciences is attempting to pull together the various activities of the science and mathematics committees and study groups. In conferences already held, the National Research Council of the Academy has concluded that the level of educational research activity is too low, that the research literature needs to be systematically organized and interpreted to make it readily available and usable to teachers, and that a central organization to promote basic research should be set up. In other words, a scientific and systematic approach in these areas of science and orderliness is being called for.

Criticism of what has been done in the past comes from outside the field too. Brameld comes to the point quickly when he says:

The traditional teaching of physics, chemistry, and other sciences is inadequate. The various fields of science have been taught as separate, compartmentalized bodies of knowledge without regard either for their relations to one another or for their relations to cultural experience. The average student is not going to be a scientist, and the science he studies should be primarily, therefore, in the form of problems selected from his familiar environment with constant concern for interrelationships of the natural sciences, the social sciences, and the arts.[13]

In 1961, more than 9000 high school students were given the opportunity by the National Science Foundation to obtain tuition-free science and mathematics training during the summer. This extensive program involved 158 colleges, universities, and nonprofit research organizations located in 43 states, the District of Columbia, and Puerto Rico. The Foundation's activities also extend to research activities for high school and college teachers of science, to summer institutes for teachers, and to opportunities for a small number of highly selected undergraduates to work with scientists during summer sessions. Through summer writing conferences, the development of high school textbooks, laboratory manuals, guides, and films, and with actual classroom experimentation with the materials already produced, the Biological Sciences Curriculum Study is seeking actively to improve education in biology; teachers and students are involved as producers, experimenters, and consumers. (Obviously

[13] Theodore Brameld, *Education for the Emerging Age,* New York, Harper & Row, Publishers, Inc., 1961, pp. 181–182.

one of the biggest problems faced in the explosion of scientific knowledge is for scientists to stay "on top" of the subject. In addition, they must organize it and pass it on to others.) Small eruptions of activity are also in evidence. Money from the Florida Foundation for Future Scientists (at the University of Florida) is made available to selected high school students to further their special projects for science fairs. *Science and Math Weekly* is published by Wesleyan University. The Science Materials Center in New York City publishes *Laboratories in the Classroom,* which specifies elementary- and secondary-school equipment and supplies. The Colorado State Department of Education's "Mobilab" (a laboratory on wheels) helps local school authorities provide adequate in-service education experiences for elementary and junior high school teachers of science and mathematics. "A Probing Mind" is a recent film that stresses the importance of the environment that a skillful teacher can create in teaching science. The October, 1962, issue of *School Life* (U.S. Office of Education) is devoted to articles on resources for improving instruction in biology, chemistry, and physics (including newer concepts) and to the new curriculum in earth sciences, and changing directions in elementary and junior high school science.

Mathematics is going through a revolution that will result in the most sweeping revision for that entire field in more than 50 years: Funds from the National Science Foundation for this purpose are now well past the $4 million figure. Added to this picture is the work of the Yale University study group under Edward G. Begle (now at Stanford University). More than 800 researchers, scholars, and teachers are working on textbooks and teacher preparation materials for the more than 3,000 teachers instructing 100,000 students. Among others in on the mathematics push are Paul C. Rosenbloom, Director, Minnesota School Mathematics Center, University of Minnesota; David Page's project at the University of Illinois; Robert Davis's at Syracuse University; Hawley and Suppes at Stanford; Gundlach at Bowling Green University. The effort is being made on all levels, elementary through university, to find new ways of "getting ideas across" and to help children discover rather than always being told.

A fresh approach in mathematics is the new Doctor of Arts in Education degree. The problem is that there are just not enough future college teachers preparing in this field; the total number of people with a Ph.D. now teaching mathematics in colleges is 3000; fewer than 300 of these degrees are received annually. Furthermore, orientation has been far more toward research than teaching. The Mathematical Association of America and the American Mathematical Society recommended the historic step of a totally new degree, a step that may lead to repercussions in other parts of college teaching. Perhaps you have recognized the need for this change in emphasis as some of your college teachers vividly display their vast knowledge of research and their limited awareness of how to teach.

In the public high schools enrollments in science and mathematics courses have shown an increase in recent years—even in physics, the last to join the rise.

CONCLUDING REMARKS

It would take many libraries, thousands of teachers, millions of students and an entire population to present the whole picture of education. This chapter has made an attempt to hit some of the highlights. Of course, everyone's highlights would be different based on differing experiences, viewpoints, and emotionalized attitudes.

An overview is essential before we move into the future; the line between what is and what will be is really rather indistinct. Conant has attempted to bridge the gap; so have Zacharias in the physical sciences, Beberman in mathematics, and the National Council of Teachers of English. With the help of all of them, and thousands of others, we are now ready to take the big plunge into tomorrow. Today's educational pioneers have guided us to innovations in equipment, machines, school organization, and staff utilization. But no additional steps will be taken unless you take them.

A cautious approach may be best for you as you look at these innovations and experiments, ready to reject the fraud, question the doubtful, and accept the reasonable, sound, and prudent. But be ready once in a while to take a chance on what is new, sometimes not fully tried, often exciting. If the young or new teacher does not slip a compassionate hand to the ones who dare to be different, we may as well toss in the towel of defeat. A visit to most college campuses indicates clearly that the pioneering, experimental spirit is riding high among thousands of future teachers. It is just too bad that all of *their* teachers do not always share the glow!

CHAPTER 3

A TIME FOR *Looking Ahead in Education*

For a profession that has not made full use of the materials and equipment already available to it, a surge ahead into an era of automation, new techniques, and frontier-type ideas may be only a vain hope. How many teachers use motion pictures, the slide projector, filmstrips, and the opaque projector as they should be used? How many use them at all?

The fear of newness and change is a quality that is part of most of us. And yet, of all people, teachers can least afford the luxury of being scared, passive or antagonistic to change. They cannot be "for" or "against," but must go on record in favor of the *best* learning for the *most* children with the *least* time and effort. Every tool and shortcut must be utilized. And although it may be more comfortable to hide away in a figurative nineteenth-century classroom, it just cannot be done. Burying one's self in administrative detail, in counting lunch money, or in teaching as one was taught years ago means exposure to the possibility of a rude awakening. Nothing new has come along that will replace the sound teacher-learner relationships; but much has appeared that can help make that relationship even more warm, human and meaningful.

A warning of the problem was apparent in an article by James Cass:

Technology in the classroom has come a cropper most often because teachers haven't mastered the simple mechanics of teaching machines, language labs, ETV, or even movie projectors and tape recorders—to say nothing of knowing how to make most effective use of them educationally. Even new teachers, just out of college, have seldom been introduced to the "new" media and their use in the classroom. It is not surprising that this should be so, because many groups in the profession—particularly those concerned with teacher education—have displayed a vast lack of enthusiasm for innovation in classroom organization and teaching techniques. They have, to be sure, cooperated on occasion, but usually they have done so fearfully and reluctantly. The development of new aids and new methods has come largely from the vision, creativeness, and energy of men outside the schools, with a relatively small number of schoolmen providing bold leadership within the profession. But now the influential American Association of Colleges for Teacher Education has initiated a study, financed by a grant from the U.S. Office of Education, to determine how colleges and universities can best use the new technological developments to teach future teachers, and how classroom teachers can themselves make best use of technology in their classrooms. It is possible that at this date the profession itself is ready to take leadership in a field where its knowledge, encouragement, and competence to evaluate the effectiveness of new departures have been sorely missed in the past.[1]

If you add to the availability of bright new approaches to education, the desperate need for their use (population explosion, population mobility, international tensions, teacher shortages in number and quality, for example), then you must realize that the race is on to find practices and devices that work. In order for education to advance, it needs "sweeping changes on the inside," said Philip H. Coombs of the Ford Foundation. And the tough part is that these changes must frequently help prepare a child for work and an entire way of life at which we can only guess.

Despite the fact that some educational seers are almost gaily optimistic about the educational future, others take a far more cautious line as they look ahead. Instantaneous reform is hardly their theme.

Although evidence appears on every side of a great tide of change that can carry the schools to a new standard of excellence, there is no assurance that this movement will succeed. Students, parents, teachers, administrators, school boards, and taxpayers will have to make millions of right decisions on the road to excellence, which is always uphill. There will be resistance from parents who prefer the easy way and from educators reluctant to try any new way. It's never easy for any group to abandon ideas and practices of long standing, and educators are perhaps more hidebound than most where their own work is concerned. But this nation will be unable to hold

[1] James Cass, "While School Keeps," *Saturday Review*, May 18, 1963.

its own in the hard and exciting years ahead unless the great change now beginning in public education comes to fruition. Community leaders throughout the U.S. have no graver responsibility and no more inspiring opportunity than to lend a hand in the remaking of American education.[2]

Sometimes sheer newness brings with it an aura of excellence, so the danger lights must be constantly blinking, warning you that new ideas, procedures, and equipment demand constant evaluation. Just because they work in a pilot study or community is no reason to go off on a wild bandwagon of promises, claims, and unrestrained enthusiasm. An increasing awareness of the dangers involved in "faddism" is essential. Questions like the following should be asked about a reform measure:

Does it make possible better learning and higher quality?
Will it relieve you of repetitive activity, and make you more available for the kind of teaching of which you are capable?
Will it help you reach more students, individualize instruction more?
Can you move past the "goodness" or "badness" of the technique or gimmick itself, and evaluate how it is *used?*
Is it worth the cost in actual dollars?

On the question of reforms in general, the following questions are pertinent:

How can you help break down the barrier of teacher (and administrator) reluctance to meet change head-on, cope with the lag between research and practice that permeates much of the profession?
Who will teach the teachers which innovations are valuable for their children and how they can be utilized with the least expense and turmoil (both physical, in the classroom, and mental, in the teacher)?
How can you keep up with the changes that seem to be pressing in, ever more demandingly? What are the best sources for finding out what they are?
For which children, teachers and school districts are the specific newer ideas of real value?

Before we go into a more detailed discussion of some of the newer approaches with which you must be at least conversant right from your first day of teaching, it is vital to give you some idea of the scope

[2] Charles E. Silberman, "The Remaking of American Education," *Fortune,* April, 1961.

of this subject. It is hardly a new one as indicated by the 1962 publication of the U.S. Office of Education entitled *Technology in American Education, 1650–1900*. The April, 1963, issue of *Educational Leadership* ("New Aids—New Opportunities") attempted to bring the matter up to date.

The teacher of today and tomorrow faces some innovations that were unknown and even unthought of a generation ago or less. To know of their existence may help lessen somewhat the threat, frustration, and mystery. That you can add to this list may be obvious from the beginning—but here is at least a start:

Programmed learning
Educational television; "stratovision"
Ungraded classes
Team teaching
Use of teacher aides; assistants, readers
Unique and flexible school structures, rooms, and facilities
"Hidden talent" projects
Place of the Peace Corps
Newer audio-visual aids, such as instantaneously produced motion pictures and low-cost video tape recording equipment
Electronic and automated classrooms installed with complete audio-visual laboratories
Changing school coverage and schedules—longer year and day; expansion in community and junior colleges; increasing adult education; emphasis on certain subject-matter areas (foreign languages, sciences, mathematics)
Paperbacks and other variations in text materials
Automated data processing and other uses of the computer in educational settings
Language laboratories; individual viewing and listening equipment
Varied approaches to grouping—large, "traditional," seminar, individual; honors classes and seminars for the bright
Changing course contents, resulting from groups such as the Biological Sciences Curriculum Study, National Science Foundation, School Mathematics Study Group, and others

Experimental work in many of these areas has moved along swiftly in recent years. Automated classrooms are receiving a thorough testing at the University of Wisconsin, where they are using slide projectors, a movie projector, a tape recorder, teleprompter units, an opaque projector, a four-speaker sound system, controlled lighting, a television projector and an extensive electronics system for automatic control. Far from eliminating the teacher, this kind of environment for learning requires even more preparation by the teacher of courses of study. From the University of Wisconsin has also come a booklet entitled *Making Teaching and Learning Better* which describes a cooperative university-school district project directed by Dr. John Guy Fowlkes; this experimental project has gone into curriculum improvement, better use of teachers, increased use of learning equipment, and development of teaching internships. Electronic classrooms are in use at the New York Institute of Technology, Long Lots Junior High School (Westport, Connecticut), and the high school in Quincy, Massachusetts.

The state-wide Oregon Program for the Improvement of Education is attempting to mobilize public and private educational institutions on all levels in a long-range effort to use promising innovations in teacher training, staff utilization, teaching methods, and instructional equipment. The Ford Foundation has made grants to two local school systems (Newton, Massachusetts, and Norwalk, Connecticut) in an effort to put the whole range of constructive innovations to work, from kindergarten through the twelfth grade.

Santa Barbara County in California is attempting to pull together all of the newer contributions to education from the elementary through the college level; experiments in teacher preparation, individualized study, television, and teaching machines are part of their work. Far across the country, the South Florida Education Center has been set up in Fort Lauderdale to see how much and how fast a youngster can learn under "ideal" conditions; these conditions include a longer school day and year, abolition of grade levels, master teachers in every subject, heavy emphasis on "basic subjects," and clerical assistants for teachers.

Some of the most forceful stimuli for change have come from J. Lloyd Trump working with the National Association of Secondary-School Principals. Among the many suggestions that permeate his writings (and they are in concrete form, ready to be put into effect by creative teachers and administrators) are these: rearrangement of the school program based on independent study, small groups, and large classes; teaching teams, with relatively fewer "career" teachers (whose salaries may be up to $20,000) and including specialists, consultants, aides and clerks; a "learning resources center" where every instrument and device, plus laboratory and workshop space are available; an "instructional materials center" with the latest and best for the teaching staff. Trump's themes center around flexibility in all school arrangements, in scheduling, in architecture, and in organization of instruction, staff utilization to its capacity, use of facilities and equipment in tune with the demanding needs of the times, and close relationships with the community. His works abound with statements such as the following: "difficult to tell where the school ends and the community begins";[3] "textbooks and chalkboards will no longer suffice"; "the bell is no respecter of students' interests or teachers' plans."[4]

Although nearly 100 schools have taken part in Trump's work, only one school (Ridgewood High, Norridge, Illinois) has put all of his commission's recommendations into operation. The school's basic beliefs are based on (1) development of intellectual powers, (2) attainment of basic skills, knowledge, and appreciations of each student to the highest level possible, (3) development of each individual's capacity to assume more and more responsibility for his education (and not stopping when he leaves school), (4) the significance of *every* area of human knowledge for *each* student's intellectual growth, and (5) tying school progress in with readiness to move from one stage to another, not necessarily with age.[5] Those may sound like a lot of words, but whether they have any meaning depends on how the school is really working out. Comments from its superintendent and teachers indicate that Ridgewood High is moving right along—and its staff apparently wonders why others haven't joined in.

A conference that had its eyes and ideas squarely on educational needs of tomorrow took place in Sarasota, Florida, late in 1960 under the title of "Designs for Learning." Chaired by an extremely creative architect (Philip H. Hiss, formerly Chairman of both the Sarasota County Board of Public Instruction and Board of Trustees,

[3] J. Lloyd Trump, *Images of the Future,* Washington, D. C., The National Association of Secondary-School Principals, 1959, p. 35.

[4] J. Lloyd Trump and Dorsey Baynham, *Focus on Change—Guide to Better Schools,* Chicago, Rand McNally & Company, 1961, pp. 35, 40.

[5] Dorsey Baynham, "A School of the Future in Operation," *Phi Delta Kappan,* May, 1961, pp. 350–354.

New College, a promising step forward in higher education) it pulled together personnel from the U.S. Office of Education, Educational Facilities Laboratories, Inc., the educational, architectural, and engineering fields, and the newspapers. J. Lloyd Trump provided the keynote address, and top educational names like John I. Goodlad, Robert H. Anderson, and Francis S. Chase gave provocative papers. Ways to permit students to advance as fast as possible, fitting teachers into teams, getting the most skillful teachers on television, and promoting unusual and flexible school designs all came up for discussion. Programmed instruction received a big play, as did automatic data processing and the use of electric computers in scheduling.

The possibility of an educational break-through has been conspicuously present several times on commercial television. A CBS hour-long presentation "The Influential Americans"[6] (November, 1960) was especially well presented. It included a nontechnical description of the more provocative experiments now going on related to educational television, team teaching, language laboratories, and other areas. Let us look at some of these new ideas in more detail.

PROGRAMMED LEARNING

I think that I may never see
A machine as wise as li'l ole me.
The only program that will go
Is one *I* plan for students slow,
Or bright; no matter, *I* know best.
There's no machine to let me rest.

But if machines will tardies check,
Relieving me of pain in neck,
Or kiddies' absence totals count,
My enthusiasm might just mount.
There'd be fewer hedges, sir,
If one would mark the register.[7]

[6] Based on the Arthur D. Morse book, *Schools of Tomorrow—Today*, Garden City, N.Y., Doubleday & Company, Inc., 1960.

[7] Joseph M. Cronin, *Phi Delta Kappan*, June, 1962, p. 407.

And with such glib comments some teachers dismiss one of the brighter of the teaching innovations. Maybe they feel threatened by its appearance. Perhaps they feel it will do them out of a job. It may even be a natural tendency to say "No" quickly before the idea is understood at all. It could be that someone has fed them the idea that teaching machines will somehow "dehumanize" learning. On the other hand, claims may be made as extreme as this one (*Time*, March 24, 1961): "Already it promises the first real innovation in teaching since the invention of movable type in the 15th Century."

However, a much more cautious (though receptive) tone was hit by a group of thoughtful men when they wrote the following:

During the 1960's the orderly development of these devices should not be marred by premature enthusiasm on the one hand nor misguided antagonism on the other. By 1970 a decade of experimental research on human learning, and application of the results to self-teaching devices and materials, should have made the best of these an adjunct to the teaching process that no school could afford to be without. . . . The best self-teaching devices and programs have proven remarkably effective, and students seem to enjoy working with them. Wisely used, they can remove a load from overburdened teachers, and give each student the luxury of a private tutor who proceeds at a pace determined by the student.[8]

What *is* a teaching machine anyway? Does the material prepared for it *have* to be presented in machine form? The answer to the second question should be stated quickly to allay some of the fears that have been involved in recent years: Not at all. The material can be in a booklet, film, or filmstrip format. As long as it is programmed (for machine use or not) and competently prepared, it can be used in any of the formats mentioned. The *method* is more important than the *mechanism;* after all, the machine itself does not teach. Take a subject (*any* subject, say some psychologists, but the burden is on them to prove that the application of the technique is that broad) and these are the rules that would apply:

1. Material must be broken down into small sequential steps leading gradually to the desired behavior.
2. Material should require frequent active response on the part of the learner.

[8] President's Commission on National Goals, *Goals for Americans,* Englewood Cliffs, N. J., Prentice-Hall, Inc., 1960, p. 90.

3. Learner receives immediate knowledge of results for every response.
4. Learner receives immediate reward for correct response (for most human beings, just knowing they are right may be enough); good programs are written so that the student usually *is* right, with mastery assured at every stage.
5. Rate of working through the material can be adjusted to fit the individual learner.
6. Sequence of materials covered can be adjusted to fit the learner.
7. Maintenance of student interest, up-to-date content, low error rate, and a testing-revision-testing sequence as long as necessary in preparing programs in the first place.

The "machine" itself into which this kind of product can fit may be anywhere from an electronic device costing as much as $5000 to a manila folder with a slider that is pulled down to reveal a correct answer after the student has written his.

It is probably logical in an era of electronic marvels to look upon any machine as a potential worker of wonders. Accustomed to hearing the computer carelessly classified as a machine that thinks, the average person is not astonished at the introduction of a machine that teaches. He does not expect to be able to understand the mysterious processes by which the computer thinks, and he naturally assumes that the processes involved in machine teaching are equally incomprehensible. So it comes as a surprise to him to learn that the machine itself is simply a handy device that presents the programmed subject matter. There are many variations but they all have one thing in common: a one-to-one ratio of student to machine.

The teaching machine was born in 1926 when psychologist Sidney L. Pressey devised a self-scoring machine that tested knowledge of material already learned by traditional methods. This machine was based on the familiar multiple-choice technique. The student indicated his choice by pushing the correct lever. It became apparent to Pressey during the course of his experiments that the machine could also be useful in introducing new material.

However, it was not until the 1950s that the teaching machine became a reality. B. F. Skinner, a psychologist working at Harvard, produced a machine that enabled the student to compose his own answers instead of selecting one of several presented to him. But Skinner's major contribution was his development of a new method of organizing and presenting the subject matter to be taught, something called a "program." The underlying principle of programming is a combination of common sense and psychological research. Psychologists call it the principle of "reinforcement." Mere recognition of a correct answer does not guarantee the ability to provide that answer when it is needed; Skinner emphasizes the point that the student must produce the answer, find it for himself. Simply stated, the basic principle capitalizes on the human preference to be right rather than wrong and to be rewarded by the immediate confirmation of this rightness. The purpose is to teach, not to test, and there may be prompts or cues along the way that help lead to correct answers.

To understand how this works imagine yourself in front of your television set watching a quiz show. You realize that you know or think you know the answer to a question. Not wishing to run the risk of feeling foolish in case your answer should be wrong, you probably say it to yourself or mutter it under your breath. A few seconds later the contestant on the show gives the same answer and the M.C. shouts, "Right!" A glow of satisfaction envelops you. You sit up a little straighter and listen a shade more intently to the next question. This time you snap out the answer in firm confident tones, startling your wife who was reading the newspaper, and once more the M.C. rewards you with "Right you are!" Now you are hopelessly involved in the process of demonstrating your mental agility to yourself and the members of your family who happen to be sharing this finest hour. So far you have been correct twice in a row. Each time your correctness was confirmed immediately and this stimulated you to further effort. But what will happen to this motivation —to say nothing of your self-esteem—if your next answer is wrong? It will probably go into a rapid decline and you'll decide to raid the refrigerator, change channels or simply refrain from any further participation. The principle of "reinforcement" is at work until you give that incorrect answer and the reinforcement of knowing you are right is suddenly withdrawn, your interest with it.

So programmed learning sets aside the old precept of learning by correcting your mistakes since it is obvious that your interest in learning is greater if you don't make the mistakes in the first place. How does a program ensure that you don't make mistakes? It isn't easy, but it can be accomplished by extremely careful writing and rewriting of materials that have been cautiously and professionally organized, and by testing the program on children and adults similar to those for whom it is being prepared. Efforts to reduce the error rate and at the same time retain the interest, and even enthusiasm, of the student are goals constantly sought in program preparation.

It may require considerable adjustment of attitude in parents and teachers to accept a system of instruction where the student makes few if any mistakes; but some startling results have emerged in classrooms where programmed learning has been offered.

A class of eighth-graders in Roanoke, Virginia, completed a full year of ninth-grade algebra in one semester. Forty-one percent of the class scored higher than the ninth-grade average score on a national examination. At Dartmouth Medical School the learning performance of a class in parasitology was found to be almost double that of a comparable class instructed by conventional methods. Gifted children moving ahead at their own pace, mentally retarded children guided step by step through programmed materials, and "average" children have all profited from the technique.

Tests are the programmer's most ruthless critic. A cherished sequence of carefully constructed frames representing literally hours of work becomes fodder for the wastebasket when testing shows that students fail to learn the material. The textbook writer never knows whether or not anyone learns his subject; the programmer's failure is a tangible record of error, and he has no one to blame but himself. He must go back and revise the material, filling in the gaps that resulted in student error.

However, when his program has undergone its final revision he can make the claim that no textbook writer or lecturer can make: This program teaches the subject to the students for whom it was designed. A good program is not published until this crucial point has been proved.

The very fact that its success can be proved so specifically brings up another unique characteristic of programmed instruction. Since the student must participate actively every step of the way by writing the answer in every blank, there is a graphic record of his learning progress. There is no way to measure the amount of material in a standard textbook that a student actually reads, nor is there any way of knowing how attentively he reads it. The same student must read every word of a sound programmed text carefully and attentively in order to give the correct answers.

One of the most highly publicized misconceptions about programmed learning is that the machine will replace the teacher. Actually the advantages of programmed instruction as a teaching tool have been applauded by those teachers who have had the opportunity to work with such materials. The teaching machine no more replaces the teacher than the automatic dishwasher replaces the housewife. In both cases the machine is a time and labor saver that releases the individual from routine drudgery. The teacher who is no longer hamstrung by the need for repetitive drill on fundamentals is free to deal with the creative aspects of a subject in its relationship to the larger field of the total curriculum. Assured of a student's grasp of the required fundamentals as taught and graphically recorded by machine or programmed text, the teacher can direct the student's further study on a level appropriate to his individual ability. It is obvious that more, rather than less, will be required of the teacher: more education, more experience, more of a professional attitude, more professional growth, more knowledge of learning theory and child development.

The implications of this individualized instruction in today's crowded classroom are not lost on the overburdened teacher who finds it impossible to deal effectively with a wide range of student differences. The student who learns quickly can move ahead without waiting for the slower learners to master the same material. For the slower learner the program alleviates the relentless pressure to "catch up" to the rest of the class. No teacher teaches every subject equally well; no teacher approaches every level of student ability with equal effectiveness, and no teacher wishes to see a certain percentage of the class, no matter how small, fail to learn essential material. Having programmed instruction is like having a specialist in each subject. It can broaden the base of student success at different levels of ability. Absences from school need not result in gaps in instruction that may never be properly bridged. Homebound students can enjoy the same quality of instruction that is offered in the schoolroom.

School boards across the nation are taking a long look at the field of programmed learning when considering plans for new buildings and changes in existing classroom design. Serious predictions have been made that the traditional but largely artificial barriers of grade levels will be erased by this new approach to learning. If these predictions prove accurate, it is obvious that the classroom as a self-contained unit will be of little academic or economic value.

Industry, too, is exploring the advantages of programmed training, and here again results have indicated great promise in speeding up on-the-job training and increasing efficiency. Programs for home use that offer instruction in games like chess and bridge are also on the market.

The number of tested programs available right now is obviously limited. A meticulously constructed program is costly to produce. It takes time to write, test, revise, test and revise again until the subject is taught thoroughly and painlessly. And it takes money, too; but most of it is going into the preparation of programs rather than machines, and despite both time and cost, there may be many programs available soon. Don't close the door on them, but don't open it very widely either until you know who produced them (company and specific people), what testing was done on them, and what value they are to *your* children. The need is obviously to select them carefully and use them well.

Teaching machines and programmed learning, at their best, increase the teacher's control over the learning activities of each child in the classroom. They are a promise rather than a panacea, despite some of the wild claims that have been made by some of their proponents.

EDUCATIONAL TELEVISION

During the past 10 years, more money has been spent on educational television than on all the newer school practices combined. The Ford Foundation alone since 1951 has allocated more than $20 million to help schools get started in this direction. And yet, in even the most ambitious programs children are receiving a half hour or less of televised instruction each day.

Although the road ahead is long and the progress to date seems limited, the steps forward *are* significant, as indicated by the following:

More than 70 educational television stations are in operation, covering a population of 75 million persons, perhaps 100 million by 1965.

More than 2100 hours of programming are transmitted weekly over these stations (in 1955, only 340 hours were presented).

Almost 1000 college courses for credit are offered on television (in 1955, there were only 222).

There are 350 closed-circuit systems in operation, transmitting programs over private wires to select audiences (in 1956, the figure was 77).

"The New Biology": CBS's "College of the Air" is televised to 8 educational television stations, in addition to 186 network affiliates, and is approved by 200 colleges and universities for credit.

"Continental Classroom" NBC's American government course is televised to approximately the same large number of institutions of higher learning, also for credit; the course on mathematics (1960–1961) attracted 5000 students for credit and 1.3 million viewers each week.

Professional organizations, representing the disciplines of science, mathematics, English, social studies and others, are cooperating in the television approach; an example is the "Continental Classroom" course in Economics, participated in by the American Economic Association, the Joint Council on Economic Education, and the Learning Resources Institute.

It has been prophesied that by 1970 educational television facilities could be available to every school in the country. They will be used to extend education to those who cannot go to school, to share expert teaching, rare demonstrations and expensive experimentation, and to enrich regular classroom experiences. A single teacher will be able to instruct 100,000 children at one time on a national educational network. But despite such ubiquitous qualities, television does not threaten the role of the individual teacher any more than programmed learning does. The major aspects of teaching will always be accomplished in the face-to-face interaction between teacher and student.

Television first made its appearance in education in 1932, but it was not used in formal instruction until 1953, soon after the Federal Communications Commission had set aside 242 channels for educational purposes. By 1960, ½ million to 3½ million students were receiving actual instruction by television, depending on which research source you use. More than 10 million students were enrolled in educational television classes in 1962–1963. Pittsburgh's school system was among the first to use television for teaching reading, arithmetic, and French. Pennsylvania State University, Western Reserve, and Iowa State were pioneers on the college level (1954), and the city of Chicago entered the adult education area in 1956. But the circle is complete in some localities. The glow apparently wore off quickly in the Washington, D.C. schools, which reportedly were the first (1960) to conclude that children do not learn effectively by watching television in the classroom. New Jersey, one of the first states to experiment with educational television (1950), eliminated it from the state budget in 1954.

What are the advantages of educational television as stated by its proponents? Here are a few of them:

In certain subjects the classes can be quite large, perhaps 500 to 1000 students, giving the classroom teacher more time for individual instruction and guidance.

Fine instructors can be made available to larger groups of children and can have more time to prepare for this demanding task. However, the master teacher in the classroom is not necessarily a master teacher on television.

The techniques and materials of these teachers can be emulated by other teachers in an in-service manner; the wall between teachers can be partly eliminated, and comparisons can no longer be avoided.

The total school curriculum can be broadened for schools where on-the-spot offerings may be somewhat limited.

Early studies indicate that students learn as much—sometimes significantly more—from televised instruction as from conventional instruction.

The opposition is summarized by Dr. Galen Saylor who at a meeting of the National Association of Secondary School Principals said:

I think that instruction by television, when it is regularly scheduled as a substitute for a classroom teacher during part or all of the period, is a travesty on quality education. Most of the television instruction with which I am familiar places a highly competent teacher in a studio and equally skilled teacher in a large lecture hall or auditorium in which a large group of students are gathered, and by this medium prevents both teachers from providing a meaningful, challenging learning experience for the pupils forced to endure the class.

Accusations have been made that television is a one-way medium and that viewing is a passive experience on the part of the child. Other problems are the inadequacy of current school design for large-group television viewing and the unanswered questions of children who are watching. In addition, the classroom teacher may be frustrated by being relegated to the role of television-set adjuster and resentful of the disruptive qualities, the superiority of educational films for bringing the child close to the subject, and the high cost involved.

In pointed language, Newton N. Minow, former chairman of the Federal Communications Commission, spoke to broadcasters of the United States about their "vast wasteland." At the same time he identified what is certainly one of the major problems of educational television when he said:

> Commercial television has no monopoly on wastelands. We all know there is room for improvement in program quality in educational as well as commercial broadcasting. . . . Television requires many skills and many talents of a high order. It also demands a large slice of showmanship. I'm afraid that many educators consider "showmanship" a dirty word. Many educators brush off showmanship as arty and gimmicky and they are leery of it. But tawdry theatrics are a world away from *true* showmanship—the art of attracting and holding an audience, of making an idea or a subject fascinating, the art of emotional involvement. Great teachers always have been exciting and challenging. Great teachers use showmanship every day. And they never bore. True showmanship demands greatness of spirit, the pioneering instinct, creative initiative, and courage. It demands imagination and daring in the treatment of ideas and techniques.

The use of educational television as a teaching tool has moved along rapidly in Canada, France, Italy, Japan, the Soviet Union, and the United Kingdom. In Great Britain a combination of private and governmental funds will make possible the creation of a television center for educational programs aimed at newly developing countries; it will concentrate on literacy education, public health, agriculture and child care. And instantaneous viewing in our own country of a presidential news conference or a flight into space provides an educational stimulus that classroom teachers would have a difficult time matching.

THE UNGRADED SCHOOL, CLASSROOM
ORGANIZATION, AND CLASS SIZE

The ungraded school has no grade labels and several basic ingredients:

One teacher stays with the same group of children for 2 or 3 years. This procedure can be tried just as well in the intermediate or upper elementary grades, but the lower academic level is where the plan is more frequently found.

No grade number is attached to the levels involved. Instead of having three grades, there may be eight or ten levels, providing much more flexibility in advancing up the educational ladder. There is less temptation here to make some children wait until others catch up, or to fill their vacant moments with busywork "just to keep them out of mischief."

An ungraded primary-level period would end after 3 years. Most pupils would go into fourth grade, a few would stay another year, and one or two might go into fifth grade. A 3-year period without the interference of annual promotions gives youngsters a much better chance of catching up than if the same stiff standard of accomplishment is used for all at the end of each year. There is no need for a pass-or-fail decision before the 3 years are completed.

Individualization is usually recognized in this plan. A class of first-grade children often has a 4- or 5-year range in ability. Some are ready to start formal reading this year, but others were ready and *did* start 1 or 2 years ago, while another group won't be ready to begin for 1 or 2 more years. So through this ungraded plan, an effort is made to individualize the program and guide children at their own rate. No, they are *not* permitted to set their own pace; the direction and speed are always under the control of a teacher who should know better than the child does.

A broad spread in achievement of each group of children is encouraged, and no effort is made to keep them together. If you think that teaching this way is much more difficult you're absolutely right!

Flexibility is the keynote. This plan is a new twist on the old one-room school; although these youngsters work on different levels, they are reasonably close in chronological age.

Competition is stimulated, but with one's own past record, and evaluation of progress is frequent and steady.

An awareness of child development is demanded of the teacher; and parents are encouraged to take a new look at their school and leave behind forever remarks that begin, "Now when *I* went to school . . ."

The ungraded class or school is obviously not a panacea for all educational ills, no more than are programmed learning and educational television. It is a type of school organization whose effectiveness depends on the personnel and the curriculum, an organization that loosens the bonds and lowers the barriers that a strict grade structure frequently imposes on creative teachers.

A pioneer in teaching teachers about the ungraded school was Central Washington College of Education, Ellensburg, Washington, which in the summer of 1957 offered a course on this subject. Many school districts have experimented with this approach, most of them happily; it has even been tried on the secondary-school level (as in Melbourne, Florida). In the key book in the area, Goodlad and Anderson report a tremendously increasing interest in the subject.[9]

Since 1947, Appleton, Wisconsin, has had a "continuous progress" plan which is almost a classic example of ungraded activities. In their program children move along as fast as their abilities can carry them, no grade promotions or failures, no report cards. Instead, there are conferences with parents and progress reports describing performance in relation to capacity. The plan includes early entry for appropriate young children, "primary school" and "intermediate school." There is a conscious effort to break the chronological lock step. One purpose of the Appleton experiment was to study the ill effects of nonpromotion on children.

Although a few schools tried out the ungraded primary in the 1920s, the strongest steps forward have been taken since 1940. Milwaukee entered the picture in 1942. In *Elementary School Organization* (1962), a publication of the relatively conservative Department of Elementary School Principals of the NEA, the ungraded school is viewed as one of the most promising educational developments of today and tomorrow.

The flexibility of the ungraded school and the experimentation with team teaching and the various Trump proposals run headlong into some of the rigid school patterns of the past. Some of the latter are stubbornly clung to under the label of "the self-contained class-

---

[9] John I. Goodlad and Robert H. Anderson, *The Nongraded Elementary School*, New York, Harcourt, Brace & World, Inc., 1963.

room." It would be ideal to have a self-sufficient classroom situation *if* it managed to meet the needs of all the children in it. Unfortunately, few teachers are fully capable of doing so, a basic reason for seeking approaches that really satisfy individual differences. Beating the drums for holding on to the self-contained environment is the Association for Supervision and Curriculum Development, which maintains that (1) it is not arbitrary and mechanistic; (2) it integrates the child's program and does not fragmentize his learning; (3) time pressures in it are not so demanding; (4) *learning* rather than exactly prescribed subject matter is the major concern in this classroom; (5) knowledge is interrelated anyway, so let's not compartmentalize it; and (6) the single teacher can know a child better than several teachers can when they see him only for limited periods of time. "To compare the average or poor aspects of an existing plan with the hoped-for potentialities of a proposed plan is to make no comparison at all," the Association says. "An organizational plan, of itself, does little or nothing to improve the curriculum."[10] The last statement is true, of course, but the six items noted above are not necessarily so. They depend on the caliber of the teacher and administrator involved.

A kind of middle approach between the self-contained and the specialized-teacher setups is the Dual Progress Plan devised by Dr. George D. Stoddard of New York University.[11] It maintains that if you are responsible for teaching most of the curriculum in a given grade you may have too big a job. If required to teach language arts, social studies, mathematics, science, and all the other subjects without outside help, you may have to rely heavily on textbooks and teachers' manuals. The results may be superficial and out of tune with the times.

The Dual Progress Plan is based on semidepartmentalization. The children spend half of the day with the same teacher, the other half with several teachers. The experimentation in Long Beach, California, and Ossining, New York (under a grant from the Ford Foundation) is based on the latter half being nongraded in the areas

[10] Association for Supervision and Curriculum Development, *The Self-Contained Classroom*, Washington, D.C., 1960, p. v.

[11] George D. Stoddard, *The Dual Progress Plan*, New York, Harper & Row Publishers, Inc., 1961.

of science, mathematics and the arts. This plan combines many features of team teaching, the ungraded approach, and the self-contained classroom.

Undergirding much of the discussion of the ungraded school and classroom organization is the very practical problem of class size. Everyone says he can do a better job with a smaller group than he can with a large one, and yet research on the subject is painfully limited. Opinions are available, of course; they state that the small class helps increase student achievement, but the proof is seldom present. In the 1961–1962 school year the average class size in 50 large urban communities was 32.2 students. Nearly three-quarters of these students were in classes enrolling 31 or more.

Alvin Eurich of the Ford Foundation became somewhat suspicious of the almost universal agreement on an ideal class size of 25. He traced it back to a statement in the Babylonian Talmud, written in the third century! More seriously, he said:

Because so much in education depends on it, the first shibboleth that requires critical examination is the fixed teacher-student ratio . . . a half-century of experimental work does not support this fixation in American education. In fact, research places the burden of proof on the proponents of small classes. Students do as well on examinations, and in many cases better, if taught in larger classes *by superior teachers*.[12]

Charles S. Johnson, former President of Fisk University, expressed his idea on the subject: "The small class merely assures the transmission of mediocrity in an intimate environment."[13]

Experienced teachers frequently have firm feelings about class size. In a 1961 opinion poll of the NEA the following figures evolved from the elementary teachers questioned:

12 percent preferred fewer than 20 students
54 percent preferred 20 to 24 students
31 percent preferred 25 to 29 students
3 percent preferred 30 or more students.

Because 52 percent of the teachers polled actually *had* 30 or more students in their classes, their preferences are clearly not being respected at the present time!

[12] Alvin Eurich, *Phi Delta Kappan*, May, 1961, p. 371.
[13] Charles S. Johnson, quoted in *Saturday Review*, October 21, 1961, p. 59.

The work of J. Lloyd Trump related to large classes, seminars, and individual study is an effort to break the barrier of rigid class size. It all depends on *what* is being studied, *who* the students are, and *who* the teachers are. Although education is on its way toward reducing the rigidity, the first steps are still isolated and faltering, but gathering strength.

OTHER ASPECTS OF STAFF UTILIZATION

Several other approaches have been made to use teaching staffs as efficiently as possible. After all, just because you will be a skillful teacher does not necessarily mean that you will be equally good with all children, all educational levels, all subjects, or all situations or organizational patterns. If you think for a moment of your own desires and abilities, you'll quickly recognize that your preferences firmly point in certain directions.

Current research and experimentation indicate that the ways of organizing classes and schools in past generations are not necessarily the best methods available. Of all the efforts toward staff utilization one of the most intriguing, popular, and discussed is "team teaching." It has not had universal acceptance by any means, but it has given the followers of the self-contained classroom the roughest jar in a generation of educational criticism.

Its basic concepts are quite simple: Teachers teach in teams based on their specialties; children are in larger groups, but can be broken into very small ones when it is desirable to do so; teaching teams may cross grade level on the basis of children's needs; there are opportunities for large lectures, small seminars, and individual study. The teaching team itself need not be strictly defined; it can consist of one or more "master" teachers, specialists, aides, apprentices, all under a team leader, and it can be used on all educational levels. There is more time for teacher preparation, evaluation and discussion of each teacher's contribution, and concern for each child's needs. Time limits of classes are also flexible. Teaching teams have made wider use of newer developments and media, such as programmed learning and educational television, than have regular classroom teachers;

the former because of their emphasis on experimental approaches to education seem more eager to try what is new and different.

Team teaching faces an uphill battle against well-entrenched educational organization and practices. It calls for a further evaluation of what we mean by teacher "equality" and "autonomy," for example. Most of our states and more than 100 communities have taken firm steps in this direction. The latter include Evanston Township High School; schools in Lexington, Massachusetts; Norwalk, Connecticut; Jefferson County, Colorado; and the southern California communities combined Team Teaching Program of Claremont Graduate School. Architectural design receives a real challenge from this approach because flexible class size, student movement, cutting across grade lines, and more use of audio-visual aids all require a new kind of school building; the old three story structures in many of our big cities dating back to the early years of this century hardly satisfy these needs.

Schools do not have to enter the team teaching picture on a big scale. It can be done simply and slowly by two teachers working together, each teaching the subjects in which he is most competent. Or it can acquire the dimensions of the Harvard Suprad project (School and University Program for Research and Development), started under the vigorous leadership of Francis Keppel, former dean of Harvard's Graduate School of Education. Master teachers will warrant significantly higher salaries in the future, Keppel maintained, just one reason why this whole approach should be attractive to teachers in general. There is a negative aspect, however, because it is possible for the junior members of a team to lose their identity or for cooperation to be stressed at the expense of initiative. As for the cost of team teaching, it need be no higher than if the teachers were all in separate classrooms. In addition, the total number of teachers and children involved need not be very different.

One innovation of team teaching is the practice of using teacher aides. Ask any teacher whether there are some activities she would just as soon pass on to a competent assistant—or wait until you are teaching yourself. The answer is almost invariably an enthusiastic, "Yes!" Since 1956 nearly 500 volunteers annually have worked in the New York City public schools through an organization called the

Public Education Association. Their activities vary from organizing a school library to vocabulary building to piano accompaniment to assistance in crafts to teaching English as a second language. High school teachers in the greater Boston area have had volunteer aides from the undergraduate honor rolls at Harvard, Radcliffe, and Massachusetts Institute of Technology; a similar program evolved from Columbia and Barnard College, to Manhattan's benefit. The most quoted demonstration of the use of teacher aides is Bay City, Michigan, where their work extends to many of the more routine activities of the classroom teacher: taking attendance, preparing simple reports, correcting papers, answering the telephone, and taking messages. Because involvements like these occupy at least one-fourth of a teacher's time, you can easily see how valuable this assistance can be and how the teacher can be freed to do more of what he was hired to do, teach children. The practice is economical because the aides are paid less than teachers (as in Bay City) or are volunteers.

Some people, however, don't want the help, resent the presence of someone else, or prefer to bear the entire burden. But just as doctors and dentists depend on the assistance they receive from others in their offices, so teachers will increasingly profit from this kind of division of responsibility. College English teachers can have helpers who can be depended upon to read student themes competently; high school teachers can have part-time secretarial help; elementary teachers can have more time to meet individual problems. The teacher aide can fit into many current "teaching" functions. The fact that we ask our teachers to be and do all things (for parents as well as for children) is evidence that we are not very clear about the teacher's professional role. And our lack of clarity often results in waste of talents on nonprofessional tasks.

"Too many teachers are caught in an unhappy cycle," observed two astute critics of the education scene. "Although they enter the profession filled with idealism they gradually lose their enthusiasm and curiosity in a treadmill of academic trivia. We take a first-rate master teacher and make a second-rate clerk out of her."[14]

A call for help is being heard more and more in various parts of

[14] Benjamin Fine and Lillian Fine, *How to Get the Best Education for Your Child*, New York, G. P. Putnam's Sons, 1959, p. 227.

the country, although it is still relatively faint, and in many positions for which you'll be considered, the assistance will already be there by the time you arrive.

USING FACILITIES WISELY

"It could be the end of the cells and the bells," said Harold B. Gores, President of Educational Facilities Laboratories, as he viewed the drastic and exciting changes in school design in recent years. Although it will take many years for the outmoded school buildings to be replaced, a significant start has been made.

As additional buildings are erected, new communities spring up, and school populations increase, the school picture of the future begins to fall into place. Because the design of buildings and classrooms influences school programs, teachers and administrators must be concerned with flexibility, appearance, and utility. The odds are on your side that in the near future you'll have space, light, and equipment available to you. What you *do* with them is, of course, another matter—and a responsibility you'll have to consider seriously. So will those who help you prepare for teaching.

The schoolhouse is not, of course, as important as the school teacher. But the schoolhouse, because it stands there to be seen, speaks of the intention of the community toward the children. Any school you build either helps to anchor the people to the community or, instead, hastens their departure. The schoolhouse more than any other structure in town declares the public intention to press on, to rest awhile, or to go back.[15]

Unfortunately, fear of new design is as prevalent in educational circles as fear of innovation in the classroom, and economy is always a nagging kind of pressure. Many implications for newer school designs have evolved from Trump's *Images of the Future;* its viewpoint is that class size is directly related to the subjects and children taught. Arbitrary preconceived ideas are to be replaced by an attitude of "It all depends."

Research, experimentation, and dissemination of knowledge re-

[15] Educational Facilities Laboratories, *The Cost of a Schoolhouse,* New York, 1960, p. 139.

garding educational facilities are still in their beginnings. In the forefront of activity is Educational Facilities Laboratories (New York City), a nonprofit organization established by the Ford Foundation in 1958, whose stories of adventurous new schools relate educational programs to building design.

In addition to rather complete revamping of over-all school appearance, efforts are constantly being made to utilize more wisely the space and equipment that are currently available: classrooms that are empty part of the day, evenings, and weekends; audio-visual materials that gather dust because teachers are ignorant or fearful of them; large meeting rooms that are seldom occupied. These are costly and should not be wasted.

THE DEPRIVED ONES

Call them "deprived," "under-privileged," or "disadvantaged," and blame their educational losses on socioeconomic status or language differences, the problem remains one that can be stated simply: Some children are not getting their fair share of the educational opportunities of which we are so proud.

Ride through the congested neighborhoods of any big city, and you'll see large buildings, narrow streets, sidewalks crowded with children. Walk into the apartment houses, down the alleys—and think a little bit about the schools and teachers that are attempting to bring knowledge, beauty, and understanding to children who spend most of their waking and sleeping hours in such an environment. Others have paved the way for your thinking, sometimes with indignant reactions to what they've seen, sometimes with considered, reasonable recommendations of what the schools can do. Conant,[16] Riessman,[17] the Educational Policies Commission,[18] and the Association for Supervision and Curriculum Development have all presented thought-provoking statements on this problem that seems

[16] James B. Conant, *Slums and Suburbs*, New York, McGraw-Hill Book Company, Inc., 1961.
[17] Frank Riessman, *The Culturally Deprived Child*, New York, Harper & Row, Publishers, Inc., 1962.
[18] Educational Policies Commission, *Education and the Disadvantaged American*, Washington, D.C., NEA, 1962.

almost a perpetual weight which American society bears. This complicated issue has two aspects: The waste of children in general—the bright, the slow, and the mass of the in-between; the specific waste of hidden talent. As you consider the total problem, keep both parts of it in mind.

When talent is discovered in unexpected places (among the poor or the physically handicapped) it is a dramatic event. It turns up in science and industry in leaders who have survived being melted into the multitudes, or overcome childhood afflictions. Rising above disparity, oppression, and prejudice is part of the American dream; but it cannot be permitted to occur by chance. From a top source, the President's Commission on National Goals, comes a clear statement of the issue:

> We should insist that regardless of the individual's economic level, regardless of his color, whether he lives in a modern suburb or the backwoods or a city slum, he should receive the best we can give in the way of opportunity and encouragement to develop whatever abilities he possesses.
> We are still losing large numbers of talented young people who terminate their education short of their full potentialities. Why do we lose them? Can we prevent the loss? We are just beginning to find answers to these crucial questions. During the 1960's intensive research should be applied to the problem of "talent salvage."[19]

Although there are many dedicated and extremely capable teachers in the schools which these children attend, the majority are often new, partially qualified, or transitional teachers. And because the parents and communities as a whole are sometimes unable to provide the guidance and inspiration needed, the school environment becomes even more important than it is for other children. Bright youngsters from limited settings find it hard to escape, said Eli Ginzberg, because "among other reasons, most of their friends have their sights set on leaving school as quickly as possible, getting a job that pays well, and having fun with girls."[20] Perhaps they are all reasons that can be justified personally, but both the individual and the rest of us are the losers. Overcrowded urban areas, farm

[19] President's Commission on National Goals, *Goals for Americans*, Englewood Cliffs, N. J., Prentice-Hall, Inc., 1960, p. 83.
[20] Eli Ginzberg, *Human Resources: The Wealth of a Nation*, New York, Simon and Schuster, Inc., 1958, p. 82.

localities where automation is helping create a population surplus, and depressed areas are all on the list for increased attention in the years ahead. With fewer than one-fifth of our high schools producing 82 percent of all college students, you may wonder what all the others are doing.

The problem is not new or suddenly discovered by a few astute and sensitive individuals. More than 25 years ago, in 1937, a book was published called *How Fare American Youth?*[21] In surveying American young people, it found large proportions of them unemployed, in poor health, poor readers, and possessing other negative factors. Recent reports find the education and health of deprived youth to be about as disturbing as it was then. The current situation is related in one way to the increasingly large numbers of emotionally disturbed and mentally retarded children that there seem to be. But are there *really* more than ever, or is it primarily a matter of our greater awareness, greater adeptness at ferreting out the problem, plus a larger total population?

The subject of deprived children is large and complex. Riessman pointed out that children from economically and intellectually poor families number one out of three in our fourteen largest cities. If present trends fail to change, half of the inhabitants of our larger cities of 1970 may be unable to participate constructively in their society. He and others have stated that we have too long ignored the affirmative aspects of their background, their special interests and creative potential, for example, and that the schools should adjust to them rather than the other way around. To insist on standards and programs totally unrelated to their lives is not a realistic approach. Negro children from uneducated families in the rural South, white subsistence-level farmers from isolated areas in the Appalachians, and immigrant children from Puerto Rico are among those who hardly find a home-away-from-home in the lives of Dick and Jane. Their cultural and economic paths are far apart, and to force them to converge may just increase the frustrations of children with another language, another home setting, and another socioeconomic environment.

Because jobs for the unskilled are becoming less and less available (in New York City alone, 8000 elevator-operator jobs were wiped out

[21] American Council on Education, *How Fare American Youth?* Washington. D.C., 1937.

by automation within the past year), because education may actually be rejected by those needing it, and because more money is spent on attempts at correction of indigence, delinquency, and crime than on education, the school's tasks related to the deprived ones will be on our hands and minds for years to come. Poverty, disease, instability, and conflict are problems that a teacher can not solve directly. But he *can* recognize that children may often be tired, ill, lonely, or hungry. A teacher who ignores these factors cannot be an effective guide to learning.

EFFORTS TO SOLVE THE PROBLEM

The most quoted project related to the problem of hidden and lost talent was set up in 1956 in our largest city and was based on early identification and encouragement of able students from poor homes. Under the title of Demonstration Guidance Project, and with the cooperation of New York City's Junior High School 43 and George Washington High School, the experiment involved Negro and migrant children in slum neighborhoods permeated by one-parent families, poor housing, and disproportionately high community and school disciplinary problems. As a result of the experiment the school dropout rate was cut in half, the percentage of graduates eligible for college increased from 9 to 36 percent, I.Q. scores rose sharply, and discipline problems almost vanished. Was it a kind of magic to which these students were exposed? You might call it that, but more specifically the improved situation resulted from concrete efforts like these: Counselors, psychologists, and social workers stepped into the picture; standardized testing was more widely conducted and interpreted; remedial reading, speech improvement, parent interviews, and remedial mathematics were introduced; classes were reduced in size. The sights of these students were raised beyond their own communities and into the arts and other areas they had never touched before. They saw Shakespearean plays, visited Hyde Park, attended concerts, museums, and football games. Children who had been ignored were now noticed; groups that drifted through became individuals with specific problems that needed and received careful attention. No miracle took place here; instead, there was more teaching and learning, more exposure to culture, more attention to each child.

In January, 1963, the progress report of the New York project (now referred to as the Higher Horizons program) indicated its expansion, into 76 schools in the city. It has spread even further—into the large school systems of other cities where thousands of children live under depressed conditions. It has gone from a quiet $40,000 appropriation in 1956 (from the National Scholarship Service and Fund for Negro Students and the College Entrance Examination Board) to a $500,000 program in 1959. It has changed demoralized and disinterested children to students with college and professional aspirations; transformed a stigma of poverty and helplessness to a feeling that "equal opportunity" is more than empty words.

Much as one might like to, one cannot ignore the relationship of educational deprivation to race and other factors. That is why the National Scholarship Service referred to above was started in the first place in 1948. That is why its president, Richard L. Plaut, can cite with pride its accomplishments with boys and girls who without this assistance probably *would* have added to the dropout rolls instead of contributing their talents to the professions which need them.

Within large cities there is a constantly moving population, from neighborhood to neighborhood, from the core of the city outward, eventually to the suburbs. Sociologists for a long time have been concerned about the areas that circle the commercial centers of cities, dominated by older housing, low income levels, migratory workers, and adults of limited education. The Ford Foundation has supported experimentation in these "gray areas" in some of our largest cities. Participating in its Great Cities School Improvement Program are Buffalo, Chicago, Cleveland, Detroit, Milwaukee, Philadelphia, Pittsburgh, St. Louis, San Francisco, and Washington, D.C. All are attempting to bring together school and community facilities to strengthen the over-all educational program. Special orientation centers for migrant children, nongraded programs for overage children, and on-the-job training with its emphasis on practical aspects of education are phases of these big-city experiments. The objectives are ones you can easily recognize: reduction in failure and dropout rates; improved attendance records; higher levels of achievement and aspiration. "Careers for Youth" spearheaded by Robert Choate, Jr. in Phoenix has similar goals.

"Malignant cancer" is Robert F. Kennedy's descriptive phrase as he notes the effect of this child neglect on the neighborhood, the city, and the nation. These problems are deeply rooted in poverty and slum conditions. Each of the cities referred to above has been actively involved in the beginnings of a solution—hard to reach, long in coming, but at least on its way. Concern for the individual—real, practical, active concern—is in the picture as we look ahead in education. The deprived ones will not vanish in the next year or two, but at least they are not being ignored. Not *all* of them, anyway.

TRAVEL, NDEA, AND THE PEACE CORPS

If we look critically and carefully at certain aspects of the education picture today, we're forced to realize that they are moving, changing, expanding. Student travel, the ramifications of the National Defense Education Act, and the work of the Peace Corps are examples of present-day education "on the move."

Your interest in the subject of travel may be of a very personal type. Unlike the depression days of the 1930s when travel by college students was limited to street cars, buses, elevated, or subways between home, school, and work, the current situation reveals these facts:

More than 100,000 United States students applied for passports in 1961 (expanding from fewer than 24,000 in 1951).

Almost 20,000 are annually enrolled in institutions of higher learning abroad. The largest number has been attracted by the University of Paris (Sorbonne), Mexico City College, the University of London, the University of Madrid, and McGill University (Montreal); but we also have student representation in Beirut, Hong Kong, Ankara, Tokyo, and Helsinki, among others.

All do not go to Europe, by any means: 1100 enrolled in Mexico in 1960; 1700 in Canada; others are as widely distributed as Ghana, Argentina, the Union of South Africa, Israel, and Guatemala.

More than 800 grants were available in 1963–1964 for graduate study or research in 46 countries under the Fulbright-Hay educational exchange program.

Other countries send out their educational ambassadors, too; UNESCO estimated an increase from 180,000 in 1957 to more than 200,000 in 1961. For study, training, and teaching, nearly 70,000 persons came to the United

States in 1960–1961; 53,000 students enrolled in 1,666 colleges and universities. The University of California alone enrolls about 2,000 annually. (Incidentally, only 5,000 of the 53,000 were here under government programs.)

More than 7000 persons from 100 countries annually participate in teacher exchange programs conducted by the U.S. Department of State. Other possibilities for teachers are not on an exchange basis; for example contract arrangements for teaching in African schools are made through the International Exchange Service of the Department of State.

Study abroad varies greatly, depending on the person, his objectives, and the place he selects. Study tours which combine travel with an academic program, "informal" study resulting from independent travel, special seminars and summer courses, regular school programs, a full year or summer abroad sponsored by United States colleges and universities, and work camps are among the situations available.

More and more of our educational institutions have been getting into the act: Scarsdale High School brought its production of *Our Town* to European teen-agers; Michigan State University conducted its doctoral research fellowship program in ten foreign countries; an entire prep school (Whiteman-Gaylord in Steamboat Springs, Colorado) was transported to Spain for a semester; Syracuse University has an Overseas Training Program, a living-working experience for graduate students preparing for overseas jobs. Foreign-study programs have also been organized by Dartmouth, Stanford, Colgate, Oberlin, Fordham, New York University, the University of Kansas and many others. The spectrum of activity extends from small colleges (Goshen in Indiana and Parsons in Iowa) to the full expanse of the Fulbright and Smith-Mundt Acts with their provisions for foreign language and culture studies, research, and government-sponsored educational exchanges.

SOME PROBLEMS OF OVERSEAS STUDY PROGRAMS

How do we limit or eliminate purposeless dabbling and happy-timing on the part of the student? How can we be sure of the caliber of his teachers, schools, and housing in the foreign setting? How can we relate his overseas education to his education, vocational future, and total adult adjustment at home? Merely being in a different environment does not mean that true enrichment takes place (any more than proximity to a great teacher means that greatness necessarily rubs off on the student). What happens depends on more factors than location and nearness.

A spring, 1961, issue of the Carnegie Corporation's Quarterly spotlighted this point when it said that "too many of the programs for study or work abroad have been shallow in conception and shoddy in execution, leading at best to a gloss of cosmopolitanism to adorn the traveler and at worst to the false belief that he has acquired more than a superficial notion of what the world is all about." A pretty brochure, a quaint town nestled in the mountains, a foreign language, and school buildings that date back to the Middle Ages may all be very inviting and might lead to a pleasant vacation. But meeting the goals of academic learning, cultural breadth, and educational achievement requires more than a colorful setting and travelogues. A foreign university should have more than a glamorous name: Is its reputation substantial? Are its faculty members really distinguished in their fields? Are its credits of the type that most institutions in this country would recognize and accept without difficulty?

At their best, travel and study abroad provide the most memorable of experiences. At their worst they can bring frustration, disillusionment, and no small expense. Mark Twain once looked at the affirmative side of the issue when he observed, "Travel is fatal to prejudice, bigotry, and narrowmindedness, all foes to real understanding. Likewise, tolerance or broad wholesome charitable views of men and things cannot be acquired by vegetating in one little corner of the earth all one's lifetime."[22] The current interdependence of the world's people encourages one to take seriously his century-old bit of wisdom.

A second example of a new and expanding educational development is the National Defense Education Act of 1958, resulting in almost as much travel as our overseas educational programs. One big difference is that the NDEA has brought it about in this country. Since the Act has been about as misquoted and misinterpreted as any activity related to the total education scene, let's cut straight through to some of the facts. The major parts of the act are as follows:

[22] Mark Twain, quoted in James F. Fixx, "Go to College and See the World," *Saturday Review*, February 17, 1962, p. 75.

TITLE I	General provisions
TITLE II	Loans to students in institutions of higher education
TITLE III	Financial assistance for strengthening science, mathematics, and modern foreign language instruction
TITLE IV	National defense fellowships
TITLE V	Guidance, counseling, and testing: identification and encouragement of able students
TITLE VI	Language development
TITLE VII	Research and experimentation in more effective use of television, radio, motion pictures and related media for educational purposes
TITLE VIII	Area vocational education programs
TITLE IX	Science information service
TITLE X	Miscellaneous provisions

This Act was passed in the welter of criticism of American education following the first Soviet sputnik. Priorities in it were given to strengthening our science, mathematics, foreign language, and guidance programs. Little difficulty has been encountered so far in authorizing time extensions for the plan which is based on State-Federal matching funds. An indication of its breadth is shown by the 55 language- and area-research centers established on college and university campuses and the offering of more than 1200 courses in "critical" languages, enrolling 7000 students, utilizing 600 faculty members, in 40 different languages. Instructional materials for 70 of the languages of the world not commonly taught have been developed. In 1961–1962, 1485 institutions applied for Student Loan Funds. In the first two years of the Act more than 5000 classrooms were remodeled to accommodate new science and mathematics equipment, 2500 language laboratories were set up, and counseling services were expanded considerably.

A before-and-after look at guidance and counseling is in order. Before 1958 the following was true: (1) Fewer than half of our high school students received assistance from a well-rounded counseling program; (2) two-thirds of the school counselors did not meet minimal certification requirements; (3) it was estimated that 15,000 additional counselors were needed in the public high schools alone. Two years later these facts emerged: (1) Professional guidance personnel employed by states expanded from 99 to 194; (2) the total number of counselors increased more than 100 percent, from 12,000 in 1958 to 27,000 in 1963; (3) more than 9.2 million high school students were tested for aptitude and achievement at least once during the second year of NDEA.

In curriculum areas, under Title III, the changes are even more dramatic. Before 1958 only a minority of our high school students studied chemistry, physics, intermediate algebra, trigonometry, solid geometry, or even a modern foreign language. In fact, fewer than half of our public high schools offered courses in modern foreign languages. During the first two years of NDEA, 56,000 local projects were approved for the purchase of new equipment in science, mathematics, and foreign languages. States now employ 193 specialists in these areas (only 33 before 1958).

A third and most widely discussed example of education moving ahead was a pet project of President Kennedy's administration. His special message on the Peace Corps was made to Congress on March 1, 1961. At the start, the Peace Corps was accused of being "too idealistic," "for beatniks and deadbeats," "dangerous . . . will incite international incidents," "a juvenile experiment." But within a year from its inception, a startling change took place. The most conservative of our Congressmen lauded it. The House Foreign Affairs Committee unanimously approved the Administration's request to double its budget. College presidents and foreign embassies shared the enthusiasm. What happened?

Performance by a group of dedicated people and increasing requests from foreign countries (in the first year 40 nations requested 50,000 Peace Corps workers) combined to alter the image. Glamour may have surrounded the original concepts, but the emerging facts were far from glamorous. To begin with, Peace Corps volunteers receive no pay other than living expenses and $75 severance pay for each month when they leave the service. They are not tax exempt. Even the top-level executives with the Peace Corps are on a limited payment basis, and its director, Sargent Shriver, receives the traditional $1 a year.

During its first year the patterns of work and location were established. These included teaching school in Ghana, Nigeria, Sierre Leone, and the Philippines; helping build roads and draw geological maps in Tanganyika; working on rural development and farm projects in Colombia, Chile, Malaya, and Pakistan; and helping control malaria in Thailand.

The request from 40 nations for 50,000 workers will be a long time in being filled. Closer to reality are the annual training figures of up to 5,000 men and women for this permanent Federal agency. Although teachers constitute a large group in the total picture (60 percent), there are also librarians, laboratory technicians, nurses aides, agricultural workers, and medical and sanitation personnel. The Corps motto frequently heard is "We came to learn as well as to teach." There is a minimum age of 18, but there is no maximum; one must be unmarried (except if both husband and wife join together) and have no dependents under 18 years of age; recommendations from at least six other persons are required.

"A substantial popular base for responsible American policies toward the world" and "a new dimension to America's world policy" are ways in which Director Shriver views the Peace Corps. That's how it's worded at the top; but where the people work there are steamy jungles, hot deserts, dusty plains, and a tough, demanding job to do in fighting illiteracy, disease, and poverty.

CONCLUDING REMARKS

We have some concrete hints of what education will look like tomorrow, and we can be certain about at least one thing: It *will* be different. The differences may be slow in coming, but they can already be heard in programmed learning, educational television, the ungraded school, team teaching, and other strong whispers of change.

That future is not appearing unannounced. In 1960, 7600 participants took part in the White House Conference on Children and Youth; they brought forth 670 recommendations as they looked toward the next decade, viewing children in their homes, schools, communities, and world.[23] One of the major goals of the Conference was to provide guideposts for citizen action. These ideas from a very

[23] Reported in *Recommendations—Composite Report of Forum Findings, 1960 White House Conference on Children and Youth,* Government Printing Office, 1960.

thoughtful group of people provide the guidelines for our teachers and future teachers. Also paving the way toward a future based on change are individuals—Conant, Bruner, Trump, Goodlad, Gardner and many others—who speak and write of educational innovation.

Change has started in school organization and architecture, with departures from the egg-crate school building, the 8-4-4-year school sequence, and the school day and year of set lengths. "Why?" is the crucial word, and the answer must be more than "Well, that's the way it always has been." In Broward County, Florida, the third fastest-growing county in the United States, a complex of schools is planned in one locality, extending from nursery through graduate school. It will be created around the newest educational facilities and experimental programs, bringing together all of the newer practices discussed in this chapter. At one time Paul Woodring (now known primarily for his editing of the monthly education issue of the *Saturday Review*) proposed a school reorganization plan based on student ability, ungraded primary school, partial grouping, and trade schools.[24] Benjamin Fine, former editor of the *New York Times'* education page suggested a ten-year combined elementary- and secondary-school program, or a twelve-year system divided into three parts.[25] The year-round school, the extended school day, and shared services of isolated rural areas are all in the wind.

We must realize, of course, that what seems new to us may actually date back many years. For example, departmentalization in our schools, pounced on by eager young enthusiasts as "the greatest ever," actually goes back to the nineteenth century. In student teaching or in your first year on the job you'll think, and perhaps say, "Why don't they group the children or use more phonics? It seems so obvious . . ." What is obvious to you was also apparent to experienced teachers, and a long time ago.

But there *are* new forces at work, exciting possibilities, whose sheer newness builds up a core of resentment in those who resist change of any sort. One of the greatest challenges you'll face is to help batter down the opponents of the new and the different. Such opposition is perennially with us, constantly fighting any alteration in the *status*

[24] Paul Woodring, *A Fourth of a Nation,* New York, McGraw-Hill Book Co., Inc., 1957, p. 147.
[25] Benjamin Fine and Lillian Fine, *op. cit.,* p. 229.

quo, and steadily losing in a world that cannot stand still. Your task is to be on the side of progress, where youth always belongs; to block it is to be unrealistic at a time when a realistic view toward our problems cannot be avoided.

CHAPTER 4

A TIME FOR *Qualified Teachers*

During the 1960 Presidential campaign, a university instructor polled his classes one morning: "How many of you watched the Kennedy-Nixon debate on television last night?" In one class 3 out of 19 raised their hands; in the other, 5 out of 25.

"How many of you attended the assembly yesterday afternoon when actress Janet Leigh spoke on a political subject?" In each class all but one raised hands in reply.

Although the efforts in many colleges and universities to attract the best and screen out the rest are becoming more refined each year, their relative ineffectiveness worries many who recognize the pressures on our country today and in the years ahead. The lethargic attitude of some future teachers toward the world around them is a deep-seated part of that concern. And it helps not at all to point out that many of their parents are also disinterested and complacent; that fact provides no consolation for those who recognize the leadership potential that good teachers can and must provide.

"It is not a job for economic or emotional misfits, for frightened, inferiority-ridden men and women seeking a safe, respectable and quickly attainable social and emotional status. . . . To be allowed to teach children should be the sign of the final approval of society."[1]

Many studies have been made of who these future teachers are, where they come from, and why they selected teaching as a vocation. In fact, if you want to prove that they are largely an intelligent, highly selected group, you can find statistical support for your contention.[2] On the other hand, if you seek support for the belief that future teachers are less intelligent and less capable than college

[1] G. B. Chisholm, "The Psychiatry of Enduring Peace and Social Progress," *Psychiatry*, February, 1946, p. 10. (Reprinted in Myron Lieberman, *Education as a Profession*, Englewood Cliffs, N. J., Prentice-Hall, Inc., 1956, p. 235.)

[2] *10 Criticisms of Public Education*, NEA, pp. 173–174.

students as a whole, you would have no difficulty finding sources to back you up.[3]

Much as you may not like to accept it (and with an apology in advance to the many thousands of bright, dedicated, able teachers we are fortunate to have), evidence on the negative side is uncomfortably strong. Sad but true is the fact that teaching has attracted and will continue to attract every year some people who are neither personally nor intellectually qualified to work with children. The burden of the incompetent and the professionally disabled is borne by the many who *are* qualified and who are denied the salaries, working conditions, and community respect they deserve.

The tragedy is that there are too many who contribute to the caricature that still sticks to our profession. It has faded somewhat in recent years—and your presence in the field will help it fade more —but its persistence is one of the discouraging factors that persuades many needed young men and women that *they* need some other goal. The stereotype, although changing, and as unfair and inaccurate as most stereotypes are, is often the buxom, dominant woman or the milquetoast man wearing drab, ill-fitting, unchanging clothes. Personality, voice, and interests also become stereotyped. We must, unfortunately, deal with attitudes such as the following:

A concomitant stereotype about teachers, which tends to persist particularly in rural regions, is a belief that employing a teacher is a genteel kind of charity. Teachers often come under supervisory and administrative pressures resulting from an extension of this concept of employment. Not only have some administrators absorbed this attitude but they have merged it with still another persistent view, that teaching involves a mystical call; that the teacher is a combination of missionary and pioneer; that he should accept the hazards and forego the rewards of his profession.

Another commonly held prejudice is that the teacher is more likely to be neurotic than the rest of the adult population, a belief for which the authors found no definitive evidence in the literature but which thrives nonetheless to further plague and degrade the teacher.

The teacher is the victim of at least one other kind of stereotype widely publicized of late. It is that the study of education is at worst a kind of scholarly astrology. At best it relates to the respectable disciplines about

[3] Educational Testing Service, reports on draft deferment tests in 1951–1952 and Paul Woodring, *Let's Talk Sense About Our Schools*, New York, McGraw-Hill Book Company, Inc., 1953, pp. 93–94.

the same way the chiropractic does to medicine, and the teacher in wasting a substantial amount of time on "education" is becoming an apprentice quack and should be treated as such.[4]

If we leave the fantasy picture of teachers and look at the facts, we see some things that may be somewhat disconcerting but necessary for you to face just the same: (1) Students attracted to education are more similar to those in business, home economics, physical education, and some of the social sciences than to those in science and mathematics. In other words, the areas which have a reputation for being "difficult" often get more of the brighter students. (2) Future teachers as a group have performed lower than prospective engineers in various testing situations. (3) Entrance requirements are traditionally low in many teacher-preparation institutions; the continuing shortage of teachers may keep them that way, but those who *graduate* may tend to be stronger individuals than those who entered because of the screening through the college years.

To meet the need for teachers in the next few years, nearly half of all college graduates must go into teaching; we are now getting only about one-fifth of them. That means that students in education will have to be below the present intellectual level if there are going to be enough teachers to go around. In a profession where recruitment of personnel is largely unplanned, it is sheer luck that we attract and retain as many bright ones as we do.

All over the country, especially in many small communities there are *some* teachers who are nice ladies, sweet mothers, and wonderful community workers; but that does not necessarily make them creative, challenging teachers. If we talk to this group about the tragic waste of our gifted children, their reaction is glassy-eyed; for how could it be otherwise when their own intelligence may be below the average for the nation as a whole? We discuss the need for communicating effectively, and the papers they turn in abound with errors like "recieve," "handwritting," and "corespond." We talk to them about world crises, and the extent of their international thinking is the Canadian border. We mention a scientific approach, and their understanding of science may include the thermometer and barometer, and then again, it may not. These teachers are not to

[4] Lindley J. Stiles (ed.), *The Teacher's Role in American Society*, New York, Harper & Row, Publishers, Inc., 1957, pp. 133–134.

blame. They work hard, mean well, and are capable of mixing the fluffiest "instant" cake batter you ever saw! But they never should have been permitted to enter teacher education, to pass the courses in it, or to be certified by their state departments of education.

Fortunately, their numbers are decreasing. Programs are attracting excellent liberal arts graduates; there is a tightening up in certification and teacher preparation in recent years; and the picture of the teacher as a person is changing. All of these are altering the hard core of the profession. The conclusion you have to draw is that the best of you will have to compete with the best of them for the most desirable jobs. Some institutions of higher learning set up committees to screen out unqualified applicants. This is most important since the desire for large enrollments should not eclipse the responsibility of the college toward children, the community, and the country as a whole. The entire point of higher education as a setting for intellectual pursuits and preparation for respectable professional performance must not be missed. To correct the accumulated ills of several generations demands a massive, conscientious effort to attract the best, reject the worst, and prepare well the ones permitted to enter.

Just as we know a great deal about teachers already in the classroom, we also know much about you as a future teacher, as part of a large group. We know all this, for example:

—that most of you are from the so-called middle class, from families whose incomes are close to the country's average—but some of you right up to this minute have never had to bother keeping the check stubs up to date or balancing the monthly bank statement, while others have literally gone to bed hungry hundreds of times and know very well what it is like to have the lights turned off and water discontinued for non-payment of bills.

—that most of you will be graduates of liberal arts colleges and have bachelor's degrees or higher—but some of you will be products of teachers colleges and may even be able to get teaching jobs in your state with less than a four year degree.

—that you may not academically have been in the top quarter of your class—but outstanding graduates of liberal arts colleges *are* going into teaching by the thousands, and they sometimes regard the preparation and certification requirements as challenging as those demanded by engineering and other professions.

—that about half of you do not expect to be teaching five years after you are graduated, or have mixed feelings about the whole thing, very much like the man who watched his mother-in-law drive over a cliff in *his* new Cadillac—but yet, most of the men do see some permanency in the field, and so do most of you aiming toward secondary school teaching, men and women.

—that your beginning salary may be around $4000 a year—but it probably will be higher if you are in a big city or teaching in the far west, and lower if you teach in some parts of the south.

—that your first teaching job may really be your first job—but on the other hand, you may have already raised a family, fought a war (or two), held three or four other kinds of jobs, taught in one or more foreign countries, or been on the "community circuit" of the hospital volunteer-Red Cross-YWCA-Symphony guild-League of Women Voters routine.

—that you may have chosen teaching because you come from a family of teachers and it seemed like the natural thing to do—but maybe it was because one day you had a heart-to-heart talk with yourself and decided that in this relatively limited time on earth allotted to each of us we should *do* something, *have* something of value to which we can look back in later years and feel that it all wasn't a waste.

—that you may ultimately leave the profession because of marriage or more money available elsewhere—but there are other reasons in the offing for some of you, like not being able to get along with people (your coworkers, administrators, parents, or the children), the needs of your own children at home, the Pied Piper come-on of Arizona, Florida, Alaska, Hawaii, or California, or the fact that this was just the wrong professional choice in the first place—the last point based on the idea that the teacher "drop-out rate" resembles student school-leaving and divorce, actually starting before it began and being the "accumulation of the trivial."[5]

So what this all adds up to is that you are not a "type" but a composite of all that is great and mediocre in the American scene. You are as frivolous and unpredictable and imponderable as a spring snowstorm in the middle west. You represent the best of modern education, and also the least worthy factors in it. You may have within you the excitement of youthful questing for answers even though you are in your forties or fifties, or you may represent the stodginess of all the ages and be in your early twenties.

You represent all of our political parties; social points of view; skin colors; peculiarities of worship on Sundays, Saturdays, weekdays,

[5] Willard Abraham, *A Handbook for the New Teacher*, New York, Holt, Rinehart and Winston, Inc., 1960.

or no-days; and belief (or nonbelief) in the beauty of the individual child.

Teachers, coming to a large extent from the middle class, represent middle-class attitudes and may attempt (sometimes with more pressure than they recognize) to enforce the manners and values of their background. This may contribute a great deal to family dissension by stressing cleanliness without recognizing that the boy's father may walk right into the living room with muddy shoes and put them up on the couch, or by stressing bathing where water is both scarce and cold.

Although change moves slowly in this profession, it is coming. And these pictures of the past and present will not always be with us. Changes will be brought about by those of you who *expect* salaries commensurate with your importance, respect in line with your abilities and professional preparation, and an education that will prepare you for the most demanding occupation of all.

ALL KINDS OF SHORTAGES

Many within this profession, through either design or stupidity, want to keep the door closed to you about the conditions you face. But you are no baby, and you should know about them, intimately and honestly. You deserve a fair look before you are asked to dedicate your life to a vocation. Tear-jerking movies and books about beloved school teachers honored in a vale of flowers, ribboned gifts, and saccharin words of endearment will not give you that truthful peek. In order for us to get the qualified teachers we need, your decision must be made after the facts are presented and weighed.

Teaching is a field complete with shortages, all varieties of them. Many young ladies think about the lack of male companionship and marital opportunities. Because there are so many entering this field on an opportunist, temporary basis it is understandable why this concern is so great. And because teaching has unfortunately become a female occupation to a large extent, this concern is very real. However, the studies of Frank Endicott, director of placement at Northwestern University, show that education graduates are "outmarrying" graduates of the liberal arts school. In a recent 5-year period 145 out of 197 (or 73.6 percent) were married, and Endicott concluded that the young men in our communities, whether teachers or not themselves, usually take high notice of a new crop of unmarried women teachers.

Many other shortages in the teaching profession stand out in bold relief in studies of why young people shun it or run out of it as soon as they can (to the tragic tune of about 150,000 each year). There is a widespread inferiority complex about teaching, revealed in a tendency to introduce oneself as "just a teacher." Can you imagine doctors, engineers, or lawyers doing that? Preposterous idea, isn't it? Negative attitudes toward teaching are changing, but they haven't been entirely removed. Here are some reasons why they persist:

Relatively poor salaries
Community restrictions and pressures
Questioning and challenging of loyalty
Picayune details that interfere with teaching
Arbitrary decisions of boards and administrators without consideration of teachers' ideas and feelings
Too many technical and outdated details related to certification
Public attitude toward teachers as inferior members of the community
Student attitude that teaching is for introverts, incompetents
Attitudes in the professional college community against teacher education
Relatively limited opportunities for advancement

Perhaps you will dispute some of those points. You may know some teachers whose salaries are excellent, some communities that respect teachers, some states that have not bowed to the super-patriot pressure groups that doubt everyone's loyalty but their own. Of course you know teachers whose mental health and image of themselves are secure and stable—and it is too bad they do not represent the entire profession.

If we turn the coin, these feelings about the profession become even more clear. Why *do* people go into teaching? Among many others, Redl and Wattenburg have come away from that question with an amazing array of reasons. Here are some of them:

Status
Family pressure
Love for subject matter

Identification with a former teacher
Love of children
Fun in teaching
Helping to build a better world
Self-sacrifice
Correcting short-comings of one's past
Reliving childhood patterns
Desire for affection
Need for security
Halfway house to other ambition
Need for power
Guaranteed superiority[6]

If you have skimmed through those the way most of us scurry over lists, you ought to go back, check them slowly, personalize them at least a little bit. Which are *your* reasons? Are they good ones? Do the facts make them realistic? How about one like "status"? Is it really so, or would you *like* it to be? What do teachers in the field say about it? And doesn't "fun in teaching" depend on who the teacher is? Just to read the list and accept or reject its parts without thought or question misses the point of approaching your decision and preparation with fact and sensitivity and in a thoroughly personalized manner.

In order to get the right perspective on this job-choosing subject, another important question to be asked is this one: Do people choose *other* vocational goals with any more insight, information, and intelligence than you have used in choosing yours? If you ask them, the answers some give might indicate they do, but don't be taken in by the glib reply. They may actually think they applied all the rules of good guidance until you dig into the real reasons why choices were made, reasons based purely on chance, parental pressure, or peer "guidance" ("Bill took accounting, so I did, too"). Of course, that does not excuse future teachers from being *more* careful in their reasons. The factors involved in selecting teaching as a goal are more serious merely because the ultimate tasks are more important and vital than in any other occupation.

In education the biggest shortage of all is a numerical one. Thou-

[6] Fritz Redl and William W. Wattenburg, *Mental Hygiene in Teaching*, New York, Harcourt, Brace & World, Inc., 1951, pp. 390–395.

sands of communities face a teacher shortage because of the small number in preparation and the many who leave permanently, temporarily (and then may or may not return), or are "stolen away" by school districts with more money, more sunshine, or more beach facilities. That we now face the need for about 2 million teachers means that one out of every 50 employable adults must go into teaching. With so many now working in the field we must face the fact that we just have not kept pace with the demand, despite our preparing more than we ever have before. The runaway requirements of the biggest education system the world has ever known make it more necessary than ever that we eliminate the reasons for young people avoiding it, and for slightly older people leaving it. This "sellers' market" also means that while the ill-chosen and poorly prepared may have some difficulty in getting jobs, they will end up in the front of classrooms anyway—in schools that already suffer from plenty of deficiencies without adding this especially heavy burden of the unqualified teacher.

Although we have talked of personnel shortages for a few years now, the stern fact is that it was not until September, 1960, that the elementary schools first felt the full impact of 4 million births 6 years earlier, and then only in first grade. By 1965, however, all six grades will feel the impact of this birth rate—and there is no indication at all that it will let up. In fact, the trend is in the other direction, toward bigger families. Add to this the increasing mobility of our population, greater demands on the schools, and more children staying in school longer, and you begin to see clearly the magnitude of the problem.

No educational system can be better than its teachers. None can improve without both quantity and quality. With our need for new teachers in the next decade being nearly one-half of *all* 4-year college graduates (and with only one in five actually entering the field), the size of the problem is apparent. With our standards sadly in need of improvement (more than 30 percent of our elementary teachers do not have bachelor's degrees), the quality factor comes into focus too. Two critics of professional education have some thought-provoking statements to make on this vital subject. Even when their ideas make sense, many teachers, school administrators, and especially college personnel who prepare teachers resent almost anything they say.

Surprisingly reasonable and sensible, however, are the comments below:

We all know of the nationwide shortage of elementary and high-school teachers. What is not evident is the real meaning of this shortage. Few classrooms are ever closed because a teacher is lost. What happens is that teaching standards are lowered or the class size is raised. Both of these accommodations have already taken place and may well become the general rule. When a teacher with the desired qualifications is not available, someone less qualified is hired. The teacher then becomes, in effect, a "baby sitter."

The result of this niggardly payment of our teachers—of those upon whom we depend to transmit our culture and our civilization—is to commit a fraud on our children. If the children were as astute as their elders supposedly are they would say: "I'm sorry, but I'm not ever going to be ten years old again. Can't you afford to give me good teachers *now?*"

The elementary and high schools would have to enlarge their teaching staffs by at least five hundred thousand in the next ten years merely to maintain the present pupil-teacher ratio; this is a greater increase than took place in the previous thirty-five years. To achieve this net increase of 500,000 three times that many will have to be recruited to take care of those who leave to get married, to take other jobs, or retire. The colleges and universities will have to add more teachers in the next fifteen years than they have in all their previous history.[7]

The vitriolic bias of the second critic comes out clearly in his glibly proposed solutions for the shortage:

We can raise teacher salaries in the hope of attracting more people of better quality to our classrooms.

We can try to find teachers who are masters of their subject matter at the level on which that matter is to be presented. . . .

We can keep the school open all year. . . .

We can shorten the length of a child's schooling. . . .

We can increase the qualitative performance of our present teachers— and possibly attract more people to the profession—by allowing them to spend more time teaching and less time doing school housework. . . .

We can limit the school's job to the essentials. . . .

We can save much of the teachers' time by driving out of the school-house a lot of dubious activity that has nothing to do with education. . . .

[7] H. G. Rickover, *Education and Freedom,* New York, E. P. Dutton & Co., Inc., 1959, pp. 108–109.

There is currently much propaganda urging young people to enter teaching, asking older people to return to school to help reduce the teacher load in one way or another. Nevertheless, it seems to me that the shortage will persist until we're ready to accord teaching a higher place in our social scheme, and that we will not be ready to do this as long as we're satisfied with competence as a substitute for excellence.[8]

These comments deserve discussion, certainly before acceptance, and with the emotional tendencies squeezed out. Later on we will find opportunities both to agree and disagree with the author. You may want to stop right now for a moment and see how far you go with or against him. It will be a good exercise in seeing how objective you can be.

A key factor related to the shortage of personnel is the recruitment of future teachers, or to be more exact, the lack of or ineffective recruitment programs. How did *you* happen to get into the teacher preparation program? Perhaps somebody came out to get you, to encourage you, to talk you into entering a field that needs your talents and services—but the odds are against that. It is far more likely that it just "happened": recruitment by accident. But this profession is growing up. And it needs a plan to attract the competent and dissuade the incompetent. It needs such a plan on a continuous basis, both before and after actual entry into teaching. Colleges and universities must have students, schools must have teachers. And there is a third group that has to be considered in this recruitment picture; it is, of course, the child. Thousands of children suffer most if no one shuts the door on persons intellectually and temperamentally unsuited for teaching.

Many institutions of higher learning have screening practices which cut down to some extent the number of unqualified persons entering the teaching profession, but they have a difficult time standing up against the pressures of (1) financial need, (2) increasingly high enrollments in elementary schools, (3) college teachers with vested interests in classes which might have to be eliminated if these students are not admitted, and (4) college students who have majored in "occupationally barren" academic fields suddenly recognizing that their only route toward making a living is to cram in a

[8] John Keats, *Schools Without Scholars*, Boston, Houghton Mifflin Company, 1958, pp. 154–160.

series of education courses as electives during that last year before they are graduated.

Screening works in the two ways already indicated: attracting the best as well as diverting into other channels of endeavor those not well suited to teaching. In order to attract the first group, we and the communities in which we are located have to recognize the factors listed earlier which drive qualified persons into other lines of work. Big words and the glad hand may not be enough to accomplish the job of recruitment. The scholarship-fellowship-loan-subsidy route may have to be the one to be followed. Foundations, local government and state organizations, fraternal groups, and the federal government are all getting into the act, recognizing that we have a big problem of neglect and shortage that is not solving itself.

Recruitment cannot be separated from two subjects to be considered later in this chapter: teacher preparation and certification. Warnings related to them come from a thoughtful source:

If the programs for the preparation of teachers are rigid, formalistic and shallow, they will drive away able minds as fast as they are recruited. Unhappily, preparation for pre-college teaching has come all too close to that condition. In some states the requirements for certification are so technical and trivial as to make it unlikely that individuals with a first-class liberal education would even apply—or be eligible if they did apply.[9]

We must recruit persons of above-average abilities in the first place to help relieve the personnel shortage. Unless the caliber of the average teacher is raised beyond the level where it now is (and even capable college instructors cannot make all the Eliza Doolittles who come their way speak well!), attracting sheer numbers of people will not get the job done. Selectively, discriminately, intelligently, they must be chosen.

Although the most dramatic shortage is in our having just too few people, perhaps we should stop trying to solve the insoluble and get at the causes behind it. In recent years much attention has been given to the working conditions of teachers and some progress has been made toward alteration or elimination of some of them. Working conditions lead directly to how people feel about their work, whether in teaching or elsewhere. It is not surprising that the morale

[9] Rockefeller Brothers Fund, *The Pursuit of Excellence,* Garden City, N.Y., Doubleday & Company, Inc., 1958, p. 24.

of some teachers takes a terrific beating in an atmosphere of low salaries, large classes, poor administration, no periods of relaxation, unsatisfactory plant and buildings, lack of adequate materials and equipment, absence of public or board cooperation, impoverished social life, and inadequate provisions for tenure. It takes even more of a beating when there is no recognition of the teacher's multiple role and pressures as a citizen, family member and provider, tax-payer, consumer, and public servant, as well as teacher. Work weeks are too long, daily schedules too continuous, and clerical work too heavy (prime teacher complaints). All the research and experimenta-tion related to teachers' aides (as in the Bay City, Michigan, effort) are still used only to a limited extent.

You will hear a great deal of talk about individualized teaching, but few teachers have the time or capabilities for doing it. They are too busy collecting lunch money, keeping seemingly endless records, carrying a high school teaching load of perhaps 175 to 200 students, counseling, attending committee meetings, being on hall guard and study-hall duty, selling tickets, and grading papers. Some *do* the individualized teaching, but not enough; not when we give lip service but frequently little else to the ideal of educating every child to his capacity. A student of the problem once figured out that if a teacher required of each of his high school students a minimum weekly assignment of three typewritten pages, his annual reading and grading load would be 20,500 pages, more than 4 million words, an equivalent of 40 books of 100,000 words each!

That is not a particularly happy thought, but it is one you should know about, now, while you are piecing together all the facts and eliminating all the fancy related to your future vocation. "The world is dominated by change," wrote Arthur Morse, "but the teacher is dominated by a relentless schedule that prohibits the reflection and study necessary to introduce change where it is most needed—in the curriculum."[10]

TEACHER SALARIES

This topic is uppermost in teachers' minds. If for some strange reason a teacher fails to give it the consideration it deserves, he can

[10] Arthur D. Morse, "Open Minds and Flexible Schools," *Saturday Review,* Sep-tember 17, 1960, p. 68.

usually depend on his wife to bring it vividly to his attention when the mortgage payment, milk bill, and doctor's fee are due and when Christmas comes round. That will not be necessary, however, for the one out of four men teachers below the college level who have at least two jobs.

Some years ago a humorous cartoon, with almost tragic Chaplinesque undertones, was making the rounds. It showed a young lady leaning back in a chair tipped on two legs, feet on the desk, cigarette dangling from her lips, speaking to a shocked middle-aged man standing nearby. The caption read, "You pay a lousy salary, you get a lousy teacher!" Luckily, most teachers do not feel that way. They do their best to overcome the difficulties already listed, and they try not to let salary limitations get them down.

Figures cited are confusing, and can prove just about what you would like them to. Want to prove that teachers are paid well? Then show that their earnings are keeping pace with manufacturing employees *(using a base date of 1929)*. Want to prove that they are lagging behind? Then do the same kind of comparison but with *a base date of 1939*. You can juggle concepts by showing their salaries are advancing faster than local government employees, but slower than automobile workers. The purchasing power of small-city elementary teachers has increased 136 percent from 1904 to 1959, but remember this, the school year is longer, their preparation is now more expensive—and besides, many other occupations have climbed much higher. That factor of preparation cost is one not to lose sight of, because many times when we compare salaries of teachers and others we fail to consider the investment in both time and money that people put into their own education.

In drawing comparisons we might as well leave out doctors, lawyers, and business men. The Research Division of the NEA noted that, on the average, teachers also earn less than architects, chemists, clergymen, dentists, dieticians, engineers, foresters, librarians, optometrists, veterinarians, and welfare workers, all of whom require a college education too. The average annual pay for five other professions in 1962 was $9803; for teaching it was $5787, or only 59 percent of the others. The NEA group concluded that in the last 15 years there has been no major shift in teachers' salaries away from the earning level of blue-collar workers and toward professional groups. As the figures in the table below indicate, earnings differ a great deal from state to state.

TEACHERS' AVERAGE YEARLY SALARIES, 1960

1.	California	$6700	26.	Wyoming	$4953
2.	Alaska	6600	27.	Utah	4950
3.	New York	6200	28.	Oklahoma	4765
4.	New Jersey	5930	29.	Montana	4680
5.	Michigan	5925	30.	Missouri	4675
6.	Connecticut	5900	31.	Iowa	4582
7.	Nevada	5800	32.	Kansas	4575
8.	Delaware	5789	33.	New Hampshire	4569
9.	Illinois	5725	34.	Texas	4490
10.	Arizona	5700	35.	Vermont	4450
11.	Maryland	5680	36.	Idaho	4400
12.	Indiana	5618	37.	Virginia	4300
13.	Rhode Island	5600	38.	Maine	4210
14.	Hawaii	5550	39.	North Carolina	4100
15.	Washington	5510	40.	Georgia	4078
16.	Massachusetts	5500	41.	Kentucky	4069
17.	Oregon	5500	42.	Tennessee	4065
18.	New Mexico	5400	43.	Nebraska	3990
19.	Ohio	5367	44.	West Virginia	3980
20.	Minnesota	5325	45.	Alabama	3850
21.	Pennsylvania	5250	46.	North Dakota	3800
22.	Colorado	5175	47.	South Carolina	3725
23.	Wisconsin	5075	48.	South Dakota	3675
24.	Louisiana	4975	49.	Arkansas	3550
25.	Florida	4960	50.	Mississippi	3415

50 states and
District of Columbia $5215

SOURCE: U. S. Department of Commerce, *Statistical Abstract of the United States*, 83rd Annual Edition, 1962.

Among the suggestions made in recent years regarding teachers salaries, the ones below seem to combine the primary recommendations:

1. Since teaching is essentially a cluster of different occupations, despite their common label, we should expect some salary differentiation according to the teaching field; this does not mean merely the elementary-

secondary dichotomy, which is unrealistic as a basis for differentiation.

2. Top teachers must be paid $10,000–$15,000 a year as a minimum, through the use of educational specialty boards. Such boards may provide for more than one rank of superior teacher.

3. Teachers should not be required to teach either full-time or not at all; older teachers should be allowed to decrease their load and salary, and we should utilize potential teachers who can teach only part-time.

4. Teachers should be given a direct economic stake in the efficiency and productivity of the school system. They should receive a fair share of the difference between the estimated and the actual costs of operating the schools at an agreed-upon level of educational achievement.

5. A school system should not be forced to give raises on a permanent basis or not at all; the salary structure should be sufficiently flexible so that systems can pay non-recurring raises.

6. The notion that the public will not pay high salaries is a rationalization of teacher weakness and must not be accepted as the final state of the public mind on the subject. The businessman who knows it is to his business advantage to pay high salaries for good personnel can hardly deny the validity of this argument to the business of the public.

7. All salary data should be easily accessible to the public.[11]

Ballooning enrollments and efforts to increase teachers' productivity, as important as they are, must not divert our attention from the practical aspects of a pay check and its size. You may want to think about it, discuss it, consider how important it is to you now and will be 5, 10, and 15 years from now.

MEN IN EDUCATION

"It's a man's world," they say; and if you're a man and are giving serious thought to the field of teaching, you begin to wonder who "they" are. Then you hear gags about this whole idea of men being the dominant of the sexes, and questions come to mind. A man's world? How about in teaching? Are the working conditions and salaries of a teacher related to the "dominant male" theme? While you're mulling over that idea, how do you feel about the following situation:

[11] Myron Lieberman, *The Future of Public Education,* The University of Chicago Press, 1960, pp. 276–277.

A lady was telling a friend that she and her husband had a fine solution for problems: they divided them up, the lesser ones to her to solve, the tougher ones to him. "I decide where we will live," she explained, "what job my husband will take, how we will spend our money, what schools our children will go to, and things like that." "But I thought you said your husband handles the more serious ones," the friend replied. "Oh, he does," the lady said. "He decides how to obtain world peace, how to solve the problems of cancer and heart conditions, and what to do about overpopulation and unemployment."

In an environment dominated by women, the need for men teachers becomes obvious. Born of women, reared by women, taught by women, and later married to women—our male population appears to be completely influenced and dominated, and the necessity for a more balanced situation seems apparent. All one need do is analyze the curriculum, especially in the primary and intermediate grades, and the conclusion becomes even more apparent. If more little boys than girls have reading difficulties (and the facts and figures all seem to point in that direction), the cause may be more than the unexciting materials with which many of them are taught. Perhaps their teachers have difficulty in understanding their problems and aspirations—and for a very simple reason; they have never been little boys themselves!

Teaching careers for men are being viewed more favorably by the public, according to a 1963 Gallup Poll. In 1953 only 5 percent of those queried would recommend teaching to young men. Ten years later the figure was 12 percent—increased, but certainly not an overwhelming choice! Men already teaching want more company. Released early in 1963 was a revision of "Teaching as a Man's Job" by *Phi Delta Kappa,* first published in 1938. Essentially an affirmative approach, it was joined by other articles on the "angry young men in teaching" (*NEA Journal,* February and May, 1963). Teachers themselves feel that more men are needed, and they ought to know. In a recent teacher-opinion poll of the NEA almost three out of four teachers (71 percent) believed that a higher proportion of men is needed on the secondary-school level. More than half (57 percent) see the same need on the elementary level. The reasons for this need are fairly obvious and freely expressed. Men are needed by children from broken homes, because of the limited time most fathers have with their children, and to handle "discipline." (Many women teachers will resent the implication that they cannot "keep order," and many of us will have to take their side. We've seen, and been exposed to plenty of women in the classroom who displayed an adroit ability to handle any situation that came along.)

The number of men going into teaching has taken a shift in recent years. In 1958–1959, for the first time since the U.S. Office of Education started collecting data on teachers in 1890, men teachers outnumbered women in the nation's high schools, 52.2 percent to 47.8 percent. The number has steadily increased in recent years from 40.5 percent in 1890, to a low of 34.9 percent in 1929–1930, up to 45.4 percent in 1951–1952. Somewhat improved salaries and at least a slight increase in public recognition are given as the reasons.

But the elementary schools remain a female-dominated situation. Only 15 percent of its teachers are men. A recent survey among freshmen college men found that only 133 of 2260 considered teaching as a life work. Of the men who had at one time considered that possibility, 71 percent no longer did. A full 28 percent of the freshmen women questioned were actively thinking of teaching as a career. These and other figures forced the writer of the article in which they appeared to conclude very pointedly: "In America, women can afford to teach. Men can't."[12]

So what are the solutions for the dilemma? As usual there are the long lists of pat answers that solve nothing. To suggest raising salaries, improving working conditions, and increasing prestige merely identifies the difficulties. Fortunately, a number of concrete suggestions have been made, but they are not put into effect often enough. Elam suggested that "differential salaries with much higher maximums be established upon some principle that will bring many of you more alert, capable young men into teaching—and keep you there."[13] Another serious attempt to nail this problem down evolved into a trio of suggestions. Its author offered them only as examples, implying that there are many other approaches.

1. A national scholarship award system should be created to provide for the establishment of a number of Junior Teaching Fellowships. These

[12] Stanley M. Elam, "Who Is There to Take Our Place?" *Phi Delta Kappan*, April, 1960, p. 289.
[13] *Ibid.*, p. 290.

would go to certain outstanding boys in the last year or two of high school in return for time spent assisting selected elementary school teachers in the classroom.

2. A new professional role sequence should be developed whereby career men in the armed forces could, upon completion of a twenty-year hitch, enter elementary teaching after appropriate training. Enlisted men as well as officers should be eligible, and a college credit equivalent should be given for experience.

3. A direct attack upon the societal stereotype of the male elementary school teachers should be made through mass media. For example, a television series of the situational type, with the central male character an elementary teacher, could be produced. The teacher could be shown with his family, in the community, in the school—not in a didactic manner but rather as a human being (slightly superior in many qualities, of course!), similar perhaps to the father in the "Father Knows Best" series. The problem would be to see whether it would affect the stereotypical thinking of different samples of viewers.[14]

If you're a young man thinking about teaching and wanting to teach, stick with it. Through the efforts of all of us perhaps this career will have the respect it deserves, and salaries to match, by the time you enter it. Much stranger things have happened. But it won't come through gripes, complaints, and self-pity. It *will* emerge through ideas like those listed above, and through the professional approach to a professional career demanded of all who cherish the education of children and adults as the greatest of life works.

TEACHER EDUCATION

Perhaps you have entered teacher education with no knowledge of it, or with only a few rumors as your foundation. That isn't fair to you. You deserve a peek behind the scenes. If you aren't mature enough for it, this early view probably won't do any harm. If you *are* mature enough to understand what we're talking about, this "open door" policy will pay off richly in alerting you to some of the major issues involved in preparing you for your profession.

Some journalists, liberal arts college professors, and parents have

[14] George I. Brown, "Recruiting More Men for Elementary Teaching," *Phi Delta Kappan*, April, 1960, pp. 295–296.

had a heyday in the past few years criticizing the way our teachers are prepared. The voices of authority have closed in from all directions, for don't they all have children in school, and aren't the schools "everybody's business" anyway? They aren't at all concerned by the Ellen Glasgow bit of advice that "wisdom is easy, unhampered by experience," for haven't they all had 12, 16 or more years of schooling themselves? The premises from which they start are usually something like these:

> The teachers' colleges are doing a terrible job.
> Everybody knows that.

> Those who can, do; those who can't, teach.
> Those who can't teach, teach the teachers.

> I'd love to teach, but oh, those education courses!

> Maybe teachers know *how* to teach, but let's be
> practical—what about subject matter?

So, as the accusations fly, many who are in teacher preparation do the human thing. They deny, defend, or use the "better-than-ever" routine. And then at the end of the argument they go home depressed and disgusted with themselves for running away, for making every effort "to get along with the cook." Their remorse can be traced to some obvious facts: Many of them know there is a great deal wrong with the preparation of future teachers; they also know what should be done about it—but their unconscionable reluctance to move quickly and decisively is a source of embarrassment and shame to many in the profession. Improvement, whether it is of a person, a country, *or* a profession, has to come from within. In the final analysis that is where the problems must be tallied and the solutions hammered out. Deep inside the field of teacher preparation itself (can't the label of "teacher training" be scuttled once and for all?) it is more necessary than ever to tabulate weaknesses rather than to hide behind accomplishments.

Even with leadership toward improvement evolving from within, the profession cannot close its eyes to criticism no matter how angrily or tactlessly offered. The criticisms and complaints come in hurricane proportions from parental malcontents sore at the world or their spouses and taking it out on the schools; from professors in the sciences, business administration, and engineering with personal grudges against "educationists"; from admirals, historians, philosophers and "ordinary laymen" who often seem to alter facts to suit their preconceived conclusions. All should be evaluated by colleges and universities which prepare teachers. All must be taken seriously by the instructors and administrators in every department contributing to teacher education, for many of the gripes are firmly imbedded in truth, and they know it. They know, for example, that some poor students are muddling through, that shallow teaching is too common, that courses in many departments need tightening up or outright elimination—but they seldom admit these deficiencies in public. ("Dirty linen and all that, you know.") There are two groups with whom it is necessary to go into battle regarding this negligence that affects thousands of our children every day of their lives:

The critics: those whose responsibilities are nil and whose words are many, who say they want to improve the selection and preparation of future teachers, but whose criticisms are based more on vilification than on careful thought and research.

The professionals: the all's-right-with-the-world boys who would rather squabble over the hundredth course in a teacher education program than eliminate it (*and* 50 others just as unnecessary), who prefer to philosophize over the heads of their students rather than recognize that nose-wiping, single-parent children and outhouse-sharing problems will face these future teachers every week-day morning next year or the year after.

In the haggling between the two groups nothing at all is gained. The critics single out masters' and doctoral theses and dissertations from schools or colleges of education on topics like "The Use of the Brake in Driver Training" or "Fly-casting and Its Relationship to the Philosophy of Progressive Education," and the professionals retaliate by finding titles just as silly (or sillier) in the academic fields. The critics study college catalogues and come up with an amazing list of overlapping and proliferated courses, and the professionals can do the same in the fields of history, psychology, foreign language, and others. The critics put their finger on dullness, anti-intellectualism, and poor teaching in the teacher preparation sequence, and the professionals say, "Ditto!" for many academic areas in colleges and universities.

Neither group constitutes a "whole"; the critics are far from the whole of society, and the professionals are certainly not the whole of teacher education. But the critics in their directionless activity and the professionals by their smug inactivity cause a lot of problems for far larger groups both in and out of the teaching profession. More meaningful criticisms and more vitality in the professionals, can be profitable. The result may help provide a sound approach to teacher preparation at a time when the teacher in our society plays the most crucial role in what our children will become.

Negative and passive attitudes toward teacher education in colleges and universities started a long time ago and continue today. The preparation of teachers began in isolated normal schools, and it required almost 100 years for teachers colleges and higher education to dominate the scene fully.

On some campuses future teachers are still thought of as "second class citizens," and even viewed with some derision by both students and faculty outside their own professional field. Some institutions of higher learning do not yet recognize their full obligation to help preserve the culture of all the ages. If they did, they would be forced to see that the task can only be accomplished by the teachers of our children.

The colleges and universities that once were normal schools and the ones not "tainted" by teacher education in their early years now graduate most of our elementary and secondary school teachers. When they brag about their graduate programs in science, commerce, and humanities, they sometimes add, "Oh yes, we still train teachers, but isn't it too bad we can't seem to outgrow that?" And when they provide campus tours they'll sometimes point to an old frame building hidden away behind tall bushes: "We keep it for sentimental reasons, our original normal school; quaint, isn't it?"

The question of who prepare our teachers must be answered by saying that *all* departments in our colleges and universities are involved. If the preparation is sound, all can take the credit; and if it is done miserably, the blame rests in many hands.

With future high school teachers studying only 18 to 22 semester hours in professional education (out of an undergraduate total of 120 to 130 semester hours), the responsibility for admitting the unscholarly, preparing the incompetent, and graduating the poorly taught leaves guilt in many places. The proportion of work taken by these students in education courses drops even further as more and more of them complete master's programs in their own subject-matter fields. Even most elementary teachers spend only about one-quarter to one-third of their college careers in a school or college of education. (Engineers and pharmacists spend 45 percent of their college study time on professional courses in their fields; business administrators, 47 percent; nurses, 52 percent; and musicians, 68 percent.) The ineptitude of some of our teacher-education programs has its foundation in four segments:

1. Many college and university instructors who teach teachers are primarily research rather than people oriented. They know the Dewey Decimal System, library archives, and their own field inside out, but their preparation may have included no acquiring of teaching skills or psychology of how people learn. The dismal environment for gaining knowledge in their own classrooms is the logical result.

2. Some college and university instructors constitute a strangely youthful segment of our "retired" population. Active for part of each working day, their partial retirement still deprives us of many of their potential abilities. They meet their classes promptly, attend committee meetings, and conduct office hours for student advising; but how about (a) keeping up with professional journals, (b) doing original research, (c) revising bibliographies and examinations, and (d) participating in scholarly meetings? An erudite facial expression or a smoke-filled office may fool some people into thinking they inwardly possess the fire of intellect. However, long lunch hours and coffee breaks and not keeping up with one's own area hardly represent the professional pride and performance needed in this era when thoughtful leadership is so essential for our preservation.

3. The best college and university instructors are sometimes isolated in research laboratories or small graduate seminars. Freshmen and sophomores who drop out of school in an air of frustration may do so because the least competent instructors, graduate assistants, or inexperienced beginning teachers too often teach English 101, Biology I, and History A. Our future teachers can sometimes go through their entire college careers and have no contact with the most profound thinkers on the campus.

4. Little inspiration or enthusiasm comes to our future elementary- and secondary-school teachers from those college and university instructors who are socially, educationally, and politically conservative to the point of dullness. Those who are strict and unalterable conformists in belief, dress, attitude, and morals, and who are satisfied that what is, is right, can hardly stimulate and guide others to satisfy the ever-questioning minds of children.

A telescoped picture of those who teach our teachers includes many fine, skilled, scholarly men and women, and some dullards; many probing, searching, intelligent minds, and some that are smug, stolid, and superficial. A profession that cannot afford the luxury of harboring *any* who are inadequate does the unspeakable by passing on *many* of them to all the children in the land.

The men and women now teaching our children and those in teacher education cannot be separated from the most controversial and castigated topic of all—the teacher-preparation program itself; controversial because almost everyone seems to have some dogmatic opinions about it, castigated because it has too often hidden behind a shield of immunity and gobbledygook of confusing and shadowy verbiage.

The question is simple: What is the best way to prepare teachers? The answer, however, is complicated by emotion, envy, and misunderstanding. The suggestions that follow attempt to avoid such difficulties. In any college or university they must be adapted or molded on the basis of personnel available. They will offend some people, perhaps cause some ill feelings, but one's eye must be on the child in our schools and not on retaining business "as is."

Basic Needs in Teacher Preparation

TO ESTABLISH FULL INSTITUTIONAL RESPONSIBILITY FOR TEACHER EDUCATION

This will mean bringing the academic and professional education departments together. It will mean that courses in history, biology, English, and other subjects will be taught so that the potential first-grade teacher can get from them what she needs to teach young children. It means that the college instructors involved will have to keep up with the current research on how to teach their subject on *all* levels, the primary grades through the university. Developing a responsible attitude by the entire institution for the preparation of teachers will take real cagey administrative handling. Many antagonisms and deep feelings will emerge. It may almost take locking professors in a room and throwing away the key for a few hours. But the result will be fewer course duplications and gaps, a better balance in the "how" and "what" of teacher preparation, and ultimately better professional relationships.

Best of all, the future teacher will find his series of "methods" courses consolidated into a sequence that is jointly sponsored by the academicians and the educationalists, and the materials in his subject matter courses more meaningfully organized for ultimate use with children. The unneeded ballooning of courses in *all* departments could be punctured, by persistent, unstinting, and relentless efforts at professional cooperation.

TO CREATE A NEW ALIGNMENT OF LIBERAL ARTS (GENERAL EDUCATION), SPECIALIZED SUBJECT MATTER, AND PROFESSIONAL EDUCATION

All elementary- and secondary-school teachers should study all three. The proportion may vary from college to college, but perhaps with something like a 50–25–25 relationship applied to the three areas in the order given. The sound foundation in liberal arts and the specifics of teacher preparation would be buttressed by a major, or several strong minor, fields of study for all future elementary teachers. (The high school teachers, of course, already are required to have these strengths.) Whether we call them teaching specialists or "built-in" consultants, we need a group of persons in every elementary school prepared in depth in *all* content fields. It would take a superperson to acquire enough knowledge to stay ahead of an average class of elementary-school children in all subjects today. History, science, mathematics, arts, and communication areas are just developing too fast.

TO IDENTIFY THE IMPORTANT INGREDIENTS OF TEACHER EDUCATION

You can almost make a parlor game out of this one. The only trouble is that matters might get a little out of hand because contrary opinions may make the sparks fly. But can a teacher of any subject, or on any level, *really* be well prepared without at least a sure footing in many academic areas? Doesn't it cheapen the whole profession to expect it to "make do" with any less? Can *any* of these be omitted?

An introduction to the physical and biological sciences
Democracy—its meaning and background
Historical, cultural, and sociological heritage of the United States
The place of the United States in current world affairs

The world today—its economic, political, and cultural conflicts and problems

Interrelationships of art, music, philosophy and religion

Ability to read critically

Ability to communicate effectively

Knowledge of the scientific method

Psychological understanding of self and of others

Education—its history, objectives, and problems

How children learn, grow, think, and differ in characteristics and abilities

Teaching methods and materials adapted to children's needs, as well as those needs can be anticipated in the world of tomorrow, including newer approaches, such as programmed learning

Increasingly intimate professional contacts with children, through observation, participation, and student teaching

Add to these an intensive knowledge of at least one academic field and you have the triple feature: general education, content, and professional education. With our 50–25–25 ratio as a guide, a fair balance should result. If arrived at objectively, that balance can soften the aggressive howls from various academic departments which may insist that regardless of what others may want, all future teachers will have at least 2 years in *their* department. Collective demands as unrealistic as that could lengthen the program proposed here to at least 10 or 15 years!

The most basic of all the teacher education ingredients—the human factor—must not be overlooked. Ralph Waldo Emerson referred to it in this way: "But they (the colleges) can only serve us when they aim not to drill, but to create; when they gather from afar every ray of various genius to their hospitable halls, and by the concentrated fires, set the hearts of youth aflame."

Whether for the freshman and sophomore liberal arts courses or in the major fields, the most skilled college teachers must be smoked out of their research laboratories, recalled from their foreign project gallivanting, and enticed from "high level" discussions in their seminar rooms. Great teachers are rare, and they must be utilized where they can influence the largest number.

Everywhere—in general education, in specialized subject matter, and in professional education—teaching vitality and spice are essential. Not just the lecture method, not just the "pooling of ignorance"

in discussion groups, not just a dull, dreary series of student reports
—but a little of each and a lot more besides. Four years may not be
long enough for the kind of preparation outlined here, and the
states with certification based on even less than four years are back in
the last century! The fifth year should include both content and
method, and should be taken after some teaching experiences to
make it more meaningful. However, let's be realistic: Strict demands
for five years of teacher preparation would close schools in some
states—and it is in just those states that they are most needed to
lower illiteracy rates and to reduce the number of school dropouts.

Sound teacher education has a long way to go in most parts of the
country. Some of the colleges and universities have started to seek
and encourage the inspirational teachers and to dismiss the dolts.
Maybe parents of future teachers can help do the job. Not trying to
tell the colleges what to do, mind you. Just interested in talking
over a subject of mutual interest. A few within and many without
have pecked away at the imperfections in teacher preparation.
PTAs, individual parents, the spontaneous combustion of "citizens'
groups," the Council for Basic Education, the followers of Rickover,
Bestor, and others (and the tirades of the men themselves) have all
been in the forefront of the needling and nagging.

Closer to the root, however, are the recent activities of the National Commission on Teacher Education and Professional Standards (TEPS). Its meetings of academic professors and educationists
seeking truth and improvement have brought together diverse ideas
in a professional atmosphere. Various organizations of colleges, universities, administrators, and teachers are trying to repair piecemeal
the teacher education framework, but the massive structure needs
more than the makeshift approach many of them attempt. It needs
the force of individual college and university teachers in all departments shaken out of their lethargy and self-satisfaction. It needs the
pressure of individual college and university administrations to
screen unsparingly courses and teachers in all parts of their institutions, related to the supply of future teachers. It needs *research,
research, research*—on preparation for different teaching jobs, on
the organization of methods courses, on who *should* teach the teachers and how it should be done, and on the best preparation of college
teachers. It needs continuing and increasing concern and financial

support by organizations such as the Ford Foundation, who with its $2.4 million grant to the Graduate School of Education at the University of Chicago, as well as other such grants, has its eye directly on the target of improved preparation of teachers.

Hopefully, these tantalizing ripples of research and activity will expand into ever-widening circles, based on the thought that "thou canst not stir a flower without troubling a star." Hopefully, too, the research will be *used* in giving vitality and intelligence to teacher education, a practice that would in itself be rather unusual in some educational settings—for teachers and school administrators do not always base their teaching principles and practices on what research indicates. ("Who bothers to keep up?" "Who has time?" "Who *wants* to have time?")

So far the forces at work are very few in proportion to the size of the task and the lateness of the hour. But they have at least made a start.

Of course, many things are good about teacher preparation. It has thousands of dedicated, capable people in it who teach with sensitivity and understanding. It increasingly demonstrates an experimental point of view. It is improving every year.

CERTIFICATION

In some states, perhaps, Schweitzer, Teller, and Von Braun would not have the "necessary courses" to become certified elementary or secondary school teachers—and no doubt that's a very good thing. They have other work to do. So do surgeons, engineers, and accountants who fail to meet certification requirements.

The fact that they are not "qualified" to teach drives some people wild. They don't object at all to state licensing of barbers, veterinarians or even liquor stores, but children are everybody's property. The gates should be wide open. These same folks feel that state certification requirements also keep many good liberal arts graduates out of teaching, all excellent potential teachers, just aching to get into the classroom. They would have you believe that these requirements discourage them more than low salaries do.

Although the growing flexibility in certification has made entry into teaching easier, the anticipated avalanche of applicants has not developed. There is no assurance at all that the complete absence of certification would result in more and better teachers. This "open shop" might even drive out some fine ones who already resent the incompetents we now have.

What are the facts on certification? Is it true that teachers are required to have more college work in "how" than "what" to teach? Not at all. The professional requirements actually extend from less than one-fifth to about one-quarter of their college work—which means they must have three to four times as much in the content fields. But certification hands are not entirely clean, and they will not be until we make deeper inroads into: (1) a reciprocal and more uniform set of requirements among all the states, and a requirement in all of at least a bachelor's degree; (2) more concentrated content for elementary teachers, rather than the present dabbling in this-and-that with which some are now permitted to be graduated; (3) a content-method link in course content to discourage the current cleavage; (4) a strengthening rather than relaxation in certification requirements because lowering the barriers will not attract competent teachers anyway; and (4) a realization that more courses, more semester hours, are not by themselves conducive to "raising standards."

Public pressure has played a big part whenever stronger state certification standards have been instituted in recent years, frequently applying more influence than comes from the professional educators. Such higher standards include a master's degree in a content field for high school teachers and more demanding undergraduate programs for elementary teachers. In California many changes have entered the certification picture: In May, 1963 their State Board of Education unanimously approved new requirements that declared either a major or minor in education to be unacceptable. They adopted a kind of "Einstein clause" that permits persons skilled in a particular field to teach it regardless of their educational background.

Sometimes absent in the certification picture is mention of *quality* in teacher preparation and *aptitudes* and *abilities* in the selection of future teachers. As long as we are satisfied merely to acquire "warm bodies who have taken courses" for our classrooms, certification must remain in the realm of unfinished business.

Martin Mayer's story of William Cornog epitomizes the questionable practice of stressing "required courses" and ignoring experience or proven ability. The bitter sequence goes this way chronologically:

> Ph.D. in English and medieval Latin
> Teaching at Northwestern University
> Principal, Central High, Philadelphia
> Principal, New Trier High School, Winnetka, Illinois
> Threat of accreditation loss by New Trier—its principal lacked 18 semester hours of education courses[15]

Mayer embellishes the story with side remarks that make it seem even worse, but the point is clear. Certification, yes, but with common sense and flexibility applied to its enforcement, two factors which fortunately have been used rather widely despite rumors of rigid certification requirements rigidly interpreted.

Arguments related to certification are bound to continue for a long time. They revolve around these unanswered questions: Who should do the certifying? Which school personnel should be certified? How do we get some uniformity among the states? How do we avoid a head-on collision of laymen and professionals claiming the "right" to answer these questions? From the professional side of the picture the TEPS book, *New Horizons For The Teaching Profession,* provides some answers—but they will not be acceptable to all who have an oar in the boat of education. You might want to try the answers to some of those questions yourself. You can start out with the assurance that your conclusions are no more open to dispute than many of those offered by professional personnel after many years of discussion. Among the certification trends in recent years are these:

Growing flexibility in some states making it more possible to hire those
    who seem qualified but who do not have all specific course requirements
Bachelor's degree for elementary teachers
Master's degree for secondary teachers
Reduction in professional education requirements
Use (and also misuse) of provisional certificates to employ "experts"

[15] Martin Mayer, *The Schools,* New York, Harper & Row, Publishers, Inc., 1961, pp. 409–413.

Lieberman has contributed a brief and penetrating analysis of the problem:

We can summarize the situation in this way: From state to state, the power to regulate the requirements for a teaching certificate is haphazardly divided between legislatures, boards of education, education departments, superintendents of public instruction, and teacher-training institutions. The policies adopted by each of these agencies are often shaped by chance factors which should have no influence at all on teacher-education. In other words, when we take into account not only who makes the decisions affecting teacher education at the state level but also the processes by which these persons acquire their positions, it becomes clear that there is neither rhyme nor reason to the way in which teacher education is controlled in the United States.

But who *should* control it? Let me approach this question first from a professional point of view. In other professions, the practitioners themselves exercise the decisive role in shaping programs for their own training. Entry to the profession is controlled through state board examinations, and the professional schools must offer a curriculum that will enable their graduates to pass these examinations. The scope of the examinations is so broad that the professional schools have little discretion to offer electives or to require subjects not required by the state boards. The crucial point, however, is that the state boards which prescribe and evaluate the examinations are controlled directly or indirectly by the practitioners of the profession concerned.[16]

And the President's Commission on National Goals succinctly summarizes the whole business: "There should be a thorough overhaul of certification requirements in most states."[17] Such a trend is clearly on. In just 2 recent years, 29 states reported significant certification revisions and 8 states completely revised their certification structures, with added work mainly in content areas. Current certification information is available to you from the latest editions of the following publications:

W. Earl Armstrong and T. M. Stinnett, *A Manual on Certification Requirements for School Personnel in the United States,* Washington, D.C., National Commission on Teacher Education and Professional Standards, NEA.

[16] Lieberman, *op. cit.,* pp. 104–105.
[17] President's Commission on National Goals, *Goals for Americans,* Englewood Cliffs, N. J., Prentice-Hall, Inc., 1960, p. 93.

Robert C. Woellner and M. Aurilla Wood, *Requirements for Certification of Teachers, Counselors, Librarians, Administrators for Elementary Schools, Secondary Schools, Junior Colleges,* published annually by The University of Chicago Press.

Teacher certification was instituted in the first place to help control the entry of incompetents into the profession. Regardless of what you may hear some people say, the present situation could be a great deal worse. Just throw out all certification requirements and see how soon the demands would be made by many of the off-with-their-heads boys to set some up again!

THE QUALIFIED TEACHER

A person may be exposed to courses, but does mere exposure qualify him for teaching? He may pass certain required tests, but does the passing of them give him the knowledge and competence needed to teach children? A person is certified and the state says he can teach, but does that mean he has the capabilities for doing so?

Think for a few moments about where you have learned something of value, and from whom. A parent? A neighbor? An older brother or sister? Your buddy when you both were 10? The chances are that, if you were lucky, there are at least a few teachers on that select list. So let us consider them for a while. What were they like? Did they have similarities in appearance, personality, background, and technique? Probably not. They no doubt were big and small, quiet and bombastic, lecturers, discussion leaders, and laboratory experts. What impressed and appealed to you may have depended on your age and maturity at the time. If you are objective about which teachers helped you most, you will have to come to this conclusion about them: *There is no single "type," personality, or characteristic of size, shape, or sex that adds up to a great or even a good teacher.* You may have rebelled unmercifully against the tough one at the time, and extolled her virtues later when you had the experience of a few more years to convince you of her rare abilities. You may have admired another at the moment, only to realize later that a glib, superficial approach may have been a classroom delight but only of momentary value. Jacques Barzun put it this way:

It is extraordinary how many diverse kinds of men and women make desirable teachers . . . Remember you need lecturers and discussers and tutors. They can differ in endless, unpredictable ways. You can take the halt, the lame, the blind; men with speech defects or men who cannot be heard above a whisper; gross and repulsive men (at first) like my blessed mathematics instructor; men who are lazy and slow, who are bright and unstable, or incorrigible *enfants terribles;* you can even risk some who are deficient in learning, and join them to form an admirable as well as an induplicable faculty. This is possible because the students also display a variety of human traits and cannot all be reached and moved by the same spells.[18]

You read statements like this, you nod in agreement, and yet you may want to know whether you as an individual can make the grade. The necessary qualities for success in teaching are listed below. Maybe you want to know whether you can deviate from the list and still succeed. Because we are dealing with human beings, with their innumerable variabilities, and not with simple measurements, the answer can be an encouraging "Yes."

Ask some of your college or university instructors what makes a good teacher. Try to keep them from hedging. That will be difficult because they will want to add an "if" or "but" here or there. Or make up your own list before you move on with our discussion here. The one important cautionary note at this point is this: Don't let any list discourage you. Keep in mind the human variations of good teachers you have known. Remember that basically a good teacher has (1) intelligence; (2) knowledge of subject matter and interest in it; (3) a liking for teaching and the knowledge of how to teach; (4) good mental health and personal adjustment; and (5) an ability to enjoy people, accept them, and respect them.

The following was compiled by a teachers' committee in Tucson, Arizona:

I. Professional Characteristics of a Superior Teacher
   A. Has complete certification requirements
   B. Spends time in reading, travel and continued study to keep abreast of the changes as they affect his professional and liberal growth
   C. Participates in professional organizations
   D. Shows professional loyalty by

---

[18] Jacques Barzun, *Teacher in America,* Boston, Little, Brown and Company, 1945, p. 187.

1. Being proud to be a teacher
2. Respecting associates and recognizing their worth
3. Evaluating self and welcoming professional evaluation of teaching performance
4. Refraining from engaging in disparaging remarks about associates or school
5. Doing whatever possible to make the profession universally respected

II. Personal Characteristics of a Superior Teacher
   A. Shows emotional maturity through
      1. Self control
      2. Sense of humor
      3. Sincerity
      4. Objectivity
   B. Shows awareness of appearance by being
      1. Neat
      2. Clean
      3. Appropriately dressed
   C. Has enduring patience and kindliness
   D. Is willing to accept responsibility for own actions
   E. Is always willing to try, use or discard new techniques
   F. Is tactful
   G. Does critical thinking and evaluation
   H. Shows enthusiasm
   I. Is not discouraged by defeats or failures, but sees each day as a new chance
   J. Likes children
   K. Passes along compliments
   L. Has ability to make adjustments to fit any occasion

III. The Superior Teacher and the Child
   A. Is an excellent organizer of time and materials for most effective results
   B. Has discipline which provides for effective teaching and results in good citizenship
   C. Instills intellectual curiosity and the desire for learning
   D. Has wide knowledge of subject matter
   E. Provides for individual differences
   F. Keeps accurate and up-to-date records

IV. The Superior Teacher, Parent and Community
   A. Makes use of community reasources
   B. Makes an effort to know parents

C. Knows what is going on in the community and exercises the voting franchise with intelligence

D. Has a sense of loyalty to parent, school, community and country[19]

Some writers on the subject like to differentiate between those who select teaching as a career and others who are in it only for a year or two. Such differences sound contrived and artificial. To children they do not exist, for they deserve and should expect imagination, preparation, vision, and understanding whether the teacher will be there a day or a lifetime. In addition to the obvious kinds of qualities itemized above, there are some off-beat ones to which you might give some consideration. Here are a few questions to start your thinking:

Do you feel threatened by or scared of children or adults? What do you intend to *do* about that?

Do you have prejudices on the basis of race, religion, nationality, culture, or socioeconomic level? Can't they *ever* be eliminated?

Is your speech irritating, uneven, in need of some attention? When are you going to correct it?

What about your appearance—weight, teeth, complexion, color sense? When will you go into action to change matters?

Do you have personal quirks or nervous mannerisms that may bother others —hair pulling, chin rubbing, ear yanking, knuckle cracking, leg swinging, hand wringing, lip wetting? What do you intend to do about *that?*

Are there serious problems in your personal life that will interfere with your teaching?

Is your own environment thin, sparse, rigid, and colorless?

Are you subject to fetishes of cleanliness, order, and quiet that are totally unrealistic in the child's world of variability, noise, and laughter?

Is your graduation from college thought of as the end of learning?

Is your eye on the impossible goal of being an expert on all things to all children?

Are your grammar and spelling in need of "tightening up" (a polite term —more exact ones might be "total reorganization" or "basic study")?

Is your knowledge of the world around you in need of broad reading and study?

The NEA's Department of Classroom Teachers has released a revised edition of a little check list called *I Look at Me,* which might

[19] Reported in *Arizona Teacher*, Arizona Education Association, March, 1961, p. 13.

help you look at yourself. You can get highly inspirational about the qualifications of the successful teacher, or you can turn a squinty eye toward the subject and dispose of it as flippantly as was done in this letter (which seemed to include teachers and the whole educational process):

> Barrytown, N. Y.
> Nov. 26: 1916

My Dear Dr. Drury:

Do you really think that if I had any ideas on the parent and the child question I'd waste them on you? But just now I am taking a loaf and trying to forget the whole subject. Is the education of the young the whole of life? I hate the young—I'm worn out with them. They absorb you and suck you dry and are vampires and selfish brutes at best. Give me some good old rumsoaked club men—who can't be improved and make no moral claims —and let me play chequers with them and look out of the Club window and think about what I'll have for dinner.

> Yours faithfully,
> John Jay Chapman[20]

WHEN YOU BECOME A "NEW TEACHER"

All the emotions you have, whether based on eagerness, anticipation, anxiety or fear, have preceded you in thousands of newcomers to the field of teaching. The pounding heart of your first day was also the loudest noise in the world on the first day of practically every teacher since the first one scratched his name on the stone "blackboard" of his cave-like classroom. The wonder you have about whether those smiling faces looking at you are aware of your damp hands and dry throat is a wonder handed down from generation to generation. Your professional family is immense, and it is on your side. This largest cheering section in the world wants you to succeed, and for some very practical reasons, too.

The teaching profession has been taking some tough raps lately, and it needs all the intelligent, enthusiastic new blood it can get. Teachers have to do more and know more than ever before, and the

[20] John Jay Chapman, "A Letter to S. S. Drury," in Claude M. Fuess and Emory S. Basford, *Unseen Harvests*, The Macmillan Company, 1947, p. 642.

evidence is strong that despite unfounded accusations to the contrary they are also accomplishing more than ever before. In the field of history you have to include a couple of complete eras that were unlived just a few years ago. New approaches in science and mathematics are demanded. The teaching of foreign languages requires insights that our rote memory teachers of years ago seldom had or used.

In this age when we are beginning to recognize that guided children are at least as important as guided missiles we are eager to welcome you with your ideas, dreams, and creativity. We know that although most of you will be straight out of college, many of you have the experiences of parenthood, military service, foreign travel, and responsible related or unrelated jobs in your background to add to your college preparation. Although the sheltered young girl is still among our new teachers, she has plenty of company. The migrant quality of most of our population since World War II has broadened the pot from which our newcomers are drawn, so that the teacher in California is likely to have been born in Connecticut, reared in Illinois, and college-prepared in Oregon—and all of that is part of the richness which you bring to this profession.

Teaching is an adventure, but also a means of earning a living. It has a lot of surprises and excitement, but also personal and professional problems. It's built on accomplishment and satisfaction, but also some elements of frustration and monotony. How terrific it would be to entice you into your first teaching experience by saying it will all be the professional equivalent of a "lead pipe cinch," but entrants now coming along are too sophisticated for that kind of fakery. You have heard and seen some of the negative factors, but you are joining us anyway. Because you've survived both the bait and barbs of other occupations and professions, you do not have to be sold all over again on teaching as a "good deal." Apparently for you as an individual it is and will be. Although the first adjustments may be a bit of a strain, you might take hope from the wise words attributed to Thomas Macaulay, the English historian, when he was 4 years old. A maid spilled hot coffee on him and then made a great fuss over him because of the accident. He gently but firmly pushed her away. "Thank you, madam," he said, "but the agony has abated."

You are expected to be an "incomplete" teacher when you start to teach, with the transition period of your last year of college continuing at least through your first year on the job. So many of the finest teachers insist that even after many years they are still learning, adapting, listening; still experimenting, still failing to reach the ultimate in their skill and knowledge. The approach of that first day of teaching creeps up and seems to be over almost like the preparation and explosion of our missiles and rockets—and the aftermath of the first day is sometimes as emotionally shattering as the impenetrable quiet that must follow for the planners if a missile fails to go into orbit.

Your questions and wonder after the first day will frequently be the results of a new experience, not a reflection of lack of preparation at all. The answer is in adequate preplanning, in getting ready for the climax of those years of study. But the advance planning implies flexibility, *not* the kind where seat work is prepared in great detail (and quantity) for children you have never seen, *not* the kind where you have made up your mind so rigidly about what you intend to do that you are liable to be confused by the realities of the situation. "Flexibility" may make you uncomfortable, but it cannot be avoided when you are working with somewhat unpredictable young human beings.

In order to start out with a sense of well-being and security, you need some information, a lot of information—and the first day of school is not the right time to get it. It is just too late. When you sign your contract, after you sign it, during the orientation week (or day)—those are the right times. But the old story is certainly true that you have to ask a good question to get a good answer, so perhaps the check list below can be helpful. Of course, there will be some items here that you don't care a bit about. Fine, concentrate on the others. Satisfy yourself on them. Get the facts that are important to you. The answers may come from an administrator, a supervisor, a teacher, or from some printed or mimeographed material the school releases. Information probably will not come in accurate form from any other source. It *may*, of course, but the "they say" route is hardly the most dependable one for a trusting new teacher to use.

Although you obviously will not want to, or have to, ask all of these questions, you might use them as a guide to be certain that from *some* dependable source you are accumulating all the data and details you need to help you glide into a smooth beginning. If you are scheduled for a conference with your principal, or another administrator, a few of these selectively chosen might help break the ice *and* give you important information.

QUESTIONS OF DIRECT CONCERN TO ME

Are there any basic school philosophies toward education, the community, school personnel, the children, or parents that I should know about?

What are some unique things about the community that will help me become oriented to it? Can I get a city or area map?

Is there a school directory and/or organization chart available to me? A building chart that will show me the locations of administrative offices, the nurse, custodian, rest rooms (children's and teachers'), auditorium, gymnasium, supply room, bulletin board for notices, audio-visual room?

Does the school or system have a salary schedule, rules on tenure, retirement regulations?

When is pay day?

What kind of housing will be available for me? What will it cost? Where is it located—how far from the school?

Is there any insurance available to me and my family through the school—hospitalization, life, retirement, accident?

Does the school have a credit union?

What are the provisions for sick leave, maternity leave, absence with and without pay?

Are there any specific requirements I should know about in case I need a substitute?

Will I be able to participate in any in-service teachers' program?

What kinds of college or university courses are available to me in this vicinity?

What are the provisions in this state and district regarding certification and renewal of certification?

What are my teaching hours?

What are my duties outside of the classroom? Are there any specific lunchroom, transportation, lavatory, and playground rules I should know about?

Are there any special building policies related to food, smoking, afterschool use of facilities?

What are the dates of holidays and vacations? Is there a school calendar?

What textbooks and supplementary books are available to me? What supplies and equipment? What art materials and games? What programmed learning materials?

How about the availability of audio-visual aids? Can I order films, filmstrips, slides, and pictures from school or other sources? If so, how and when?

Do you have some recommended guides or courses of study?

What community resources are available for our use?

Are any written plans required of me for supervisory or administrative personnel? If so, when and in what form?

How far in advance of the first day of school will I know where my room is? Will I have an opportunity to get it ready? What bulletin boards, desks, and tables will I have?

Is there a professional library I can use in this building or in the system?

How are teachers' assignments made to grades and schools in the system?

Questions More Directly Related to the Children

Which teacher(s) did my children have last year? When will I be able to speak to her (or them)?

Will I see cumulative or other records of the children before school starts? How long in advance of the beginning of school can I see them?

What is the school's testing program? What tests? When administered? By whom?

What special personnel and services are available in this school or district: special teachers, psychological or guidance personnel, nurse, physician, special people to deal with hearing, sight, speech, orthopedic, and miscellaneous physical handicaps, and mental retardation?

Are there any special practices or procedures now being used, or contemplated, in connection with gifted children?

What are the regulations for absences and excusing students early? Fire and air raid drills? Homework? Promotion and retention? Corrective discipline?

What are the bell arrangements for fire and air-raid drills? For the start of school, recess, lunch and dismissal? What are the specific entry and dismissal rules?

Are there any prescribed opening exercises?

What are the forms, and how are they to be filled out, regarding daily, monthly, semester, and annual attendance; pupil progress; cumulative folders; accidents; transfers; collections; field trips; and also those not specifically related to children, like inventories and requisitions for supplies and books?

You'll learn the rules. They'll be clear enough. But it may take a little time to know *how* and *when* to bend them. It may take a little more security in your new job, too. You certainly do not want to be the kind of teacher who is so rigid in his daily planning and so satisfied with his own perfection that he covers his bulletin boards and their materials each June, uncovers them each September, and keeps them clean—but more yellow all the time! Regulations, as well as all other practices related to your classroom, call for understanding, for knowing the reasons why, and for being able to accept those reasons. Blind obedience was a trait of the army the Nazis built up, but quiet consideration, adjustment, and full comprehension are more nearly the characteristics of teachers in a democracy. Being able to interpret the intent of those who make or write a statement is as important as hearing it in the first place.

With all the planning, all the questions, all the concern and worry, the first day itself may still not run as smoothly as you hope it will. No one can tell you exactly what you should do on that day, for some obvious reasons: It will depend on the grade level you are teaching, the specific things you have been able to find out in advance about these children, and your own preparation and personality. It will also depend on any specific first day requirements of your school.

If you make a decision in advance to be either "tough" or "a real guy," you are liable to have made a mistake if either characteristic is foreign to your own personality. The teaching situation calls for some characteristics that all of us share in varying degrees: firmness, warmth, humor, humility. It calls for being able to listen and observe and adapt. And it demands that we remain true to the personality we have and the basic respect toward the other human beings without which no one in the field of teaching can succeed.

Accepting your new school, the teachers in it, and the experience they represent (at least temporarily) may pay dividends. Maybe it seems to you that nothing has changed since you were in elementary school, and what may even be worse is the feeling you have that you will be unable to teach as you want to. And perhaps you will be wrong on both counts, as you may find out if you give others a chance to show you that they have not been sitting around doing nothing all the years you were getting an education. As you cement relationships, practice the listening routine, and get to know your own youngsters, you will no doubt find that experimentation and the desire of others to learn from you will gradually develop. Acceptance in a school *is* a gradual process, seldom nurtured by a mouth in perpetual motion based on ridicule, impatience, or the feeling of not being appreciated.

Disappointment can be a two-way street, because the expectations of the experienced teachers also may be high. They may be surprised at *your* reluctance to adapt a little bit, at your conviction that all your learning has already been done. They may have kept up with developments even more than you have, may still be taking courses, reading, and using the research; *and* they may have a broad background of experience into which to fit all they are finding out. They might even be a little miffed because you come right in and have a great deal to say about the records (on which they have worked for years), the courses of study (in whose preparation they were proud to have participated), and the school regulations (set up by their committees). They will like you, all right, especially your friendliness and fresh approach to things, but they might feel, "Can't he wait just a little before he tries to tear down or change all we've done?" Just as you may wonder why an old course of study has to be recommended for your use, they may wonder why, after they have worked for years to get them detached from the floor, you arrange the desks in firm, unchangeable rows!

Among the publications of value to the new teacher are the latest available edition of *Teaching Opportunities,* U.S. Department of Health, Education, and Welfare, Washington 25, D.C.; *The New Teacher,* New York, Ford Foundation, 1963; and *A Handbook for the New Teacher* by the author of this book, New York, Holt, Rinehart and Winston, Inc., 1960.

CONCLUDING REMARKS

Who is really qualified to teach? Ask some parents and they may tell you in negative terms, "Anyone but Miss Jones! What a ————!" Ask the state certification board and they will list some courses for you. Ask a college liberal arts instructor and he may put his emphasis solely on knowledge of the subject. Ask a person who teaches professional education courses and he may stress the personality factors.

Ask a school principal and his reply might belie his background in subject matter, athletics, or finance.

The conclusion you must draw is that there is no composite, no one type of person, no single kind of preparation, no isolated point of view, aptitude, appearance, or sets of opinions or facts. "Let each of us become all he is capable of becoming" might be a good start.

CHAPTER 5

A TIME FOR *Being Professional*

I don't keep up with the literature in my field.

I never contribute to that literature.

I'm not aware of recent research.

I don't go to conferences, attend meetings, or participate in seminars to help me keep up with things.

Am I a professional person? Of course I am!

Whether we are talking about law, medicine, engineering, or teaching, the first four statements just cannot lead up to the last one. A point of confusion exists among teachers themselves who debate year after year this matter of their professional status as it pertains to working conditions, salaries, and other factors. There are endless conversations and discussions on this point at conferences, meetings, and seminars. For many teachers the realization that their work is in a profession comes too late, if at all. It must develop early, in the preteaching years. The first seed leading to the conviction that teaching is an important calling must come right at the start of your preparation for it.

It is time—and way past time—for calling a halt to unnecessary haggling. Teaching *is* a profession for many obvious reasons. One publication states that a professional—regardless of the particular profession of which he is a part—

Is a liberally educated person

Possesses a body of specialized skills and knowledge related to and for the performance of his function

Is able to make rational judgments and to take appropriate action within the scope of his activities, and is responsible for the consequences of his judgments and action

Places primary emphasis upon his service to society rather than upon his personal gain

Actively participates with his colleagues in developing and enforcing
standards fundamental to continuous improvement of his profession and
abides by those standards in his own practice
Practices his profession on a full-time basis
Is engaged in a continuing search for new knowledge and skill[1]

There is room for improvement in all professions in the standards
for actual entry, in the selection of those who enter, and in the
preparation to which they are exposed. Teaching is more vulnerable,
among other reasons because its language is more readily understood
than the technical verbiage of some of the others. Teaching is certainly not alone in professional failings. And yet that is no excuse for
incompetence, even less of an excuse than other groups can point to.
Law has its quacks, dentistry has its inefficiencies, medicine has its
poor judgments. But in teaching the accusations of quackery, inefficiency, or erroneous judgment affect children, large groups of
them. Such accusations must be steadily countered with study, evaluation, and correction.

Teachers, through one of their own organizations, the Department
of Classroom Teachers of the NEA, have taken a penetrating look at
themselves as professional persons. In fact, their theme for 1961–
1962 was "Teaching: A Profession," with accompanying posters,
conferences, and letters to local segments of the Department. They
have singled out, for special attention, the possession of a unique
body of knowledge and skills, autonomy, a national accrediting body,
an effective professional organization, advancing "in the interest of
society the cause which society has entrusted to it," and the unselfish protection of the welfare of its members.[2] Of course, as too
often happens among our people, they became bogged down in
terminology that abounds in words and phrases like "responsibility
and accountability," "policy decision on teacher status," and "goals
and methods." Maybe these are necessary to get some ideas understood, but one cannot help wondering whether such verbiage hinders
more than it helps.

A major stumbling block in the way of our being fully recognized

[1] National Commission on Teacher Education and Professional Standards, *New
Horizons For The Teaching Profession,* Washington, D.C., NEA, 1961, p. 6.
[2] Department of Classroom Teachers, NEA, *Classroom Teachers Speak on
Teaching as a Profession,* Washington, D.C., 1961.

as a profession is, as they say in advertising, our public image. Don't you think it creates the wrong image when we do things such as the following?

Approach our jobs as stop-gaps

Say we are "just a teacher"

Make do with too little time, money, and resources for the job we want to accomplish

Put on the martyr complex and the "humble bit" as we sometimes accept large classes without even a murmur

Fail to join our professional organizations

Take foolish pride in running them down even if we do join

Ridicule our own preparation without *doing* something about it "within the family"

Do not realize which are our professional tasks and which are subprofessional ones that less skilled persons and mechanical means can handle (sometime ask *your* teachers about the clerical activities that weigh them down!)

Fail to understand that within our profession we must differentiate among our skills, rather than thinking or saying that we can all do anything within the teaching gamut

Give little consideration to recruitment of the kind of future teachers who can help us out of the backwash of the professions

Do not keep our knowledge current and our techniques imaginative

Ignore our role of leadership, as citizens in a democracy, sometimes cowering behind the seen-but-not-heard philosophy of the rural teacher of the nineteenth century

Settle for fringe benefits (like sick leave, coffee breaks, vacations, and hospitalization plans) which peg us as nonprofessional personnel in the eyes of the public

Put in longer and longer hours for no additional salaries, thus garnering a kind of condescending gratitude rather than the sturdy respect which accrues to other professions with their large hourly stipends

Limited individual and group goals and salary objectives, the closed-door-leading-to-closed-mind sort of isolation, false zeal, fake satisfaction, and questionable adjustment, a repetitive, rote approach to a job that for many has the aspects of an exciting, thrilling adventure—these are some of the aspects of stagnation (even though they may be possessed by only a relatively small proportion of teachers) that make many within and even more without raise an eyebrow when we refer to ourselves as a profession. And our case also loses some of its weight when an upper-grade teacher asks to be transferred to the first grade because she falsely assumes that she can then "relax for a year," when fear permeates a whole school prior to a visit by a school system administrator or board member, or when the new teacher is ridiculed because he or she "dares" to suggest that there are new ways to teach mathematics, that phonics *may* have an even stronger place in the teaching of reading, or that the unit method has on occasion been abused by lazy, incompetent teachers. These examples may be isolated but they sometimes, unfortunately, get more attention than the thousands of fine dedicated teachers we have.

We started out by saying that teaching is a profession. It is—but some of the practices of its participants and attitudes of its public are not professional. The rest of this chapter will help us take a closer look at our shortcomings and our promise. We certainly have plenty of both.

EFFECTIVE TEACHING

According to a recent report,[3] more than 50 years of research on teaching ability have failed to produce sound knowledge about what the ingredients of that quality are. Even after all that effort they are defined only in a fuzzy manner. However, poor discipline and lack of cooperation are pegged as important factors, with health, educational background, preparation, age, and knowledge of subject matter pointed out as of lesser importance in terms of teacher failure. Viewing those items (especially the one based on knowing the subject taught) as less important reasons for teacher failure will have quite a shock effect on many people.

The implications of that report can lead to a fascinating discussion. Persons who read it carelessly may assume that no matter how poor the preparation, how limited the subject matter, or how advanced the age, the teacher can be fairly successful just so long as he

[3] Department of Classroom Teachers, American Association of School Administrators, National School Boards Association, *Who's a Good Teacher?* Washington, D.C., NEA, 1961.

or she keeps children quiet and cooperates with the administration!

Others have viewed effective teaching from different vantage points: They look for the "showman" characteristic, such as the one attributed to comic Jerry Lewis about whom it was once said that whenever he opened the refrigerator and the light went on, he put on a 30 minute performance; they assume that the Aristotelian philosophy of teaching made sense when it said that the things we are to do when we have learned them we learn by doing them; they believe that Laura Zirbes, the grand old lady of Progressive Education, had a good point when she insisted that students must be active, they must not "sit and soak"; they side with Comenius when he admonished teachers to teach less so that students could learn more; they see some sense in Confucius' advice to guide without pulling, to urge and not suppress.

What is effective teaching anyway? Does anyone know what the size, shape, voice, and looks are of the teacher who fits into that framework? Of course not. There is no single physical or mental compartment that invariably constitutes "the good teacher." Clara N. Ady was the best or worst teacher that many students ever had, and for some of them she was both. Year after year fearful students dreaded the Labor Day weekend because it meant that the next day they would enter eighth grade at Avondale School in Chicago and face Miss Ady. A hulk of a person, a deep voice, a shock of light brown, graying, wavy hair with a comb in it, pince-nez glasses, with quiet and order the "law" of every day, she ruled her roost; and every child knew from long before the first minute who was boss! English grammar and historical and geographical facts were drilled and drilled and drilled. The result? Many dropped out of school as soon as they could after that experience; but some stayed on and never forgot those facts after the drudgery and dreariness of their eighth grade class in the 1920s.

On the other hand, there was Margaret Helen Cain at Senn High School in Chicago—competent, kindly, and challenging. She was also able to infiltrate facts and a respect for literature that remain with her students through the decades. Without mental turmoil she guided the students toward her goals, and in many instances made them theirs too.

You know many like Miss Ady and Miss Cain, and thousands

between. Both taught effectively for *some* students, and their personalities and approaches could not have differed more. So perhaps there is no teaching performance that meets the needs of all students under all circumstances. Many have tried their hand at identifying what effective teaching is, and some of their efforts are worth your consideration. Unfortunately, most attempts lack specificity and practicality, and their values are somewhat restricted.

In some succinct remarks Paul Woodring uses the themes of "enjoyment," "interest," "hard work," and "discipline." He says:

A classroom should be a happy place where pupils enjoy living. Learning will proceed most effectively if the pupils are deeply interested in their work. But a good teacher can lead a normal child to be interested in almost anything within his range of comprehension, and the school program need not, and should not, be limited to the interests which the child brings to school with him.[4]

Kenneth H. Hansen writes:

Any school can be thought of today as a kind of laboratory for learning. The modern, progressive school is very accurately described as such a laboratory, and is clearly seen as such. Within the more traditional patterns of the conventional school, however, we are increasingly seeing signs that even these schools are taking a "laboratory" approach. So we are not restricted to just one kind of school when we try to generalize an answer to the question, "What are children doing in today's schools?" In and out of the classroom, but still mostly in, the boys and girls in American schools are daily doing these things:
1. They are learning specific things systematically, by reading, writing, talking, listening, figuring, practicing, reviewing.
2. They are setting up and solving problems.
3. They are creating and expressing.
4. They are living together as a group.
5. They are developing individually.
6. They are being examined, judged, evaluated.
7. They are developing and modifying attitudes.[5]

But Woodring and Hansen only begin to tell the story of what

[4] Paul Woodring, *A Fourth of a Nation*, New York, McGraw-Hill Book Company, Inc., 1957, p. 141.
[5] Kenneth H. Hansen, *Public Education in American Society*, Englewood Cliffs, N. J., Prentice-Hall, Inc., 1956, p. 162.

effective teaching is. A fully professional approach to the subject can begin with their remarks, but it must go on. You know that is so, merely because you have been exposed to teaching at both ends of the scale. You could make a list of your own of the most memorable and effective approaches to teaching in your experience. A few moments spent on what good teaching is can be important to you even this early in your preparation. Here are four factors you might think about:

Interest: Interest is the major factor in any learning situation, and skillful teachers capitalize on it at every opportunity. Do you have any doubt about whether a baseball-happy fourth-grader learned "Roman numerals" as he wrote the following: "Mickey Mantle hit LII home runs in MCMLVI. Roger Maris hit LXI home runs in MCMLXI. Babe Ruth hit LX home runs in MCMXXVII. Lou Gehrig hit IL in MCMXXXIV. How many did they hit in all?"

Success: Encouragement, stimulation, and reinforcement based on success are keynotes for learning in the future. The prime symbol of those ingredients is the programmed-learning movement. "Wisdom . . . needs no external authority," wrote Sidney Hook.[6] Instead it comes from the facts, from the materials themselves. It can never emerge from "ridicule, cold indifference, or the show of outraged dignity." John Masefield, the poet, has been quoted many times in terms of a variation on that theme: "The days that make us happy make us wise."

Personality: "Perhaps we have made a sad and serious mistake in erroneously singling out what we feel is the core of the teaching situation. It is the child, most people say—but maybe that's an error." George Polya of Budapest, Zurich and Stanford University, a short, wiry man with the large head and long white hair of popular imagination, who is generally regarded among mathematicians as the greatest mathematics teacher of our time, likes to say that "in education, one thing is certain. If the teacher is bored, the child will be bored. We know that for a fact. All else is guesswork."[7] At least his idea is worth thinking about; especially if you intend to be a "stopgap teacher."

Progress: Too much emphasis is placed on the order in which subjects should be learned. Jerome S. Bruner recently put it this way: "Any subject can be taught effectively in some intellectually honest form to any child at

[6] Sidney Hook, "The Danger of Authoritarian Attitudes in Teaching Today," *AAUP Bulletin,* Autumn, 1951, p. 529 and Autumn, 1960, p. 276.

[7] Martin Mayer, *The Schools,* New York, Harper & Row, Publishers, Inc., 1961, p. 26.

any stage of development."[8] Boswell, many years ago, quoted Johnson as saying: "Sir, it is no matter what you teach them first, any more than what leg you shall put into your breeches first. Sir, you may stand disputing which is best to put in first, but in the mean time your breech is bare. Sir, while you are considering which of two things you should teach your child first, another boy has learnt them both."[9]

Perhaps the time is ripe to put the cold spotlight of emphasis on teaching *something*. Define it as you wish, but maybe the proper word to use is *skills;* those useful today and tomorrow, by themselves or as part of other learning subjects. Although we leave the specifics of effective teaching techniques to other books, there is a limited place for them here too. Sometimes the what-not-to-do approach tells the story best. Rousseau tried it when he wrote the following little lesson with a moral:

MASTER	You must not do that.
CHILD	Why not?
MASTER	Because it is wrong.
CHILD	Wrong! What is wrong?
MASTER	What is forbidden you.
CHILD	Why is it wrong to do what is forbidden?
MASTER	You will be punished for disobedience.
CHILD	I will do it when no one is looking.
MASTER	We shall watch you.
CHILD	I will hide.
MASTER	We shall ask you what you were doing.
CHILD	I shall tell a lie.
MASTER	You must not tell lies.
CHILD	Why must not I tell lies?
MASTER	Because it is wrong, etc.[10]

It took the past few years to provide some of the most exciting guidelines to effective teaching yet published. Unfortunately you will seldom find all of them used in your college courses, so let's be

[8] Jerome S. Bruner quoted in *Phi Delta Kappan*, May, 1961, p. 360.

[9] James Boswell, "Dr. Johnson on Education," in Claude M. Fuess and Emory S. Basford (eds.), *Unseen Harvests*, New York, The Macmillan Company, 1947, p. 115.

[10] Jean Jacques Rousseau, "On Reasoning with Children," in Claude M. Fuess and Emory S. Basford (eds.), *Unseen Harvests*, New York, The Macmillan Company, 1947, pp. 502–503.

certain right now that they are pin-pointed in your direction. Perhaps the most provocative are from A. S. Neill's *Summerhill*. Whether you like them, or agree with the ideas, doesn't matter much. What is important is that he offers a way of looking at what is commonly written for future teachers.

In all countries, capitalist, socialist, or communist, elaborate schools are built to educate the young. But all the wonderful labs and workshops do nothing to help John or Peter or Ivan surmount the emotional damage and the social evils bred by the pressure on him from his parents, his schoolteachers, and the pressure of the coercive quality of our civilization.

Parents are slow in realizing how unimportant the learning side of school is. Children, like adults, learn what they want to learn. All prize-giving and marks and exams sidetrack proper personality development. Only pedants claim that learning from books is education.

Books are the least important apparatus in a school. All that any child needs is the three R's; the rest should be tools and clay and sports and theater and paint and freedom.

Most of the school work that adolescents do is simply a waste of time, of energy, of patience. It robs youth of its right to play and play and play; it puts old heads on young shoulders.[11]

Bruner in his stimulating little book called *The Process of Education* attacks the unnecessary postponement of school subjects on the mistaken premise that they are too difficult. He maintains that the basic ideas that lie at the heart of all science, mathematics, literature and life are as simple as they are powerful, and he calls our attention to the "spiral curriculum" that turns back on itself at higher levels. He notes the relationships of ideas rather than their isolation and stresses starting such relationships right *at* the beginning (some of his examples go into the kindergarten). Set theory, metric geometry, and physics are all fair game for the elementary school, he believes; their basic notions are perfectly accessible and can contribute toward the building of intuitive and inductive understanding in the early years as a prelude to more formal courses later. Social sciences and literature are as ripe for this kind of basic approach as science and mathematics, and Bruner points out that "there has been little research done on the kinds of concepts that a child brings to

[11] A. S. Neill, *Summerhill: A Radical Approach to Child Rearing*, New York, Hart Publishing Company, 1960, pp. 25, 28.

these subjects, although there is a wealth of observation and anec-
dote."[12]

Bruner's ideas are attracting attention, and they may be one of the
prime forces for curriculum revision in the next few years. Maybe
they will scare you away from teaching because of the demands that
will be made on you. Maybe they will urge you to reevaluate the
preparation you are receiving. Whichever of these directions you
follow will be a healthful one—for you and for the children spared
from or exposed to your knowledge and skills.

Another recent and exciting contributor to several books and
articles is J. Lloyd Trump. His activities are more probable as course
reading list entries than those of Neill or Bruner because they are
more "respectable" to those who teach you. Although his ideas look
calm and unruffling from the schools' point of view, don't be fooled!
Give just a little thought to the implications in statements like these:

A first step in curriculum reorganization involves an analysis of what is
now being taught and studied by students in conventional classrooms, study
halls, libraries and laboratories, and in the usual assignment of homework.
Teachers in a subject area should then ask themselves which of these purposes could be better served by large-group instruction, by small-group discussion, and by increased independent study by students.

In effect, these are the questions that teachers will answer for each unit
in their present courses:

What content and purposes could students of different levels of ability
learn and accomplish for themselves with little or no help from me?

What content and purposes require motivation, explanation, demonstration, or other presentation by me or by some other competent person?

What content and purposes actually require personal interaction among
students and between me and the students?[13]

A sound approach to new ideas in education—whether they relate
to the current subject of effective teaching, or to the phonics, grading, social promotion, or foreign languages in the elementary school
—is to make some effort to get more than one side of the picture.
Instructors may help you, but don't depend on them for the whole

---

[12] Jerome S. Bruner, *The Process of Education,* Cambridge, Harvard University
Press, 1961, p. 46.

[13] J. Lloyd Trump and Dorsey Baynham, *Focus on Change—Guide to Better
Schools,* Chicago, Rand McNally & Company, 1961, p. 114.

story. However, some future teachers, unfortunately, don't know what they think until they are told what it is acceptable to think. They go along on the same monotonous note of the famous Uncle Fud of Bob Burns, the old-time Arkansas comic, who played a one-stringed cello and the same squeaky note on it. One day his wife heard another person playing the cello, varying the notes as he went along. When she raised a question about the musical monotony in her own living room, Uncle Fud replied, "That fellar's still searching for the right note. I've found it!"

Too many of the teachers we already have amble along on that unchanging, dogmatic trail. Our main hope is in you, the ones coming along, so try not to freeze your ideas yet. In the growth possibilities offered in the next section are many that can help you be the kind of professional person needed in teaching.

PROFESSIONAL GROWTH

In John Keats' diatribe against teachers and those who teach them, his approach seemed too antagonistic, but a few of his points hit the spot.[14] There *are* some teachers, hopefully not too many, who mark time until the next pay check, take "snap" courses rather than useful ones during summer sessions, fail to keep up with the research in their field, and as a result, lower the entire professional level of the far larger number of competent, enthusiastic, bright teachers who represent the other side of the coin. His accusations also comfortably fit a few of the sometime scholars who teach in teacher preparation programs.

Just as there are no sudden starts or stops in the total educational process, there are no sharp beginnings in preparing for the teaching profession. The first step was before you remember, when you were first taught something—the distinction between Mother and the rest of the world, between a bland cereal and tasty apricot, between bright red and pale pink. The other steps were in a continuous process of learning stages, through the grades, high school, college, and then teaching itself. But the preparation doesn't stop at that

[14] John Keats, *Schools Without Scholars*, Boston, Hougton Mifflin Company, 1958.

point. It can't—especially in the current race against international disaster. It can't—if teachers are to provide the leadership that their communities have every right to expect of them.

Negatively, professional growth "is a reflection of the occupational neurosis, the fear of shrinking to the size of one's students. The long vacations, the sabbatical leaves, the distressing eagerness of culture with a capital C—all are necessary decompression chambers for the teacher out of her classroom."[15] Positively, such growth comes from a real desire to keep up and move ahead, a desire that cannot be imposed by others through lengthy assignments, cajoling, or arguments. Growth during the preparatory period and after actual entry into teaching is necessary to avoid stagnation, archaic attitudes and techniques, and a *status quo* which means a steady drifting back, back, back. "Schools without scholarship are apt to become prisons for the minds of children and shackles for a society."[16]

Opportunities for moving forward are as varied as your own creative mind. They include the expanding of horizons through making you a more complete person and almost invariably, therefore, a person better qualified to open doors to eager, absorbent youngsters.

In-Service Preparation

More and more schools and school districts face the fact that young teachers (just like young engineers and doctors) are not quite finished products. Before you can do a first-class job for your school, it in turn has a responsibility to you. This doesn't mean the college or university hasn't accomplished its task well; it may have, but there are still plenty of sharp edges to be rounded off.

The route of in-service courses, lectures, and conferences is one way of helping smooth out some of the rough spots. Administrators, supervisors, and others can all get into the picture, providing orientation to the school system, going into the difficult subjects such as the preparation and proper use of materials in cumulative folders, and discussing topics of personal and professional concern to *this* school district.

[15] Mayer, *op. cit.*, p. 21.
[16] National Society for the Study of Education, *Social Forces Influencing American Education*, 60th Yearbook, pt. II, Chicago, 1961, p. 42.

College and University Courses

Summer workshops and extension classes, degree or nondegree courses, lecture series adapted to your school district with one professor or a team of them can usually be almost as flexible as your needs and the creativity of your school demand. Many times these are eye openers. One teacher took a summer course on mental health and discovered the following fall that for the very first time he had a number of emotionally maladjusted children in his class!

You may have to travel to take advantage of such courses, but the key point isn't distance. It is more likely to be your answer to these questions: "Have I had it? Have I had enough education? Can I face almost any educational contingency, today or tomorrow?" A series of staccato "Yes" answers may be enough to make you stop for a moment and wonder, especially if the limit of your education is a four-year degree. In the competitive market we always have for good positions, a higher degree takes on added importance. No one would be foolish enough to say that it provides the total answer, but "all things remaining equal," it acquires significance in the job-seeking picture.

Your Alma Mater

Follow-up questionnaires, alumni magazines, and the opportunity to keep in touch with your former teachers are all connections to be nurtured. You never know when you might want a reference letter from someone who knew and liked you years ago. You may be able to go back for graduate work, and the wisdom of doing so (rather than choosing another institution) depends on various factors such as time, money, personnel, courses offered, and alternatives available elsewhere. A rule of thumb is that it's better to have degrees from different places, but there are too many variables for one to generalize.

A sad commentary to support Thomas Wolfe's idea that you can't go home again came from a study conducted on graduates of Carleton College in Minnesota who become high-school teachers. There seemed to be a pattern of indifference and rebuff when they sought the counsel of their academic professors, apparently driving them into the receptive professional arms of "those who teach teachers."

Not a particularly happy thought for "antieducationists" to face, but one they ought to recognize just the same.

Expanding Horizons

Less formal ways to expand professional horizons may be more obvious to you than the three routes itemized above, once you think about them a little bit. They may be more fun, but that doesn't make them any less valuable. It is the old story of man not living, thriving, or gaining by work alone.

No one can make you extend your activities beyond your work. Maybe you're satisfied to limit yourself that way—but the fact remains that you have no right to limit your children. They are entitled to educational relationships with adults who live richly, and not just for 2 weeks each summer on "conducted tours" consisting primarily of other teachers.

Some sample kinds of enrichment can only begin to tap the vast expanse of possibilities open to any person entering the profession of teaching. Here are just a few of them:

Working on a hobby, whether it is building toothpick castles or breeding rare birds or writing commercial verses for birthday cards

Being a collector of pictures, kitchen gadgets, songs, poems, stories, or rhythms

Traveling, within the limits of your city, state, country, or world, weekends or summers or, if you're a fortunate one, around the calendar some year

Attending conventions, if the administrative powers can help you arrange for the time and money

Keeping up with world events, but by balancing the printed "facts" from the various, conflicting sources available

Making friends, and gaining a great deal for yourself and your children from the variety of occupations and interests they represent

Experimenting in science, dance steps, flower growing—or you choose the area

Your growth can also come in a way that teachers too seldom consider, the writing they might do for professional or popular publications, running the gamut from the *NEA Journal, Grade Teacher* and *Educational Leadership* to *This Week, Today's Health* and *Saturday Evening Post* to your local daily or weekly newspaper. Reasons (or excuses) for nonactivity in this direction are plentiful:

too many other things to do; disinterest; no writing skill. But the main one is usually just plain inertia. And yet who can tell education's story better than the classroom teacher? Who knows the school's problems, the teacher's frustrations, and the children's dreams better? An added incentive is that there is no match for the personal satisfaction of getting one's name in print. A list of publications may be just the weight needed to swing a wanted position in your favor. And—just in case it hasn't occurred to you—some publications pay for what they publish. Generally the broader the public they reach the higher the rate, so don't let anyone belittle the mass media to you on the basis of either the reading coverage or the possible income.

Growth into a "full teacher" is also aided by reading of three types: professional, expansive, and "slice-of-life."

PROFESSIONAL READING

Your undergraduate classes may make you feel that perhaps there is an overabundance of publications; and it would no doubt be the same if you were in business administration, engineering, advertising, history, or the physical or biological sciences. Maybe you feel (as you also would in most other fields) that a publishing moratorium by some of the journals would be welcomed by both readers *and* staff (perhaps *after* the writing contribution suggested to you above is accepted for publication).

If your undergraduate assigned reading in some of the professional journals builds up an "anti" feeling on your part, a conviction that it all adds up to very little, take a rest from it during the beginning months of your teaching; but then give it another chance, and add some materials your undergraduate years may not have included. Others have done just that after feeling as strongly as you do; and somehow, in what seems almost a miraculous way, the articles take on new meaning and vitality. They haven't changed very much, but something, or someone, did. The techniques, materials, insights, philosophy, or ideas they represent (some of them, anyway) now fall on receptive and understanding ears. You may subscribe to one or more, or locate them in a nearby college, university or public library. They're good company for a new teacher; they provide consolation as you face decisions and seek answers for recurrent daily climaxes in your classroom. Here are a few which new as well as more experienced teachers find valuable; and there are dozens of others:

Child Study	Instructor, The
Childhood Education	Journal of Educational Research
Children	National Parent-Teacher
Clearing House, The	NEA Journal
Educational Leadership	Personnel and Guidance Journal, The
Elementary English	Reading Teacher, The
Elementary School Journal	Review of Educational Research
Exceptional Children	School Life
Grade Teacher	Teachers College Record
Harvard Educational Review	

Not exactly appropriate for that list, but perhaps even more valuable in some ways are the Sunday New York Times education page and the monthly education supplement of the Saturday Review. And, as an undergraduate student, you have perhaps already seen the Student NEA News.

In addition to the journals, you may find more exciting educational reading in book form, exciting because it's controversial and the words used are not always so polite. It is fun when the professionals take off their kid gloves and swing hard (and sometimes wildly) to prove a point that seems to be pretty precious to the swinging individual.

You may be surprised to find yourself taking sides on issues that never before aroused more than a yawn. Don't be so sure you're passive until you give Flesch, Rickover, Bestor, and their companions a chance to get at your blood pressure—and then be honest with yourself by giving Brameld, Harold Hand, and others rebuttal time. You'll be agreeably surprised to note that all educators do not spend all their evening hours grading papers (if you ever did think so).

Everyone who teaches has his favorite list of professional books and pamphlets. Naturally it would take a ricochet kind of defense to support the inclusion of each of these, or to explain the exclusion of others. If you take some time to thumb through these, part of the professional mission of this section will have been accomplished.

Barzun, Jacques, Teacher in America
Benjamin, Harold, The Cultivation of Idiosyncrasy
Bruner, Jerome S., The Process of Education
Conant, James B., Slums and Suburbs

Goodlad, John I., and Robert H. Anderson, *The Nongraded Elementary School*

Lieberman, Myron, *Education as a Profession* and *The Future of Public Education*

Mayer, Martin, *The Schools*

Morse, Arthur D., *Schools of Tomorrow—Today*

Neill, A. S., *Summerhill*

Trump, J. Lloyd, *Images of the Future*

Trump, J. Lloyd, and Dorsey Baynham, *Focus on Change—Guide to Better Schools*

Perhaps you would like to expand this list by adding some writers in the profession who are especially readable and whose written work has a commonsense approach. Unfortunately, the list wouldn't be expanded as much as one might hope; but it would no doubt include names like James L. Hymes and Kenneth H. Hansen.

Although magazines and books may dominate your professional reading now and in the future, organization and government publications might also be included. Yearbooks, catalogues, and research materials can be obtained from the organizations listed in the next section of this chapter (Professional Organizations) and from the American Council on Education and the National Committee for Children and Youth (following up the 1960 White House Conference). "Education" lists are available through the Superintendent of Documents, Government Printing Office; "Selected References" is a series of the Office of Education, Department of Health, Education, and Welfare; and curriculum and other materials can be obtained from state and county departments of education.

EXPANSIVE READING

Not completely in the professional realm, and not as far out as the "slice-of-life" reading referred to later, are many books and pamphlets that a well-educated teacher today should know, think about, discuss, accept—or reject for a reason. Again, no two lists will agree, but that may be part of the enjoyment of bringing up the whole subject. Whenever you have a chance you might react to these:

Barzun, Jacques, *The House of Intellect*

Gardner, John W., *Excellence*

Ginzberg, Eli, *Human Resources: The Wealth of a Nation* and *The Uneducated* (the latter with Douglas W. Bray)
Jessup, John K., et al., *The National Purpose*
McClelland, David C., Alfred L. Baldwin, Urie Bronfenbrenner, and Fred L. Strodtbeck, *Talent and Society*
Murphy, Gardner, *Human Potentialities*
President's Commission on National Goals, *Goals for Americans*
Rockefeller Brothers Fund, *The Pursuit of Excellence*
Stern, Edgar, Family Fund, *Recognition of Excellence*
U.S. Department of Labor, *Manpower, Challenge of the 1960's*
White House Conference on Children and Youth, *Conference Proceedings*

Remove some of these—add your own—but keep in mind that no teacher can be well educated who restricts himself to readings based only on course assignments. And it doesn't broaden you sufficiently if you attempt to justify your limited reading by referring to courses you've "had" in the liberal arts and sciences.

"SLICE-OF-LIFE" READING

Our third category is not of a professional nature. But it can help fill the gaps left in your reading during college days because you didn't have time, or so you said anyway. Later on we will discuss the almost impossible goal for all adults working with children, seeing through their eyes. Some of these books will help us face that problem. Some will just help us open our own a little wider, take away the blinders that are imposed by our restrictive environment, personality, exposure to intellectual exploration.

This list has 20 writers on it, and a little library browsing can add to it, giving it increased personal depth. It reminds one of the statement made by John J. De Boer of the University of Illinois: "The main thing wrong with the undergraduate college program is that it interferes with one's education." And it is a controversial list, too, among many college and university faculty members as well as the library boards of some communities. Most of these will be pleasurable to read, maybe even exciting, but that doesn't make them any less worthy of your time.

Cousins, Norman, *In Place of Folly*
Dreiser, Theodore, *An American Tragedy*
Fontaine, Robert, *The Happy Time*

Griffith, Beatrice, *American Me*
Hersey, John, *The Child Buyer*
Hunter, Evan, *The Blackboard Jungle*
Huxley, Aldous, *Brave New World* and *Brave New World Revisited*
Kerr, Jean, *Please Don't Eat the Daisies*
Krauss, Ruth, *A Hole Is To Dig*
Lindner, Robert, *Must You Conform?*
Linkletter, Art, *Kids Say the Darndest Things*
Maugham, W. Somerset, *Of Human Bondage*
Owsley, Jennifer, *A Handy Guide to Grownups*
Packard, Vance, *The Hidden Persuaders, The Status Seekers, The Waste Makers*
Runbeck, Margaret Lee, *Our Miss Boo*
Smith, H. Allen, *Write Me a Poem, Baby*
Smith, Robert Paul, *Where Did You Go? Out. What Did You Do? Nothing.*
Steinbeck, John, *The Grapes of Wrath*
Weill, Blanche, *Through Children's Eyes*
Whyte, William, *The Organization Man*

It certainly should also be a "must" to know more about the world in which we live, the undercurrents and forces of politics as they affect us every day, the surge of power in Africa and Asia as the twentieth century ebbs, the changing influences of the United States in world affairs. All sides of these issues belong in your present and future reading and in the professional library of the school where you will teach.

Summary

All of the suggestions in this section on professional growth are ways of adding breadth to you as both a person and a teacher. Whether it is formal course work or travel or writing or reading, the objective remains the same of filing away the ragged edges of immaturity and inexperience. A concrete summary of what and who you are is the cumulative personal record of your education, teaching experience and related information, a realistic picture of your professional potential, status, accomplishments, and growth.

During the depression years practically all job seekers knew what a "personal data sheet" was. This summary on paper of what one had done educationally and occupationally was essential as one filled out job application forms and answered help wanted advertisements by the dozens. Fortunately we have become less concerned about this purpose of the form, with jobs plentifully available. But another point related to it has taken on considerable significance. Despite the job-hunters' market since World War II, the most desirable position will continue to have more than one applicant interested in it. So who will get it? How will the decision be made? What would *you* do? The answers should be obvious. If two or more apply and they all look and sound good, then the next step is their personal and professional record. How will you stack up in years to come on questions like these:

Does he change jobs often? What are the reasons?
Are his professional references good?
Has he been productive in writing? community affairs? professional organizations? school affairs?
What education has he acquired beyond a bachelor's degree?

In other words, will he (will *you?*) let the future take care of itself; or will he (will *you?*) try to help it along? We can believe implicitly in fate, and yet realize that what happens tomorrow is the direct result of what we do today.

PROFESSIONAL ORGANIZATIONS

Maybe you have always prided yourself on not joining an organization unless you could be active in it—and maybe that was either a laudable objective or an excuse. Now you have available to you a vast array of organizations that are directly or partially related to your profession, plus many others in your community that might attract you.

There is, of course, no necessity for restricting your activities to groups in the education field. In fact, some of your best "missionary work" can be done by participating in groups outside our field, letting them know that we *do* work hard, are *not* in an ivory tower, *have* similar dreams, ambitions, fears, laughs, and desires as they do. If you think "missionary work" is a pretty strong way of putting it, reserve judgment a little while until you listen to some of the misunderstandings and nonunderstandings you pick up as you go along

—some apologetically stated, some inadvertently uttered, some blatantly blurted out.

Organizations of a community nature you will discover very easily on the basis of your own needs. They may be social, religious, theatrical, or artistic groups, based on a "cause" or just the desire to get together, consisting of various ages or limited to a narrowly defined age level. Although you may join as a "teacher," you will no doubt be accepted as a "person"; and that is when you begin to do your profession some real good. Keep that objective on an incidental level, however. Just have a good time, and the rest will take care of itself.

In the organizational possibilities of a professional type, the list is equally long, equally diverse in interests and objectives, local, national, or international in scope. You may find one in your teaching area of English, social studies, mathematics, or in another field that is just right for you. Or perhaps one of the many aimed at the elementary-school level will serve your purpose better. Maybe more than one will attract you.

Classroom teachers are the backbone of many of them as their publications indicate so well. Those publications are frequently the main reason for your wanting to be part of the organization, although the national and regional conferences are another fine way of keeping up with latest developments in your area of interest (if you don't attend too many too often where you are forced to suffer through the dreary efforts by some persons to make old oft-repeated ideas sound new). Getting time off and money to cover expenses for attending them are something else again, however.

A list of organizations in which you might be interested is given here, admittedly incomplete, and subject to numerous supplementary suggestions from your more experienced co-workers who can help keep you from being "a lonely island." Complete lists are also given in the *Educational Directory* which is published annually by the U.S. Office of Education (the 1961 edition devoted 128 pages to educational organizations). In the list below, the first five are in Washington, the last three in Chicago.

Association for Childhood Education International
Association for Supervision and Curriculum Development

Council for Exceptional Children
Department of Classroom Teachers
National Education Association (and state and local education associations)
International Reading Association
National Congress of Parents and Teachers
National Society for the Study of Education

Other organizations about which you should be aware are the American Federation of Teachers (and its official publication, *The American Teacher*), the World Confederation of Organizations of the Teaching Profession, and honorary organizations such as Phi Delta Kappa, Pi Lambda Theta, and Kappa Delta Pi.

You can join and be active or join and be passive. It is also easy to stay out, of course. But on the other side of the coin, it's easy to become stagnant in one's job!

The NEA is by far the largest of all, and in fact includes three of those listed above at the same address. It was organized in 1857 under the name of the National Teachers' Association, and now has more than 800,000 members (with a goal of "A Million or More in '64"), 33 separate departments, and more than 7,000 local associations affiliated with it. Its publications in book and other form total more than 1,000 and run right through educational subjects alphabetically, from "administration" to "television" and beyond.

Late in 1961 the NEA initiated a Professional Priorities Project through its membership ranks, soliciting ideas in areas like these: excellence in educational programs; professional and citizenship status of teachers; working conditions and welfare for teachers; financial and organizational structure of the schools; public understanding and support of education; vigorous professional organizations. Room was left on the back of a form widely distributed by the Project after the statement, "My dream for the long run—If I could chart the future of our profession for the next decade or two, I would:————." Take a hint and check up on the results of this Project later on.

Another major activity of the NEA was its Project on the Instructional Program of the Public Schools, concluding its two years' work in August, 1962. Its objectives were high: "to upgrade the quality of, and give direction to, American public education"; "what constitutes a sound program of elementary and secondary education in today's world"; "over-all consideration to improvement and adaptations required if the instructional program is to be adequate for the issues that confront us"; emphasis on "what to teach" and "organizing for instruction"; "a final summary report that will have an incisive and fresh edge." "Action" was the keynote of the Project from the beginning—and no profession has needed it more. (Through its National Commission on Teacher Education and Professional Standards the NEA has also set up the National Council for the Accreditation of Teacher Education.)

From various directions, both within and without, the pressures are heavy to close the teaching ranks more tightly, to organize more completely. Bernard Iddings Bell makes that plea in order to arouse the public, to get more financial support, and to resist political control. His major fear is that the schools will become "agencies for the spreading of government-devised propaganda"; organizing the teaching profession will in some strange way remove what he sees as a threat.[17] Jean Grambs calls for solidarity to increase salaries and respect. "Away with our feeling of inferiority, our fear of offending public opinion, our innocuous social action" is her theme; we envy the strength of the American Medical Association but we fail to exert the group effort necessary in order to attain it.[18] Our mistake has been that we concentrate on immediate needs rather than on long-range goals, says Lindley Stiles; indifference or outright hostility to political or even to everyday citizenship activities, and a lag far behind the unified front often shown by manufacturers and industrial union groups, are the pictures we present.[19]

A particularly touchy phase of professionalism (or lack thereof) is represented by the controversial issue of whether teachers should ever go out on strike. The New York teachers' strike of April, 1962, brought heated comments in newspaper editorials and from political leaders, teachers, and laymen. Also widely discussed was the pledge by members of the Utah Education Association not to sign

[17] Bernard Iddings Bell, *Crisis in Education*, New York, McGraw-Hill Book Company, Inc., 1949, p. 202.

[18] Arthur Foff and Jean D. Grambs, *Readings in Education*, New York, Harper & Row, Publishers, Inc., 1956, pp. 45–46.

[19] Lindley J. Stiles (ed.), *The Teacher's Role in American Society*, New York, Harper & Row, Publishers, Inc., 1957, p. 123.

contracts unless the quality of Utah education was upgraded. Can teachers have professional status, respect, and security—and at the same time have and use the economic weapons of a labor union? What do you think?

RESEARCH, FOUNDATIONS AND GRANTS

"Research" is a word about as scarey to many undergraduate students in teacher preparation as logarithms, a required course in the physical sciences, calculus, or statistics. It is also about as poorly understood. *Webster's Third New International Dictionary* pedantically defines it as "studious inquiry . . . critical and exhaustive investigation or experimentation having for its aim the discovery of new facts and their correct interpretation, the revision of accepted conclusions, theories, or laws in the light of newly discovered facts. . . ."

In a particularly thought-provoking attack, Jacques Barzun lays wide open the too-frequent tendency to attach a mysterious, sacred quality to research methods.[20] Instead of our standing in awe of anyone who says he is "doing research" we ought to ask, "Into what?" and insist on a response that we can understand. The label is applied much too loosely to such activities as pupil collections in elementary schools, tabulating answers to poorly prepared questionnaires, uncontrolled interviews, busywork bases for promotions in universities. One's own curiosity and the goals aspired to are far more basic reasons for doing research than imposed requirements; the money of business, foundations, or government seeking a place to dissipate itself; or the desire to impress someone, even if it is only one's self.

Too much attention to the mechanics and statistics involved frequently interferes with the richness of the results that might be available. Stopping short of interpreting those results so that the public and the average classroom teacher can read, understand, and use them is another frequent fault in the whole research picture. Merely "measuring" is a common weakness in research. Other weak-

[20] Jacques Barzun, "The Cults of 'Research' and 'Creativity,'" *Harper's Magazine,* October, 1960, pp. 69-74.

nesses are a fear of experimentation with ideas and a preference for status studies; a lip-smacking pleasure in using words that are too big and whose definitions are frequently not even agreed upon by the authorities who use them; an inability to distinguish between "good" and "poor" research; and a tendency to ignore the scientific method. The whole subject reminds Roger Williams of the scriptural saying, "Where there is no vision the people perish."[21]

Educational research is not a test-tube product; lacking strict control over all variables, it remains open to criticism. Much of it in early stages shows fantastic results—but why shouldn't it if accompanied by teacher enthusiasm and novel materials for the children?

Unfortunately, the lag of teachers in educational research applies in all three directions of doing, reading, and using it. And that lag begins early in the undergraduate program, maybe even before that, in the failure to instill thoroughness and insight much earlier. (We can push back the blame more and more—to the secondary school, elementary school, nursery school, parents, and to all the in-laws on the father's side of the family!) It takes only a casual conversation with many undergraduate and graduate students, as well as with teachers in the field, to show how limited their acquaintance is with recent research even in their own area of concentration. Parents would look with abhorrence on the practice of using a doctor who had no professional source materials in his home or office and who had not kept up with developments and research in his field. Yet, without knowing so, in many cases they are entrusting their children to persons who not only are not keeping up with research but in some instances were not even introduced to it during their period of preparation. Whether it is lack of training or disinterest which causes this void in some teacher preparation and growth doesn't really matter. The important fact is that many of our teachers are uninformed and doing nothing about that situation.

When a student nearing the end of an undergraduate program in teacher preparation defines the *Education Index* as "a file in the library to look up books on education" or "the classes a person has taken in different areas," when he thinks the *Mental Measurements Yearbooks* are published by the Metropolitan Life Insurance Com-

[21] Roger J. Williams, *Free and Unequal*, Austin, University of Texas Press, 1953, pp. 76–77.

pany, and when he cannot identify the *Encyclopaedia of Educational Research,* there is something drastically wrong with him, his teachers, or both. In addition, when these source materials are not recognized, it must be true that they have not been used effectively nor can they be in the future.

And what about the teachers who have already completed their preparation? Do they use these and numerous other research sources in order to keep their teaching up-to-date? Isaac Newton once said something about seeming to see farther than others because he stood on the shoulders of giants. Similarly, our own perspective can certainly be broadened if we make use of the knowledge unfolded through the research published by others and if we are critical of that research. The fear of research has actually cheated us out of one of the major satisfactions in teaching: studies in our own laboratories —our classrooms. But let's take one thing at a time: first, use the research of others to improve our teaching, and then attempt some ourselves to direct more attention to "individual interests and needs," a phrase which many of us use so glibly.

And as you read what others are finding out in what we hope are well-controlled situations, you will gain new insights to ticklish topics like discipline, grading, parent interviews, and methods of teaching. Your contacts with research may also be in the broader realm of subject matter or content, in science, social studies, arithmetic, and the rest. Throughout the wordy expanse of educational literature are ideas for future research. They tantalizingly peer through the faulty conclusions we draw on the basis of inadequate evidence: small classes are "better"; a 5-year (or 4- or 6-year) program of teacher preparation is "better"; doctoral programs need (or don't need) foreign-language requirements; and on and on. Ideas appear also in the broad gaps that still remain in our knowledge of who is a good teacher and what good teaching is. Here are just a few of the major areas that will have the mystery peeled away in the first years of your teaching. Maybe you'll help remove it. Perhaps you will be fortunate enough to land a job in that rare school system that provides teacher leaves of absence for research of this kind.

Meeting the needs of individual children—sounds hackneyed, but still in the area of unfinished business
Utilizing research data already available by the bushel load

Nonteaching tasks of teachers and the waste involved in them

Systems analyses of what goes on in a school; what happens to a child all the way through

Causes for the educational lag—the lag behind research, science, medical knowledge, political events

School inefficiencies and the reasons for them

The child in the school, home, and community of the 1960s

Experimentation that brings scientists, sociologists, engineers, architects and others into the education framework, with the richness of their own research

Specific child development problems; example—"the fourth grade slump"

Use of new educational materials, such as programmed learning

The beginning efforts to meet these and other unsatisfied research needs are appearing in the literature now. But it will take some real selectivity on your part to filter them out. The series of pamphlets, "What Research Says to the Teacher," of the NEA; the bulletins, *Research Relating to Children*, of the Children's Bureau, Department of Health, Education, and Welfare; releases from the Cooperative Research Branch of the U.S. Office of Education; reports from the Office of Statistical Information and Research of the American Council on Education, and issues of the *Review of Educational Research, Journal of Educational Research*, and *Phi Delta Kappan* —all of these are at the cutting edge of this subject. Perhaps it's too much to expect you to keep up with them. Maybe so, but it's necessary that you know about them, and even look at them once in a while. That's not a particularly unrealistic hope to express to someone who will help carry the most important occupational burden of the years ahead.

Educational experimentation has frequently been the victim of professional buck passing. Teachers won't try out new methods and materials—many are still scared of the motion picture projector available to them—because "the principal won't let me." Administrators fail to encourage them because "the teachers won't do anything new anyway." The resulting stalemate and frustration keep educational progress in many communities on dead center. But not everywhere, fortunately, for there *are* teachers and administrators who have an inward push to move ahead. Besides, there are also external forces at work. As an example, James E. Allen, Jr., New

York State Commissioner of Education, appointed a Consultant on Educational Experimentation to work with superintendents and other school administrators around the state. Identification and evaluation of new practices, initiation and expansion of experimentation, and acceleration of activities that prove successful are part of his task.

However, the most vibrant force, the kick where it will do the most good, has been provided by the various foundations. There is "supreme merit in risking spirit in substantiation," said Robert Frost,[22] and the foundations are sharing the risk by providing the stimulant that seems to work best: money.

The most complete record of all comes from The Fund for the Advancement of Education of the Ford Foundation. It has given its attention to five major areas of American education:

The recruitment and preparation of teachers

The better use of teachers' time and talent (teacher aides, team teaching, educational television, programmed learning and teaching machines)

Extension to all of full educational opportunity commensurate with ability (Virgin Islands project, proposed by Hampton Institute, Virginia, 1953; Kentucky mountains project, Berea College, 1953; Puerto Rican study, New York; Great Cities School Improvement Program; National Merit Scholarship Corporation; Southern Project of the National Scholarship Service and Fund for Negro Students)

Improvements in curriculum (Portland, Reed College study; early admission to college programs; advanced placement programs)

Improvements in school management and financing (surveys to bring about specific improvements in the management of colleges and universities; studies to document the need for rising faculty salaries; creation of means for promoting greater private financing of higher education; establishment of norms for cost comparisons among institutions of various sizes)

Its emphasis is on relatively untested activities rather than on the sure thing, no matter how worthy, and it has kept hands off projects that rightfully belong within regular institutional budgets. Its major purpose is to support ideas "that hold some promise of helping the distressed educational system meet the manifest needs of modern society more effectively."[23] In its fiscal year of 1961, the Ford Founda-

[22] In a speech at Arizona State University, May, 1958.
[23] Fund for the Advancement of Education, *Decade of Experiment*, New York, The Fund, 1961, p. 16.

tion as a whole spent $161 million with the major stress on education.

In connection with the recruitment and preparation of teachers, the Fund has attempted to make its greatest impact. An example is the emphasis it has put on fifth-year programs in teacher preparation.

Through its projects and publications the Fund has tried to answer questions like these: What kinds of schools does the United States need? What should they do? What are the facts in the really important issues in education? Its grants, conferences, workshops, and fellowships have all helped provide answers. So have the original National Citizens Commission for the Public Schools, the monthly supplement in the *Saturday Review* called "Education in America," and Mortimer Adler's Institute for Philosophical Research.

The Fund's bibliography includes these publications:

Bridging the Gap between School and College 1953
Encouraging the Excellent by Elizabeth Paschall, 1960
New Directions in Teacher Education by Paul Woodring, 1957
Schools for Tomorrow: An Educator's Blueprint by Alexander J. Stoddard, 1957
Teachers for Tomorrow 1955
Teaching by Television 1961
Teaching Salaries Then and Now 1955
They Went to College Early 1957
Tomorrow's Professors by John S. Diekhoff, 1959
White and Negro Schools in the South: An Analysis of Biracial Education by Truman M. Pierce *et al.*, New York, Prentice-Hall, Inc., 1955.

The Fund for the Advancement of Education is far from being alone. Other family fortunes have also been put to work for education. The Rockefeller Foundation spent $32,833,971 in 1960 for projects as varied as a center for Tibetan studies at the University of Washington, graduate study in the Faculty of Agriculture at the University of Khartoum in the Sudan, and workshops in Indian art at the University of Arizona. Carnegie fellowships have been set up for selected liberal arts graduates in order to attract some of the most able ones into teaching. Fellowships from the John Hay Whitney Foundation are aimed primarily at high school teachers and school administrators, encouraging them to broaden their backgrounds in the humanities.

An integral part of the whole professional improvement picture are (1) the National Science Foundation's institutes for high school and college teachers of science and mathematics; (2) the foreign language and guidance institute, loan, and fellowship programs for present and future teachers provided under the National Defense Education Act; and (3) the Woodrow Wilson National Fellowship Foundation which financially encourages graduate study in preparation for college teaching.

Academically poor natural science students have a better chance for financial support in graduate study than do superior students in the social sciences and humanities. But that is just a sign of the times, and always subject to change.

PROFESSIONAL PROBLEMS
OF THE FUTURE TEACHER

Becoming and being a professional person requires the hurdling of countless obstacles, the maturing of traits you already have in embryo form, and the development of some that you never seem to have had in the first place. Frustration, dissatisfaction, and a gloomy outlook are all, strangely enough, the launching pad into a successful teaching career. Oscar Wilde once wrote that "discontent is the first step in the progress of a man or of a nation." If that is true, then no one in any professional field is in for quite as much progress as new teachers! Some of you will be as happy as larks, of course, but the complaints of many others might accumulate uncomfortably. The major reason sometimes rests squarely with those of us who preceded you; we have frequently failed to see the classroom, school, and community through your eyes.

No complicated statistical survey is necessary to determine the problems of the young teacher. Just ask a question, and you find out what the beginning teacher *feels* is the main difficulty, which is close enough to the truth for our purposes here. First, let's list some of the problems most often mentioned. You'll no doubt find one or more that hit home for you as you anticipate your entry into professional life. We'll cling to the hope that you won't find more than one or two. On the list may be some you feel you can solve, partially or fully yourself. There will be others alleviated by persons, printed materials, and resources you consult. Time will take care of a few. But there may be some left which when matched with a particular personality are incapable of solution. They can add up to the tragedy of a human being (plus his family) and a loss to the teaching profession.

Here are some as new teachers have actually expressed them. They are not in any order of importance; if one will fit you, it obviously belongs at the top of your list, regardless of where others may place it. And don't some of them tell a great deal more about the individual speaking than they do about our profession?

That back-biting gossiping! I thought teachers were different; maybe that was expecting them to be more than human.

I can't take the rigidity of the curriculum. It keeps me from being as creative as I want to be. It even keeps the children from learning as fast as they should.

So where can I meet a man? It's too strictly a female field!

My only problem is discipline. What little monsters they can be! Parents say they have a tough time with 1 or 2 and expect me to act like an angel with 35!

Where is a person supposed to find a decent place to live in this town? The only livable places are too expensive; the only inexpensive ones are holes.

There's nothing to do here after school hours. My records are always kept right up to the minute because the recreational opportunities are just plain nil.

Sure, we have a supervisor and a principal and a lot of people around with lots of experience. But who can get to see them? It's almost like Macy's with everything marked down to 98 cents!

I know I was hired to teach, but I've never known any more than that about my job. I want to be left alone, of course, but not that much alone.

We're supposed to set examples of broadmindedness, acceptance of differences, and the most literate and educated type of understanding. But I certainly don't find it in *this* school.

I want to be part of the school scene, but because I'm a new teacher I'm left out. Where's the "team" they talked about?

If I only knew how to get started! After that I wouldn't face any real problems, but what to do that first week is my worry.

So they give me a folder for each kid, with the biggest bunch of subjective claptrap and indecipherable test results you ever saw. A lot of good all that stuff does!

My class has I.Q.s from 63 to 147, one who can't see, another who can't hear, a quiet little guy who never says anything to anybody, a pale little girl who has *petit mal* seizures—and where in my teacher preparation did I find out about all of *them?*

When I came to apply I asked for work. I know that. But I didn't expect to have to work nights to keep up with reports. When am I supposed to do the ironing, clean the house, make dinner, and buy groceries?

The theories I learned! How I wish they'd fit!

They put me in front of the toughest class in the toughest school. Why don't they place their experienced teachers in classes like these? As soon as I can apply for a transfer I will; let them find another sucker for this room.

I'd do a better job in math and science if I liked them, but I don't find them at all interesting. So my children are being penalized as I probably was by teachers who just couldn't care less.

And there were many many more, sometimes stated very cryptically ("It's just not for me"), sometimes sadly ("If I only didn't have to worry about money"), sometimes hopefully ("Nothing wrong that time won't correct"). Seldom is a problem expressed that can't be solved by someone, some book, some bit of advice, or some thoughtful reasoning.

When new teachers were asked in a survey for one-sentence suggestions for you who are about to enter the profession, the answers came speedily. A lot of hope and humor permeated their recommendations.

Realize no job is perfect.
Adapt to the idea that money isn't everything.
Learn the school policies and adjust to them—at first, anyway.
Try out new ideas as much as you can, but be ready to explain objectives and procedures to doubters.
Attempt to find a school where the philosophy is similar to yours.
Remember the "what" and "how," but especially the "why" of education.
Keep your eye on teachers you consider to be successful.
Make every effort to know each student, *really* know him.
Don't get emotionally involved in children's problems.
Keep your sense of humor.
Establish pleasant relationships with parents and community.
Don't be timid about asking questions.
Realize it's a dull routine only if you let it become one.
Learn from your failures, but don't brood over them.

Stay out of school politics as much as possible.
Get married.
Use your college preparation as a guide.
Don't gripe, belittle, or gossip—at least not too much!
Know your materials.
Keep on living, laughing, reading, learning, enjoying.
Give it a fair chance—but then if you don't like it, do the school and the children a favor by getting out.
Don't expect a "thank you" every time you do something.
Realize it can be the most rewarding job in the world.

Problems and their answers are personal things—involved, intense, intimate. No one should be so presumptuous as to tell you what to do about them. But it helps to expose and share them early in the game, as you anticipate your professional goals. With that idea in mind, maybe we can profitably single out a few of the most obvious examples for you to think about. Feelings of inferiority, home pressures, theory versus practice, and democracy in the classroom are all discussed below.

Sometimes the requirements of the work accumulate and bear down on an individual so quickly (especially during the crucial first year) that you may feel the decision to go into teaching was ill-advised. It may seem to you it all adds up to a kind of numbing effect, and perhaps you should have chosen, instead, the most routine, repetitive kind of work you could find—operating an elevator, for example. Although in some instances the latter, or something like it, really *may* have been a more appropriate choice, it'd be a rare case for college graduates who have successfully completed at least an undergraduate program. Apparently you've already demonstrated your scholastic ability, success in adapting to new situations, and aptitude for getting along with others. Your teaching situation will call for new adjustments, and they may come more slowly than you had anticipated. But they *will* come.

Did you ever see the cartoon of the lady with three arms, one holding a baby, the second washing clothes, and the third ironing? Her husband has just come home and is saying, "How about something to eat?" She replies plaintively, "But dear, you can *see* I only have three hands!" So it sometimes seems to new teachers, especially the married ones. The number of working wives has been on the increase, and the need arises to ask some pertinent questions, which have to be answered before the family splits up over too much pressure on one of its members:

Is it necessary that you work, or are you doing so because of the pin money, new car, or new house routine? In other words, how important is this job to you financially?

Are you teaching because you feel very strongly the need for teachers, for *good* teachers, and you want to help alleviate the shortage?

What about your children at home—are their basic needs for the three A's of achievement, acceptance, and affection being met?

Do you and your husband have enough understanding in common so that you can share the home as well as the money-making responsibilities?

Can you get some other help around the house, either from your older children or from someone who can come in once or more a week to lighten your burden? Can you afford to pay for the latter kind of help?

These are merely questions for discussion, but the answers can be quiet revealing in nailing the importance of the future job for you and for your family. Even if all of these questions are answered satisfactorily, the real problem may not be solved if the cause is a disorganized mind. If running a house requires an orderly thought process to accomplish all the tasks of cleaning, shopping, cooking, washing, and the rest, then it obviously becomes even more necessary when the work is doubled. A disorganized person can confuse two jobs more easily than she can one, and if her husband is disorderly too and fails to care about the mess in which they both live that doesn't make the situation any more palatable—not to the children whose education is in the hands of this erratic individual.

Now this isn't a hopeless situation about which we're talking. Thousands of mothers and wives who teach give eloquent evidence that it can be done successfully, even adding immeasurably to the rich environment at home and school because of the dual responsibilities. But at least two steps are necessary: (1) Realize it's complicated to run two "homes" well, that the pitfalls are many. (2) Realize that the setting up of a "priority list" and a weekly "block schedule" can come in very handy.

If you've ever worked with (or are) a college student in academic trouble because of too many activities, you'll readily understand how valuable the priority list and block schedule can be. So many students (and they are frequently very capable ones) overload themselves with school and social activities, all desirable, important, and of some value to their maturation. There's one simple fact of life that gets in the way, however: The day is just so long, and despite all the advances in science, it can't be expanded. Teaching wives and mothers face an identical problem. So what has a priority? What needs to be done first? You can make out your list, plot it into a time schedule, and find that sometimes you're blacking in the same hour over and over again. That means the list has to be trimmed somewhere; doesn't it? Hours for sleeping have to be cut, or television watching, or dish washing—or maybe even the job of teaching school. Perhaps a half-day teaching position in a school on split sessions or a nursery-school job is the answer.

When a distinction is made between what one *must* do and what one would *like* to do if there is time, then a sound weekly schedule might evolve. Until that time a lot of us continue to run the rat race of the confused or the greedy, becoming more involved, frustrated, and hard to live with. You will know the result, and so will your husband. So will the children you're trying to teach—and after all, if they lose, then what is gained from all the grief you may bring to yourself by trying to carry too heavy a load?

Another problem you may face is the presumed conflict of theory and practice. It is epitomized by the story about a man who had a trained flea. He put it in the palm of one hand, and said, "Jump!" The flea obeyed promptly by jumping into the other outstretched palm. "Jump!" and he jumped back. Back and forth he flew as the man called the command. "Now I want to show you something," said the trainer. "I'll remove the hind legs, and then give the command again." He did both things, but the flea no longer jumped. "My conclusion? Only this: Removing the hind legs of a flea interferes with its hearing acuity!"

That was his theory, but was it really true in practice? Or was there something wrong with his theory in the first place? In the latter question is posed the crux of the whole issue. If it's really a *good* theory, it will work in practice; not necessarily in every instance, but in the majority of cases anyway. The conflict is apparent more than it is real. Actually it's merely a convenient device to combat or reject theories we may not like. It's about as convenient as using the debating device of name-calling, pegging the other fellow as being "unrealistic" or "superficial," whether or not he is.

As a new teacher you will have theories and ideas that sound good to you. They are backed up by both common sense and research. It is foolish for you to accept at full value every between-you-and-me-word-to-the-wise from experienced teachers and administrators as a substitute for ideals and convincing explanations of how children learn. Listen, of course. Evaluate what you hear. But don't dismiss your own new, creative ideas because they are lumped by others into the basket of "fuzzy" or "impractical" theories. The labels attached don't necessarily make them so.

Our theories related to feeding of babies (demand versus schedule) and toilet training have changed. So have our theories related to educational practices, but you're entitled to keep yours until *you* decide otherwise. Besides, if they work out well for you in practice, then maybe that's a good reason for you to retain them as part of your own "tools of the trade."

You may have fondly cherished theories, for example, related to respect for human beings, or more specifically based on democracy in the classroom. Unrealistically you may be intent on carrying them to an extreme, as a group of first-graders once did. They were discussing their pet hamster, and one of them brought up the sex question, saying you could tell by the length of its hair. A second insisted that eye color was the determining factor. The teacher was about to change the whole subject when a third youngster proudly stated, "I know what we can do! Let's vote on it!"

Democracy in the classroom has to be very carefully understood, and based on the ability of the children to determine and regulate their environment. But behind our discussion of this subject must be the belief that (1) the teacher is basically responsible for the learning that takes place, (2) the teacher has the most to contribute on the basis of his knowledge, experience, and maturity, and (3) although children may enjoy making decisions, they enjoy even more receiving the guidance of a well-qualified adult who helps them set limits on their activities.

Pupil-teacher planning with the teacher in the driver's seat can be fertile territory for the development of future adults who will be able to think for themselves, evaluate critically what they hear and read, and become active, responsible members of a democracy. Aren't these among our major educational objectives?

"Anyone who expects to do good," said Albert Schweitzer, "must not expect people to roll stones out of his way, but must accept his lot calmly if they even roll a few more into it." Perhaps it will sometimes seem to you as though the stone-rollers ought to take a rest, give teachers a chance to catch up.

But if you help one child over a learning hump, you will know it was worth it, worth all the work and worry. It generally doesn't take new teachers long to come to that conclusion. When children (particularly those from whom you least expect it) get through the first preprimer, learn to use the dictionary, can explain what fractions or decimals are, enjoy surprising you with an interpretation of a scientific discovery or historical event, show any bit of accomplishment, it is the thrill above all others in teaching. This profession is sometimes tough and without reward, but when the dividends *do* come, they constitute a gift beyond comparison. For now you've brought a human being closer to his capacity, helped him learn, and can anyone do more than that?

In her little book, *The Arts in the Classroom,* Natalie Cole says, "When children are engaged in what they love to do, the barriers are down. The teacher has access to the child within." She goes on to talk about freeing children from fears and tensions, building up faith and confidence, enriching experiences, and taking care of mechanics so that spontaneity doesn't suffer. What may seem to be obvious and easy for an experienced teacher frequently comes only through laborious and intricate channels for the newcomer. However, because help is available just for the asking, the task that appears so difficult in anticipation takes on manageable dimensions. Even the goals Mrs. Cole so eloquently sets up seem completely attainable.

Perhaps all of the following sources won't be available to you, but some of them will be. Identify them, cement your relationships with them, realize what they can do for you and you for them; their importance cannot be overestimated.

The administrative staff: superintendent's office, principal's office, assistants in both places, the school board, *and* the very important secretaries and other administrative office personnel

Supervisors: grade level supervisors, subject area supervisors

Helping teachers: those assigned to work with new teachers, those assigned to work in particular problem areas

Consultants and special teachers: art, music, home economics, physical education, industrial arts, academic fields, exceptional children

Special services: psychological services, reading clinic, audio-visual aids, radio-television, social workers, home visitors, librarians, medical and nursing services, guidance counselors

Co-workers on the teaching staff: custodial staff, adult safety patrol, transportation

The children themselves

Their parents

People in the community

Others known to you as you start looking around your school and community

All of these people may not agree on the best way of creating the school they want, but their goals are strikingly similar, even for the children. The more mature ones are quite outspoken in their hopes for a sound education in the hands of competent and professional teachers and administrators. We could spend a lot of time arguing the point of who is on "top": the superintendent, the school board, the people themselves, and so on. But the real question is something like this: To whom will *you* be responsible? Who will send you directives, evaluate your work, approve your request for a leave or for books and supplies? Although your answers may vary from situation to situation, it's vital that you know who it is, for the smooth running of any classroom depends on a teacher who knows the channels for getting something done and who has established a good working relationship with the people in those channels.

Generally your school principal will be the most important person to you in the administrative setup. In a small system you may have many contacts with the superintendent, but more frequently the principal will be the one most directly concerned in helping you do your job well. It would be a rarity if a person in that position did not understand just about every difficulty you encounter as you adjust to the role of the teacher. Having been a teacher himself and knowing many others who have gone through the initial problems, he usually will see things as you see them and welcome your questions (and suggestions too, but perhaps more so *after* you've been teaching a little while). He may visit your class at intervals, and

your reaction will depend entirely on the relationship you've established with each other. Those visits can be friendly, informal, and
helpful. Or they may be tension-provoking and disruptive. Until you
know otherwise, why not assume they'll be in the former category?
When one occurs, just go on with your program without quick shifts
or fancy adjustments. Continue to feel that the children come first,
and proceed as you were.

Just as your children, at school and in your own family as well,
study you almost as much as they seem to study their subject, so it
will pay for you to know something about your administrative head.
Of what does *he* most approve educationally? What are his educational pet peeves? What is his professional background? It may do no
harm at all to find out, as you go along, what his hobbies are, what
family members he has, and the professional organizations and
publications that are part of his career. No deliberate effort need
be made to pick up these details; you may accumulate them effortlessly. The objective in mentioning them is to alert you to a possibility that may aid you in getting help toward doing the best job
you possibly can.

Administrative personalities obviously differ as much as do those
of people in any occupation. Their ideas may come to you in clear-
cut, specific directives, in more general written or oral statements, or
in indirect suggestions handed out through intermediaries. In whatever form they reach you it's important for you to get the message.
The various titles, functions, and services of supervisors, consultants,
and helping teachers will depend largely on funds available for
such assistance and the basic school philosophy toward auxiliary
personnel aids to the teaching staff. The trend is toward more help,
more understanding of the bigger job teachers face these days, and
more awareness of how to keep supervision and service free from the
administrative tasks of ratings, salaries, and promotions.

From one or more of the persons mentioned earlier will come the
experienced shoulder to lean on when you're upset by an assignment
that nobody else wants, by the heavy load of reports and records, by
a teacher clique, tale carrier, chronic griper, or by a scanty pay check
that won't quite cover a new suit or dress (or food for the next 14
days). Perhaps by title you'll locate the person who can help carry
burdens; but it isn't at all unusual for the librarian or nurse or bus

driver or physical-education teacher to be the trouble sharer, based more on a receptive personality than on a descriptive job title.

It's vital to recognize that as a teacher you will not be a trained psychologist, psychiatrist, speech therapist, or other specialist. You won't be an educational "know-it-all." Realize your limitations, and through such recognition avoid some of the frustrations that will inevitably result if you try to be all things to all people.

Another note is appropriate about the job objective of the supervisor. It is *not* to stand in judgment, find fault, criticize unconstructively, or lead to a "war" based on a personality conflict or a professional difference of opinion. It *does* have the same purpose that every good administrator and teacher shares: to get the best teaching and learning accomplished, and to use the techniques of cooperation and understanding to reach that goal. Taking suggestions in the spirit in which they are offered (and let's hope you're lucky enough for that spirit to be one of friendly persuasion and helpfulness) will be vital for you, despite any warnings or fears that may have been instilled in you in advance. Just as you may some day run into a principal who long ago forgot the problems in the classroom, you may be saddled with a supervisor equally oblivious to your difficulties, but the odds are on your side.

The main reason for losing one job or not liking another may have nothing at all to do with competence; there's more of a chance that it will result from not getting along with people. What are a few of the hints for being liked and wanted and needed? One thing is certainly true: they do *not* include sticky subservience or indiscriminate imitation. A sound substitute for foolish imitation would be a blending of the following characteristics:

Be willing to talk more than "shop." Hobbies, movies, clothes, vacations and anything else in which you're interested are appropriate. But betraying a child's confidence, adding to school or community gossip, and expressing concern about already formed teachers' cliques are the types of things to avoid.

Ask for help if you really want it or need it. Being consulted is flattering, but not if asking questions is in the realm of what they used to (or may still) refer to in the Army as "sharp-shooting"—tossing out questions to impress an instructor or audience rather than with the objective of receiving an answer.

Request assistance of the engineering or custodial staff. A little common sense will tell you that the least effective way to get heat in the room, waste baskets emptied, windows shined, lights lit, and shades fixed is to give orders, demand service, or expect unreasonable speed. Just try it and see how far you'll get!

Express interest without being competitive; show eagerness to learn without undue aggressiveness; be friendly without clinging to one who says the first kind word. The middle ground between "going it alone" and tapping the rich human resources in the school is a sensible goal to have in mind.

A few pitfalls are possible in relationships with the experienced teachers, however, who may feel threatened because children sometimes confide in the newer teachers more readily, or resent youth and starry eyed dreams regarding our profession, or are concerned over the easier adjustments of the new ones when memory tells them their own were unforgettably rough. You may have to discount their tagging a child as "bad," "unmanageable," or "disagreeable" as you seek the reasons *behind* the labels, and they may not like your dismissing their "analysis." They may not approve of your referring to their contemplated field visit to a planetarium or zoo or museum as "fun" when they view it as a strict "learning experience" without any relationship to enjoyment. Or they may not like your picking up an overwhelming interest in planets and satellites when the course of study "specifically states we will study them in *my* grade, *not* in yours."

But don't let all of that bother you too much. For each one like that you'll find at least ten who seem to attract children like bees to honey, who welcome your dreams and plans for teaching, smile warmly over the ease with which you're adjusting, and seek with you the answers behind what makes Jimmy such a terror in the classroom. Whatever traits you new teachers have they have too, except perhaps theirs are a little mellowed or accentuated by time. So maybe now you'll agree that no man (or woman) in teaching is a lonely island. The bolstering up can come from many directions if you'll only look or ask or be at all receptive to the helping hands that are out toward you, eagerly hoping you'll let them assist whenever the going gets rough.

Although organizations, publications, research, and people can provide a great deal of information for you as a professional person, other sources are the laws of your state and country, and the professional rules under which you work. The latter may be in the realm of "rights" and "ethics," and not necessarily in legal opinions and court proceedings. For example, they may tell you that you *should* not break a contract rather than that you *cannot* do so. The contract that you sign will have two sides, of course, and your rights of employment are protected by it just as much as are the rights of the school district to the services of a potential employee. The rules of your position and its future may be stated in detail, or they may be in the less accessible regulations of your school board. Although they may not be on display anywhere, they should be available to you for the asking. Among the kinds of information of importance to you of a more-or-less legal nature are the following:

Duties of various individuals and groups
School financing and the record of the community toward it
Certification requirements—your present position and any you may be contemplating
Salary deductions: retirement, insurance
Sick leave; other kinds of leaves of absence
Tenure and (let's hope of little or no importance) grievance rules
State laws regarding textbook adoptions, religious exercises, and flag displays and activities

Another whole raft of legal facts are just as important to you as next week's pay check. They are in the area of income tax regulations, especially on the side of deductions. Each year during the few months before April 15, some of the professional journals run articles that carry hints of how you can save money on your annual tax. They also often have advertisements of recent books and pamphlets that can help you out. Of course, a competent accountant who keeps up with the latest rulings may be your best bet; but if your financial life is relatively uncluttered you will no doubt be able to handle the return yourself. The best advice is to take all deductions to which you are entitled, and the official instructions and inexpensive annual pamphlet from the Internal Revenue Service are designed to help you accomplish that goal. Because your allowances change every year or so, checking the regulations once doesn't do the job. It takes annual watching to save that elusive dollar that belongs to you.

CONCLUDING REMARKS

A few years ago Paul Woodring ably pointed out some important limitations on the professional responsibilities of the school. Any soundly professional person must realize that his power and strength can just go so far and no further. Woodring's list provides a great deal of consolation for future teachers. It includes items like these:

The school is not responsible for the total development of the child; that responsibility is shared with the home, the church, and the community, with its final resting place being with the parents.

In connection with health (both physical and mental), the school's responsibility is preventive and educational, not diagnostic and therapeutic.

Social reform and character development must be shared by the school with others.

All children cannot be educated in the "regular classroom." Exceptions include the educable and trainable mentally retarded and the seriously emotionally maladjusted.

The school is not set up to reform criminals or delinquents, although help toward prevention is among its many duties.[24]

Any teacher you speak to can enlighten you on the pressures and inappropriate detail that keep him from doing the kind of professional job he wants to and can do. But time too frequently runs out, and everyone can't be satisfied. So if choices have to be made, the satisfaction should accrue to the children, a satisfaction determined by the qualified teacher on the basis of what the children need and what is good for them.

Your growth into becoming a teacher begins early and lasts long. And whenever you close the door and face your children, the moment arrives when your resources and abilities combine to help you become a fully developed professional person. The time for being that person started long ago. If you are realistic, you will know that your preparation should continue until the day you close your classroom door for the very last time, from the outside.

[24] Woodring, *op. cit.*, pp. 140–141.

CHAPTER 6

A TIME FOR *Controversial Issues:*
Some of the Big Ones

Great fleas have little fleas upon their
    backs to bite 'em,
And little fleas have lesser fleas, and
    so ad infinitum,
And the great fleas themselves, in turn,
    have greater fleas to go on;
While these again have greater still,
    and greater still, and so on.[1]

Perhaps the persons who have written variations of this rhyme
have not had the education profession as their target. However,
many in this field have frequently been among the bitten or the
biting, related to the larger issues discussed in this chapter or the
smaller ones in the next. Many efforts have been made to identify
the major educational controversies of our day. Usually they come
up much later than the introductory courses in teacher preparation,
and it's sad that they are delayed so long. Here is where much of the
excitement in education is, and to bring it to the attention of
future teachers early in their preparation seems like a commonsense
approach.

To expose our differences rather than shelter the young college
students preparing to teach can help attract and hold them in a profession that desperately needs the brightest among them. Among
Cleveland Amory's "least favorite quotes" is this one: "the stressing
of both sides of a controversy only confuses the young and encourages them to make snap judgments based on insufficient evi-

[1] "Editor's Notebook," *NEA Journal,* February, 1961, p. 72.

dence. Until they are old enough to understand both sides of a question, they should be taught only the American side."[2]

Future teachers are old enough to serve their country militarily, sometimes considered old enough to vote, and it certainly is in the realm of reason for them to discuss seriously two (or more) sides of a situation, whether or not a national or other division is involved in the issue. The lists of such issues as they apply to education are long, deep, and involved. They have raised blood pressures by the thousands among parents, teachers, administrators and laymen, between and within groups. They attract rational, logical thinkers as well as irrational hotheads with axes to grind that are only superficially hidden, result in sound scholarly discussions as well as heated arguments, accusations, hurt feelings, and destroyed careers. They evolve in academic treatises, popularized editorials and newspaper features, and television documentaries. What are some of the subjects that have controversial overtones? In an address before a national conference of classroom teachers, Philip H. Phenix of Columbia University identified these twelve:

1. *Curriculum.* What should be taught in the public schools? Should we teach more, or less, mathematics, science, social studies, English, foreign language, health, art, driver training?

2. *Teaching methods.* How should instruction be organized? According to disciplines, or projects, or life situations? Should teachers teach by lectures, by discussions, by assigned readings, by teaching machines, by television, and in what proportions? Should classes be conducted with strict discipline or with maximum freedom for the students?

3. *Classification.* How should students be grouped? By age, by intellectual ability, by social maturity? Should we have a one-track or a multiple-track system? Should we have mixed groupings and comprehensive schools? What should be the criteria for promotion and graduation? What techniques should be used for evaluation reporting?

4. *Extra-curricular life.* What are the limits of school responsibility? Should the school engage in non-intellectual forms of instruction? What is the place of athletics, dramatics, clubs, student organizations, social affairs, and personal counseling in the life of the school?

5. *School finance.* How should education be financed? Do school boards and officials use tax monies efficiently and responsibly? Are the present systems of taxation fair to various groups of citizens?

[2] J. Evetts Haley quoted in the *Saturday Review,* November 4, 1961.

6. *Policy-making.* Who should control the schools—local boards or state and federal agencies? Who should be on the boards? What is the role of professional educators—administrators and teachers—in policy decisions? What place do parents, students, and citizens in general have in educational policy-making?

7. *Teaching as a profession.* Are teachers really professionals? What standards are applicable to them? Is this or that person qualified to be a teacher? How should teachers be prepared? Should teachers organize and bargain collectively?

8. *Communism.* What are the schools doing and what should they be doing about communism? Are they teaching it, either for information or for indoctrination, intentional or otherwise? Is this or that teacher a loyal American? How can loyalty be insured and disloyalty be detected and eliminated?

9. *Internationalism.* What should the schools do about the place of America in the world? What is the proper role of the schools in the national defense effort in the atomic age?

10. *Economics.* What is the responsibility of teachers toward our economic system? Should teachers advocate capitalism, or may they also teach socialistic ideas, or should they stay clear of any discussion of these matters?

11. *Segregation.* Was the 1954 Supreme Court decision on segregation in the public schools right? How, if at all, should desegregation be accomplished?

12. *Religion.* What should the public schools do about religion? Should they be entirely secular, or can they properly engage in some sorts of religious activity or instruction?[3]

In February, 1962, school administrators meeting in Atlantic City for their national convention trimmed their list of issues down to five of major importance: Federal aid; fall-out shelter policy; national standards; extension of public education to 14 years (junior colleges); national test programs.

A few years ago three men edited a book they called *The Great Debate: Our Schools in Crisis.*[4] After an introductory section of pros and cons (are the schools doing their job; mediocrity; John Dewey; "adjustment") it considered these as the larger areas needing discussion and decision: Neglect of fundamental subjects; the challenge of

[3] Philip H. Phenix, "How to Analyze and Evaluate Educational Controversies," *Arizona Teacher*, March, 1962, pp. 20–21, 29.

[4] C. Winfield Scott, Clyde M. Hill, and Hobert W. Burns (eds), *The Great Debate: Our Schools in Crisis.* Englewood Cliffs, N. J., Prentice-Hall, Inc., 1959.

Soviet education; do we do enough for the gifted child; are school buildings too fancy; can teacher training and certification practices be justified.

Although it may be more exciting to answer questions and dig into issues on an either-or, black-or-white basis (and incidentally, sell more books and be quoted more frequently), it is vital that we be more careful in our analysis. This bit of advice seems appropriate: "It is easy to mistake our prejudice for patriotism, our rationalization for reason, our littleness for logic, our theories for truth, and our fervor for fact."[5] One-sided presentations seem to have a special appeal for the naïve and ill-informed, for those who enjoy making up their minds without an adequately balanced presentation of facts. Criticism that is both warranted and constructive in its effort to further the aims and practices of education in the United States is far more acceptable to the thoughtful student of the school scene than are subtle schemes to undermine our confidence in school people and community support of education. However, this approach does not negate the advantages to all of objectivity rather than neutrality merely for its own sake, of one's taking a positive stand both within and outside of the school setting.

The over-all question is not whether our children are as well educated as they once were, but rather whether the education of each is as sound and complete as it *should* be. It is on the basis of this issue that our approach should be formulated for the topics under discussion in this chapter and the next one. Phenix proposed some valuable and systematic guidelines when he suggested this logical approach to "matters in controversy":

1. Semantic analysis. Language is full of ambiguity. Misunderstandings arise when the same word is used without warning in different senses.

2. Definition of positions. The matters in dispute should be clearly defined. Precisely what is asserted by both sides? Part of the logic of controversy is to secure definite statements of the positions being advanced by both sides.

3. Separation of problems. It is impossible to analyze everything at once. The secret of intellectual progress is "divide and conquer." Many controversies are compounded of a variety of components which need to be attacked one by one.

[5] William Arthur Ward, *Phi Delta Kappan*, November, 1961, p. 91.

4. Sharpening the issues. The good analyst of controversies knows how to put his finger on the key matters at issue. What are the fundamental convictions upon which a whole argument rests? What is essential and what is merely supportive or auxiliary to the main contentions?

5. Schematizing the argument. Every argument includes certain premises, from which conclusions are inferred. The defense of any assertion requires the introduction of evidence.

6. Checking the validity of inferences. After the argument has been set forth, the final step in logical analysis is to check the validity of the inferences drawn.[6]

Sometimes in our discussions of controversial issues we fail to utilize more than a superficial approach. Skimming along the surface, we might neglect the basic problems, the real causes, the power structure in which policies are made. Obviously, the issues discussed below can be only a few of the ones already listed as important to the educational picture. Omissions will be apparent to you; some of your most enjoyable class discussions and maybe even scholarly arguments will evolve from topics not touched on here, but which you consider basic to the future of education.

FEDERAL AID TO EDUCATION

Gluyas Williams, the cartoonist of "Suburban Heights" fame, once wrote a book about commuters called *Daily Except Sunday*. In it he had a cartoon that showed a line of people walking through a commuters' train with the caption "Where did they come from? Where are they going?" So it seems to many who have heard and read the repetitive articles and speeches on the topic called federal aid, control, support, interference, or assistance, depending on one's point of view. "When did it begin? When will it end?" There is a mass of biased and not very much objective information and discussion of the subject; the basic pros and cons are itemized below.

In favor of federal aid or support
1. The provision of public education is in part a federal responsibility because our form of government and national survival depend upon the adequate education of our entire population.

6 Phenix, *op. cit.*, p. 20.

2. The federal government is the only agency able to bring about nation-wide provisions of necessary facilities and services.

3. The principles of federal action and appropriations are firmly established by a long history of laws and federal educational activities.

4. There is a great and increasing need for further federal support related to school construction, teachers' salaries, and operating expenses.

5. A program of federal assistance can help reduce the larger differences in educational opportunities among and within the states.

6. The partial discharge of the federal responsibility in education through financial aid to the states is feasible and can be effective.

Against federal aid or support

1. There is no need for aid from the federal government; communities and states are adequately meeting the educational needs of their populations.

2. Federal aid leads to federal control and interference; schools should be controlled entirely by local persons.

3. According to the Constitution and tradition, education is a state, local, and private matter.

4. To involve the federal government in education would lead to unsound fiscal practice.

5. Federal involvement may interfere with our fundamental practice of separation of church and state.

6. Our system of federal, state, and local taxation can be revised to the extent necessary to provide adequate funds for public education from state and local sources.

A revealing series of attitudes was expressed in congressional hearings conducted during the spring of 1961. Some of the representative comments quoted below are certainly not unexpected when you note the affiliations of these persons at the time of their remarks.

Abraham Ribicoff, Secretary of Health, Education, and Welfare:

Our future requires that appropriate educational opportunities be freely available to all children and youth no matter what their background, circumstance, or place of residence. We have made substantial progress toward meeting this goal, but rising enrollments and increasing costs have placed great pressure upon the States and local school districts. . . . Another problem confronting many a school district is the great mobility of our population. Each year more than 5 million people move from one State to another. Today's resident of a high-income State with a better-than-average school system may well find tomorrow that his children must attend a less-than-average school in a low-income State. Moreover, the

States exhibit varying degrees of ability to support education. . . . The next decade holds no promise of lessened impact upon our resources available for support of education.

John B. Swainson, governor of Michigan:

It has become increasingly evident to us in Michigan that the problems confronting education in 1961 must be attacked on all three levels of government. Only by a total mobilization of our Nation's resources can we meet the current and future demands on education. ·

Peter T. Schoemann, vice president, AFL-CIO:

The real problem facing America today, it seems to us, is whether the National Government is playing its fair part in support of education. We think it is not; we urge that it should.

Harley L. Lutz, government finance consultant, National Association of Manufacturers:

(1) Public education is not a Federal responsibility. The sphere of Federal services and functions should be limited to those matters which can be handled only by the National Government. (2) There is no "crisis" in education, present or impending, that would justify assumption by the Federal Government of responsibility for a service completely outside the area of its truly national tasks; (3) The Federal Government is in a precarious financial situation . . . (4) Federal support inevitably leads to Federal control and this control will distort and devitalize the educative process. (5) Federal money cannot buy excellence in learning.

K. Brantley Watson, speaking for the Chamber of Commerce of the United States:

The people of the United States have proved that they are more than equal to the challenge to meet their educational needs via local and community action. Their efforts have made it possible for us to boast, proudly, that more Americans receive a better education, are taught by better teachers and do their learning in better facilities than is possible in any nation on earth. We conclude then with the contention that grant-in-aid legislation . . . is not only unnecessary, but might slow down local and State action upon which needed improvements in the quality of education actually depends.

W. W. Hill, Jr., speaking for Member State Chambers of the Council of State Chambers of Commerce:

Federal control will follow Federal aid just as surely as night follows day, but it may not be apparent until the schools are so dependent on Federal support that they cannot conveniently relinquish what appears to be a free subsidy.

In addition to individuals, representing their own or their organizational points of view, many professional and other groups have clearly expressed their feelings on this subject. The National Council of Independent Schools polled its members, who overwhelmingly (88 percent) opposed federal grants to private schools and federal loans to private schools (65 percent); they were strongly (74 percent) in favor of tax relief for those paying tuition, however. Going on record approving federal financial assistance are the following: National Conference on Higher Education (representing college and university leadership); Phi Delta Kappa; President's Commission on National Goals; American Council on Education. Showing discrimination on various phases of the issue is the National Schools Boards Association: No general federal aid to education (55.2 percent); support of the National Defense Education Act (62 percent); assistance to federally impacted areas (69 percent); own school districts cannot manage with funds from presently available sources (22 percent).

This subject is not one that can be decided now or in the near future. Based on the question "Should the federal government step into the education picture?" one important fact must be stated: The federal government is in education, and has been for a long time. No one can dispute that fact. A brief history of the highlights in federal aid to education shows the following:

The Survey Ordinance of 1785 provided that, from the public lands west of the thirteen colonies, one lot in every township should be dedicated to the maintenance of public schools.

The Northwest Ordinance of 1787 declared that "schools and the means of education shall be forever encouraged."

The Morrill Act of July 2, 1862, set aside public land for each State to maintain at least one college for promoting "the liberal and practical education of the industrial classes"—the basis of state colleges and universities, 68 of which now benefit from federal funds.

The Vocational Education Act of 1917 (the Smith-Hughes Act) was the first step in a long program of Federal assistance to vocational education of less-than-college grade.

The G.I. Bills for World War II and Korean War veterans both bestowed educational benefits.

Public Laws 815 and 874 by the 81st Congress, September 1950, provided funds to help individual school districts build and operate schools for the children of people connected with Federal activity.

The National Defense Education Act, September 1958, authorized more than a billion dollars for a dozen separate programs of assistance to schools, colleges, and students.

Washington stated in his first annual address to Congress: ". . . there is nothing more deserving your patronage than the promotion of science and literature . . . whether this desirable object will be best promoted by affording aids to seminaries of learning already established, by the institution of a national university, or by any other expedients will be well worthy of a place in the deliberations of the Legislature." Hamilton observed that whatever concerned the general interests of learning was within the federal jurisdiction "as far as regards an application of money." Jefferson declared that Congress could appropriate public lands for the support of education, and he proposed a tariff on imports for "public improvement" including education. All three men either stated or implied that the "general welfare" clause of the Constitution sanctioned federal financial aid to education.

In addition to the seven major federal types of assistance cited above, the following should also be noted:

Hatch Act, 1887: experiment stations in agricultural colleges
Smith-Lever Act, 1914: instruction in agriculture and home economics
George-Deen Act, 1936: education in distributive occupations
George-Reed Act, 1929; George-Ellzey Act, 1934; George-Barden Act, 1946; all in vocational education
Support of the American Printing House for the Blind
Columbia Institution for the Deaf
Howard University
Education of Indians
Federally maintained schools in Panama Canal Zone and other localities
National School Lunch Act

Of all the examples of federal aid now in existence, none is more vivid than the story of the land-grant colleges which celebrated its one-hundredth anniversary in 1962. It began with the signing of the Morrill Act by Abraham Lincoln on July 2, 1862, in the midst of a heavy load of military decisions and tragedy. It was "An Act donating public lands to the several states and Territories which may provide colleges for the benefit of agriculture and the mechanic arts. . . ." It granted each state 30,000 acres of federally owned land for each of its members of Congress. All states and Puerto Rico have one or more institutions of higher learning under the Act, from which 25 of the 42 living American winners of the Nobel prize earned at least one degree. To it are also attributed the birth of the R.O.T.C., the awarding of nearly 40 percent of Ph.D.s in all disciplines, more than half of all engineering doctorates, and the enrollment of 600,000 students a year (one-fifth of our total college and university enrollment).

On the joint topic of federal aid and the land-grant colleges, President Edward D. Eddy, Jr. of Chatham College said in an address at West Virginia University, a land-grant institution:

Those who continue to claim that federal aid means federal interference have not studied their history well. In the past one hundred years, there has not been a single instance of a serious attempt by a federal bureaucracy to dictate policy in opposition to state determination. . . . One wishes that the same could be said of the state governments in their relationship with the colleges. The history here is not as tidy. Time and again the individual land-grant colleges have had to fight off political interference on the part of a state legislature or a less-than-highly-motivated governor.

The National Advisory Committee on Education appointed by President Hoover (1931), the Advisory Committee on Education appointed by President Roosevelt (1939), and the Educational Policies Commission (1939) all agreed that federal activities in education throughout the history of our country were extensive and would no doubt continue. The latter drew attention to the issue in this way: "The Federal Government has been the founder of the public school systems in most of the States, and its influence on educational development has been both positive and widespread." President Hoover's Committee reported finding 14 warrants in the Constitution for federal activities in education, none authorizing control over state and local school systems.

The political support for federal assistance has traveled various routes, with chief advocacy by Republicans in the 1870s and 1880s and support by one large segment of the Democrats in the 1950s and

1960s. Although the current discussion by some politicians and laymen seems to be *whether* we should have federal aid, the more accurate approach on the basis of our history should be *how much* and under what limitations. In monetary terms, how large has the federal involvement been in recent years? The U.S. Office of Education estimated that during 1961 the states used approximately $518 million in federal funds administered through the Department of Health, Education, and Welfare. The most extensive part related to the National Defense Education Act of 1958 (extended to continue at least until 1964) in areas like mathematics, science, languages, guidance, graduate fellowships, new educational media, and student loans. The National School Lunch Act serves food to more than 14 million children; the cost in federal cash assistance is $94 million; but $610 million comes from the children, $130 million worth of food from the Department of Agriculture, and $250 million in state and local contributions. In all, the federal government is involved in almost 100 broadly defined educational programs administered by 20 different departments and agencies, but primarily by (1) Department of Health, Education, and Welfare; (2) Veterans Administration; (3) Department of Agriculture; and (4) Department of Defense.

Whether funds come from federal, state, or local funds, or a combination of two or three of them, there has been a certain amount of agreement on some of the needs that must be met, needs related to *scholarships, tax equalization, population mobility,* and *illiteracy:*

To make educational opportunity effectively equal there must be a broad scholarship program that reaches down into the high school and extends through college and graduate school. . . . The number of scholarships must be large enough to care for some 5 per cent of the boys and girls of high-school age.[7]

The public lower schools and high schools are almost wholly supported from *local taxes on real and personal property.* These taxes in a super-industrialized country like our own, where income depends on more than real-estate investment, are not and cannot be productive of enough revenue to run the schools. In consequence, the public schools are overcrowded and their buildings often in bad repair, the teachers grossly underpaid, the

[7] W. Lloyd Warner, Robert J. Havighurst, and Martin B. Loeb, *Who Shall Be Educated?* New York, Harper & Row, Publishers, Inc., 1944, p. 165.

whole enterprise limping financially. Hence there is more and more demand for *subsidies from the Federal Treasury,* which can raise the necessary
money by way of income taxes, profits taxes, corporation taxes, and so on.[8]

We have a mobile population. The forms of wealth have changed to the
extent that the federal government is the only unit that can properly tax
them at the source. Wealth is mobile; it can originate in one state as raw
material, be processed in another, and sold in all states. The profit from
such transactions may be located in a favored state, either in terms of
property wealth—or stocks and bonds. In any event, the corn grown in
Iowa, the timber of Washington, the coal of Pennsylvania, the iron ore of
Minnesota, and the oil of the southwest, are processed, shipped, and used
in all states. The fruits of national wealth should go to all our citizens, who
by their purchases are the creators of the wealth.[9]

. . . the responsibilities that confront the nation—not only for its own
future but for the future of the free world—to raise and maintain large
armed forces and at the same time to be as productive as possible in raising
food and in manufacturing goods. It is beyond argument that the Armed
Forces were handicapped in the scale and speed of their mobilization of
manpower in World War II by being forced to make a series of special
adjustments to cope with the very large numbers of illiterate and poorly
educated persons in the draft-eligible ages. . . . What, then, are the options
that face the country with respect to the elimination of illiteracy at the
source—among those now of school age and those who will come of school
age in the future?[10]

Among the most active barriers to federal aid is the place of
church-related and other non-public schools in the issue. The con-
stitutionality of assistance to private schools, freedom of parents to
educate their children where they want to, and church-and-state
separation are all heated aspects of the problem.[11] Another barrier,
of course, is in the realm of statistics. Whose are used? How are they
interpreted? Do they show how good we are or how much we need?
Do we go back to original sources, or do we quote what somebody

[8] Bernard Iddings Bell, *Crisis in Education,* New York, McGraw-Hill Book
Company, Inc., 1949, p. 192.

[9] Maurice J. Thomas, *The Concern of All,* Pittsburgh, The Tri-State Area
School Study Council, 1960, p. 3.

[10] Eli Ginzberg and Douglas W. Bray, *The Uneducated,* New York, Columbia
University Press, 1953, pp. 228, 234.

[11] See "Federal Aid to Church-Related Schools," *NEA Journal,* May, 1962, pp.
26–28.

said somebody said? How consistent is the opposition to federal aid and the support of it? Do the former say "education has failed" *and* "our taxes are too high"? Do the latter stress "how wonderful our education system is" *and* "let's have much more money for it"? Or— can we go back to the beginning in our *intent* to educate all children to their capacities and *settle for no less,* regardless of the source of the funds? Evaluating our systems of taxation and educational power structure all up and down the line and viewing objectively the services needed to meet the goals that must be reached by the richest and most competent country and population the world has ever known are necessities of our time.

CRITICS AND DEFENDERS

The heat of controversy in the entire field of education never burns so highly as it does when the critics and defenders of the schools get together. The main trouble is that they seldom *do* get together, on the same platform, in the same book, or even on the same topic. But these reluctant, belligerent, argumentative protagonists, and their points of view, will be displayed here for your edification. Much of the vitality in the professional scene in education comes from those who spar and battle in this arena. They do not pull their punches—and neither will I in presenting the following framework in which they are displayed. It is necessarily lengthy, but the huge cast is to blame.

That both sides exaggerate and overstate their cases you must expect, for as it is so often in politics, the louder and more repetitious a statement is, the more its exponent feels it will be accepted. Although you obviously were not in on the first act of this drama, the current review will provide you with a prologue for a play that will be with us for many years.

Bertrand Russell once said, "The trouble with the world today is that the stupid are cocksure, while the intelligent are full of doubts." This matter of jumping to conclusions without proper evidence or experience is supplemented by another fact that contributes to controversy and the excitement that sometimes envelopes it! Many newspapers and magazines have the attitude that attack makes better news than defense, that lively and picturesque charges build up circulation. A few years ago the NEA discussed what it identified as the ten major criticisms of education. Its list consisted of the following:

Control of public school policy
Progressive education
Life adjustment education
Promotion and reporting practices
Discipline in the public schools
Instruction in classical and modern foreign languages
Science and mathematics in high school
The education of gifted children
Moral and spiritual values
Teacher education[12]

None of these has yet been settled with any definiteness. More fuel has been added by the hassles over phonics, grouping, guidance, certification of teachers and administrators, merit pay, tests, testing procedures, and the place of homework in school and home. All continue to receive considerable popular and professional attention, some of it rather objective in approach,[13] although objectivity is usually not a basic ingredient. Others have attempted to simplify the issues involved, lighten them, change their construction so that they might just blow away. No one has nailed this approach for its foolishness and deceit better than John H. Fischer, President of Columbia University. In "It's Never Simple" he takes the "simplifiers" to task, first by putting them into four groups:

The advocates of the single-track approach whose prescriptions invariably begin: "All we need to do is . . ."
Those who point out the alternatives, one good, the other bad. "Thus we are warned against the evil of a single national curriculum and urged to retain full local control of schools. That a single national curriculum is hardly a practical possibility and that pure local control is to be found nowhere in the American public school system are facts of little moment. Setting up straw men just to shoot them down makes dramatic conversation. . . ."

[12] NEA, *Ten Criticisms of Education*, Washington, D.C., 1957.
[13] See Mauritz Johnson, Jr., "The Rise and Fall of Life Adjustment," *Saturday Review*, March 18, 1961, pp. 46–47. See also Lawrence A. Cremin, *The Transformation of the School: Progressivism in American Education, 1867–1957*, New York, Alfred A. Knopf, Inc., 1961.

The "more-of-the-same" group, those who would improve weak schools by doing things on a bigger scale.

The "simplifier" who meets difficulty by discrediting the opposition, lumping all aspects of it together and labeling it "bad."

"The point is not that the single-minded critics are wrong," Fischer concludes, "but that they deal with only fragments of the total situations."[14]

Laying all the shortcomings of our society on the doorstep of education is as erroneous as education's taking full credit for all advances our society has made. It may be convenient to establish a scapegoat for juvenile delinquency, divorce rates, Russia's advances in science, and economic depressions. But one can hardly expect people in education to be badgered continually and still seek the bright light of improved educational methods and materials in their day-to-day teaching and administering of a financially overburdened and understaffed program. Still, the housecleaning must go on, from within as well as without.

Critics

Let no one tell you that all persons critical of public education today are misguided, misinformed, or stupid; that they all have personal little axes to grind; or that they are all "enemies of the public schools." In *any* large group there may be misinformation and deliberate juggling of ideas and figures to promote a selfish end, but no surge of criticism of this type can be dismissed so cavalierly. Represented are scholars, public figures, professional writers, and persons who classify themselves as professional educators. By and large, they take pride in the accomplishments of our public schools but feel that definite improvements are long overdue. Some of the force of their most cogent arguments is considerably lessened by undue vehemence and emotionalism that a few proponents permit to seep in. For an indication of the magnitude of the "anti" effort see *Teacher Education Criticisms: An Annotated Bibliography*.[15] This list of 59 sources from books and magazines could be amplified considerably if it were brought up to date and if newspaper stories were added. A few of

[14] John H. Fischer, "It's Never Simple," *Saturday Review*, April 21, 1962, pp. 53–54.

[15] James W. Popham and Suzanne A. Greenberg, *Teacher Education Criticisms: An Annotated Bibliography*, Pittsburg, Kan., Kansas State Teachers College, 1959.

the major critics are presented below along with some of their own comments.

BERNARD IDDINGS BELL

At one point Bell accused all of us of developing a nation of Henry Aldriches, of putting our primary emphasis on pleasure seeking and money grabbing. We must transmit the basic wisdom of the ages, as well as basic skills and decent manners. One tragic mistake is the cleavage between religion and secular learning. Another is the anti-intellectualism that is the foundation of most colleges and universities. In addition, too many responsibilities that belong at home are loaded on the schools, which are too eager to accept them.

. . . the virtues of American education . . . are considerable, but . . . its faults—basic faults . . . result, in spite of the virtues, in immaturity of our culture and thought, an immaturity increasingly evident as year follows year, an immaturity that endangers the social structure and prevents a reasonable amount of happiness for Americans individually as well as weakens and undermines the nation. The intention of the book, as was stated at the start, has been to disturb complacency: if possible to wake up the citizenry to the fact that they and their children are being provided with a low-grade education which pretends to be first-class; perhaps to make our educators a little ashamed of themselves. . . .

Thought needs to be given to what may be done in respect to teaching morals and manners. . . . We might well have a moratorium on discussion of methods and organization of education until we come to some decision about the moral ends of education.[16]

ARTHUR E. BESTOR

Bestor insists that the lowering of educational standards for the great mass of students is a fact, and that it reflects an antidemocratic attitude on the part of the public schools. He holds professors of education primarily responsible and puts on battle garb in his opposition to what he feels is their domination of the profession and their responsibility for its low academic level.

. . . schools exist to teach *something*, and . . . this something is the power to think. To assert this, of course, is to assert the importance of good teaching. Professional educationalists are fond of beclouding the issue by sug-

[16] Bell, *op. cit.*

gesting that those who believe in disciplined intellectual training deny the importance of good teaching. Nothing could be farther from the truth. It is sheer presumption on their part to pose as the only persons in the academic world with a concern for good teaching. . . .

Across the educational world today stretches an iron curtain which the professional educationists are busily fashioning. Behind it, in slave-labor camps, are the classroom teachers, whose only hope of rescue is from without. . . . American intellectual life is threatened because the first twelve years of formal schooling in the United States are falling more and more completely under the policymaking control of a new breed of educator who has no real place in—who does not respect and who is not respected by—the world of scientists, scholars, and professional men. . . .

As a prospective teacher looks out over his future career, one hard, inescapable fact stares him in the face. He must acquire a certain number of hours in "education". . . . In the university itself the department of education will constantly remind him of the fact that there is no way to get a teaching certificate except by entering the classroom of a professor of education, taking down what he says, and handing it back to him on an examination. . . .

A bureaucrat in the state capital must shuffle the papers and certify that the prescribed education courses have been taken . . . . Pestalozzi himself, after a lifetime of teaching, could not be regularly and permanently employed by the school board of the smallest hamlet in the nation, because, forsooth, the official standards would prove him ignorant of and incompetent in pedagogy.[17]

Classroom teachers have a right to professional standing and to the prestige that goes with it. They will never attain it by plodding along in the educationists' treadmill. . . .

However lamentable the fact may appear to the educationists, the public will always judge the teaching profession by what its members know about the subjects they profess to teach. . . .[18]

Of all the critics, Bestor has probably stimulated the most reactions within the profession—and they result in some heated arguments, a fascinating "welcome" to your life's work!

[17] Arthur E. Bestor, *Educational Wastelands: The Retreat from Learning in Our Public Schools*, Urbana, University of Illinois Press, pp. 10, 121, 131–132.

[18] Arthur Bestor, *The Restoration of Learning*, New York, Alfred A. Knopf, Inc., 1955, pp. 271–272. See also "We Are Less Educated Than Fifty Years Ago," *U.S. News and World Report*, November 30, 1956; Will R. Burnett, "Mr. Bestor in the Land of the Philistines," *Progressive Education*, January, 1954; and Walter D. Cocking, "A Reply to Arthur Bestor," *The School Executive*, March, 1957, pp. 7–8.

ROGER E. FREEMAN

Freeman views our public schools almost exclusively in terms of cost. Although no one can deny its importance, there may be considerable difference of opinion about whether it is the *only* dimension that should be used. The framework he uses for his comments consists of the following: Our school graduates are less prepared than the European boys and girls; our curriculum and academic standards are watered down; we can save money by large classes, double sessions, the 12-month school year, less space per student, and educational television.[19]

JOHN KEATS

John Keats says that the public schools offer an education "that is anticultural, anti-intellectual, narrowly utilitarian at best and utterly vapid at worst." It is "bad in theory, bad in practice and abysmal in its results." Our schools have failed because they "pamper the jackasses, stuff the geniuses under the rug, and meanwhile envelope everyone in that fatuous diaperism they call life adjustment."[20]

His romp through words and ideas continued in his book, *Schools Without Scholars*, certainly one of the most readable diatribes on which you can put your hands. It abounds in passages like these:

If there is a national tendency to sell our children short—and I am convinced there is—I believe the fault lies with those educators who know better How To teach than what to teach. Further, I believe the overworked social conscience of these same educators to be partly responsible for a leveling influence in our schools; their fear of establishing, or even admitting, of an intellectual elite has had the effect of scaling the offerings down to a level which might lie well below the average ability. I believe another effect of this same conscience leads these educators to a false, overly sentimental concept of the child, and that one result is an emphasis on happiness at the expense of a request for a little hard work.

Questioning, questioning, always asking, Is the course necessary? is not talking poor-mouth. These days of rising school construction costs and chronic teacher shortages are very good days indeed to take our school

---

[19] Roger E. Freeman, *School Needs in the Decade Ahead*, Washington, D.C., Institute for Social Science Research, 1958.

[20] John Keats, "Are the Public Schools Doing Their Job? No" *Saturday Evening Post*, September 21, 1957.

apart and see what really makes it tick, and what is pure fluff. Perhaps we can save construction costs by weeding such rank growths as domestic arts and driver training from the curriculum. Perhaps we can spend the money saved on better salaries for better teachers. Perhaps we can remove some courses and reassign teachers and thus help reduce the teacher shortage. At the very least, questioning the worth of a course is one way of guaranteeing its value.[21]

JAMES D. KOERNER

Strong in its criticism but less vehement in its exposition is a book Koerner edited. Its chapters go through much of the curriculum, expressing the ideas of academic specialists in the fields discussed. He definitely holds the olive branch out to professional workers in education as indicated by the comments quoted here.

The root of our trouble does not lie in an unbalanced curriculum, or in an inadequate emphasis on any one subject, or in poor teaching methods, or in insufficient facilities, or in underpaid instructors. It lies in the circumstance that somehow the average high school graduate does not know who he is, where he is, or how he got there. It lies in the fact that naturally enough he "will settle for shallow and trivial meanings." If nothing in his early education has convinced him that Newton, Shakespeare and Lincoln are both more interesting and more admirable than Frank Sinatra, Jerry Lewis and Pat Boone, he will find answers to his questions in Sinatra, Lewis and Boone, and not in Newton, Shakespeare and Lincoln. If he has learned little or no history, geography, science, mathematics, foreign languages, or English he will, naturally enough, learn (for even if all men do not desire to know, in Aristotle's sense, surely they desire to know *something*) golf, quailshooting, barbecuing, and some specialized technique of buying and selling.

In accordance with his luck and his temperament, he may become happily lost, or unhappily lost. But lost he will become. Lost he will remain. Lost he will die.

And if we allow these lost ones to multiply indefinitely, they will see to it that our country is lost also. . . .

We will achieve success if we encourage professional educators at the public school level; not if we seek to destroy them. In pointing up the deficiencies of our schools in a manner which invites improvement in specific areas, we should recognize that it is at least in some part due to the

[21] John Keats, *Schools Without Scholars*, Boston, Houghton Mifflin Company, 1958.

professional educators that offerings in foreign languages, literature, mathematics and science are now available to most high school students.[22]

ALBERT LYND

As a business man, ex-teacher, and parent, Lynd was one of the first spokesmen accusing teacher-preparation institutions of undermining our total public school program. In a vividly written article, he stated his case with no holds barred.

Your local high school may be in the charge of a "fresh Kiwanian," he said, and "he may even wear the splendid title of Doctor, earned through researches into the theory and function of a school cafeteria." He explores the "inner mysteries of the pedagogical cult," "educational panjandrums," "professorial millinery," "head-rubbing by a professor of education," "these boys in the educational back room," "adulterated pap." But consolingly he concludes, "you may draw some comfort from the knowledge that the greatness of this nation lies in its infinite capacity for surviving hocus-pocus!"[23]

PHILIP MARSON

No less gentle are the remarks of Marson as he heaps ridicule on topics like social promotion, the concept of "the whole child," objective tests, permissiveness, and social studies. He feels that something must be done about the low salaries and the shortage of well-prepared teachers, putting the blame for the latter on the "interlocking directorate of educationists."

In Lynd's spirit he carries forward the themes of chaos, anarchy, tragic inertia, elective sweets. He sees in education a need for "a militant guardian angel," a maelstrom of utter confusion, a gigantic numbers racket, a crazy patchwork quilt, a hodge-podge of ideas and action, the floodgates of radical theories, a complete breakdown and a national disgrace. In a more controlled moment, he pursues one of his major themes:

Our classrooms must become workshops instead of rumpus-rooms. Children must be conditioned at home to consider school their serious occupa-

---

[22] James D. Koerner (ed.), *The Case for Basic Education*, Boston, Little, Brown and Company, 1959. See also Koerner, *The Miseducation of American Teachers*, Boston, Houghton Mifflin Company, 1963.

[23] Albert Lynd, "Quackery in the Public Schools," *The Atlantic Monthly*, March, 1950, pp. 33–38.

tion, nothing less. Parents must insist that boys and girls are appropriately dressed for school, not as if they were heading for the beach or the barn. They should assume that unsocial behavior will not be tolerated in school any more than it will at home or in business. Interference with scholastic progress must be looked upon as injurious to the family, to the community, and the nation.[24]

H. G. RICKOVER

One of the most widely read, listened to, and quoted critics of American education is a man highly respected for his contributions in a totally different area, one of great importance to our national destiny. In many speeches, three well-circulated books and a group of magazine articles, the educational ideas of Admiral Rickover have become known to a mass audience.[25]

As a guest on television ("Meet the Press," January 24, 1960) he summarized his basic thoughts on this subject. He feels very strongly on these ten points:

1. Our children cannot pass the academic examinations taken and passed by European children.
2. The children in our schools waste a great deal of time on subjects unrelated to education.
3. We need federal standards of education. "I advocate that a federal permissive standard be set up for what every boy or girl at age 18 should know."
4. We should try to give every child a "liberal education" at least through high school.
5. Too many persons are going on to higher education who are not prepared for it.
6. "I would get better teachers . . . I would knock off some of the administrators who are really running our schools."
7. If parents did their job we would have better educated children.
8. "I believe that every child in this country no matter where he comes from, what the financial status of his parents is, what his social status

[24] Philip Marson, *The American Tragedy—Our Schools*, Cambridge, Berkshire Publishing Company, 1958.

[25] H. G. Rickover, *Education and Freedom*, New York, E. P. Dutton & Co., Inc., 1959; *Swiss Schools and Ours*, Boston, Little, Brown and Company, 1962; *American Education—A National Failure*, New York, E. P. Dutton & Co., Inc., 1963; "Let's Stop Wasting Our Greatest Resource," *Saturday Evening Post*, March 2, 1957. "The World of the Uneducated," *Saturday Evening Post*, November 28, 1959. "Don't Hamstring the Talented," *Saturday Evening Post*, February 18, 1960.

is, should have an equal opportunity to develop himself to the maximum. I would give federal aid to education as is necessary to accomplish
this."

9. "I would not stop any youngster who is brilliant. I would not have him
held back by anyone else."

10. The school should be used to train the intellect.

As a "customer" for the product of our schools, Rickover has found
that product quite unsatisfactory. Emphasizing education as our first
line of defense, advocating increased financial support to improve
the quality of public education, and noting our failure to identify
the gifted and talented are factors that bring little disagreement.
But other ideas expressed by him have brought strong rebuttals.
Stressing intellectual development and ignoring the development of
character in our schools, setting up national standards of achievement, and disposing of the comprehensive high school are among the
most controversial of his suggestions. In an unusually conciliatory
tone, he expressed a conclusion with which few can disagree:

If we do not realize that the education of our children is our most important task; if we are more concerned with their clothes or with their
recreation and entertainment than with the training of their minds, then
we need not be surprised that our schools do not produce either an adequately educated citizenry or a sufficiently large and competent corps of
professional men and women to maintain our culture and civilization.

There is a much-quoted story about a presumably fictitious teacher
who went up to him after one of his talks on education and said, "I
enjoyed your talk, Admiral Rickover. Now if you have a few minutes,
I'd like to give you some ideas on how to run the navy." This is
hardly worthy as a reaction, but to debate the accuracy of his
information and conclusions is a permissible professional task.[26]

MORTIMER SMITH

Smith is high in the ranks of the angry opposition and executive
secretary of the Council for Basic Education. He has summarized his
major points in several books. Our reading, spelling and grammar
are deficient; we need less of the "reading series" and more phonics.
Guidance, with its probing techniques, is dangerous, and so are

[26] Richard I. Miller, "Admiral Rickover on American Education: An Analysis
of His Viewpoints," *The Journal of Teacher Education*, September, 1959.

accrediting agencies and the concepts of "readiness," "child development," and "individual differences." European countries do a far better educational job than we do. Our "average" children can take a much tougher school program, our professional educators are too dominant in the whole field, our textbooks are oversimplified and filled with triviality.

His pros are Advanced Placement Program, essentialism, general education, merit pay, phonics. The "anti" list is much longer: American Council on Education, child-centered school, College Entrance Examination Board, core curriculum, driver training, Educational Policies Commission, Educational Testing Service, exceptional child (his opposition is to the inclusion of the gifted), Life Adjustment Education, National Congress of Parents and Teachers, NEA, objective testings.[27]

About the "modern educator" and method versus content, he said:

. . . anti-intellectual and anticultural, practical and narrowly scientific. Though he has been exposed to cursory training in the liberal arts, he is usually a specialist in some narrow field: ventilation, physical training, vocational agriculture, psychology, finance or home economics. And these specialists are expected to set the tone of the teaching of academic subjects.

. . . the glorification of "technique" . . . new teachers are selected on the basis of efficiency in the mechanics of pedagogy . . . teaching as a human relationship and the body of serious knowledge to be imparted are relegated to second place . . .[28]

About "those who teach the teachers" he said:

. . . no dyed-in-the-wool Educationist really seems to believe that knowledge of a subject has much to do with teaching that subject.

. . . sets the standards of American education . . . a racket . . . concerned not with improving standards, but with maintaining and strengthening a set of meaningless, mechanical requirements . . . these theorists sold to an unsuspecting public and a drowsy academic world a strange bill of goods: the notion that there is a special branch of learning, a *science,* called "Education."[29]

[27] Mortimer Smith, *A Citizens Manual for Public Schools,* Washington, D.C., Council for Basic Education, 1959.
[28] Mortimer Smith, *And Madly Teach,* Chicago, Henry Regnery Company, 1949.
[29] Mortimer Smith (ed.), *The Public Schools in Crisis,* Chicago, Henry Regnery Company, 1956.

Others have helped make education big news in recent years by stressing its shortcomings. Sometimes they have been school people like Glenn McCracken, who gave the reasons for what he called our national failure in reading instruction and proposed solutions on the basis of experimentation in New Castle, Pennsylvania.[30]

Others have names well known to the public at large. In the August, 1958, issue of *Holiday*, Clifton Fadiman was critical of the "good time" theory of education, of eliminating report cards and introducing compulsory promotion, of air conditioning the non-academic rather than the academic parts of the school plant. Aldous Huxley pointed out that "during the past half century every other nation has made great efforts to impart more knowledge to more young people. In the United States, professional educationalists have chosen the opposite course."[31]

The critics already quoted are almost polite in their comments on professors of education in comparison with the bitter criticism of Virgil Scott:

. . . every Professor of Education has been run through the same mold and has emerged with the same dry, expressionless voice (if you walked from class to class with a tuning fork and a metronome, you would find that they all maintained a perfect middle-C pitch and a constant speech tempo throughout every forty-five minute lecture), and these men also have the same scaly skin which looks sandpapery, and the same suits, brown tweed or gray pin-stripe, and the same brown-stained brief cases, sagging and limp-looking when they are laid clip-up on a desk, and the inevitable rubbers on the inevitable black oxfords, and the inevitable rimless glasses on the inevitable thin bridges of noses, and the inevitable smell of chalky dryness about their bodies.[32]

As James D. Finn said in recalling this vitriolic passage, "Virgil Scott hated. No man could write like that if he didn't hate."[33]

Groups have joined the critical brigade too. A leadership role is occupied by the Council for Basic Education, which sees the primary purpose of the school as fourfold:

[30] Glenn McCracken, *The Right to Learn*, Chicago, Henry Regnery Company, 1959.

[31] Aldous Huxley, *Tomorrow and Tomorrow and Tomorrow*, New York, Harper & Row, Publishers, Inc., 1956, p. 40.

[32] *The Hickory Stick*, New York, Swallow Press, 1948, p. 95.

[33] James D. Finn, "The Good Guys and the Bad Guys," *Phi Delta Kappan*, October, 1958, p. 3.

(1) To teach young people how to read and write and figure; (2) to transmit the facts about the heritage and culture of the race; (3) in the process of (1) and (2), to train the intelligence and to stimulate the pleasures of thought; and (4) to provide that atmosphere of moral affirmation without which education is merely animal training.[34]

The Council is a zealous advocate of strong academic content, and takes pride in advances it notes in recent years in the public's interest in "basic education." Progress has been made, it feels, in the teaching of mathematics and science, a little in reading instruction due to a trend toward systematic teaching of phonics, very little in social studies, and none in English. Teacher education still receives the brunt of the blame.

Few would debate the point that responsible citizens' committees are capable of making a contribution toward the improvement of our educational programs. The full story has not yet been told of who their members are, what their goals are, whether their theme is always cooperation or merely provides a sounding board for malcontent reflections of home, family, or community relationships. The majority who are affected are strangely quiet, leaving the expression of various school criticisms to the vocal few.[35] Soundly organized and representative citizens' committees can be effective examples of democracy at work. Selfishly oriented groups that apply pressure or impose pet theories can be detrimental to the schools they may profess to support.

Much more space could be devoted to "the critics," but you no doubt get the picture. Now it's time to turn the coin.

Defenders

Just as the critics are certainly not all misguided, misinformed, or stupid, the defenders are not all selfish, blind supporters of the *status quo*, and antiintellectual. They, too, include scholars, public figures, professional writers, and persons who classify themselves as professional educators. Some of them, too, lose part of the force of their arguments through undue vehemence and emotionalism. Many times they ask questions which are difficult for the critics to answer:

[34] Mortimer Smith, *A Citizens Manual for Public Schools*, Washington, D.C., Council for Basic Education, 1959, p. 3.

[35] Howard Whitman, "Speak Out, Silent People," *Collier's*, February 5, 1954, pp. 23–28.

What is your evidence? What are your qualifications for evaluating it?
Have you read our *good* research?

Is your criticism based on a scientific approach?

Is your complaint isolated, personalized, or is there a basis for generalizing?

Are you aware of the great accomplishments of our country? Isn't education at least *partly* responsible?

If education is responsible for the relatively small number who are delinquent and can't read, are you willing to give it credit for the far greater number in neither of those categories?

Are the schools responsible for professional shortages—or did the depression and low birth rate of the 1930s have something to do with them?

Questions that are even more specific are implied in the comments of various persons we will turn to for the defense. As in other fields, their best defense is sometimes a vibrant, stirring offense.

THEODORE BRAMELD

Along with some others on this side of the fence, Brameld concedes that there is at least partial justification for the criticisms which say our schools are overweighted in skills, procedures and "tricks of the trade" at the expense of subject matter. Those who are most vociferous in leading the attack he feels "are also most likely to suggest as a solution little more than a differently dressed reversion to traditional subject matters traditionally organized."[36]

He pin-points the "fashionable" quality of setting up John Dewey and "progressive education" as scapegoats. In a review of Rickover's book, *Education and Freedom,* he compliments the author for his admission that "Fortunately, progressive educational methods have not found too wide application in our schools." Then, he asks, how can we blame these methods for the "present sorry plight of American education"? If they haven't been tried, they shouldn't bear the blame for deficiencies we note in our schools. Dewey's philosophy, he explains, is *not* based on "life adjustment," on helping the child adjust to life as it is. On the contrary—it is based on a desire "to develop a capacity in learners to engage in constant *re*adjustment by the disciplined application of scientific methods to all important problems of human life. A much stronger case could be made that American school programs are frequently dull or otherwise mediocre

[36] Theodore Brameld, *Cultural Foundations of Education,* New York, Harper & Row, Publishers, Inc., 1957, pp. 19, 255–257.

just because they continue to practice the author's [Rickover's] own obsolete brand of learning and teaching."[37]

Although the language Brameld uses is frequently too heavy for the uninitiated to interpret without help, it provides ideas which, ultimately accepted or rejected, are worth pondering. He is one of the few professional educators, however, willing to admit that there is often much busywork in schools of education, that their instructors are too frequently limited in quality, and that their students are often low on the intellectual ladder.

PAUL BRANDWEIN

Brandwein, whose background is primarily in the sciences, suggests that the objectives of American schools are competence and compassion. The latter is based on "the second chance," an opportunity not provided by European schools which he knows firsthand. In his stimulating speeches, he takes the opposition to task and affirmatively presents his own point of view. The following are from three speeches of his: at Arizona State University February 21, 1958, and February 22, 1958, and at Osborn School District, Phoenix, March 19, 1958.

Scientists who practice the scientific method in their own field should do the same when they approach professional education. To draw conclusions on the basis of their own experience or that of one or more of their own children is unreasonable and unprofessional.

The schools should not promise too much or receive more blame or credit than is reasonable for the time they devote (6 out of 24 hours versus society's 18 out of 24).

The function of teaching is not "to tell" (except in connection with safety). It is to teach by questioning—and the answers are not necessarily in textbooks.

The needs of children will not be met until the needs of teachers are met.

We expect too much of teachers. They cannot do "everything" any more than students, sales persons, accountants, or lawyers can.

In European schools children are taught by an attitude based on contempt; and that is one reason the children can evolve into adults contemptuous of others, so vividly demonstrated by the Nazis.

Let's give the schools a chance; they have been made available to all the children for little more than one generation.

[37] Theodore Brameld, *Education for the Emerging Age*, New York, Harper & Row, Publishers, Inc., 1961, pp. 232, 233.

If our teachers really are poorly prepared, let us blame the liberal arts colleges which produce most of them.

The only "fundamental" worth pursuing is this one: "Let each child do the darnedest with his mind—no holds barred."

Let us ask, and demand answers, regarding every school criticism: Is it true? Is it kind? Is it necessary?

Brandwein may antagonize certain members of his audiences, but he never fails to arouse a response.

WILLIAM W. BRICKMAN

The recent trend toward emphasis on science as an academic foundation for most of our children has aroused Brickman's ire. There is far more to education than a grounding, no matter how professionally provided, in the sciences. Many of the critics are eager to get on a science-and-mathematics binge, sometimes as though only these subjects provide "learning," "discipline," and the basic needs of our society, all others being of secondary importance. He makes his point this way:

There is little doubt of our right to expect rigorously trained scientists to think along scientific lines, in and out of their recognized fields of competency. If scientists cannot apply the scientific method except in the laboratory, then it is reasonable to raise more than eyebrows when they use their prestige to make the public believe that the road to national survival and salvation is mainly, if not solely, through a stress upon the teaching of science and the training of scientists.[38]

He also feels that too often an eminent person misleads the public regarding education by transmitting inaccurate information, subjective judgments, and irrelevant remarks. "Perhaps he should be even more careful with the public than with the profession, because the latter can see through shoddy work while the former may not easily be able to distinguish between a great man's considered judgments and his snap conclusions. . . . When everybody is an expert on everything, nobody is an expert on anything."[39]

[38] William W. Brickman, "Stressing the Teaching of Science," *School and Society,* March 15, 1958, p. 139.

[39] William W. Brickman, "Rickover as a Comparative Educator," *Phi Delta Kappan,* November, 1958, p. 67.

HERBERT L. BROWN, JR.

In a pro-and-con debate on education with John Keats,[40] Brown pointed out that the schools' problems are far from simple. With the number of children and schools, the variations in approaches, attitudes, and administration implied in local control, and with the added demands of individuals and groups (health programs, driver training, citizenship, family-life education), the schools' tasks have increased in scope, intensity, and difficulty. He reminds us that children are not all the same (they mature at different rates), and that drill has limitations as well as advantages. "Life adjustment," he writes, does not spurn basic skills or discard academic subjects. Nor does it necessarily mean there will be little discipline, with children doing exactly as they please without adult authority or control. He brings "social promotion" into his discussion, maintaining that to fail a child will not necessarily encourage him to move ahead and catch up academically. Evidence that secondary schools often do a good job is available in scholarships earned, college academic records, and College Board examination scores, he says.

WILLIAM A. BROWNELL

We have an impressive story to tell, says Brownell, former Dean of the School of Education of the University of California at Berkeley. But we don't put our best foot forward when we deprecate the schools and teachers of earlier years. By stressing our concern for the individual child, it sometimes seems as though we're insisting that no consideration for him was given *until* we came along.

"It is obvious to us," he writes, "that the child-centered curriculum, while putting renewed emphasis upon non-intellectual learning outcomes, does not thereby minimize intellectual outcomes." In educational circles it is assumed that subject matter will of course be attended to when the child and his development are discussed, he feels. But "our critics exactly reverse the relationship; they talk about subject matter, assuming that their children will be properly treated and encouraged toward good conduct."[41]

[40] Herbert L. Brown, Jr., "Are the Public Schools Doing Their Job? Yes," *Saturday Evening Post,* September 21, 1957.
[41] William A. Brownell, "The Three R's in Today's Schools," *NEA Journal,* September, 1952, pp. 335–337.

Brownell discerns one unifying idea in the welter of conflict: Education for our children must be "functional," in the broadest sense of that word. He rejects the answers to criticism that are based on a do-nothing policy, angry denunciation of all critics, and attempts to prove that current school achievement is higher than it was 20 or 30 years ago. (Why shouldn't it be, we might ask; it costs us more; we're 20 or 30 years more mature in our research and basic understandings; our teachers are presumably better prepared; and there are more and better educational materials available.) Instead, he prefers a fourth route: A continuous program of educating, confiding in, and making friends with the community. This seems to him a much more practical approach than defensive measures to quell criticism.

WALTER W. COOK

In a single article, Cook summarizes his attitudes; one passage is representative of them:

The current tide of public interest in public education is welcomed by all competent schoolmen—even the panic-striking books, pamphlets, and journal articles crying that we are neglecting our gifted children, that Johnny can't read, that children can't spell, that schools have no discipline; written with sweeping generalizations made from two or three horrible examples and showing no more psychological insight than is commonly apparent at a supermarket or over the bridge table; blaming the whole sorry mess on that overworked, underpaid, and unappreciated group of men and women who have dedicated their lives to the improvement of public education.[42]

ARTHUR COREY

In many speeches and articles Corey has reviewed criticisms of education and emphasized ways to meet them. Particularly filtered out for comment is the subject of the "what" and "how" of teaching.

The method with which young people are taught as well as the subject matter they are taught makes the difference between training and learning, the difference between the technician and the intellectual, between the pedant and the scholar. We are being told that method makes no difference.

[42] Walter W. Cook, "The Gifted and Retarded in Historical Perspective," *Phi Delta Kappan,* March, 1958, p. 249.

It is being said that it is not only unimportant but unnecessary. This is my very deep concern.[43]

Affirmatively, he points out that one of the major emphases of present-day education is to develop in children the ability to think —the importance of the intellect. Important, as part of this approach, is the freedom from dogmatism, prejudice, superstition, and ignorance. Among the basic conclusions he comes to are these: We cannot afford the luxury of stupidity: "the stupid man is the one who refuses to think when he has the ability, and could if he would." Although men are reluctant to change their ways, "we must adjust or perish and . . . we will not adjust by what are called the 'good, old methods.' "

NORMAN COUSINS

Perhaps you didn't expect to find the editor of the *Saturday Review* among the defenders of education. But he is frequently there, in his many speaking engagements before state and other conferences of teachers and school administrators, and in his writing too. Cousins points out that among the misconceptions harbored by some noneducator groups and individuals which need interpretation, clarification, and better understanding are the following:

1. Educators regard their profession as a closed corporation.
2. Educators communicate with each other in academic gobbledygook.
3. Educators turn their backs on fundamentals like the three R's.
4. Educators have become exponents of an alien system known as "pragmatism."
5. Educators are antireligious.
6. Educators are in a conspiracy against American institutions.[44]

The implications are that we must determine *which* educators and *what* evidence is referred to in such assertions. He feels it is necessary that parents, school people, and others bring to the "great debate" more positive ideas related to the opportunity (1) to do one's best in an atmosphere that makes possible one's best, (2) to be free from stagnation, and (3) to partake of the spirit of adventure.

[43] Speech reported in *The Teacher of Teachers*, Arizona State University, November 15, 1961.
[44] Norman Cousins, "The Great Debate in American Education," *Saturday Review*, September 11, 1954.

LAWRENCE G. DERTHICK

In his position as United States Commissioner of Education, Derthick often expressed himself on educational controversies, usually defending the public schools and their workers against all opposition. He emphasizes five themes and questions related to them. As a little test for yourself (not a very difficult one) decide whether you think his answers will be "yes" or "no."

1. Character and intellect: Should the school be concerned with intellect alone? Should not the school be concerned with the development of character?
2. A high school for all: Should we substitute the specialized secondary school systems of Western Europe for our comprehensive high school?
3. Standards for quality: Should there be national standards specifying what every boy and girl should know at age 18 so that every parent could tell how well his children and teachers have done in school?
4. Schools here and abroad: Are the European systems of education superior to the American system?
5. Our school leadership: Is the American school administrator prepared and competent to carry out his responsibility?[45]

In reply to the questions, he insists that though the schools are primarily concerned with the intellect, they have other goals, including character training and the development of special talents. As Conant does, he feels that our comprehensive high school is a distinct contribution, and that it is as innately suitable for our society as the more selective schools are for European countries. National standards, he maintains, would fail to meet the diverse needs of people in different parts of the country with varied intellectual levels, parental desires, and local goals. Our commitment to universal education precludes our copying the European systems of education; if someone thinks they are superior, someone else should ask, "For whom?" Pointing to the strong academic backgrounds of school administrators, he concludes that they are well prepared for their work. You, of course, may or may not agree with his conclusions.

[45] Lawrence G. Derthick, *Schools in Our Democracy*, Washington, D.C., U.S. Department of Health, Education, and Welfare, 1960.

EDUCATIONAL POLICIES COMMISSION

In many publications of the Educational Policies Commission of the NEA, efforts have been made to stem the tide of criticism when it is of an irresponsible nature. "Citizens must recognize that careless criticism of education may actually result in a deterioration of quality rather than in improvement. An atmosphere of fear, distrust, or emotional antagonism is not conducive to those changes and tests of new ideas which are the basis of improvement."[46]

The Commission has frequently pointed up the need for accurate information and the ability on the part of the citizenry to interpret it correctly. Just because numbers are stated so precisely does not mean that they can always be accepted without challenge.

JAMES D. FINN

Finn has been devoting much time in recent years to the newer technological developments in education, related mostly to programmed learning, teaching machines, and audio-visual aids. Once in a while he makes a foray into this educational battlefield, on the side of the professional educators of whom he feels a part. In a rather picturesque manner, he indicates why he feels there is so much criticism:

. . . Books that have good things to say about our society do not sell very well; very few orders for pamphlets and reprints are received when the pamphlets and reprints have something worthwhile to say in favor of a person or institution. It's small consolation, but the last best seller that sang praises was probably the Book of Psalms.

At the moment, there's money, prestige, and almost sure publication without much chance of getting slapped back awaiting anyone willing to kick an educationist in the stomach. Aggressions are also relieved. By creating a new minority group (the educationists) to push around, most of the critics . . . (but not all critics) have discovered a form of therapy that brings wonderful release . . . and money. Lecture on education, anyone?[47]

On the subject of the Council for Basic Education he is especially

[46] Educational Policies Commission, *The Contemporary Challenge to American Education*, Washington, D.C., NEA, 1958, p. 20.
[47] James D. Finn, *op. cit.*, p. 31.

verbal, criticizing their point of view, style of writing, and almost everything else about the organization. He accuses them of presenting a distorted picture of teacher certification, points out that they apparently are opposed to teacher tenure, and indicates that almost anyone who finds something good in education is subject to their scolding pen (with Conant and the Rockefeller Brothers Fund not exempt). He describes the writing style in their Bulletin as "a talk-down, let's-laugh-at-the-peasant-educationists, throw-barbs-in-'em approach," one based mainly on emotion-laden words, although it castigates educationists for doing the same thing.

HAROLD C. HAND

They must have had some gay times in recent years on the University of Illinois campus, with Bestor ripping into the whole field of professional education, and Hand using attack against him as the strongest type of defense. However, Bestor isn't the only target. Hand is willing to "take on" all of the critics, and on several occasions has shown sufficient vitality to do so. In fact, he is so eager to meet the challenge that on many occasions he has flown his own plane to the site in order to be on time at the proper place.

He has stressed several points that represent his major views on education today:

Educational research has not paid off often enough. Too frequently its results are ignored and the *status quo* goes on and on.

Our seeming lag behind Russia in scientific endeavors is not the fault of education but is due to the opposition of high governmental officials to pure research in the fields of missiles and satellites. (He quotes Wernher Von Braun, I. Keith Glennan, and Donald H. Menzel on this point.)

A false diagnosis of the place of schools in our whole national picture has resulted in their being a scapegoat for many of our problems. Because the schools are everywhere, are defenseless, and *do* have some things wrong with them, they are the perfect scapegoat.

It is fine to be in favor of "high standards", but they cannot effectively be the *same* standards for all children everywhere. They would result in frustrations for the less able ones and "make academic bums out of brighter youngsters." A single rigorous standard of achievement for each grade level could result in a reversion to practices of 50 years ago: 15-year-olds spending 10 years in first grade; young adults 11 to 18 years of age progressing no further than third grade, and in the same classes as 7- and 8-year-olds; only one in three getting as far as eighth grade in "the good old days."

The high school curriculum of 1900–1910 will not satisfy the needs of our greatly increased school population today. Even then it resulted in a very high dropout rate. A truly democratic education will not result from offering the conventional academic subjects to *all* students indiscriminately.

He maintains that children exposed to education of the type criticized by the Council for Basic Education and others tend to do better on standardized achievement tests. We must relate school subject matter to the life of the child, and we must bring into our classrooms actual examples of the kinds of situations to which we expect our teaching to transfer.[48]

MYRON LIEBERMAN

Among the most literate spokesmen on educational controversies is one who has his sights largely on the future as his writings vividly indicate. Lieberman feels that the outcry against education for its life-adjustment tendencies comes with poor grace from the liberal arts colleges. After all, isn't it the latter who frequently seek the "well-rounded" student, who reject students because they may not "adjust" well enough, and who desire a geographic distribution of students?[49]

He feels, too, that criticisms of the schools are often magnified much beyond their importance by school administrators whose jobs are so dependent on public opinion. There is a tendency of the school people to exaggerate the political strength of their critics. Valid criticisms without popular support will not bother them nearly so much as completely invalid ones with popular support. The latter can pose a threat to occupational security.

AGNES E. MEYER

When a woman gets into the fray, a new dimension of excitement can enter—especially when the woman is intelligent and dedicated. On many occasions Mrs. Meyer's remarks have been direct and her

[48] Harold C. Hand, "Black Horses Eat More Than White Horses," *AAUP Bulletin*, June, 1957, pp. 266–279; "On Ways of Preventing Regression to the *Status Quo Ante*," address to Association for Supervision and Curriculum Development, March 5, 1959.

[49] Myron Lieberman, *Education as a Profession*, Englewood Cliffs, N. J., Prentice-Hall, Inc., 1956; *The Future of Public Education*, The University of Chicago Press, 1960.

point of view unmistakable. The following statements are from a speech at the convention of the Association for Supervision and Curriculum Development given on March 6, 1960 in Washington, D.C.

National achievement standards would destroy local control; we can't have both.

Admiral Rickover is wrong; we must build both brains *and* character.

Education must treat each child as an authentic individual, not as a basic ingredient of national defense.

The critics who say our children don't work hard enough are correct, but their solutions are essentially wrong. They *will* work hard—if they're interested.

Education must not restrict itself to imparting facts without meanings; we cannot preserve freedom that way.

Knowledge must liberate thoughts, emotion, and imagination.

In an address to the American Association of School Administrators (February 17, 1953), Mrs. Meyer stressed the importance of the noneducator's role on the stage of educational controversy:

As a rule, a layman is diffident when addressing a large group of professional educators. But today, which for the whole field of education, is a time of crisis, the layman has a definite place, yes an important place, in meetings devoted to a consideration of our public schools. For it has become the moral duty of every American citizen who values academic freedom to take a stand on the controversial issues which revolve about our educational system.

The "today" she referred to in 1953 is no less current as you read her statement now. With both children and money as basic ingredients of public education, and both coming from the population as a whole, informed opinions from that population are the foundation for improved educational resources.

MAX RAFFERTY

A novel approach to the criticisms of education has been taken by an administrator actively involved in the school scene, although certainly not always defending or even kindly toward school people. In recent months he has become an extremely controversial personality, opposed by many in the profession. It's our fault, he says, and it's time to take off the kid gloves. Here's how Rafferty puts it:

"How," we ask ourselves pathetically, "has a profession which tries only to do good and tell the truth accumulated such enemies?"

Well now, let's not get sickening about it. A lot of this is our own fault. We have striven too long and too hard to be all things to all people. We have been guilty, too, of the sin of Pride. We have been willing to see Education gorged with all sorts of extraneous projects and problems until it swelled like a force-fed goose. Conversely, we have been unwilling or unable to state our case to the American people strikingly enough to silence our foes.

But our greatest mistake has been the image of Education which we have presented to the nation. It has been for a generation and more an essentially feminine image—gentle, non-combative, benevolent, maternal, a little fussy.

With all due respect to the thousands of devoted and dedicated women who labor so diligently in our countless classrooms, Education is not feminine. It never has been until just the other day. Since the days of Socrates and Plato, and before, it has been masculine in its outlook and appeal. It seeks to change concepts, to conquer ignorance, to fight evil. It brings not peace, but a sword. In its final, triumphant form, it will sweep the planet like some mighty besom, smashing aside dykes and levees like matchwood, and fulfilling its ancient role as the guardian and mentor of the human race.

Yes, Education is male.[50]

So, perhaps the whole area of educational controversy is simple after all. At least that's one man's opinion.

WILLIAM VAN TIL

A leading spokesman representing all education is the man who is Chairman of Secondary Education at New York University and former president of the Association for Supervision and Curriculum Development. Van Til has frequently taken to task the people he refers to as "unscholarly scholars," the ones who quickly become experts in fields other than their own. He calls their references to courses with names like "fly-casting" and "basket-weaving" their comedy gems, and challenges them to name schools where they are offered. The most newsworthy part of all their accusations is their anger, he feels, as unrighteous as it is.

[50] Max Rafferty, "Children of Uranus," *Phi Delta Kappan*, October, 1960, pp. 22–23.

In a widely read article he maintained that progressive education might be considered outmoded except for the stubborn fact that the questions it raised have not been satisfactorily answered. These questions are related to the basic aims of education, the foundations upon which the school program should be built, and what the schools should teach.

"One of the myths of our times," he wrote, "is that the several tendencies which characterized what is broadly termed progressive education prevailed, were fully achieved, and are now being repudiated. This sedulously cultivated myth is incomprehensible. The reality is that progressive education has never been tried on any significant scale."[51]

In other words, why set up a straw man who can then be beaten down as if he had really been and is still dominant in the school picture? He asks those who want to understand fully the problems of education today to go to the writings of Dewey, Bode, Counts, and Kilpatrick—not to what others said these men said, but to the original words.

ADDITIONAL THOUGHTS

One of the major difficulties, as you'll soon discover, is that these men do not always communicate their ideas so well; but that doesn't mean that it isn't worth the effort. Anyone who wants to be fair and avoid prejudging must also take the time to tap the resources of the defenders even though they may not always be as colorful as the critics. Some additional thoughts from this camp are summarized in the following paragraphs.

C. C. Trillingham, Superintendent, Los Angeles County, attacks the false picture of our schools painted by some of the critics: children making complete decisions of what they want to do in school, no discipline, promotion without effort or accomplishment, no standards. To lump together all the abuses, mistakes, or evidences of weak teaching and administration and label them "progressive education" or to attribute them to the entire school system is faulty and dangerous, he feels.

Charles H. Wilson, superintendent in a Chicago suburb, wants to

[51] William Van Til, "Is Progressive Education Obsolete?" *Saturday Review,* February 17, 1962, pp. 56–57, 82–84.

know how the professors of education are able to wield such a tremendous influence over future teachers when they have them in classes such a little bit of the total class time available. He asks the question of Arthur Bestor, and implies rather clearly that if our elementary and secondary teachers are poor, perhaps at least *part* of the responsibility for their deficiencies should rest with the college teachers with whom they have done most of their work—the liberal arts faculties.

Sloan Wilson, novelist, who has attacked the schools in scathing terms, on another occasion said: "More education is being passed on to more children than ever before in history, as well as more health care, entertainment, and all the rest. . . . [His] children learned to read beautifully in the public schools. . . . They're contentedly curled up with books which I at their age found incomprehensible."[52]

Fred M. Hechinger, the Education Editor of the *New York Times,* generally tries to retain a stance of objectivity. But he dropped it in at least one article, pointing out that a pragmatic, antiintellectual approach dates back to our pioneering frontier background (not to teachers' colleges) and that the elimination of school subjects like Latin and other languages was due to the pressure of "practical" men on the school boards (not the educators).[53]

Mary Anne Raywid attempted to analyze the motivations, associations, and pressures of public school critics about as thoroughly as anyone has.[54]

All is not attack and defense, however. Some try to dodge, even discourage, the barbs of anger and accusation, sometimes with moderate success, more often arousing the ire of both sides. John Hersey in his citizens' group in Fairfield, Connecticut, suggested that we base our efforts on common sense: work closely with the schools, engage in prolonged study, and avoid both apathy and hysteria. To walk the thin line of compassionate inquiry and action is obviously not easy—not when there are unbending efforts to copy European centrally controlled systems (and at the same time retain our emphasis on local control of schools) and attempts to pile more activities

[52] Sloan Wilson, "Public Schools Are Better Than You Think," *Harper's Magazine,* September 1955, pp. 32–33.

[53] Fred M. Hechinger, "The Fate of Pedagoguese," *Saturday Review,* December 12, 1953.

[54] Mary Anne Raywid, *The Ax-Grinders,* New York, The Macmillan Company, 1962.

on schools (and at the same time insist they are already infringing on what the home and community should be doing).

In a two-part series dating back some years (but surprisingly timely today) an effort was made to awaken the public to what they have, what they need, and what they might lose in their schools. In September and October, 1952, John Bainbridge wrote a penetrating appraisal of some school controversies in *McCall's*. One of the most valuable parts of the series is a list compiled by Virgil M. Rogers, former superintendent of schools in Battle Creek, Michigan, a sort of "formula" for differentiating between honest and dishonest groups that are critical of the schools. An honest group shows the following characteristics, he said:

1. Meets under auspices of regular organization—P.T.A. or School Advisory Council.
2. Has the sanction of and cooperates with school authorities and teachers.
3. Makes criticisms that are constructive and specific.
4. Welcomes teachers and administrators in meetings, usually jointly held with them.
5. Avoids use of propaganda literature, shuns sensationalism.
6. Rejects the inflammatory orator, radio commentator or newspaper-letter-writing addict.
7. Uses American way of getting at the truth—let all be heard, listen to both sides and make up your own mind.
8. Keeps on the issues and avoids bringing in personalities.
9. Makes decisions based upon all available evidence and only after exhaustive study.
10. Makes open and objective reports that are first submitted to the whole group for study and consideration.

Dr. Rogers associates the dishonest critical group with these characteristics:

1. Meets initially under an honest authorized group; may then begin holding secret or off-the-record sessions.
2. Tends to work under cover and use devious means of evading school officials and faculty.
3. Attracts emotionally unstable people, who are often given command of the group.
4. Uses smear literature, poison pamphlets, usually imported from the outside, or lifts phrases and slogans from them.

5. Introduces extraneous issues instead of concentrating on the agreed-upon area of discussion.
6. Accepts rabble-rousing techniques, "dust-throwing," "name-calling."
7. Permits only one side of the issue to be presented fully.
8. Frequently passes resolutions without thoughtful deliberation and regardless of all the evidence.
9. Attacks personalities—the superintendent or principal becomes the "whipping boy."
10. Makes a pretense of getting the facts, then issues ultimatums to be answered in a limited amount of time.[55]

In your orientation to your chosen profession you will read and hear remarks representing all points of view. And in this wilderness of ideas you will sometimes want to throw up your hands in despair. "Isn't there any middle ground for all these arguments? Isn't there anyone who can provide a platform to which the newcomer can return occasionally to help catch his breath?" One man whose writings frequently cut through much of the verbiage and dissension is Paul Woodring, editor of the monthly education issue of the *Saturday Review*. He has created a niche for himself that is unique in educational publications. To him—and unfortunately to not enough others—the fundamental issues are these: What is good education for American children? How can its primary purposes best be accomplished for all of them? Too often he sees us going off on tangents of lesser importance, and he is concerned about the somewhat superficial treatment of our problems by some among both the critics and the defenders.

He feels that those who teach the teachers *have* expanded their course offerings beyond all reason, that their catalogs sometimes rival the phone book in size, that simple ideas which could be developed in a few hours have been expanded into full five-credit courses a semester long. Overlapping and a special language that is meaningless to the uninitiated (and which has no very clear meaning to anyone) are subjects for legitimate criticism, he feels, as are questions of how our future and present teachers are selected and the ways in which school policies are arrived at.

But the critics are not entirely on firm ground either, he says. They

[55] Virgil M. Rogers in John Bainbridge, "Save Our Schools," *McCall's*, September, 1952, p. 83.

frequently insist on the right of every child to a high school education
—and then blame teachers for the lowered standards which inevitably result. They ask the schools to eliminate fads and frills—and
then become a pressure group which insists on a winning football
team and a marching band. They insist on higher values—but arrive
at no agreement on *which* values. They hold the school responsible
for children's bad manners, juvenile delinquency, high divorce rates
and popularity of poor television—and forget in whose environment
our young people spend three-quarters of their time.

He, in turn, is critical of those who say the academic scholars
should be more deeply involved in planning the curriculum for the
elementary and secondary schools. They are not equipped to do so,
he said. Few have any true educational philosophy, any understanding of the needs of a fourth-grader, a child with an I.Q. of 80, a girl
who wants to prepare for motherhood rather than college.

He feels the critics have too seldom undertaken the difficult task of
formulating a philosophy of education. And if they did formulate
one, he is certain it would not be acceptable to the majority of our
people. No one can satisfy all participants in our continuing educational squabbles, and even Woodring's tact, knowledge and writing
skill fail to please them. All one need do is read the letters to the
editor of the *Saturday Review* to see how widely he misses the mark
in satisfying both sides. But the most valuable part of his efforts is
that he views the scene with comparative objectivity and attains the
rare achievement of putting a complex area of conflict into simple,
clear terms. He doesn't arrive at conclusions without carefully
catalogued evidence, setting an example for the protagonists in the
educational fights and for all who hope to enter the profession with
an understanding of its difficulties as well as its accomplishments.

THE EDUCATION OF NEGRO CHILDREN

"Middle class America runneth over with sentimentality," said
Francis Keppel, U.S. Commissioner of Education in a recent talk. In
the same presentation he identified "equal opportunity" as education's first priority. But neither sentimentality nor mere recognition
of a problem is enough when it comes to the education of the chil-

dren of a full 10 percent of our population. Recent events indelibly impressed on the history of our country in Little Rock, New Orleans, the University of Mississippi, Chicago, and numerous other localities both above and below the Mason-Dixon line give vivid evidence of the problem all of us must face. You might as well include it in your repertoire of "matters of urgent concern" long before you face your first class.

Your own prejudices, as well as misinformation and lack of information, step prominently into the picture. First, let's get a few facts in hand. In a nationwide broadcast on June 11, 1963, President Kennedy made the following statements about the Negro child, in comparison with the white child:

> About one-half as much chance of completing high school
> One-third as much chance of completing college
> One-third as much chance of becoming a professional man
> Twice as much chance of becoming unemployed
> About one-seventh as much chance of earning $10,000 a year
> A life expectancy which is 7 years shorter

Action on the part of these deprived ones in our society sprang forward with the May 17, 1954 Supreme Court decision ordering desegregation of our public schools. Entangled in a total situation of which none of us can be proud are all the factors which contribute to educational inequality of our Negro children: gerrymandered school districts in the North which result in *de facto* segregation; relatively fewer qualified teachers and less teacher preparation of many who teach in predominantly Negro communities; far higher illiteracy and school dropout rates among our Negro youth; employment prejudice which often penalizes Negro young people even when they are as well qualified as their white competitors for the jobs both want; areas most in need of modern schooling frequently with the lowest tax rate, with the low socioeconomic level perpetuating the low caliber of schools.

One in four Negro 18- and 19-year-olds are out of work contrasted with one in 10 white youth. With automation eliminating factory jobs at the rate of 200,000 a year, with 70 percent or more of the 16- to 21-year-old Negro young people with no jobs in some of our large cities, and with improvement coming too slowly in the teachers and teaching for the children who will join these ranks in years to come, the total problem begins to crystallize in its full significance.

Facing south for a moment we see that school desegregation is moving along, not swiftly but steadily. In the fall of 1963, these facts emerged:

About 37 percent of the biracial school districts have desegregated (1119 districts, a gain of 293 in just 2 years).

Alabama and South Carolina desegregated for the first time—leaving Mississippi alone with wholly segregated public schools.

Most districts desegregated voluntarily—119 districts; 21 did so on the basis of a court order.

Much of the desegregation is on a token, reluctant basis, sometimes violent, sometimes begrudgingly accomplished, but the trend is firm and sure. The number of Negroes admitted to what were formerly all-white schools has increased each year. The differences in community attitudes were astounding: the screaming, spitting, and violence in New Orleans that must have been welcome grist for Communism's propaganda mill contrasted with the orderly transition represented by a quiet enrollment of the first eleven Negro students in the Charleston, South Carolina, public schools.

Many schools which Negro children attend, particularly in the rural South, are old, ramshackle, and unsanitary. Attendance frequently drops after fourth or fifth grade, and the literacy rate for our country gets more human weights to pull it down.

Negro students represent only 1 percent of our interracial college and university population, but 10 percent of the total college-age group. Most of the segregated junior colleges available to them are unaccredited, and the number of Negro Ph.D.'s, engineers, physicians, and dentists is limited by the facilities available for preparation. Their own colleges and universities are interracial, in disobedience to many local and state laws, and many have some white students. But the basic problem which seems so apparent at the college level really originates elsewhere:

A leading educator said recently, "Any Negro who is qualified can get a college education." The statement is approximately true but dodges the big issue. The fate of most talented Negro children is sealed long, long before college. The relevant question is this: "Does the intelligent Negro child enjoy a family, neighborhood or school environment which will stimulate and nourish his gifts and inspire him to high educational effort and achievement?" For too high a proportion of Negro children the answer is clearly "No." And as long as this is true the availability of college education will be a secondary issue: most Negro children with the intellectual capacity for higher education will fall by the wayside long before they get there.[56]

All but four Negro institutions of higher learning are in the South. Apparently they will continue to draw large numbers of students who are not intrigued by the idea of attending suddenly desegregated schools that admit token representation from their race.

As you know very well (if you haven't permitted your own education to interfere with what you can learn from TV documentaries), no part of the United States has a monopoly on the problem of how best to teach children who happen to belong to races other than the dominant one. The "black belt" in Northern metropolitan areas often provides educational levels lower than those of all-white communities.

Many efforts have been made to remove or limit the educational handicaps imposed on these children. After all, children in these neighborhoods need the most skillful teachers available, not the new ones or those who aren't wanted elsewhere in a system. Teacher turnover can be least easily absorbed by youngsters whose economic, family, and sometimes physical security is subject to radical change on a moment's notice. New York's Higher Horizons program, textbooks that deviate from the lily white well-dressed family complete with convertible automobile, two-story house, and picket fence, and selection of well-prepared teachers for these less-chance neighborhoods are among the steps forward. Afterschool study centers, parent education, earlier start in reading, and human relations courses for teachers are recent suggestions that also attempt to help equalize educational opportunity.

Although northern schools in many localities might never have been segregated by deliberate plan, they may actually be because a color line is drawn on housing. Since the schools in those neighborhoods are often attended only by Negro children an effort is some-

[56] John W. Gardner, *Excellence,* New York, Harper & Row, Publishers, Inc., 1961, p. 103.

times made to create a balance, deliberately transporting children by bus into and out of neighborhoods to "even out" the races in their school attendance. What happens is hardly a realistic adjustment of the school scene and in drastic contrast to the neighborhood setting when they are transported back to their totally Negro or white neighborhoods. Just give a moment's thought to the child transferred from an economic slum to a middle-class community. Disaster will really strike if, in addition to that adjustment, he ends up in the "slow section" populated by Negro children who also were "shipped in."

Among the affirmative moves are those on the college level through the efforts of the National Scholarship Service and Fund for Negro Students in New York and its Community Talent Search (CTS). Its counseling and advisory services, scholarship aid, and precollege talent hunts have meant the difference between unskilled and highly professional occupational goals. The Higher Horizons program and New York State's Project Able were helped in their start by CTS. Some institutions of higher learning are making deliberate efforts to find qualified Negro students to enroll. The University of California at Los Angeles has its sights on these potential students for graduate and professional school entry. In a rare display of cooperation, the Ivy League (Brown, Columbia, Cornell, Dartmouth, Harvard, University of Pennsylvania, Princeton and Yale) and the Seven Sisters schools (Barnard, Bryn Mawr, Mount Holyoke, Smith, Vassar, Wellesley and Radcliffe) are working together on a "talent search" among Negro students in the South.

But merely opening doors isn't enough. When some knowledgeable people talk about the social or educational "unreadiness" of a segment of Negro youth, they are being neither callous nor misled. Maybe they are being more realistic than others who gloss over the limitations imposed on at least a significant part of the Negro young population by poor teachers, run-down schools, scanty supplies, equipment, and textbooks. Desegregation will not necessarily solve these problems. It may only add to the feelings of inferiority, frustration, and anger that so dangerously become a habit of childhood and extend into adulthood among thousands in our largest racial minority.

Perhaps these feelings are the reason we hear talk about *more* than equality to make up for the years of second-class citizenship. This talk implies that educational and job opportunities should not only be opened wide, but wider than for the rest of our population. It is an idea based on common sense in the school picture for it recognizes that the teaching and guidance have been so limited that extra funds, personnel, and materials are needed if we are to come even close to equalizing opportunities in this generation.

Because we so often talk about issues in broad settings, based upon thousands or even millions of people, we may lose touch with the immediacy of a problem. In his anecdotal kind of writing, Harry Golden has sometimes been able to cut through the generalizations, and he has done so very effectively in connection with this subject. Humor helped in his proposal of a Vertical Negro Plan, based on the premise that integration is a problem only when Negroes and others *sit down* together. So let's use something like the old-fashioned bookkeeping desks in our schools, he suggests. If only the issue could be resolved that easily!

In a poignant little story he pin-points part of the problem, rather than an easy solution. It is as told to him by a former school-bus driver in a segregated school district. The driver said he spent a few uncomfortable days at the start of each new term.

"I had a very bad time of it," he reported, "when the Negro mother put her child on the bus for the first time. She would get on the bus holding the kid by the hand and she would show the child how she must go and sit in the back. The kid would look up front toward the empty seats—just look. And then for the next few days that kid would jump on the bus and take the first empty seat, like kids will do, and then the mother would run up and down the length of that bus watching anxiously through the windows, and then she would mount the bus again and again, day after day, and take that kid by the hand again and again and lead it back to the back again and again, until it understood." I asked my friend what he was doing during this process and he told me, "I just kept my eyes on the floor in front of me until I was ready to start that darn bus again."[57]

Perhaps you're asking or thinking at this time, "What's so controversial about this whole subject? Isn't it a foregone conclusion that equality of educational opportunity is part of the American

[57] Harry Golden, *Only in America*, Cleveland, World Publishing Co., 1958, p. 133.

way of life?" The answer to the second question, unfortunately, is "No." It depends on what part of the country and what part of cities, south and north, you are talking about. It requires your realistic recognition that adult job opportunities and the racial prejudice involved tell a great deal about the limited educational opportunities for these children. It demands your awareness that even now much school integration has been accomplished on only a token basis, or not at all. The most important question is not "whether" but "how quickly," for our schools and our country are on the move toward the educational equality so sorely needed for us to play fair with our heritage.

RELIGION AND THE SCHOOLS

The major controversies related to religious activity in our schools and involving both the courts and the classroom are how much religion should be taught in public schools and how much money should go to schools set up by religious groups. While legal decisions affect classroom activity, your own situation will really depend much more on the community in which you will teach. Community attitudes may dictate local policy in the area of religion just as they do for classroom discipline, kinds of report cards, homework, and which method will be used in teaching reading. But often this subject is decided at an intensified emotional level. Although we like to think that teachers and school administrators establish the patterns, they are frequently reedlike in their bending to parental and other attitudes.

Perhaps a little history is appropriate to give you a quick picture of the major issues that lawyers and courts have tried in courtrooms all over the country right up to the Supreme Court. This list is somewhat representative:

1930 Cochran versus Louisiana State Board of Education: tax funds approved for textbooks in private schools
1940 Cantwell versus Connecticut: the "Jehovah's Witnesses case" acknowledging religious freedom to believe and to act
1947 Everson versus Board of Education: payment from public funds of bus transportation for parochial school children (New Jersey)

1948   McCollum versus Board of Education: released-time religious instruction not to be given in public school buildings (Illinois)

1952   Zorach versus Clauson: released-time religious instruction permitted outside schools if there is no teacher coercion or persuasion to attend such classes (New York)

1962   Engel versus Vitale: opening school prayer declared unconstitutional (New York)

1963   School District of Abington Township, Pennsylvania versus Schempp; Murray versus Curlett: overruled the state's requiring the holding of religious exercises (Bible reading and recitation of the Lord's Prayer) even if majority affected give consent (Maryland)

The verbiage in these and other decisions, and in the legal interpretations which preceded and followed them, can be boiled down into questions like these:

Should religion be taught in public classrooms?

What is "religion" anyway? What words or ideas constitute a religious thought?

Should public money be spent for teaching religion in the public schools? In private or denominational schools?

Should public money be spent in other ways to help support private or denominational schools? Does it matter whether they are on the elementary, secondary, or university level?

Can the courts be protective and, at the same time, neutral?

Aren't we confusing the subject by not separating the *kinds* of schools we're talking about—private or independent (like Exeter, Andover, and Groton) from denominational or parochial?

The answers to these, and other questions which evolve from them, are complex and unsatisfying. For years the courts have haggled over them, and they are still unresolved and subject to more disagreement, misunderstanding, and litigation. With more than 250 Christian denominations, plus scores of others, perhaps we shouldn't expect consensus, at least not until we've taken even more time to debate the issues.

The relationship of school, church, and state is not a new topic of conversation. But it doesn't date back as far as our colonial days when school and church melted together, with the church dominating the educational offerings. All may not have liked that idea, but it satisfied most of those who were intent on getting an education for their children. When the Constitution was written, public schools as we know them today were not in existence, so we have to read it and understand its interpretations of religion and the schools with that thought in mind.

The importance of the state as it affected education grew during the nineteenth century, not only in the United States but in France and England as well. One of the pioneers was Horace Mann in his work with public schools in Massachusetts; but he agreed whole-heartedly with the idea that religion had an important place in them. However, he rebelled against restricting such instruction to one religion and thus perhaps alienating all the others. Then, as now, the problem was in teaching religion in a "broad sense" and avoiding sectarianism.

Lutherans, Episcopalians, and Presbyterians were among the prime movers for schools of their own that could teach religion as they wanted it to be learned. But their commonly held opposition to Catholicism (which in turn was strongly against public schools) brought them into line as strong supporters of the public schools. From the beginning public education was supported to a large extent by the Baptists, Methodists, and Congregationalists. Politics and prejudice in the pre-Civil War days combined to split communities and make the growth of the Common School Movement a jagged enterprise.

Because the public school was viewed by many as a Protestant-oriented enterprise and a bulwark against Catholicism this conclusion was logically reached: If we're *against* denominational schools, then we must be *for* schools that have no religious orientation. However, until recent times Bible reading and morning prayers were an accepted part of many school programs.

But the debate is on and it will continue. The families of children in religious schools pay taxes, so shouldn't they receive some of the fruits of those taxes through financial assistance to their schools? And anyway, aren't they relieving a burden on the public schools in this period of population expansion by setting up their own? Within the public schools, shouldn't children be free *to* study religion as well as free *not* to if their families' inclinations go in that direction? Shouldn't every family have the right to select the kind of school they want their children to attend and shouldn't there be financial assistance for those schools, public *or* private? Is our banning of religious activity in public schools the reason why "people say" we are less religious these days? Will public funds used for religious activity destroy our separation of church and state? violate the Constitution? interfere with public education? increase conflicts among religions? Is "shared time" part of the solution, with students of religious schools studying their academic subjects in public schools?

Congress has argued the point of public funds for religious schools for years, in its committees and on the open floor. So have our courts. So can you if the subject interests you. It's a topic that currently and in the years ahead will continue to attract diverse opinions and hot tempers.

Maybe before you head into the battle you ought to orient yourself through materials like the following, and there are hundreds of others that they and your college or university library can lead you to.

Bailyn, Bernard, *Education in the Forming of American Society,* Chapel Hill, University of North Carolina Press, 1960.

Blanshard, Paul, *Religion and the Schools: The Great Controversy,* Boston, Beacon Press, 1963.

Brickman, William W., and Stanley Lehrer (eds.), *Religion, Government and Education,* New York, Society for the Advancement of Education, 1961.

Butts, R. Freeman, *The American Tradition in Religion and Education,* Boston, Beacon Press, 1950.

Cremin, Lawrence A., *The American Common School: An Historic Conception,* New York, Bureau of Publications, Teachers College, Columbia University, 1951.

McCollum, Vashti Cromwell, *One Woman's Fight,* Garden City, N. Y., Doubleday & Company, Inc., 1951.

McGrath, John J. (ed.), *Church and State in American Law,* Milwaukee, The Bruce Publishing Company, 1962.

O'Neill, J. M., *Religion and Education Under the Constitution,* New York, Harper & Row, Publishers, Inc., 1949.

Phi Delta Kappan, more than 20 church-school articles since 1954; note especially the December, 1963 issue.

Thayer, V. T., *Religion in Public Education,* New York, The Viking Press, Inc., 1947.

An interesting exercise in semantics can evolve from the First Amendment of the Constitution which reads, "Congress shall make no law respecting an establishment of religion, or prohibiting the free exercise thereof . . ." It can be carried a step further by a discussion of how the Fourteenth Amendment is related, the one that contains these statements: ". . . No State shall make or enforce any law which shall abridge the privileges or immunities of citizens of the United States; nor shall any State deprive any person of life, liberty, or property, without due process of law . . ."

How do *you* interpret those words which sound so deceptively simple and which are the basis for most of our discussions and legal tangles on this subject?

STANDARDS—DOES ANYONE WANT TO LOWER THEM?

To say one is opposed to high standards is like saying one is against motherhood and country. It just isn't done. And yet the meaning of words like "standards" and "excellence" is too frequently associated with the trappings in education rather than with the basic materials. Instead of limiting standards and excellence to grades, the length of school periods and terms, test scores, and added quantities of science and mathematics, we should be thinking deeply about the more important factors.

Equating high standards with hard work and more of it can be depressing when quantity is everything and quality fades out of the picture. One cannot assume that standards are a factor only for those students capable of the highest intellectual excellence. What about the less capable students? Shouldn't they, too, be expected to perform at the top level of which they are capable? No one has stated the issue more capably than John W. Gardner:

Our society cannot achieve greatness unless individuals at many levels of ability accept the need for high standards of performance and strive to achieve those standards within the limits possible for them. We want the highest conceivable excellence, of course, in the activities crucial to our effectiveness and creativity as a society; but that isn't enough. If the man in the street says, "Those fellows at the top have to be good, but I'm just a slob and can act like one"—then our days of greatness are behind us. We must foster a conception of excellence which may be applied to every degree of ability and to every socially acceptable activity. A missile may blow up on its launching pad because the designer was incompetent or because the mechanic who adjusted the last valve was incompetent. The same is true of everything else in our society. We need excellent physicists and excellent mechanics. We need excellent cabinet members and excellent first-grade teachers. The tone and fiber of our society depend upon a pervasive and almost universal striving for good performance.[58]

Many factors interfere with the search for and establishment of standards of which we can be proud. Attitudes that too frequently permeate our society and are transmitted to our children are revealed in such slang expressions as "doing someone in"; "beating someone out"; "cutting someone short"; giving a "needle," "shaft," or "dirty end of the stick." Also part of the atmosphere are the what's-in-it-for-me attitude, the condoning of laziness, complacency, and buck-passing, and the search for the easy dollar.

Free men must be competent men, Gardner writes, for competence is an elementary duty. "And the man who does a slovenly job—whether he is a janitor or a judge, a surgeon or a technician—lowers the tone of society. So do the chiselers of high or low degree, the sleight-of-hand artists who always know how to gain an advantage without honest work. They are the regrettable burdens of a free society."[59]

The whole subject takes on a lowly meaning when high expectations, achievement, and standards are equated in schools in terms of grades attained or sought. Instead of "What did I learn?" the theme becomes "How did I do?" Instead of "Did I succeed?" the question is "Did I pass?" On all levels, but especially in colleges and universities, a disproportionate importance is placed on grades, the belief being that the lower the grade the tougher the instructor and the higher the standards. Conduct a little informal survey on almost any campus by asking: "Who are the best instructors? Are their standards high? Are their grading patterns low?" You will find that high standards are not equated with skillful teaching or keeping up with one's field, but with loading on the work, grading low, giving

---

[58] Gardner, pp. 131–132.
[59] *Ibid.*, pp. 159–160.

tough exams. (A response sometimes given to this approach is that a teacher should take no more pride in his failures than a hospital does in its deaths.)

Rigor as its own goal will not improve any school setting. It will not result in better teaching, studying or higher achievement. But it can be part of a total school situation from which children will profit greatly. The more rigorous new school as seen by many who want to "tighten up" our educational programs is not viewed as reversion to a barren past based on "rote, rod and repetition."[60] But it is also distantly removed from the extremes of more "liberal" programs advocated by some in the 1930s and 1940s. This kind of school puts emphasis on mastery of oral and written expression and on reading. It gets past the arguments of *which* method to use and shows a willingness to use *all* methods, the key point being "Will it work for this child?" It has a carefully planned curriculum but retains an element of flexibility which permits adjustment to various children. Since the timing of learning is less exact than in the past, this new school is less sure that geometry has to wait for secondary school and that formal reading begins in first grade. It says that learning, even in a formalized way, can be as much fun as play is.

One of the disciples of the new school is Carl F. Hansen, superintendent in Washington, D.C. His prime example of what can be done is the Amidon School with its "phonovisual" approach to reading (a combination basically of phonics, words, and word pictures), strong emphasis on writing and early mathematics, and formal grammar in the fourth grade. Hansen feels that this is a determined effort to walk an unswerving line between "basic" and "progressive" education, borrowing the best from both. He insists that the approach to learning must be direct and not buried in units or other roundabout methods, that geography should be taught with emphasis on specific places and history approached in chronological terms.[61]

The curriculum at Amidon School is firm, predetermined, and based on discrete subjects. Hansen feels that grouping tends to fragment instruction time, believes in a textbook in each subject and

[60] Fred M. Hechinger, "Rout or Progress: The Rigorous New School Is Seen as More Than Counter-Revolt," *New York Times*, October 15, 1961.

[61] Carl F. Hansen, *The Amidon Elementary School*, Englewood Cliffs, N. J., Prentice-Hall, Inc., 1962.

regular homework assignments. The school has received parental approval (there are waiting lists to get in) and support and acceptance of its techniques by all elementary-school administrators in Washington. This has all come quickly. Its methods are said by some professional educators to be rigid, reactionary, and reversionary to the "old days." But even some of the top people in the NEA (Stinnett, for example) have only praise for many parts of it.

Higher standards may evolve from the efforts of schools like Amidon. They may also result from the work going on year after year by dedicated and well-qualified teachers wherever they are located, teachers who teach the classics to those who can absorb their deepest meanings, who use other versions for those who cannot. The highest standard to set for each child is to offer him the best, most profound, most challenging ideas in every subject area, and expect him to do all that he is capable of. Few disagree with such a standard. The disagreement concerns the method.

TEACHING ABOUT COMMUNISM

In some schools, until recent months, even mentioning the word "communism" was tantamount to subversion, to being a person suspected of dire motives. What is a respectable subject for discussion changes frequently in our schools as it does in our homes and communities. Mental retardation, various aspects of sex education, and religious holidays have all gone through these attitude changes, but none with the turbulence of communism as a subject for discussion and understanding among our children. In the hectic years preceding and during World War II the political aspects of Naziism never prompted such arguments. It was recognized for what it was, and there was very little difference of opinion. But teachers who have brought the subject of communism into their classes, even using the best documented materials from the most authoritative sources, have faced problems from many parents. In some instances the accusations have been intense. In a few they have even resulted in dismissals and court cases.

But times are changing. In March, 1962, a group of 150 educators met in Washington, D.C. under the auspices of the U.S. Office of

Education to discuss this and related issues. Among the recommendations that came from the meeting were these: (1) Officials in charge of school curricula should intensify efforts to teach about "isms," including both communism and fascism; (2) parallel study between the American and other systems should be considered; (3) regional conferences should be called to discuss techniques of teaching about freedom and different cultures.

An American Bar Association committee recently published a handbook *(Instruction on Communism and Its Contrast with Liberty Under Law)* which said that separate high school courses should deal with "communism in depth," contrasting its doctrines, methods, and objectives with ours. The handbook stresses the importance of viewing this instructional program as educational rather than as a form of counterpropaganda. Materials related to teaching about communism are also products of a joint committee of the NEA and the American Legion. A 1962 list of publications on various aspects of communism as released by the Superintendent of Documents, U.S. Government Printing Office, includes 63 titles.

The seriousness with which this whole subject has been approached recently is indicated by the setting up of a "Research Institute on Communist Strategy and Propaganda" at the University of Southern California. It was initially financed by a private gift of $325,000. The contributors, Mr. and Mrs. Henry Salvatori, felt that its results could be of great value to educational leaders.

A survey showed 63 percent of the nation's school administrators to be strongly in favor of high school seniors studying about communism; 57 percent felt that such a course should be required. Several warnings accompanied the replies pointing out the many difficulties involved and the need for thoroughly competent and positive teaching. There were differences of opinion about length of time needed for the subject. Florida secondary schools are required to offer a 30-hour course on "Americanism versus Communism." The Louisiana legislature appropriated $30,000 annually for high school seminars on the tactics and strategy of communism. In California, an advisory committee to the state's Superintendent of Public Instruction has been working on methods of teaching about Communism. A New York state education law took effect in the fall of 1962 which stated that courses of study beyond the first 8 years of full-time public day schools may provide a course on communism, its methods, and its destructive effects.

In a quiet way one of the country's outstanding private schools has set up a "Russian Studies Center for Secondary Schools." The Choate School in Connecticut opened the Center in January, 1963. Its emphasis is on the study of the language, history, politics, economics, and culture of Russia. Materials are available to high school teachers anywhere in the country. It hopes to help meet the danger of superficial teaching and special courses on the dangers of Communism by providing materials and techniques that can result in real understanding of these dangers.

A national survey of our 58 largest city school systems showed the following: only 2 have a full semester course on communism; 22 require that some time be given in social science courses to this subject; 43 assume that a certain amount of time will be devoted to it. The North Atlantic, Great Lakes, and Plains states have more required work in this area than other parts of the country—but they also indicated they have more difficulty obtaining suitable instructional materials.

Perhaps this doesn't seem to add up to a strong disagreement, but in certain circles tempers still flare when the subject is mentioned. Should we try to be objective or always show a bias toward our own system? Should we let teachers teach this subject freely, on the basis of their own discretion, or must strict curricular aspects be worked out in advance? Should communism be taught by itself or in a framework that includes all totalitarian philosophies? Should it be based on a comparative approach (with our own system) or taught factually by itself? Should it approach the future as an indefinite period of cold war, inevitable hot war, or what? Should we use education, propaganda, or a combination? Should the subject be ignored entirely, on the premise that to teach about it may call undue attention to it and thus in some way aid and abet an enemy? Can we trust our teachers to bring moral judgments as well as information into their classrooms? Can facts be taught without criticism or evaluation? What is the place of emotion in the whole affair? What source materials should be used? Which agencies and organizations can be trusted to approach the subject with at least some effort at objectivity in their published works? How should teachers be prepared to do the job, and who should prepare them? Although we seem to agree on the dangers of communism, can we ever agree on the best ways of fighting it? Whether teachers can or *should* be neutral on a topic as fraught with emotional overtones as this one is basic to the whole issue.

In your early years of teaching, this subject will be an area for concern, regardless of your level, kindergarten, elementary, secondary, or university. As long as the U.S.S.R. remains strong, challenging us in science, trade, and other areas, as long as the world's power structure is based largely on our two countries, as long as there is an overwhelming feeling in our country that this problem dominates practically all others, the teacher will remain in the center of the picture. Children will come to him for guidance, facts and understandings. They do so in the academic areas, and they do not draw a line of distinction between these and a vital subject like communism. It is essential that all teachers be as well prepared as they possibly can be to cope with some of the questions as they arise. The sources they use will no doubt depend on which members of the community or university campus they go to for suggestions—and what their own common sense and intelligence dictate. A recent article said:

We must do better than be "against," we must be "for". . . . Not only should the raw material of our own nation's story be open to the student but also the corresponding raw material of the history of other people. Democracy has nothing to fear from such a seeking after the truth. . . . There is a need for teaching about communism, not as a crash program in answer to the excitement of the current crisis, but as a rational part of a broader approach to citizenship education. . . .[62]

ACADEMIC FREEDOM

Many of you will not have been much aware of an era that resounded with arguments over loyalty oaths and varying opinions on the dedication of teachers to their nation. Unless you go back

[62] Curtis C. Jennings, "Teaching About Communism," *Educational Leadership*, May, 1963, pp. 507–511.

through the voluminous literature on this entire subject, you may not know or care that hundreds of teachers have been dismissed or threatened with dismissal because they expressed opinions in their classrooms that someone didn't like. In some communities a teacher earned the label of "un-American" or "Communist" because he stated ideas with which others differed—especially if those others happened to be influential persons in the community. And the struggle began: Who said what, under what circumstances, and what did the words mean? Seldom was as much consideration given to the actual effect on the children as to what some members of the community *felt* the effect might be. "I've never known a teacher yet who got fired because the kids didn't learn anything. But if the teacher says something unpopular ..."[63]

The need for speaking one's mind isn't the crucial issue. The need for doing so with responsibility, on the basis of accurate information, with deep understanding of the meanings involved, and with full respect for the children, their parents, and the community in which one is teaching comes closer to the crux of the problem. Any interpretation of this issue must go back to essentials, to the first amendment to the Constitution and earlier, to freedom of speech in its broadest sense. But it must also take into consideration the redefinitions of that guarantee by the Supreme Court, Congressional committees, and various state and local laws.

It is true that relatively few teachers have been touched directly by this issue; few have been investigated or questioned. Many, on the other hand, are totally unaware that there *is* an issue as they go on teaching freely and with complete security, teaching as they always have taught, using materials and techniques that are accepted by those who set policies. But some do feel the pressures, through groups and individuals who want textbooks re-edited or eliminated, controversial subjects toned down or not discussed at all, lectures revised in accordance with their own points of view. Force used on the academic scene to make teachers and materials conform can have a disastrous effect on the creativity of both teachers and children. This subject came into focus during the early 1950s in some unbelievable ways:

[63] Martin Mayer, *The Schools*, New York, Harper & Row, Publishers, Inc., 1961, p. 32.

In 1951, . . . one professor, a gentle (even innocuous) man, told me that he no longer discarded papers in his office wastebasket because he feared that a janitor might find something written by him or to him which would be reported, and for which he would have to answer to an investigating committee. This he could not face, for though he knew his life to be inno-cent of any traffic with "the enemy," he was sure that to be called for public investigation would blacken his name and quite possibly cost him advancement or even his job.

Such are the fears that enforce conformity! Such was the temper of the McCarthy era, in which traditional and constitutional guarantees of free-dom reeled under the daily headlines and under the power of the voice which proclaimed, "I hold in my hand a list . . ." Never mind that it might be a laundry list. Heads were falling, and suspicion among men grew to monstrous proportions.[64]

Some people have become a little bored with the whole concept of "freedom" as it is discussed in newspapers and magazines, in mushy editorials and feature articles. Such passive, reluctant, and disinterested attitudes lack a full understanding of how important the total concept is. Freedom to think a thought through, to say what one wants to, to reject the ideas and opinions of others, to seek and transmit the truth as one sees it—these kinds of freedom belong in the classroom as well as in the home and neighborhood. Always it has to be limited by one factor—the welfare, under law, of another person or group. Maintaining free expression in the academic setting is difficult whenever bigotry is at work. An individual teacher may face it in various forms—religious, racial, moral, political. And usu-ally there is little or no redress, even through the professional organi-zations to which the teacher may belong.

An important aspect of academic freedom is related to instruc-tional materials. Who selects them? What are the qualifications of those who do? What criteria are used? (In May, 1963, the *NEA Journal* devoted a special feature to "Censorship of Textbooks.") In a supposedly fictitious case, Lieberman poses the problem:

Suppose a high-school history teacher decides to have his class study whether the Communist party in the United States is or is not a tool of Russian foreign policy. What materials should he use in the classroom? He should have the official statements of Russian foreign policy and those

64 H. Harry Giles, "Intellectual Freedom," *NEA Journal,* March, 1961, p. 11.

of the Communist party in this country. For the latter purpose, he would need copies of the *Daily Worker*. By reading them, students could see for themselves how the Communist party in the United States did in fact follow every turn and twist of Russian foreign policy.

All this seems reasonable enough—or does it? I doubt whether a single public school teacher, superintendent, or school board in the country would dare to order such materials, even though they provide the most devastating information on the Communist party obtainable anywhere. The teachers are not going to take any chances with a school board which, if it is typical, divides instructional materials into such ridiculous categories as "subversive" or "patriotic." And the board is not likely to "take any chances" on a teacher who requests such material. "School Board Approves Daily Worker In the Schools"—a millennium of explanations would not undo the damage of one such headline.[65]

How free is the high school history teacher Lieberman referred to? How much faith do communities generally have in the professional judgments of teachers who are hired to do a particular job and who are then watched and "corrected" if any of the "right" people are offended? To be specific, have we always distinguished clearly between calling an innocent man a Communist and calling a Communist a Communist?

No matter how irresponsible an accusation might be, a question about a teacher's loyalty often arouses suspicions regarding that loyalty. One remark is sometimes enough to bring the tag of "controversial," even "subversive," on an individual, despite all the proof of its falsity. The old line of "where there's smoke there's fire" has been used in situations of this kind. A sad thing may result from this accusation-label-suspicion sequence. It may force us to lose unspoken speeches, unwritten words, unexpressed ideas from some of the brightest members of our population. It may convince them, before the accusation is even uttered, to melt quietly into the environment, to teach the necessary classes, counsel the necessary students and then go home and lie in the sun.

The losers, of course, are the children directly, all of us indirectly. The creative person who conforms cannot very well inspire creativity in the youngsters he teaches. If his words are rounded off to satisfy all possible objections from any quarter, he may arouse no ire—but

[65] Myron Lieberman, *The Future of Public Education*, pp. 65–66.

he also may inspire no response other than the answer to the next problem on the page. Fear, subservience, and textbook mimicry can hardly help this generation cope with the unfathomable problems in this last part of the twentieth century.

The opposite of academic freedom may be termed "thought control," a concept against whose beginnings we must always be on guard. The Japanese and Germans bowed to a portrait and "heiled" a symbol as a result of it. The Russians and their supporters bend fully in approval of the vagaries of the U.S.S.R. as a result of it. We usually feel it cannot happen to us—and yet it already has happened. In some communities thoroughly responsible, capable, professional teachers face the task of teaching what a vocal minority dictates they should teach.

Each teacher must answer some questions which frequently are unasked. You have to answer them, too: If a subject that has two or more sides to it comes up in your classroom, should you take a stand or be an impartial moderator? Should you encourage students to take a stand? Which is preferable—student indecision or student value judgments? How will you evaluate student maturity, information that is available and capable of being understood, your adeptness at controlling the discussion, your emotions, whether your approach to the issues is systematic? Is it ever appropriate for the teacher to play the role of political partisan, to indoctrinate with views privately held?

To be eligible for a teaching position in most states one must take an oath to support the Constitution of the United States and the state, and swear that one does not believe in or advocate the overthrow of the government by force and violence. Many statutes also require that a teacher say he is not and will not become a member of any organization advocating the forceable overthrow of the government. Most of the test cases, publicity, and discussions have centered around oaths on the college and university levels.

Book censorship, recognition of holidays in various religions, and sex education are also topics for heated discussion. The attitudes of both teachers and communities get right back to our basic concept: Any controversial issue should be approached with responsibility, accurate information, deep understanding, and respect for all the persons who may be touched by it. But to keep issues out of school is to keep life out of them.

"THE GOOD OLD DAYS"

"Our youth now loves luxury: they have bad manners, contempt for authority: they show disrespect for elders and love chatter in place of exercise. Children are now tyrants, not the servants of their households. They no longer rise when elders enter the room. They contradict their parents, chatter before company, gobble their food, and tyrannize their teachers."

So said Socrates in the fifth century B.C. And being reminded of his remarks makes one wonder whether it has ever been different. It is always the present generation that seems to have the greatest problems. So it is, too, with education. In the days gone by schools were presumably run smoothly, children learned, materials were not as foolish as the present "readers" in the primary grades, teachers were better prepared and more qualified for their jobs. Or is that really true?

Some people try to dispose of current criticisms of the schools by saying that the critics want to turn the clock back. But many of the accusations against educational programs, materials and personnel cannot be dismissed that easily. All of them are not based on reverting to an earlier era. Hansen insists that changes put into action in the Amidon experiment are not a reversion to "stilted education of the turn of the century." He sees these changes as moving education in a forward direction.

It is sometimes fun to look back at the schools as they were a generation or more ago. For a few moments let's break through the time barrier. Let's go back for a while and look at schools in the "good old days," skipping back and forth through the years.

When we were boys, boys had to do a little work in school. They were not coaxed; they were hammered. Spelling, writing and arithmetic were not electives, and you had to learn. In these more fortunate times, elementary education has become in many places a vaudeville show. The child must be kept amused and learns what he pleases. Many teachers scorn the old-fashioned rudiments; and it seems to be regarded as a misfortune and a crime for a child to learn to read and spell by the old methods. As a result of all the improvements, there is a race of gifted pupils more or less ignorant of the once-prized elements of an ordinary education.

New York Sun, October 5, 1902

Now, what I want is, Facts. Teach these boys and girls nothing but Facts. Facts alone are wanted in life. Plant nothing else, and root out everything else. You can only form the minds of reasoning animals upon Facts: nothing else will ever be of any service to them. This is the principle on which I bring up my own children, and this is the principle on which I bring up these children. Stick to the Facts, sir!

Charles Dickens, *Hard Times*

The air is full of theories, schemes, frills and fads. Especially do we fear that with so much that is new and old, fundamentals are in danger of being neglected. The children may learn these new things, but they must first learn to read, write, spell, and cipher.

The Popular Educator, 1883

(The frills referred to here were history, science, drawing, music, and manual training. As an example of recent changes in parental attitudes, Charles T. St.Clair, superintendent of schools in North Haven, Connecticut said that he once fought to retain Latin, and now has to fight to hold on to physical education.)

There are doubts concerning the business [of education] since all people do not agree in these things which they would have a child taught, both with respect to improvement in virtue and a happy life; nor is it clear whether the object of it should be to improve the reason or rectify the morals. From the present mode of education we cannot determine with certainty to which men incline, whether to instruct a child in which will be useful to him in life, or what tends to virtue, or what is excellent; for all these things have their separate defenders.

Aristotle, 300 B.C.

Our schools are in a feeble and backward state. We think the modern mode of instruction is decidedly bad.

School committee minutes, New England, 1856

Almost universal lack of distinct articulation, proper pronunciation and correct spelling.

Citizens' Committee, Madison, Wisconsin, 1901

. . . more than eleven-twelfths of all children in the reading classes in our schools do not understand the meaning of the words they read . . . they do not master the sense of the reading lessons . . . the ideas and feelings intended by the author to be conveyed to and excited in the reader's mind still rest in the author's intention, never yet having reached the place of their destination.

Horace Mann, 1838

Written examinations are impossible in the Medical School. A majority of the students cannot write well enough.

Dean of Harvard Medical School, 1870

It's the common complaint among business men that young people seeking employment are not well grounded in the fundamentals.

President of Chicago Board of Education, 1909

Our civilization is doomed if the unheard-of actions of our younger generations are allowed to continue. They are rowdy and disrespectful and they stay up late at night.

An ancient tablet unearthed at an excavation site in Ur

We could continue almost indefinitely with the dissatisfactions expressed toward schools throughout history. They include the 1845 survey in Boston which expressed shame, embarrassment, and "melancholy consideration," summing the whole thing up by referring to the exhibit of "frightful ignorance." They abound with figures like this one from 1900 in a metropolitan school system: 36 percent of the elementary-school pupils were unable to read. John Erskine expressed disgust with the spelling of his Amherst freshmen in 1903.

Education in years gone by is hardly seen objectively through glasses or eyes or memories dimmed by the intervening years. Certain facts must be brought into the picture. Only a minority of the population went to school at all in some of the eras cited above. Only an infinitesimal group went to or finished college. The knowledge and preparation of teachers, the classroom conditions, the materials for study were crude and extremely limited. Let's be fair— few of us would prefer those settings for ourselves or our children. Frequently we make the error of comparing the best of the past with the worst of the present, Aunt Minnie's beautiful handwriting with Jim's series of smudges that are supposed to communicate. No actress has been more beautiful than Billie Dove, no actor more daring than Douglas Fairbanks, Sr., no song more beautiful than "Stars Fell on Alabama," and no teacher or school better than the ones *we* were exposed to.

Such statements, unhappily, are based on emotion rather than actual facts. The past, whether it was 500 B.C. or 1900 A.D., left much to be desired educationally as well as in other directions. We worry about income taxes, but they (depending on which age we select) worried about typhoid, flu epidemics, death in childbirth. We feel our schools do not do well enough with all the money, facilities, and personnel available, but they also knew their schools were failing them—and the criticisms of them, as already indicated, are disturbingly current in their wording and meaning. Most of their adults couldn't read at all, and many of ours are addicts of comic books and poor television, have poor or no home libraries, and spell poorly. They wasted time in school with spelling bees based on meaningless words and faulty geography facts, and we frequently tie together a school day based on too little learning and too much unstructured activity of one type or another.

The most important issue related to "the good old days" is often overlooked. It is simply this: Are our schools today as good as they *ought* to be, as good as they *have* to be to prepare children to live as adults after 2000 A.D.? Whether our children read, figure, and understand as well as children did years ago isn't of any real importance. Are we teaching and are they learning as well as we and they *should?* Comparative statistics of the then-and-now type are far less important than an analysis of what we are doing, are capable of doing, and must do today and in the years you will be teaching. Getting bogged down in past-and-present comparisons may be interesting, but too often it forces us to lose sight of the real issue. As Paul Woodring said,

. . . some of us are convinced that teaching these things just as well as we did in 1920 or in 1900 is not nearly good enough. We ought to be teaching them far better if our increased knowledge of the psychology of learning has been of any use to us. And when a parent protests that Junior cannot read, it does not comfort him to be told that the *average* child reads as well as did his grandparents. Junior still cannot read, and the parent will understandably remain unhappy until something is done about it.[66]

Although many people nostalgically look back at days long gone, others are glad they are over! And whether we are talking about travel, cooking, sickness, utilities, plumbing, or education, it seems far more challenging and important to look ahead rather than back.

[66] Paul Woodring, *Let's Talk Sense About Our Schools*, McGraw-Hill Book Company, Inc., 1953, p. 128.

CONCLUDING REMARKS

The major issues in this chapter and the somewhat less vital ones in the next cannot tell the entire story of controversy in our schools. Arguments and discussions of the greatest importance may be restricted to a local situation—to the qualifications of a particular teacher, whether a certain book should be in the library or banned, who decides on academic standards. Or they may be state-wide, regional, or national. They may plumb the deepest feelings aroused by the subject of religion, by Supreme Court decisions on segregation, or by the mere mention of the United Nations, UNESCO, and World Health Organization.

It is always surprising that so many people have rabid feelings on these and other subjects about which they know very little. And therein lies the crux of this entire discussion. Other people may misuse, misstate, and misinterpret facts, but you can't. You're a teacher, and the truth must be sought at all times and from all sources. More is expected of you than of others. Such is the very welcome responsibility of the teaching profession.

CHAPTER 7

A TIME FOR *Controversial Issues: Some of the Smaller Ones*

Controversy can be as distinguished as a debate between candidates for the highest office in the land or as traumatic as a wifely query regarding lipstick on a handkerchief. It permeates our homes, our communities, our country, and the world in which we live. So why should anyone assume that the very human environment of people working together in a school should be immune, or that there should be no conflict between the school and those who support it financially? Expecting academic relationships to be perpetually without differences, difficulties or dispute is to expect what never was, never will be, and never should be. Progress evolves from discussion based on varying points of view. A number of the vital topics for such discussion have already been brought to your attention. Now let's look at a few of the lesser problems.

DISCIPLINE

Discipline can be defined as narrowly as a rap across the knuckles or as broadly as the whole area of preventing emotional problems and delinquency. Some who have written on this subject permit the educational "disease" of definitions to get in their way. (Oliva compiled a list of 25 of them[1] and earlier Bagley devoted an entire book to the subject.[2]) Future teachers are seldom as concerned about discipline as first-year teachers; and some of the latter fail to realize

[1] Peter F. Oliva, "High School Discipline in American Society," *Bulletin of the National Association of Secondary School Principals,* January, 1956, pp. 5–6.

[2] William C. Bagley, *School Discipline,* New York, The Macmillan Company, 1916.

that discipline isn't the basic difficulty at all. More frequently it may be a deficiency on the part of the teacher: lack of knowledge about subject matter, children, one's own philosophy of education, or something else. Perhaps the climax comes in Johnny's throwing a spitball, but he isn't the cause of his own action.

Nor do we always have clearly in mind the distinction between corrective and preventive discipline. Hundreds of available articles, pamphlets, and books delve into all aspects of this topic. You may find these of value:

Association for Supervision and Curriculum Development, *Discipline for Today's Children and Youth.*

James L. Hymes, Jr., *Behavior and Misbehavior,* New York, Prentice-Hall, 1955.

"Special Feature on Discipline," *NEA Journal,* September, 1958 (and other references on page 379 of that issue).

But maybe you want some hints here, with no promise attached that they will solve all your potential problems in this area. Let's list some things you can at least begin to think about:

Do you understand the importance of knowing everything you should about your children? Are they really "mean," "troublesome," "cheating," "belligerent" without a cause that can be determined—or does the cause lie in their not hearing, seeing, or mentally absorbing what is going on? In other words, does a disciplinary situation arise because you don't know what is actually behind it, what is basically bothering the child?

Do you realize how vital it is to adapt your program to what they are capable of accomplishing? This question does *not* mean "watering down"!

Do you know what "marginal vision" is? Do you know that it can help you anticipate and prepare for problems before they arise? (Perhaps you don't know how well you can see marginally, so try this: Look straight ahead with arms stretched out in front of you—slowly move your arms stiffly toward the sides—stop when your hands fade out of your line of vision. It's a mighty broad eye span, isn't it?)

Do you know the importance of classroom environment as far as temperature, light, ventilation, and the size of furniture are concerned?

The hickory stick, the cold look, the hurt expression, the challenging activities, the bright new book—whatever will work for you and whatever is encouraged in your school and community can be used for preventing and correcting disciplinary situations. Here is a keynote, however: In the classroom where children are learning and happy, where they and their teacher demonstrate daily the best practices of respect for human beings, where there is variety and humor, this is the place where discipline is seldom a problem. Children are human, devilish, and fun-loving (and teachers have moods!), but it may be possible to reduce the clash of personalities and increase cooperation.

Psychologists have told us for decades that the most and best learning takes place during the first 5 years. Children learn to walk, talk, get along with others (reasonably well!), and take care of their most pressing needs. Nothing they learn later can hold a candle to the accomplishments of those early years. What were the circumstances under which all that learning occurred? Did we say, "Learn how to say these new words today and you'll get a star—or be placed in the corner"? Did we draw a chalk line on the floor and insist, "Learn to walk this in a straight way. Keep trying until you do. If you don't, you'll learn the reason why"? Did we demand, "You stay right there until you learn what you're sitting there for—if it takes all day"?

The "three D's" (drudgery, drill, and dreariness) are least necessary—if they are *ever* appropriate—in the first few grades. Have you talked to some little children lately who are going to school for the first time next year? What's their attitude? Generally it is one of eagerness and curiosity, a desire to be there and to learn. (Except perhaps when Mother or Dad has unknowingly hammered away at, "Wait till you get to school! You'll learn to be quiet or eat or go to sleep or not talk back then!") Usually they want answers and are easily stimulated to find those answers. The "Why?" of the four-year-old still comes a year or two later for a wise, friendly teacher to capitalize on.

If, as parents or teachers, we insist that our children be exposed to and exploited by "three D's," let's add a fourth D, for it is there whether we welcome it or not: Despair. Or let's ditch that whole unpleasant array and move on to the next letter in the alphabet; E is for empathy, enjoyment, encouragement, and the resulting excitement that comes with the learning of young children. Sometimes something happens to the bright-eyed eagerness with which they first come to school. Or maybe we should say some*body* happens to them, somebody who stifles that eagerness.

Is complete quiet always necessary in order to learn? Tell that to the thousands who studied accounting or law to the clacking of public transportation as they attended "streetcar colleges" during the 1930s. Hearing the clock tick, having hands folded, going to the blackboard "by the numbers," keeping feet flat on the floor, using corners for "problem children" until it looks as though an octagon-shaped classroom is needed—although these outer manifestations of sound discipline and a good learning situation may get an approving nod from certain school administrators and teachers, these are not necessarily the ingredients of a scholarly atmosphere.

However, neither are factors like turmoil, tumult and talking, elements that it is more frequently vital to warn new young teachers against. They may have a tendency to "group it up" or encourage children to collect haphazardly into "buzz sessions." The stimulating results they seek may melt into a sad morass of classroom confusion where both discipline and learning have joined hands—and left the room.

The use of corporal punishment with children has been argued for years, and your attitude will be a direct result of your own experience. In a Teacher-Opinion Poll conducted by the NEA Research Division this question was asked: "Do you favor the judicious use of corporal punishment as a disciplinary measure in elementary schools?" Almost 72 percent said, "Yes." A slightly higher proportion of men than women teachers, and of secondary over elementary teachers, favored these measures in the elementary grades. A similar question was asked of secondary teachers regarding such action in the secondary schools, and the affirmative reply was 58 percent.[3]

A study of pupil behavior conducted by this same research group reported some interesting teacher opinions. Among its conclusions were the following:

69 percent replied that pupil behavior was "not nearly so bad" as portrayed by the press, movies and radio.

In answering a question about students who were "trouble makers," 29 percent said none, 35 percent said less than 1 percent, and 23 percent said 1 to 4 percent.

Only 1.6 percent of the teachers reported an act of physical violence against themselves in their school that year. (Seems like a small figure, but not if you are the one or two involved!)

[3] Reported in the *NEA Journal*, May, 1961, p. 13.

Almost half of the teachers classified students as exceptionally well behaved
in neighborhoods with good living conditions; but the figure fell to less
than one in six teachers in slum areas. (James B. Conant's book *Slums
and Suburbs* sheds additional light on this subject.)

Most parents cooperate with the school on behavior problems, the teachers
felt; but 4 percent of them reported that in the majority of cases they
received no home cooperation. Only 8 percent of the teachers said students as a whole were well behaved when parents did not cooperate.

When asked about misbehavior compared with 10 and 20 years earlier,
they felt there were increases in impertinence and discourtesy to teachers, failure to do homework, and drinking. But in the column headed
"No occurrence, then or now" the figures were high for gang fighting,
use of narcotics, carrying switch-blade knives, and physical violence
against teachers.[4]

Some people feel that the abolishment of physical discipline is a
major cause of juvenile delinquency and contributes to its increase.
Others counter by referring to the evidence that such discipline has
been retained, that teachers and administrations favor its retention,
and that we *still* have behavior problems. They point in other directions, toward home, church, and other community resources and
agencies that share the responsibility for helping young people develop healthfully. Although we often look for the pat answer, we
are forced to realize that misbehavior has many causes. It's easy to
make up a list of them. You could start with this question: Why did
you misbehave at certain times in your past? Could any of the following be among the reasons: poor teaching; poor home conditions;
rundown neighborhoods; lack of guidance or supervision at home
or school. Separating child behavior from environment and from the
state of the world as a whole may be a convenient thing to attempt,
but it is hardly a realistic approach. Misbehavior (a temporary state
of affairs for practically all of us at one time or another) and delinquency (highly dramatized in press, television, and films, but actually at the 1 to 3 percent level for the country as a whole) are
certainly not the same thing. We have to be careful as we toss terms
around.

Although the so-called "new concept" of discipline is more discussed than practiced, corporal punishment, despite the support for

[4] NEA, Research Division, "Teacher Opinion on Pupil Behavior, 1955–56,"
Research Bulletin, April, 1956, pp. 51–107.

it, is not as widely used as it once was (Bob Hope said, "I was reared in Philadelphia—about twice a day"). The positive approach may not work all the way through; but the current feeling apparently is at least to give it a chance.

A recent survey in Great Britain on this subject indicates that we are not alone in this trend.[5] The use of "caning" (their equivalent of paddling) is an admission of the teacher's failure, it concludes. The report indicates that in school where there is little or no caning, behavior is on the whole better and delinquency less prevalent than in "medium or heavy" caning schools.

The most vibrant recent contribution to high blood pressure among those who support unstintingly a strong-arm approach in school comes from the British headmaster A. S. Neill, as he tells about the school he founded in 1921. Based primarily on his belief in the basic goodness of children, he builds a case for an atmosphere for child growth where unhappiness will not develop, where children are free "to be themselves." His school renounces all discipline, direction, suggestion, moral training, religious instruction, and required class attendance. Rules are determined at meetings where each person (child and teacher alike) has one vote; learning comes after play; self-regulation is the order of the day; repression and guilt feelings are not permitted. Neill's philosophy related to discipline is represented by these comments:

I believe that to impose anything by authority is wrong. The child should not do anything until he comes to the opinion—his own opinion—that it should be done. The curse of humanity is the external compulsion, whether it comes from the Pope or the state or the teacher or the parent. It is fascism in toto.

Most people demand a god; how can it be otherwise when the home is ruled by tin gods of both sexes, gods who demand perfect truth and moral behavior? Freedom means doing what you like, so long as you don't interfere with the freedom of others. The result is self-discipline.

. . . in the main, Summerhill runs along without any authority or any obedience. Each individual is free to do what he likes *as long as he is not tresspassing on the freedom of others.* And this is a realizable aim in any community.[6]

[5] Reported in the *New York Times,* October 29, 1961, education page.
[6] A. S. Neill, *Summerhill,* New York, Hart Publishing Co., 1960, pp. 114, 155.

As if all of that weren't horrible enough for those who really feel that physical discipline will solve our educational problems, a Summerhill Society has been formed in this country. Its objective is to set up a school here based on Neill's principles, including the ones of "freedom without license," equal rights of teachers and children, and no compulsion related to class attendance.

GROUPING

For generations teachers have looked for "like factors" in the children who face them in the classroom. The word that describes this quality in milk is "homogeneity"; but in human beings close similarities continue to be evasive. The teacher of the old one-room school frequently cut across age lines and brought together two or three youngsters who at least had in common certain phases of arithmetic ability or language skills or science concepts. The most widely used effort today along these lines is based on age alone—if you're 6 years old by a certain date, you go into first grade, and no other information about you is of comparable importance.

But some teachers and administrators do attempt to go beyond age classification and acknowledge that there are other differences that must be considered. How about intelligence, maturity, knowledge? All of these must be reconciled in some way, they say—and that is where the problem arises. Identifying each of these accurately, keeping the school program flexible enough to accommodate temporary grouping arrangements on the basis of student need, and satisfying parents and teachers in the process are all vital points in this area. Parents of those not grouped often provide a stubborn opposition. Commonly brought into the discussion is the fallacious claim that grouping is in some way undemocratic. (Have you ever heard that accusation made related to the selection of football players, band participants, or choir members?)

Many rash claims and counterclaims have been made about grouping practices, so we must see what research—sound research—says about them. Here are a few of the more acceptable conclusions on the subject:

1. If ability grouping is used by itself it does not inevitably result in a more complete knowledge of subject matter by the children.

2. Special grouping for the mentally retarded pays off; to a lesser extent it has been worthwhile for the lower levels in the so-called "normal" range. However, it is important to realize that being deprived of the stimulation of brighter children can also be detrimental. But let's not stop there. Does a poor golfer or bridge player profit from the example of experts when they play with them—or is frustration the more common result? What has been *your* experience?

3. Teachers generally feel that their job is lightened by grouping patterns.

4. Because no two children are cut from the same mold, no classroom can honestly be referred to as "homogeneous" no matter what factors are used in attempting to limit the range within it. (However, it *is* possible to reduce somewhat the range of abilities or other measurable factors.)

5. Teachers may fallaciously assume a stereotype for a class where the range has been limited to a modest degree. They may therefore do a greater disservice to individual students than they would if those students were in classes recognized as being heterogeneous.

6. Grouping practices have a tendency to limit the socioeconomic and cultural relationships of children. So the point to discuss is this: Is that good or bad?

7. When affirmative results are attributed to the fact that children have been grouped in some way, it may not be grouping at all which is the controlling factor. Far more important may have been the class size which might have been cut appreciably or the competence or enthusiasm of the teacher. "The philosophy and ability of the able teacher are undoubtedly more important than any grouping plan, however ingenious it may be, with respect to creating a good environment for teaching and learning."[7] However, teaching ability does not preclude *also* having an "ingenious grouping plan" or maybe even one that is not so clever but that limits some factors in the class range and adds to the teacher's capabilities by making him more satisfied. Because teachers consistently favor some kind of grouping, despite the pessimistic research results, their desires should play a big part in the whole proceedings.

Most grouping recommendations have been based on subject matter, with flexibility and frequent regroupings conspicuously in the

[7] Harold G. Shane, "Grouping in the Elementary School," *Phi Delta Kappan*, April, 1960, p. 318.

picture. Conant suggested ability groupings in grades 7 through 12 in English, social studies, mathematics, and science, and on three levels, fairly small top and bottom groups and a large middle group. He makes a special point to "mix together all pupils, regardless of ability, in a twelfth-grade course in problems in American democracy."[8] These ideas have not changed since his earlier books on the junior and senior high school.

If subject-matter grouping is used, it certainly does not mean that a child will necessarily be placed in the "high" group in all subjects. His placement should be related to achievement in each area of the curriculum rather than based on a single, unalterable kind of assignment.

Because the major objective of grouping is obviously to help students work up to their capacities, a guard has to be set up against the common fallacy of "enrichment" for them as too frequently practiced. Johnny finished his five problems—so he receives five more to keep him busy. Susan finishes this book—so she receives another that covers the same material. "There is a phrase of purest educational jargon for this procedure—it is called horizontal enrichment."[9]

Grouping presents problems in addition to those in the classroom. Handling transfer students, testing, keeping records, scheduling, and informing parents are among them. Many conscientious teachers, however, have felt that their burden is lessened by grouping—and that feeling is enough to assure its presence in many of the schools where you will teach. Those who are most adamant in their conclusions that grouping fails to meet the needs of individual children sometimes stop at that point. "Being against," in recent years especially, has become a kind of badge of honor among many in our society, whether we're talking about education, government, social conditions, or taxes. But it isn't enough here, as the more enlightened members of the education profession insist. They indicate other ways of creating school flexibility to satisfy individual differ-

[8] James B. Conant, *Slums and Suburbs*, New York, McGraw-Hill Book Company, Inc., 1961, p. 64.

[9] Arthur D. Morse, "Open Minds and Flexible Schools," *Saturday Review*, September 17, 1960, p. 68.

ences. They step right to the forefront of current practice and research, and point to the newest developments in areas like programmed learning, ungraded schools, individualized reading programs, team teaching, and the Trump suggestions related to small classes and individual study. They are pleased with recent refinements in guidance practices.

Let's note and capitalize on the few advantages of grouping when it is done most carefully, they say, but let's not forget its severe limitations. And let us never feel it is the only solution for our problems. Not by a long shot in this experimental decade of the 1960s.[10]

GUIDANCE

Some children may not need much guidance. Perhaps that was so for the 9-year-old about whom this was written: "Once upon a time there was a little girl named Clarise Nancy Imogene Ingrid La Rose. She had no hair and rather large feet. But she was extremely rich and the rest was easy."[11]

Some people may think that guidance is a dangerous thing that drives a wedge between the child and his home. It is the old story of competence and skill, however, and in the right hands a problem already with us or one that may develop can be handled painlessly and professionally. Teachers have a vital guidance function as part of their teaching, and they also have one in recognizing when their abilities have run their course and outside help is needed. That's when it is smart to yell down the hall for the expert in guidance techniques and materials.

Special counseling and guidance have never been more necessary than they are now. The reasons are easy to identify. Never have school activities been so competitive. Never have good colleges and universities been so hard to get into. Never have financial, social, and mental pressures and conflicts been so great in the homes from

[10] Some of the better articles on grouping appeared in the April, 1961 issue of *Educational Leadership.*

[11] H. Allen Smith, *Write Me a Poem, Baby,* Boston, Little, Brown and Company, 1956, p. 45.

which our children come. Never has the world faced the kinds of problems that create those and many other pressures and conflicts. Each child is right in the claws of the giant pincers to which those difficulties add up, and what's more, the pincers are getting more powerful every day.

So shall we let all children float through? Here's the scholastic diet, take it or leave it? Where you've been and where you're going isn't my business? The professional teacher must answer a stern "No" to questions like that. Even though each child has to live his own life and the best guidance is to help him help himself, assistance can come from those with more experience, maturity, and knowledge, those who have been around the track once themselves, and many times with other children.

Guidance has educational, personal, and vocational aspects. The good teacher certainly doesn't want to separate completely guidance from teaching. Guidance does not begin at a certain time or age. A peculiar claim is sometimes made by specialists in the field who refer to it as being "continuous." It is no more "continuous" than is learning or teaching, speaking or listening, reading or writing. But that doesn't detract from its importance. Exactly the opposite, for its periodic or spasmodic quality means that when it is needed it is needed very much indeed.

Regardless of the type of guidance one is talking about, its major purpose is to help a child find his way through the storms all of us face, to lessen their impact and strengthen the child's ability to cope with them on his own. Cutting through family and other personal entanglements, smoothing the educational road, and guiding young people vocationally are among the objectives of a sound school guidance program.

The school's job does not end when the student leaves, whether he drops out or is graduated. Although it obviously will cost money, going beyond the usual cut-off date for guidance help at the age of 16 makes sense in the world as it is today. A smooth transition from school to work, an extension of both educational and vocational guidance—these are essential. And your shrug-of-the-shoulder comment that "I'm *just* a first-grade teacher" is the most lame kind of excuse for disinterest in this subject. Attitudes are formed early, and they last long. So you're in the act whether you know it or not.

HOMEWORK

Following the advice sometimes given that it pays to go right to the top man, one parent a few years ago wrote this letter to President Truman:

There are thousands of mothers and fathers who can't plan to do anything or go anywhere at night because the children have so much night work. How can a mother teach her daughter how to cook and sew when the daughter has so much homework to do that she is up until two or three o'clock in the morning getting it done? Or how can a dad teach his son how to build or play ball or do anything with all the night work a son has?

Our children have to go to school 5 days a week 12 years of their lives 7 to 8 hours a day. Surely the mother and father deserve a little time to enjoy their children while they are young. So, please, Sir, will you see to it that children do their studying in school instead of at home?

Because they feel they are bearing the major burden, parents are the obvious complainers about homework. But they're not the only ones. Teachers often see it as just so much busywork that either gathers dust from the next morning on or that needles and nags until finally out of complete frustration they grab and grade—or merely check it in. School administrators are seldom enthusiastic about it; if it helps children learn, they may be all for it; but most of them are not convinced that it really accomplishes that task. Youngsters themselves frequently state the entire problem of homework most clearly. Here is what a few of them have said:

I went to sleep about 10 o'clock after thinking of as many rhyming words as I could for that poem I was to write. But my parents told me that they struggled with them until about 1 A.M.! Sure, it was a game for the first few minutes early in the evening, but it was painful for all of us by the time I went to bed—and I won't ask my folks how *they* felt about it around midnight!

When I asked my high school math teacher why we have so much homework, he said it's a departmental policy. When I asked him how we're supposed to get our other homework done when we have at least 2 hours of it every night in math, he just shrugged his shoulders as though to say, "Beats me!" It beats me too—except that I'm one of the lucky ones. You see, my dad's an engineer!

So we all had to write "To be or not to be" and the whole passage that it introduced 100 times all because Jerry threw a spitball. Sure, we knew who'd done it, but no one tattles in a situation like that. You just couldn't live with yourself if you did; could you? No, it wasn't a class in literature— second semester of physics!

Despite the consensus of children's opinions about homework, there is no *complete* agreement. Gifted students frequently object to repetitious homework activities, but often are enthusiastic about creative, challenging kinds of assignments. On the other hand, slower (but conscientious) high school students frequently welcome the definite, specific, cut-and-dried assignment which gives them the opportunity to succeed. Few students object very much, if at all, to homework which is interesting or exciting for *them*. Just as it is for most of us in adult life, some enjoy the most routine and most obscure jobs, and some the most dynamic.

Teachers assign homework for various reasons. Here is a rundown on the ones most often stated:

All the work can't be covered during the day; the classes are too large and the time is too short.

It strengthens home-school relationships, keeps parents informed about what's going on in school, and taps the valuable resource that parents can provide.

Homework develops good habits of responsibility, scholarship, initiative, and independence in thought and action.

It broadens knowledge and experience, introduces new interests, and builds character.

It provides repetitive exercises and drill on what is attempted during the day, developing a carry-over of school activities.

Homework assignments can help children who were absent, who need special assistance, or who aren't working up to capacity.

It keeps children out of mischief.

Keeping busy is a virtue—regardless of what one is doing.

Some of the objectives stated above are certainly reasonable. After all, we do want our children to be independent and scholarly, to acquire breadth of knowledge and experience, and to stay out of mischief. And many parents do want to know what the schools are doing. But does homework accomplish those objectives? Even if it does for some children and families, is it the *best* way to reach the goals indicated? In order to find out whether those purposes are attained, one has to peek into various homes during the afterschool hours. If any one of the following questions can be answered "Yes" on the basis of the environment in homes you know, then maybe we're ready for the new look at homework proposed later on.

Do parents ever help their child with his homework just to get it done faster, so they can move on to other activities, such as meals, bedtime, practicing of musical instruments, or just plain family fun?

Do parents ever wonder why a particular assignment was given? Even though they may try hard to figure out the reason, do they still fail to come up with a rational answer? And does their child share their confusion?

Do children sometimes lack the proper study aids at home, such as encyclopedias, maps, dictionary, or special paper?

Do homes provide an adequate study environment, or are they too noisy, too cluttered, frequented by too many younger children, or inadequate as far as sufficient light, desk space, or distance from television are concerned?

Do parents ever yell, argue, nag or just "clam up," and then later trace the original irritant to a homework assignment which frustrated their youngster and/or them?

Are there any homework assignments that encourage copying, cheating, false values, other bad habits, or mistaken notions regarding the world as we'd like youngsters to understand it? Does the bright child ever copy merely to get a dull, routine assignment out of the way?

Have you seen or heard of assignments which are vague, contradictory, repetitious, which encourage waste of time, energy, or materials?

Do parents ever encounter a homework situation where they are working themselves into a state of strenuous competition with a friend or neighbor whose child is in the same class with theirs or where children seem to be in unhealthful competition with each other?

Do parents ever feel a personal kind of challenge from their child's homework assignment while he couldn't care less? Do they feel their ability, literacy, and intelligence being challenged while their child goes off to watch television or to bed? And then do they do a "double take" on the situation, and end up angry at themselves, their child, and maybe even the whole school system?

Many rather scholarly studies have looked at the effects of homework on home, school, and actual learning. Children, teachers, and parents have been questioned, groups of students have been matched (one group receiving homework, the other not), and many schools and school districts have been involved in carefully conducted self-studies on this subject. The results have been revealing—but not always conclusive.

For example, Irving W. Stout and Grace Langdon reported on interviews with 900 parents, and concluded that they generally "believe in homework" *if* it is reasonable in amount, is geared to the child's abilities, takes family living into account, and "really teaches." A 2-year study in Connecticut conducted by laymen and educators concluded that homework did not necessarily add to the students' knowledge of a subject or improve work habits or mental discipline. Another study compared two matched groups, one receiving supervised study in school, the other homework; a significantly larger gain in school achievement was shown by the former. Other investigations have indicated the following: Students who received no assigned homework in elementary school have competed successfully in high school subjects with students from school systems favoring homework; home assignments have been found to improve the scholarship of the average and slow, more than the bright students; tests given in high school history and economics and elementary-school spelling, geography, history, and arithmetic have shown little difference in the achievement levels of the homework and no-homework groups.

In an atmosphere where parents often feel they are unnecessarily burdened by work which others are being paid to perform, it is time to set up a kind of creed or "bill of rights" related to the assigning and doing of homework. Ten rules have been presented to many parents and teachers, and the agreement on them is usually immediate and enthusiastic. The only homework assignments to be given are ones that meet the following criteria:

They are personalized and adapted to the individual needs of students or groups of students.

They are of the type that can be done *better* at home than at school. That means that the time is more readily available at home than at school, that facilities, equipment, and study aids are at home, and that the home environment is at least as conducive to the study situation as school is. The advantages of home study versus supervised study at school will be resolved on the basis of which is better for *this* assignment and *this* child, rather than on a blanket decision for *all* kinds of work and *all* children.

They are based on the full understanding of the teacher, student, *and* parents regarding objectives, length, and the place of parents in them. It is, of course, essential that parents be fully aware of what methods the teacher has used in school activities related to the assignments.

They are at least started in school, so that the student knows the next steps involved without full dependence on his parents. Implied in this rule are the demand that homework be an extension of, and closely re-lated to, the day's activities in school, and the need for respect by teachers of the finished product.

They are not restricted to book, study, or writing assignments of a re-petitive nature, but are activities related to home projects, primary research based on experimentation, and recreational reading.

They do not interfere with wholesome home activities in which the par-ents and all the children participate. In fact, they should contribute to and frequently be an active ingredient of those activities, relating whenever possible to known hobbies, outdoor play, and special family and individual interests. They should be of the type that can be shared with the family and should have a clear relation to family life.

They do not have a strict "time limit" on them (for example, 30 minutes for certain elementary grades, 1 hour in junior high school, 1 or 2 hours in high school). If the other rules are seriously followed, there will be no need for concern about time. In fact, there will also be no need for the kinds of suggestions that say, "No homework on weekends" or "One night free of it during the week." Putting the emphasis on the meaningful, on respect for home life, and on the needs of the individual youngster re-moves the requirement for special attention to time. This type of emphasis also eliminates staggering assignments by subject areas and giving undue attention to children with delicate physical or emotional conditions.

They are *not* to be for the exclusive purpose of keeping parents informed about what the school is doing (parent-teacher conferences, room meetings and larger PTA meetings are far more effective in accomplishing that objective) nor for the questionable reason that homework is required on the next level. The more appropriate question is, "Is it needed on *this* level of instruction?"

They are definite—but not so definite that the open-ended quality of a science or construction activity is ruined because the limits are too strictly delineated.

They are preceded by careful attention through the grades to appropri-ate study skills, such as keeping notes, reading for major ideas, using a dictionary and encyclopedia, and setting up time priorities based on the significance of the work attempted.

The basic objective now becomes clear: *homework as an integral part of the teaching and learning process; homework as part and parcel of the expanding, growing, reaching to which a good family and home life contribute from infancy on.* No longer should it be considered as an activity isolated from the mainstream of both home and school, but rather as a thread woven completely into the fabric of both.

In years gone by, homework may first have been introduced because a heavily burdened teacher didn't have enough coal or wood to last through the day and the children's houses were more comfortable; work of any kind was considered better than the "ugly thoughts" that leisure might encourage. But now when our American philosophy of education is based more than ever on the education of each child to his capacity, the time is here for evaluating a vital teaching tool that has often been misunderstood and misused. A full appraisal of its power cannot help but increase the productive learning of our children and decrease the pressure on the two adult populations most concerned, our teachers and our parents.

An obvious little exercise for you is based on the two lists below. Which activities would make homework more meaningful and enjoyable for children and for you as their teacher?

GROUP A

Weather records: temperature, rainfall, barometer readings

Studies of community, neighborhood, or city history

What makes things work: clocks, watches, weather vanes, electrical appliances, tools

Our family tree: how far back can we trace?

Safety in home and community: development and use of a check list; accident prevention

Visits to factories, art galleries, museums, libraries

Recipes: trying them out; relationships to diet, health, fractions

Art, literature, and music appreciation—selective television watching related to these and other activities

Motion pictures: discriminatory viewing; history of the industry; acting, directing, sets, research needed; relationships to literature

Collections: stamps, insects, models, maps, coins, dolls
Writing activities: stories, plays, letters, thank-you notes, invitations; others
   based on actual experiences of a special nature
Experiments with clay, wood, paper, paint, scrap materials and crayons
Current events: what they mean; how different mass media report them;
   what led up to them; the persons involved
Care of pets: growth, development, animal families
Developments related to health, medicine, causes of illness and disease

Group B

"Do the next ten problems."
"Complete pages 33 to 36 in the Workbook."
"Read the chapter on how our country was founded."
"Memorize any poem about an animal."
"List the birth dates, birth places, and death dates of all of our presidents."
"Write on the subject of 'What I did last summer.' "
"Answer every other question at the end of the chapter."

Activities such as those listed in Group A may be reasonable and productive homework assignments *if* they are related to specific school activities and to the ten homework rules cited above. Adaptations would, of course, have to be made on the basis of school level and individual need. Activities listed in Group B may be satisfying for some of those who are interested primarily in teaching children as they themselves were taught and who forget the dreariness of the unadulterated "memory routine" of their own childhood. But they are rejecting the right to experiment and try out new methods, materials, and ideas, a right we support wholeheartedly in medicine, engineering, architecture, retailing, agriculture, and other areas of human endeavor.

An integral part of all this, of course, is how teachers and parents feel about homework. Most teachers are in favor of it, even in the elementary school (83.5 percent in one study, with 3 hours per week as a median in the primary grades, 5 hours in the intermediate grades). Of 1822 parents queried in Valley Stream, New York, 1611 (or 88 percent) favored homework for their children.

So you can expect to give homework, and be lauded by some and criticized by others for doing so. If you stick close to the suggestions offered above, however, you might be able to justify what you do and, what's more, be satisfied with the whole process. A defense that you have here, even more than on other educational topics, is that "the research is inconclusive."

INDEPENDENT SCHOOLS

Although most of you will teach in the public schools, it isn't fair to assume that the whole story is told if our entire discussion centers around them. They are, and will continue to be, the core of our educational program, but they are not *all* of it. Even if we consider size alone and skip quality for moment, we must not overlook the place and contribution of independent schools in American education.

Overlapping terms sometimes confuse the statistics and the opinions related to this subject, terms like "independent," "private," and "parochial." For convenience, "private" may be the most inclusive label, with "independent" referring primarily (but not entirely) to those without a basic religious affiliation, and "parochial" to those with such an affiliation. It was estimated that about 16 percent of our school-age population in 1960 attended nonpublic schools, a great increase over 1930 when only 9 percent were in attendance. The "independent" schools (the ones we want to comment on mostly here) number about 3000, with an enrollment of more than 1.3 million out of 5 million in *all* private schools. Their recent physical expansion has been almost startling, ranging from the addition of science, observatory, art, and auditorium buildings at schools like Taft, Lawrenceville, and Horace Mann to the founding of totally new schools, like the beautiful Phoenix Country Day School established in the Camelback Mountain desert area of central Arizona.

Arguments continue on the comparative merits of independent and public school education—and they are essentially very foolish ones. Parents often feel a school is a fine one if a particular teacher accomplishes a great deal with a particular child. Excellence is frequently based on such personal relationships and specific accomplishments. To lump together *all* schools, whether independent or public, and draw conclusions on the basis of their manifold activities is as futile as doing so for *all* teachers, actors, repair men, salesmen, or for that matter, all people. For most parents there is little question about which kind of school their children will attend. The obvious, and only, choice is the one in their own neighborhood. But if they are not satisfied with that school, and if they either have the money or can travel the scholarship route, or if there is a family tradition of independent-school education or a health problem, they may begin to look around.

The advantages and disadvantages of the two types of schools are not clear-cut. Some of the items listed below you will relate to public schools you know, but the effort here is to itemize a few of the factors usually associated with independent schools.

ADVANTAGES

Selectivity among children, with corresponding intellectual competition and stimulation.
Smaller classes, more individual teaching and guidance.
More intensive preparation for college.
Development of social and athletic potentialities for all.
Not required to conform to community pressures.

DISADVANTAGES

Cost.
Withdrawn from the family, neighborhood, or community group; limits coeducational opportunities.
Individualized attention may result in less self-reliance.
Teachers may be low on the ability and preparation scales because they usually do not have to meet certification standards.

Points like these depend, of course, on the specific school and child, and should therefore be qualified. For example, although costs may range from $200 to more than $2000 a year, scholarships may be available. The child may be withdrawn from his family (a disadvantage listed above, and pertaining only to boarding schools), but it matters a great deal about the *kind* of family we're discussing. And although exact certification standards may not be met, the teachers might match the child and his family and far exceed the values attributed to those standards.

These comments are examples of the independent-versus-public school discussion:

I certainly don't mean to imply . . . that all public schools are bad and

that all private schools are good . . . . But . . . in most communities under
our present mass-education system, your child, if he's above average and
is college material, stands a better chance of having his academic capabilities developed in an independent, or private, school. . . .[12]

The notion that private education per se is superior to public education
is assiduously cultivated by private school interests at all levels. It is a myth
insofar as it pretends to be a generalization or even a statement of probable
tendency. This myth results in outright tragedy at the elementary and
secondary levels if parents assume that exorbitant fees automatically purchase educational advantages not available in the public schools.[13]

For the average boy or girl, with ordinary health and ordinary ability, I
believe the public school is better than the private. It is true that in a
public school there are many undesirable pupils—it is often a school of
bad manners. Girls may become vulgar and slangy, boys may become
coarse and foul-mouthed. Good home influences, religious training, refinement, and the real companionship of father and mother will more than
offset this. The small boy is a naturally dirty little animal, and the language, pictures, and associations in his environment at a public school are
often atrociously bad. Still, the public school is an absolute democracy—
the only pure democracy to be found in America. He lives in a field of
free competition—he rises or falls, swims or sinks on his merits. In scholarship he competes fairly with all his classmates, and the son of the
labourer has the same chance as the son of the millionaire. If he does not
keep up to a certain grade, down he goes to the lower room, and no influence or outside aid can save him. The schools are all crowded, and those
who cannot or will not study must drop out under the the the merciless law of
competition. His comrades, both boys and girls, are imbued with the spirit
of democracy, and God help the little snob! If he is fair and square, asking
no special favours, he will form many friendships and stand high with his
fellows. If he is selfish, conceited, eccentric, his classmates will take it out of
him, or drive him away. He sees all kinds of life, learns the pure and
noble along with the vulgar and obscene, and literally fights his way upward. He learns to respect boys and girls for what they are and for what
they can do, rather than for the backing they have or the homes that support them. If he does not go to college, he cannot graduate from a high
school without some knowledge of all sides of human nature, and he is
prepared to meet and to understand all sorts of people. If he does go to

[12] Mortimer Smith (ed.), *The Public Schools in Crisis,* Chicago, Henry Regnery
Company, 1956, pp. 70, 75.

[13] Myron Lieberman, *The Future of Public Education,* The University of Chicago Press, 1960, p. 41.

college, he will probably go with better habits of study, with more ambition to excel in scholarship, and with more self-reliance than if he came from a private fitting school.[14]

(If something doesn't ring *exactly* true in the above statement, it is only fair to tell you that it was written in 1912!)

Efforts have been made to equate the academic results of the two types of education on the basis of comparative student grades on College Board examinations. In other words, which group does better? Again, the cautionary flags have to be waved regarding the application of generalizations to a particular child or school.

	Mean Score of Students	
	Public High Schools	Nonpublic High Schools
Scholastic aptitude, verbal	489	486
Scholastic aptitude, mathematical	518	496
English composition	515	514
Social studies	518	505
French	527	548
Chemistry	544	522
Physics	551	526
Intermediate mathematics	535	499
Advanced mathematics	598	599

SOURCE: Henry S. Dyer and Richard G. King, "College Board Scores: Their Use and Interpretation," no. 2. Princeton, N. J., College Entrance Examination Board, 1955, pp. 151–159.

In this study, public high school graduates were higher in seven of the nine tests; on three the differences were negligible. Other studies that follow the public school students into the college and university report that, in general, their academic achievement is as good or better than the others. "It would certainly indicate," wrote Jerome Bruner, "that at the very least American high schools are not ruining these students for later outstanding work."[15] They also constitute a larger proportion of the student body in the so-called prestige colleges, but they should—there are so many more of them.

[14] William Lyon Phelps, "School-Teaching and Discipline," in Claude M. Fuess and Emory S. Basford (eds.), *Unseen Harvests*, New York, The Macmillan Company, 1947, pp. 60–61.
[15] Jerome S. Bruner, *The Process of Education*, Cambridge, Harvard University Press, 1961, p. 71.

The creativity that is sometimes more possible in an independent school than in a public school which is part of a large system is reflected in the many experiments and pilot programs now being conducted by them: cultural anthropology, automation for individual teaching, paleontology, human relations and intercultural education, humanities, assistance for children who have learning difficulties, field trips, summer studies in India and Africa, teacher preparation on the job.[16]

It must be emphasized in any fair discussion of this whole subject that there is nothing inherently good or bad in either the public or independent school setup. Fine teachers and poor ones, stimulation and boredom, cleanliness, safety, and the absence of both good and bad influences, all of these and many other extremes can be found in schools on both lists. The parent whose child is not challenged sufficiently in the public school may find the solution in an independent school nearby or 2000 miles away and at a substantial cost. Or he might find what he wants after one conference with the public school principal and a transfer to another teacher's room.

We ought not pick up and run from our public schools, or assume that a solution for all of our educational difficulties will come if we withdraw support or lambast them uncritically. They deserve our continuing confidence. In only a minority of cases is it worth giving up family and neighborhood relationships and the sense of belonging with the majority in order to transfer to a different type of school setting. The highest goals can usually be attained in the channels through which most of us passed, especially with the added research, refinements, and evaluations of the intervening years.

MERIT PAY

How much you are to be paid and on what basis your salary schedule is set up are questions that may not seem pertinent at this moment. But there will come a time when their importance will be great. So you might as well begin thinking about them now and have your ideas and conclusions evolve gradually. Discussions on this

[16] David Mallery, *New Approaches in Education*, Boston, National Council of Independent Schools, 1961.

subject have been hot and heavy for many years, and we seem to be about as far away from agreement now as we ever were.

To relate your salary exclusively to your years of experience and education is to ignore the quality of your teaching. But in order to evaluate that quality some standards and human judgments have to be involved. Therein, simply, lies the dilemma. In the professions the skill of the worker (whether it is in medicine, law, or engineering) is an important factor in his income, and yet many teachers and administrators view payment on the basis of performance as a step away from the professional and toward the "hired help" status.

The NEA has gone on record on this subject. Read this comment and judge for yourself how helpful you think it is.

> The Association . . . believes that use of subjective methods of evaluating professional performance for the purpose of setting salaries has a deleterious effect on the educational process. Plans which require such subjective judgments (commonly known as merit ratings) should be avoided. American education can be better served by continued progress in developing better means of objective evaluation.[17]

The position of the American Federation of Teachers was expressed in a speech by its president, Carl J. Megel:

> The American Federation of Teachers, representing classroom teachers, has vigorously opposed this specious practice [merit rating] for more than thirty years. Our organization has seen merit rating fail in city after city. We have seen school board after school board abandon it as unworkable and not conducive to improved educational practice.
>
> The American Federation of Teachers knows that merit rating is a device designed to wreck the single salary schedule and to make teaching rewards appear higher than they are. We know that merit increases will be given to a relatively few teachers in order to blunt demands for across-the-board increases for all teachers.
>
> Ideally, to speak of basing teachers' salaries on merit rating sounds completely plausible. But it is the impossibility of fairly judging and rating one teacher above another on a dollar-and-cents basis which makes the merit system unworkable. Experience has shown that the only way to protect the superior teacher from unfair, inadequate, inept, or vindictive rating is by the use of an adequate single salary schedule based upon training and experience.

[17] Representative Assembly, NEA Convention, June, 1961.

Lest you think no case can be built on the affirmative side of merit rating, note this recommendation from a very reputable source as a starter: "Merit pay [for teachers] is [a] means of providing rewards commensurate with performance and should be universally adopted, with appropriate safeguards to insure fair treatment."[18] If we assume that salaries based on merit rating will help increase income levels, then perhaps the use of such ratings will alleviate the teacher shortage and turnover, cut down the number of teachers who must take on a second job to make ends meet, attract more well-qualified men and women into the field, and encourage them to turn down school-administration positions that pay more.

Starting salaries for teachers aren't too bad, especially in the cities, say the merit-rating advocates, but the rub comes in the limited ceilings. The essential point, they insist, is to raise or eliminate those ceilings and thus bring salaries in line with individual contributions. How to evaluate teaching performance is their next step, and they say it can be done. In fact, as children and parents we do it all the time, even though not in any exact sense. It could be attempted, and successfully so, by levels like these: (1) failure to meet minimum standards; (2) satisfactory; (3) better than average; (4) outstanding. To reject merit rating on the basis of teachers not being motivated by money or its destroying morale are equally fallacious, the "pro" boys state.

School people worry about the subjective qualities of merit rating, and for that reason are frequently pushed into a corner of negative head-shaking regarding the whole subject. "True" merit rating to the tune of $100,000 or more a year based on the real worth of great teachers is not in the cards, say the "anti" brigade. Even in districts where merit rating is used, the top of the salary scale may be only $8,000 to $10,000. They agree that teachers do vary in ability, that superiority should be rewarded, that job evaluation is used in other occupational areas. But can *valid* evaluations be made? Are they to be based on knowledge, skill, discipline, popularity, parents' attitudes, or what? Are they to be related to the teacher's success with gifted or "average" or slow children? Are there teachers whom *everyone* agrees are "bad" or "good"? There is no evidence that

[18] President's Commission on National Goals, *Goals for Americans*, Englewood Cliffs, N. J., Prentice-Hall, Inc., 1960, p. 82.

merit rating encourages better teaching (the real objective of the whole subject) or secures financial justice. It may, in fact, do just the opposite.

So run some of the arguments for and against merit rating. They are far from resolved, and the many repetitive discussions shed much more heat than light on the subject. Perhaps you will join most teachers in opposing such rating. On the other hand, you may turn out to be one of the fine ones who need more money and feel your ability should be recognized in a very practical way, through your salary check. Or maybe you should reserve your energy to do the best teaching of which you are capable and work through organizations, old and new, to get the much-delayed recognition that your profession deserves.

READING

The conflict on what reading is and how it should be taught seems endless to the point of no return. With the publication of Rudolf Flesch's book *Why Johnny Can't Read* in 1955, the battle came into high gear. Then it simmered down, but only until the Economy Book Company released its *Phonetic Keys,* the Council for Basic Education published *Tomorrow's Illiterates,* and the book entitled *What Ivan Knows That Johnny Doesn't* appeared on the scene.

Nobody questions the importance of reading or the school's responsibility for teaching it effectively. But some say it has never been taught worse, children have never read less, and the whole outcome is a population that is supposed to be educated but instead is practically illiterate, failing dismally in meeting even the rudimentary standards of what an educated man should be. Teachers and administrators are thus pushed into a defensive position and frequently make claims for their current accomplishments that in a rational mood they would not make. Some critics view phonics as the answer to all reading ills, while many professional persons caution that the subject is more complicated than that.

To get back to fundamentals, they don't even agree on what "reading" is. (You'd think *that* would be understood by everyone, but if there's something you should learn quickly in your educational travels it is that nothing should be taken for granted.) Is it just a matter of identifying sounds and words? In his book Flesch says, "I once surprised a native of Prague by reading aloud from a Czech newspaper. 'Oh, you know Czech?' he asked. 'No, I don't understand a word of it,' I answered. 'I can only read it.'" Others define reading as based on full understanding of the meanings intended by the author. Ernest Horn pointed out that fourth-graders can read the following words but cannot understand what they mean: "The square of the sum of 2 numbers is equal to the square of the first added to twice the product of the first and second added to the square of the second."[19]

It should be obvious to anyone who is a student of the educational scene that children by and large can and do read. To say that they cannot, and to condemn our largest profession on that basis, is the same as to point to our divorce or juvenile-delinquency rates and condemn all marriage and family life. But this same fair observer can't help but be aware of the fact that we have many nonreaders and poor readers, extending into the upper elementary grade, high school, and adult populations. Despite the more regular phonetic quality of other languages, nonreaders have also been found in substantial numbers in other countries. Research is not sufficient to show whether reading abilities have actually declined in recent years; nevertheless, our reading ability is clearly inadequate for the mass media pumped out in avalanche proportions and the heavy reading load required of every business man, lawyer, teacher, doctor, and engineer to keep up with the swift move of events in every country and locality as well as in outer space.

To assume that there is only one right way to teach reading is fallacious. Teachers and parents have been successfully using different methods for generations, and some children even learn on their own. Dr. Omar K. Moore at Yale and Edward I. McDowell, Jr. of the Hamden Hall Country Day School in Connecticut obtained astounding results (in both reading and writing) with selected 3-year-olds by use of electric typewriters and individualized attention. Any bright teacher who is enthusiastic about his methods can almost

[19] Mabel Alstetter, *The Place and Use of "Gimmicks" in Teaching Reading*, A Monograph for Elementary Teachers, no. 76, Evanston, Ill., Harper & Row, Publishers, Inc., 1955.

invariably show affirmative results. But those methods may not succeed for other teachers.

READING READINESS

One of the most misunderstood concepts related to learning is "readiness." It isn't restricted to 5- and 6-year-olds, nor even to the field of reading, the area with which it is most often associated in people's minds. Somehow there is a kind of ageless quality about the concept. A newborn baby isn't ready to walk and talk, but the potential is present. The sounds and movements that time will help refine are all accounted for, just waiting for experimentation during the months of play-pen confinement and encouragement from cooing cuddling parents and relatives to bring them to meaningful fruition. The physical beginnings, the curiosity, and the desire are all there, waiting to be awakened and developed.

An adult may not be ready to learn Norwegian if he plans to live in Spain, or to study chemistry if he wants to write music. As grown-ups we are ready to learn something new only if we are motivated, concerned, or challenged enough. The potentialities exist, but they need internal and/or external stimulation. It is not any different basically when we consider a 6-year-old and his readiness for reading. He wants to read because he's seen others do so; because he's curious about advertisements, signs, and labels on television; because on every road, in every store, and in almost every room of the house are these mystifying symbols which keep from him a full understanding of this wonderful world in which he lives. But he isn't necessarily ready just because he looks big enough or because many schools follow the policy that all first-graders must learn to read at the same time.

If we narrow the broad spectrum of readiness down to the subject of reading, it merely means that a child's interest and physical, mental, and emotional development have reached the point where he is ready to learn some formal reading processes. Both the schools and the parents have tremendous contributions to make toward that preparation, toward expanding interests, toward helping abilities mature. And neither can do the job alone.

Because some strange misconceptions exist in many minds about the reading-readiness program and the process of reading itself, a

little quiz has been prepared for you. Try yourself out on the statements below, and see how well you understand recent thought on
the subject. Do you agree with them—or don't you?

1. A child begins to learn to read in school, and not before.
2. The "reading readiness program" is based on waiting until the child
   recognizes he is ready and asks to be taught to read.
3. It is important that every child know the alphabet before he can be
   taught to read.
4. Strong, exclusive emphasis on phonics will get reading off to a good
   start.
5. If he can't read by the end of first grade that means he is mentally
   backward.
6. We should get his exact test score, and then we'll know what to do.
7. Television is causing most of the reading problems today.
8. Comics are causing a tremendous number of them too.
9. The classroom games they play in kindergarten and first grade have
   no importance in the educational process.
10. If children want to read, they are capable of doing so.

Let's put to rest some of the most widely held *and* most erroneous
ideas about reading. *All ten statements above are false.* If you find
yourself in agreement with even one of them, perhaps your ideas on
the subject need bringing up to date. We'll attempt to do that
briefly:

1. A child begins to learn to read in infancy, not at the age of 6. Think
about it for a minute. The first differences a baby notices are in light and
darkness (but not soon enough for new parents!), the face of his mother
versus the rest of the world, baby meat versus baby sweet desserts—and on
and on, until he knows this color from that one, this toy from that one,
this picture from that one, and finally, this word from that one. The
ability to differentiate begins very early and continues on a gradual, refined basis right into the thick of the reading program.

2. "Reading readiness" is based on action, and lots of it, on questioning
that makes children think, on observing likenesses and differences, on
broadening all the vocabularies a child has (speaking, listening, understanding), on discussing, reasoning, experiencing, following directions. It
helps relate their everyday experiences to words and books, and is about
as far from thumb twiddling as it can be. It is a planned series of activities
that lead by design into the intricacies of a formal reading program.

3. If a child really *wants* to learn the alphabet, let him, even help him; but it isn't necessary that he have it down pat before he goes to school. It'll come in time, and when it does, he will almost effortlessly have learned both the names and sounds of letters. It'll seem so easy because he'll be *ready* to learn them.

4. No capable research person in the field of reading belittles the importance of phonics. But there is a vast difference of opinion about its place in the reading program, especially the best timing for it. Agreement is fairly complete on its *not* belonging at the start of the program as the *only* technique to be used. Success in early reading stems more often from learning that these symbols called "words" have meanings, from clues related to word forms, structure and context, and from giving a child a chance to read words rather than memorizing by rote some meaningless combinations of sounds. But, as already indicated, phonics or memorizing and using combinations of sounds has a firm, vital place in the whole process. This cannot be done on an "incidental" basis, for to many teachers that will lead to sloppiness and perhaps to outright omission.

5. All children don't walk, talk, teethe, or toilet train at the same age. There is a *normal range* rather than an *exact time* for these developments. Why should we assume that reading is so different? Eye muscles, manipulative skills, and attention spans develop at different rates from child to child, and the reading skills based on them are bound to vary in their appearance on the scene. Mentally backward because he's past 6 and not reading fluently? Are there other indications that he's mentally slow? No? Well, then, he probably isn't. There is certainly nothing magic related to reading that takes place on his sixth birthday, except perhaps reading his name and age on the all-important cake!

6. Tests *are* important, but in recent years we've become almost a test-happy nation. They don't tell everything—they do have limitations—they cannot consistently give us exact scores. And they become completely invalid if a teacher deliberately uses workbook and other materials that "prepare" children for a specific test; the value of the test is destroyed by that practice, and yet some teachers persist in following it, with some parents condoning this foolish use of workbooks.

7. Television's effect on a child frequently depends on its use by the whole family. Is a family the 5 P.M.-through-late-late-movie type? If it is, then television may be interfering with the reading of their youngster. On the other hand, television if used well has been a boon to library loans, vocabulary growth, and broad expansions of knowledge in fields like history and science.

8. Ditto for comic books: they can be troublesome, but not if the read-

ing program is balanced with materials recognized as worthwhile. The Association for Childhood Education International refers to "comicbook-itis" as being a natural, normal symptom of the time. If one is seeking something or someone to blame, perhaps the search should extend beyond television and comics, to other children, teachers, or parents.

9. The games, fun, and activity in a well-run kindergarten or first grade all have a reason, a purpose. For the parent who merely drops in after the start and leaves before the finish there will be little understanding of the objectives involved. But if one gives the teacher a break by asking her sometime what her aim was, a surprise may come in how sensible and scholarly the answer will be.

10. The desire to read isn't enough. It has to be accompanied by readi-ness, ability, and teaching. Ask the wife of almost any shower baritone, and she'll set you straight!

There is no hope at all that the arguments and lack of communi-cation regarding the oft-repeated issue of how reading should be taught will be resolved during your college years, perhaps not even during your lifetime. So maybe you have to be prepared to turn off your hearing apparatus. Otherwise there will probably be no relief. Before you do that, however, a few of the more readable protagonists on this subject should be listed for you.

CRITICS

Bloomfield, Leonard, and Clarence L. Barnhardt, *Let's Read: A Linguistic Approach,* Detroit, Wayne State University Press, 1961.

Flesch, Rudolf, *Why Johnny Can't Read,* New York, Harper & Row, Pub-lishers, Inc., 1955.

McCracken, Glenn, *The Right to Learn,* Chicago, Henry Regnery Com-pany, 1959.

Trace, Arther S., Jr., *What Ivan Knows That Johnny Doesn't,* New York, Random House, Inc., 1961.

Walcutt, Charles C. (ed.), *Tomorrow's Illiterates,* Boston, Little, Brown and Company, 1961.

Whitman, Howard, "Why Don't They Teach My Child to Read?" *Collier's,* November 26, 1954, pp. 102–105.

EDUCATORS

Gates, Arthur I., "The Teaching of Reading—Objective Evidence Versus Opinion," *Phi Delta Kappan,* February, 1962, pp. 197–205.

Gates, Arthur I., *Reading Attainment in Elementary Schools: 1957 and 1937,* New York, Bureau of Publications, Teachers College, Columbia University, 1961.

See also Paul Witty, William S. Gray, David Russell, William D. Sheldon, and many others to whom they will lead you.

READING MATERIALS

Reports of Clifton Fadiman on teen-age reading which periodically appear in *This Week Magazine* represent an encouraging aspect of this picture. Also enlightening for adults in every generation who feels the next one is going to the dogs is the book list, compiled by librarians all over the country, of what teen-agers read (as of September, 1962):

> *Abominable Snowman* by Ivan T. Sanderson
> *Anna and the King of Siam* by Margaret Landon
> *The Cool World* by Warren Miller
> *Devil Water* by Anya Seton
> *The Golden Warrior* by Hope Muntz
> *The Guns of August* by Barbara Tuchman
> *Hiroshima* by John Hersey
> *A Night to Remember* by Walter Lord
> *PT 109* by Robert J. Donovan
> *Seven Science Fiction Novels* by H. G. Wells

Earlier surveys included:

Jane Eyre	*Ben-Hur*
The Diary of a Young Girl	*The Bridge of San Luis Rey*
Lost Horizon	*The Good Earth*
Gone with the Wind	*All Quiet on the Western Front*
The Ugly American	*Catcher in the Rye*
Rebecca	*God Is My Co-Pilot*

Both in quantity and quality these lists provide a hopeful sign for those who feel schools and teachers today are the worst we've ever had. But, as indicated earlier, we can still do better and more. What is your opinion on the following questions?

Should so-called classics be rewritten in simpler form for certain children? ("Watered down" is the expression used by the "anti" faction.) Is there any value in such materials for older children who read on lower levels? What about the whole topic of high-interest-low-ability materials?

Will anything come of a recent British experiment to devise an alphabet based on a limited number of speech sounds, and then to prepare primary-grade textbooks consisting of those sounds? It is "the wildest educational experiment since Froebel established the first kindergarten," wrote one professional journal.[20]

Are all the claims for "speed reading" to be believed? A little serious checking may be in order before you contribute to the private "fund raising" of those who cannot back up the fantastic promises made.

One of the most sensible statements made on reading can close this discussion, as it did the excellent article from which it came:

Reading should not be a battleground. We hope that the specialists and critics of many persuasions will climb down from their barricades and quit taking pot shots at each other. If they will read more carefully themselves many of them will discover that they have been misinterpreting what their opponents are trying to say. We hope that they will regain their sense of balance, examine all the evidence more carefully, and quit beclouding the issues with wild charges and extravagant claims.[21]

REPORT CARDS

When you went to school the report card sent home to your parents each month may have consisted of a series of numbers. They might have been arrived at "very objectively" by averaging all the grades you received on papers and recitations. What they actually meant, you may want to mull over a little bit. Did they represent what you learned—or how well you memorized? Did they reflect teacher knowledge of your ability—or teacher opinion and prejudice? Were they used to encourage better performance in an affirmative way—or through fear? Could a teacher support in a meaningful manner his conclusion that your grade in geography was 67—or would his explanations fail to carry substantial weight?

Reports to parents have gone through many stages since that time. Efforts are still being made, often in vain, to find out what a number or letter grade really means. One thing should be made clear right at the start: Grades on report cards do not always mean the same thing to all those who fill them in. They can be based on how well

20 Editorial, *Phi Delta Kappan*, January, 1962, p. 149.
21 Paul Woodring, "Can Johnny Read?" *Saturday Review*, January 20, 1962, p. 40.

the child performs in accordance with his own ability; they can measure the effort he is exerting; or they can indicate how he compares with the other children in his class. Most people in education today feel that whatever symbols are used should be fully understood by all involved—child, parent, teacher, administrator—with everything possible done so that all interpret them in the same way. Many current student reports are issued less frequently, sometimes only two or three times a year, and include teachers' comments and reports on behavior as well as achievement.

In addition, parent conferences are catching on. The difficulties encountered have caused some schools to eliminate the traditional report cards altogether, replacing them with narrative reports or parent-teacher conferences. Parents don't always like them, and teachers often disapprove too; some feel that they take too much time. Whether they like it or not, parents are sometimes being invited to help determine the kind of report that should be used. It almost goes without saying that some schools have lived to regret their ever having given out that invitation; the haggling and dissatisfaction that result hardly cement home-school relationships. School people sometimes recognize and take pride in their knowledge of their field only too late—after they have invited the unqualified to determine policy, a privilege relinquished in sad error.

The questions "Why give grades at all?" and "Why not just pass or fail and let it go at that?" are easy ones to answer. Parents just wouldn't be satisfied. And teachers who suggest the pass-fail practice are often among those who yell the loudest when *their* instructors suggest it. It will take many years to prepare the public and the profession to accept a sharp shift away from the grade-conscious environment that we have all known. The parent-teacher conference points in that direction, but it's only the beginning. Other reasons given for retaining grading systems are the motivation they may provide and their contribution to a permanent or cumulative record.

On the opposite side of the street, grades are claimed to be unreliable, to encourage dishonesty, to augment emotional difficulties, and to be vague in meaning. Report cards have "deteriorated to a level bordering on the ridiculous," said one critic of them. "Some of these report cards are so complicated and confusing that parents receiving them are unable to decode the mass of double-talking symbols and statements into any sensible or meaningful evaluation of their children's progress."[22]

Underlying much of the argument regarding report cards is a basic disagreement on motivation and rewards. Should the latter be extrinsic or intrinsic? If we want children to learn, to enjoy the process as well as the results, then don't curiosity, awareness, wonder, exploration, and success step into the picture, replacing the older concepts of fear and failure? No one has summarized the problem, put the emphasis in the proper place, or posed the challenge more pointedly than Jerome Bruner:

> Students should know what it feels like to be completely absorbed in a problem. They seldom experience this feeling in school. Given enough absorption in class, some students may be able to carry over the feeling to work done on their own . . . Where grades are used as a substitute for the reward of understanding, it may well be that learning will cease as soon as grades are no longer given—at graduation.[23]

A sad commentary on our educational process, but is it wrong? You might ponder it a bit.

SOCIAL PROMOTION

Maybe it's the word "social" that causes the argument. For some people the route from social-to-socialism-to-communism is unquestioned, so their opposition to social promotion is almost instinctive. But the issue isn't that simple. The differences of opinion on the failure-promotion problem are wide, with neither parents nor school people in any clear-cut camps. Here are a few samples of attitudes that come from both sides of the fence:

If you keep them back, they'll never catch up.
    If you *don't,* they'll slide along and learn nothing.
Imagine what failure will do to him; he's already discouraged.
    We have to maintain standards. Flunk them!
Send them all on. Success works better than failure.
    Receiving an extra year of education is a privilege.

[22] Glenn McCracken, *The Right to Learn,* Chicago, Henry Regnery Company, 1959, p. 37.
[23] Jerome S. Bruner, *op. cit.,* pp. 50, 51.

Let's try to get at the facts behind this crucial decision of whether a little boy or girl should pass or be held back at the first step in formal schooling. Let's look at the implications for later promotion decisions. We are not talking about mentally retarded children, the seriously emotionally disturbed, or deaf or blind children whose needs are distinctive. The children we will discuss are the "average" ones who are off to a slow start in acquiring skills related to numbers, science concepts, social living, and especially reading. The causes for their slowness may be numerous, intricate, and frequently beyond their control. In the youngster who is having, or has had, "trouble" in first grade, there may be a trace of one or more of the following problems:

Slow physical development	Irregular school attendance
Slow emotional development	Family mobility
Intelligence just below "normal"	Sickness
Poor home environment	Truancy
Family squabbles	Experiences based on failure
Short on affection, food, sleep	Family cultural deviations
Limited childhood experiences	Family language deviations
What he's seen and heard	

These are among the major causes for lagging behind. Parents may be reluctant about putting the blame on their own personal situation and want to look elsewhere, perhaps to the most maligned scapegoat of all in recent years—the schools. Not that school hands are lily-white; few schools would insist they are free of involvement in the sluggish educational send-off. They might admit some of these as contributing factors:

Excessive teacher absences
Large classes
High, rigid, *and* inappropriate standards of achievement
Unwarranted administrative and teacher prejudices
Use of unsuitable methods and materials
Teachers' subjective judgments
Teachers' inadequate preparation
Just plain poor teaching

Whatever the cause is, the results are the same: It is estimated that more than 2 million elementary-school children fail each year. Each

June, 6- and 7-year-olds by the thousands face another year in first grade. Of the 12 years of schooling most of our youngsters receive these days, the highest rate of nonpromotion is right at the start. Of course, it varies by communities; in some as many as 25 percent of all first-graders are held back. Although the trend since 1900 has been downward (in that year about 50 percent of all elementary-school graduates had experienced failure), it is common for 10 percent or more in a first-grade class to be required to repeat the year. And in many cases the odds are two to one that the "failure" will be a boy! Maybe you feel that's the way it should be. "Get them off to a good start," "you can't build a building on a shifty foundation," and that sort of thing. But before we jump to conclusions, let's ask the most important question of all, and then try to answer it: Does repeating first grade help a child catch up academically?

Research is plentiful on this subject, and its conclusions are crystal clear for children *as a group*. But it doesn't make any pretense of stating what is best for any *particular* child. To generalize on the basis of studies already made would be unfair to any individual child whose situation demands personalized consideration and solution. The generalizations are revealing, but especially for those who tend to draw conclusions exclusively on the basis of limited and biased experiences and desires. Here is how they add up:

The average child who repeats first grade learns no more in two years than the nonrepeater of the same mental age does in one year. Nor do most repeaters ever catch up academically.

Being unready for the work of a grade will not be corrected by repeating that grade. In other words, doing the same thing twice when one isn't ready to do it either time will not bring success.

Success and praise work better than failure and reproval in the educational setting, just as they do elsewhere.

A threat of failure and impending failure do not necessarily result in better work. Those threatened with failure do no better academically than those told they will pass regardless of their achievement.

Children who drop out of school have frequently been first-grade failures. In fact, one community found that more than 99 percent of the students who didn't finish high school had been held back in first grade. "These youngsters learned to fail," concluded the researcher.

Cost of failures is very high, much more expensive than the solutions which will be suggested later on for preventing them. Perhaps this touches an especially sensitive spot in the practical men and women on most of our local school boards.

Research concludes: (1) Pupils who are promoted each year gain more educationally than those with similar abilities whose progress in school is irregular. (2) Contrary to popular belief, nonpromotion does not spur students to greater action, but discourages them to the extent that they see little or no reason to put forth effort. (3) Children of normal ability gained more from trial promotion than children of equal ability who repeated the grade. So, if educational achievement is the objective, we're liable to be disappointed by having a child repeat a grade.

Some defend the practice of failure for young children by pointing to instabilities of adult life; but are such early defeats really good preparation for our later years? Being confused and mystified is often the beginning of a pattern of failure and defeatism and a self-concept based on weakness and unhappiness. Many children held back at the start of their school careers lose their self-confidence and initiative, feel little or no satisfaction in school activities, fear trying new activities, and develop poor social relationships. Inability to get along with others may result when a child suddenly finds himself the oldest, biggest, and heaviest in the classroom although he's quite normal for his age. All of these developments depend, of course, on how the adults in the situation act and whether the parents and teachers prepare the child adequately.

Despite the best-intentioned efforts, however, feelings of humiliation and bewilderment frequently materialize. In some extreme cases, emotional upsets may even result in stuttering. In less severe ones, it is sometimes possible to see an active distaste emerging for learning and education, demonstrated by a short attention span and poor work habits. Maybe a combination of some of those factors wouldn't be so bad *if* the child at least caught up academically as a result of nonpromotion. Mastery of subject matter may certainly be worth all the effort, but since this does not usually result from being held back, we have to assume that the turmoil for the child and his family is often in vain.

But what does the other side of the coin show? If failure is not the answer is indiscriminate promotion any better? What about "social promotion" for the "normal" youngsters who are off to a slow start? Many schools in recent years have tried it, and the reactions have been varied. Defenders of automatic and guaranteed promotion say that children work best when they are placed with others their own age, that success brings more success, and that failure leads to more failure. They point out how much it costs for each child held back and then ask, "Isn't there a better use to which we can put school funds?" They ask for proof that failing a student will increase his mastery of school skills, and the proof is unmistakably absent. They point to rigid standards and wonder how compatible they are with a philosophy of education for all based on individual differences.

The opponents of "social promotion" claim that school is the only institution this side of heaven that rewards intention as generously as it does accomplishment. Making a gift of success is based on wishful thinking of what life is like, so let's be realistic, the critics say. Life just isn't that simple and good. It's rough and tough and unpredictable, and children might as well start preparing for it early. Besides, if you remove your school standards you destroy scholarship and initiative. You pile additional burdens and frustrations on the slow student if you promote him to a level far beyond his ability.

The arguments for and against automatic promotions are most pointed when one talks about young children, about those in first grade. We all want the start to be strong, healthful, and encouraging, and yet we also want it to be based on a sound appraisal of a child's capabilities. Perhaps, as in the solution of so many problems, the answer to the promotion-failure question is somewhere in the gray zone between rigid standards resulting in the stigma of failure stamped on many children, and "social promotion" which takes some of the meaning out of achievement. In an era when schools are being evaluated more frequently than ever before, when experimentation is finally being encouraged in a field where something new used to be automatically suspect, a number of approaches are being tried. "Only men who do nothing are always right" is the old saying that frequently teases pioneering spirits into at least attempting something new. Following are a few encouraging efforts to help first-graders avoid outright failure in their introduction to a new world. Of course, no one guarantees their success.

UNGRADED PRIMARY PROGRAM

Call it the continuous pupil-progress plan, primary school, or primary unit. The objectives are all fairly similar. They get away from the rigid grade-to-a-year idea, and attempt to adapt a program to children whose capabilities fail to bend, squeeze, or stretch to the strict demands of chapters in a textbook, semester and school years of an arbitrary length, or teachers who plan programs in detail for students they have never seen. Such a program avoids pinning the tag of failure on children, for they have as long a time to catch up as most of them need. At the end of one year they may not have the needed maturity or sight vocabulary, but at the end of three years both will probably be sufficiently advanced.

FLEXIBLE SCHOOL ENTRY

If a child's birthday is January 1, and the school's cut-off date for September entry into kindergarten or first grade is December 31, he will have to wait a year to begin school. Thousands of parents who felt sure their child was ready to go to school have had this frustrating experience because of a birth date that was too "late." Parents who think their child is smarter and faster than one permitted to enter could be absolutely right. Although some schools cling tenaciously to chronological age as the single standard for school entry, this is not an effective way to determine readiness for school.

Faced by the postwar avalanche of children, many administrators have little choice but to stick to the strict cut-off date of their district. But as long as they do, they will continue to have children old enough for school who are incapable of doing the work expected of them. It's in this climate that failure begins to breed. They will also continue to reject children who are too young but are easily capable of reaching realistic grade goals.

The obvious solution is flexible school entry. Where the cut-off date is December 31, an arbitrary 4-month period could be used as a flexible factor. Any child who reaches age 5 between November 1 and February 28 would be eligible to enter kindergarten if his potential for school work—judged by tests, teacher observation, health, parent and child interviews, or any criteria the school district wants to set up—is sufficiently high. Any youngster who has a potential *lower* than the district requires cannot enter school until the following year. Here's where the parents may howl the loudest, especially if their child is 5 before December 31 and would have been admitted under the old system. And here's where the school must be certain its criteria are sound and that its preparation and public relations are "howl-proof." Through flexible school entry there is a good chance that the fast child won't be delayed too long in his formal schooling and the slower child won't be hurried with his before he is ready.

THE BOY-GIRL PROBLEM

Despite insignificant differences in intelligence- and achievement-test scores, boys fail more frequently than girls in first grade. Some interesting reasons for it might come to your mind as you think about it. Could it be that a boy is sometimes penalized because he is mischievous or troublesome? Could it be that the neatness of his work is evaluated more than the content of it? Is there something in this picture related to the primary reading materials, usually prepared with great skill but sometimes inappropriate and diluted for the active physical and mental development of a 6-year-old boy? And might one wonder whether the female world that dominates his infancy, early childhood, and early years in school has ill-prepared him for the new school situation in which he finds himself?

Despite the differences in a boy's development, interests, and needs, his first years in school (and frequently many that follow) are exactly the same in content, techniques, and materials as those of the little girl next door. The fact that it is unfair not to adjust his school program comes to light as we see the tremendously greater number of boys than girls who are held back in first grade despite the similarity in their capabilities. Some fine teachers *are* making adjustments, and many others should try to do so. If we are to profit from what we know of child development we'll give most boys more number and science concepts in first grade. The youngsters who need them are frequently those who fail to make the grade in reading. So perhaps the accompanying suggestion should be for a slower approach to the formal reading program for boys—and the controversial idea of some male teachers in the primary grades.

THE PRIVILEGE OF ANOTHER YEAR

The person who said "receiving an extra year of education is a privilege" was on sound ground if certain considerations are included. Although repetition for its own sake is hardly a satisfactory answer for a youngster who seems to be lagging behind the others, a reasonable and selective approach often works very well. So let's ask a series of questions about him, and if the answer to most of them is "Yes," then perhaps the additional year is exactly what he will need.

Is the child to be held back being considered as an individual?

Is he physically and mentally in the broad range of the so-called normal?

Is he too young chronologically or emotionally for the program in which he is enrolled? Will a reasonable length of time fail to take care of his immaturity?

Were efforts made early in the year and continued during the entire year to accumulate information about him from all available sources?

Are the facts being weighed by competent professional personnel who agree that he will profit from another year in first grade?

Were the parents impersonally involved in the school procedures on repeating grades before their own child became a subject for discussion? Are they now personally involved?

Is the contact with parents made personally, at home or at school, rather than through a form letter?

Have efforts been made to adapt the curriculum to the varying needs of children and to the specific needs of this child?

Has an effort been made to cut classes on the primary level to the smallest size possible in order to encourage individualized teaching for all, including the child under discussion?

Do the parents agree that retention is a good thing?

If you nod your head affirmatively with strong conviction to all but the last, the plan to retain may be a fizzle. Parental agreement will be one of the most important ingredients of the whole thing.

A good school district may consider retention in first grade as an answer, and a sound answer, to a child's school problem. If the questions just listed are considered carefully, the slower send-off could result in a longer but more satisfying educational career. No understanding parent, wise administrator, or conscientious teacher would ever stand in the way of using this method (or any other) if it made school for any particular little boy or girl more meaningful and profitable.

TESTS AND TESTING

For some people a test can answer any question: How smart is Eddie? How well has Amy learned her arithmetic? What should Andy be when he grows up? Unfortunately too many believe that a test provides a sort of magic answer that will solve a problem specifically and for all time. But that isn't the way it works. Test results can point out a direction for a child's present and future growth. They can provide indications, trends, hints. But there are many "ifs" involved. Are the tests valid and reliable, well administered and interpreted, and part of a sound framework of other materials? Are all the items on the test justifiably included? Since tests have limitations, their results should be supported by school grades, teacher opinion, and other evidence.

It is awkward to lump all tests and test procedures together. Finding out how well Peter has learned to divide through the process of long division is not the same as determining Jill's aptitude for college. Content, procedures, and goals are different, as are the people who design tests (teachers and test companies, for example) and formats (oral, essay, objective). The arguments on this subject revolve mainly around the usefulness of tests. In defense Gardner and Barzun have said the following:

Anyone attacking the usefulness of the tests must suggest workable alternatives. It has been proved over and over again that the alternative methods of evaluating ability are subject to gross errors and capable of producing grave injustices. Whatever their faults, the tests have proven fairer and more reliable than any other method when they are used cautiously within the limits for which they were designed.[24]

Examinations are not things that happen in school. They are a recurring feature of life, whether in the form of decisive interviews to pass, of important letters to write, or life-and-death diagnoses to make, or meetings to address, or girls to propose to. In most of these crises, you cannot bring your notes with you and must not leave your wits behind. The habit of

[24] John W. Gardner, *Excellence,* New York, Harper & Row, Publishers, Inc., 1961, p. 49.

passing examinations is therefore one to acquire early and to keep exercising even when there is a possibility of getting around it.[25]

Strong opposition comes from Martin Mayer in this way:

Most of the more important objections to standardized or objective tests apply equally well to essay or oral tests. Indeed, in almost every area where the standardized tests are deplorable, teacher-made tests are even more deplorable—they show greater insistence that every child must have learned the same things, greater marking error, greater class bias, greater influence on the child's educational future. But the weaknesses of teachers' own tests were well known, while all the hocus-pocus of science and publicity and propaganda have been employed to conceal the weaknesses of standardized tests. The danger is that the standardized test will be taken far more seriously than it should be. And the test-makers, despite their pious remonstrances in conversation and in technical journals, have been pushing the schools ever harder to accept these instruments as expressions of a Larger Truth . . . about the only people who believe in the tests completely are those who make their living through testing . . . tests and testing are at best a necessary evil.[26]

If teachers were always bright and insightful, if those who give and score tests were always accurate, flexible and well prepared for their jobs, if parents always accepted test interpretations as tentative and within a range, then we would have less to worry about. In fact, then we might not have to give tests at all. But people are not that accomplished and understanding. So it becomes necessary to indicate in no uncertain terms that tests, whether teacher-made or well-standardized, have limitations and inaccuracies. Although they may solve some problems, they provide many more. The real difficulty is when parents and school people aren't aware of test limitations and problems and go right on blithely accepting exactness where it doesn't exist. Too frequently our biggest problem is not even knowing we have one.

Subject-matter tests which stress trivialities and unrelated "facts" that are memorized and forgotten all too quickly encourage teaching in the worst tradition of the profession. But tests need not do that. Instead, they can emphasize broad principles and relationships

[25] Jacques Barzun, *Teacher in America*, Boston, Little, Brown and Company, 1945, p. 215.
[26] Martin Mayer, *The Schools*, New York, Harper & Row, Publishers, Inc., 1961, pp. 376, 372, 375.

among areas of knowledge. Isn't it obvious, however, that the latter type is more difficult to construct and therefore is found less often in our classrooms? It isn't always a matter of teacher laziness either. Time just runs out.

In some discussions of this subject the term "evaluation" is used, broadening the context and giving an impression (though an unreal one) of continuity. An ambitious approach to this broader concept has been offered which may not yet be fully practical: "Far from being only a matter of giving tests, evaluation will cover the total school program and operation. Thus it will concern each student's total development as well as his acquisition of knowledge. . . ."[27]

It is logical that serious questions should arise from the public and school people alike regarding the millions of hours and dollars devoted to tests. Here are some of the specific objections: too much duplication among the 20 national testing programs; too much teaching for the taking of tests instead of just good teaching; too much testing for entry into prestige institutions; too much of a statistical nature that fails to indicate student "staying power" and desire to learn; too much answering of questions without knowing how to study to think independently.

TEXTBOOKS

It isn't only in the field of testing that education is big business. There are 172 textbook publishing companies competing for an annual business of $336.6 million with elementary- and secondary-school sales accounting for almost 70 percent of it. Although the *total* expenditure has more than doubled in the past 10 years, the *percentage* of the total school expenditure for textbooks has actually decreased. Always small, it is now just above 1 percent of the total. When one thinks of our schools as being "reading" institutions and considers all the yelling about the quantity and quality of reading, the minuteness of this figure hits home.

Drastic changes are in the works in the textbook industry. Curriculum reforms make it increasingly more difficult to rely on one

[27] J. Lloyd Trump and Dorsey Baynham, *Focus on Change—A Guide to Better Schools*, Chicago, Rand McNally & Company, 1961, p. 58.

text. Attention to individual differences and needs means that a greater variety of text materials will be required. Publishers are also influenced by criticism for either avoiding or including controversial issues. They can't win in this one, whether they use their profit and loss statement or their conscience as a guide, and whether they accept the responsibility for lack of courage or shove it back to their customers (school boards and administrators), where it may more often belong. With the development of programmed learning it will become a choice of battling them or joining them, and some publishers have already taken the latter route. In addition, the vast expansion in availability of paperback books will affect the selling-back-to-the-bookstore routine. But no problems put into the laps of the textbook publishers are more demanding of solution, and less easy to solve, than the ones posed by Mayer. His description of the situation is as follows:

Class bias hits the American schoolchild from the moment he begins formal instruction. The reading books are all about nicely dressed children with a pet dog and a lawn to play on; Daddy comes home from the office; the family takes a trip in the car to the seashore or to visit a farm; there is great excitement over birthday parties, and much stress on people like Evangeline Booth, Florence Nightingale and Buddha, who gave up a comfortable existence to Help the Poor and Unfortunate. In the arithmetic texts the problems deal with how much money a well-scrubbed child can make by mowing lawns at forty cents an hour, or how long a little girl practiced the piano each week if she practiced forty minutes a day, or how much money the children's club raised for the Junior Red Cross if each child contributed forty cents.

All this is real enough (if not very interesting) to the middle-class child, but for nearly half of American school children the textbooks might as well be written about life in another country. The circumstances of operating a school—the fact that instruction can be carried on only if the classroom is relatively quiet, that it costs money to clean the halls, that everybody can smell his neighbor—demand stress on the middle-class virtues of order, neatness and cleanliness. Schoolwork takes place in an atmosphere where everybody sends and receives letters, where the "community helpers"—the milkman, the fireman, the policeman, the mailman, the garbage collector—are creatures one never meets socially, where the smiling dockworker happily unloads bananas to feed little boys and girls. . . .

Textbooks are written by teachers . . . Usually there will be a committee of three or four authors, at least one of whom is a professor at a teacher-training institute. On the secondary level, one of the authors may be a college professor. The authors are responsible for the content of the book and for the method of treatment—but not, generally speaking, for the actual writing, which will be done by the editors with the help of "readability" formulas. (These devices, typically, add the number of words in a sentence, multiply by syllables, punctuation marks, clauses, etc., and divide by an arbitrary constant to give an Arabic numeral which scientifically expresses "readability.")[28]

But the textbook controversy isn't only on the elementary and secondary level. Don't you have some questions to raise about college texts, too? What about *their* readability, content, redundancy? What do you think about publishers who feel they must have a complete list, a book in every subject and part of every subject, regardless of what is already available?

For all the reasons you can list, plus the others stated earlier, we will see changes in textbook publishing. A skillful job has certainly been done in the use of color, paper, bindings, and sometimes in content. But many new developments are coming.

CONCLUDING REMARKS

The spice of a profession is in the differences of opinion it harbors, both within and without. Perhaps too few of the participants in this one express their ideas, sometimes because of fear but more frequently because they just don't have any. Others have spoken their thoughts freely and may now be in another field, either by choice or demand. Teaching needs more variation in ideas than any other occupation because it affects our future so directly. For those coming into the fold, the welcome mat should say: "Through these portals enter the most dedicated *and* the most thoughtfully outspoken members of our society."

However, don't expect all those you encounter in education to agree that those are proper words of welcome. The reluctance of some teachers to try any new material or technique and the fear of a new or controversial idea are major problems in your chosen profession.

[28] Mayer, *op. cit.*, pp. 114–115, 378.

CHAPTER 8

A TIME FOR *Every Child*

Most mothers find time for every child regardless of how many there are in the family and how crowded the day is. In our large classrooms many teachers do not find enough time for each one. The day is too short, the room too filled up, or the teacher too inept; and for some particularly unfortunate children there is a combination of all three.

And yet, a dedication to the individual and his importance permeates all of the key documents in American history, politics, and education. It undergirds many of the newer school techniques and practices which have already been brought to your attention, whether they are based on programmed learning or on refreshing approaches to student and class organization such as those proposed by J. Lloyd Trump.[1]

Maybe you feel it's complicated enough to think in terms of 30 children who are doing the *same* thing at the *same* time. Although many in your future profession may be at that stage, they will not be for long if some of the vocal thinkers in your chosen field have their way. Of course, they have thousands of teachers and school administrators still to convince, with at least as many on their side to help them do the convincing, fortunately. But the struggle will continue for a long time toward consideration of children's individual educational needs.

Many concrete steps have been taken in that direction. For example, at the University High School in Urbana, Illinois, they have experimented with free time and independent study in connection with science and language classes. Melbourne High School in Florida has set up a program called "Education by Appointment," where selected students conduct advanced independent study and research,

[1] J. Lloyd Trump and Dorsey Baynham, *Focus on Change—Guide to Better Schools*, Chicago, Rand McNally & Company, 1961.

budgeting their own time and developing their own schedules, but in consultation with a "directing teacher." New College in Sarasota, Florida, is concerned with tutorial and other individualized approaches to learning. In these and other experimental programs the wishes and talents of individual teachers must be considered as well as the abilities and needs of individual children. Thelen stressed the point with clarity when he wrote:

All sorts of people go to school: toddlers, tomboys, thirsters; squirmers, dreamers, thinkers; men and women; widows, adolescents, housewives, teachers; and persons who just want to learn to tie flies for the fun of it. Teachers are of all sorts too: they range from nimble piccolos to thumping basses, from mellow horns to clashing cymbals; from sparkling champagne to flat beer; from lovable lizzies to champing Cadillacs.[2]

INDIVIDUAL DIFFERENCES

Choose any age and select ten children at random. Their range in height and weight may be as much as 12 inches and 25 pounds. Do the same with a group of adults, and you'll have some who look young at 20, 30, 40, and 50 years of age, and some who look old.

In almost any elementary classroom you will see a range of 5 to 8 years based on knowledge, capacity, and achievement. In fact, if the lowest achiever were moved from eighth grade down to fourth grade, he might *still* be the lowest achiever in the class, or at least below the class average. Similarly, the brightest fourth-grader moved up to eighth grade may set the academic pace there just as he did back in his own room.

Our emphasis in the United States on the average child and adult is a point for current discussion, but it also attracted attention more than 100 years ago. As far back as 1835 a relatively dispassionate observer stated: "There is no class, then, in America . . . by which the labors of the intellect are held in honor. . . . A middling standard is fixed in America for human knowledge."[3]

Our tendency to be satisfied with the stunted growth of a large

[2] Herbert A. Thelen, *Education and the Human Quest*, New York, Harper & Row, Publishers, Inc., 1960, p. 16.
[3] Alexis de Tocqueville, *Democracy in America*, vol. I, New York, Alfred A. Knopf, Inc., 1945, p. 52.

part of our population should weigh heavily on our collective national conscience and on the conscience of every teacher, school administrator, and parent. This applies particularly to those who in preparing teachers in our colleges and universities, ignore the differences in children's backgrounds and opportunities and the place of poverty, prejudice, and ignorance. Included in the picture are migrant children, dropout figures, delinquency charts by neighborhoods, and contrasting income patterns across the country.

In his effort to stress *similarities of groups,* without ignoring the importance of *differences among individuals,* Brameld wrote:

. . . with all their differences, races and nationalities everywhere possess similar endowments. On this score, those of our century who insist upon the innate inferiority of some and the innate superiority of others deserve to be excused far less readily than those who held such a belief in centuries past. Whereas the latter belief was completely untested, today it has been thoroughly tested—and found false. Anthropologists and social psychologists are agreed that, both biologically and psychologically, no scientific basis exists for the view that large human groups are above or below others in their inherent structures or capacities.

. . . it would seem that, among other things, they generally make love; they nourish themselves; they take care of their bodies; they play; they work; they learn; they worship; they create aesthetically; they make rules; they sorrow; they communicate; they govern; they shelter and clothe themselves; they protect one another; they count; they possess; they visit and trade; they cooperate and organize.[4]

Because our national philosophy has accepted and emphasized the similarities of groups, the strange conclusion has resulted that these groups should receive equal treatment. As a teacher it is vital that you recognize that children should have equal opportunities to fulfill their potentialities. But it is just as important for you to understand their individual differences:

Children are not equal biologically, in their native gifts, nor in their achievements. Practically every human being deviates from the so-called normal in some important ways. Equality of opportunity and before the law rather than of endowment must be our theme. Although we all can't hit home runs, we all deserve our chance at bat.

We like the idea that "all men are equal" and also the one that says

[4] Theodore Brameld, *Education for the Emerging Age,* New York, Harper & Row, Publishers, Inc., 1961, pp. 127, 128.

"may the best man win"—but aren't they in conflict? Being equal, being "as good as" another person is hardly true as we look at our physicians, lawyers, and sales clerks and realize that there are great variations even in the technical skills of persons in the same work.

The academic lock step, the assembly-line doctrine which moves all children ahead at the same pace in many of our schools regardless of their intelligence and abilities has been supported by those who feel that comparisons should be avoided at all costs, and that "any school system in which one child may fail while another succeeds is unjust, undemocratic, and uneducational."[5] Is it really "undemocratic"—or is it more so to enforce a rigid promotion and curriculum policy that fails to recognize individual differences?

Small mounds of ability can often give teachers a hint of where a peak may be developed; to capitalize on such hints requires a precise use of child-study information, a tack too seldom followed because of teacher limitations in time or ability.

A crucial undercurrent of the tendency to assume that all "normal" children are alike and to teach them accordingly was pointed out by Williams when he wrote: "We are contributing to the too-prevalent tendency toward regimentation which can make any people easy prey to dictatorship. If, however, we want to foster the love of freedom, we will teach as if we really believed in individuality and its importance to free men. . . ."[6]

Regarding the individual differences of children, two basic conclusions can be drawn: (1) Diverse educational programs must be developed to take care of individual diversity, and each of these programs must have both stature and respect. (2) You must be alert to your error if later on you note only obvious mental and physical differences and permit the faceless mass of the "average" to drift through.

John H. Fischer, President of Columbia University, summarized a sensible point of view when he wrote:

If our schools are to be genuinely dedicated to individual fulfillment, our work must go far beyond merely recognizing individual differences in the sense that we ordinarily do. What is required is genuine respect for such differences, respect which carries us to the point of giving all our

[5] Marietta Johnson, *Youth in a World of Men,* New York, The John Day Company, Inc., 1929, p. 13.

[6] Roger J. Williams, *Free and Unequal,* Austin, University of Texas Press, 1953, p. 79 (also *Biochemical Individuality,* New York, John Wiley & Sons, Inc., 1956).

pupils adequate attention and comparable encouragement. The regard for personal worth which is the fundamental principle of our culture is justification enough for such an approach. But if we want a more practical reason, we can remember that in a democratic society it is the quality of the ordinary citizen which ultimately determines the course and destiny of the nation.[7]

Maybe that clarifies your task as a teacher; it certainly doesn't ease it. But nobody who really knows ever believes that teaching is an easy way of earning a living anyway.

Working with children as distinct personalities means the development of techniques for meeting the needs of one child without neglecting the rest. The children's seats should be arranged so that needs based on size, vision, and hearing are all met. We know how important it is for the regular classroom teacher to identify children who differ from the so-called normal and to adapt the program to them or refer them to specialists. The teacher's tasks include learning how to interpret, use, and add to cumulative records; analyzing the meanings behind I.Q. and other test scores; knowing the symptoms of illness. He must realize that a "slow learner" can be a very bright child who is only working up to his grade level or a borderline mentally retarded one who is achieving to the limits of his ability; and that individual attention applies to the kindergarten child who *can* read as well as to the sixth grader who *can't*.

An unusual approach to the subject of variations among children can be found in the works of W. H. Sheldon: *The Varieties of Human Physique* (1940), *The Varieties of Temperament* (1942), and *Varieties of Delinquent Youth* (1949) published in New York by Harper & Row. (However, in the years since publication his research has often been challenged.)

Closely related to this subject of individual differences and the necessity for respecting them is a little fable that has become an educational classic; it was written many years ago by Dr. George H. Reavis when he was an administrator in the Cincinnati Public Schools. Few who have read it forget its moral:

Once upon a time, the animals decided they must do something heroic to meet the problems of a "new world." So they organized a school.

[7] John H. Fischer, "Our Changing Conception of Education," *Phi Delta Kappan*, October, 1960, p. 19.

They adopted an activity curriculum consisting of running, climbing, swimming, and flying. To make it easier to administer the curriculum, *all* the animals took *all* the subjects.

The duck was excellent in swimming, in fact better than his instructor; but he made only passing grades in flying and was very poor in running. Since he was slow in running, he had to stay after school and also drop swimming in order to practice running. This was kept up until his web feet were badly worn and he was only average in swimming. *But average was acceptable in school, so nobody worried about that except the duck.*

The rabbit started at the top of the class in running, but had a nervous breakdown because of so much make-up work in swimming.

The squirrel was excellent in climbing until he developed frustration in the flying class where his teacher made him start from the ground up instead of from the treetop down. He also developed "charlie horses" from over-exertion and then got C in climbing and D in running.

The eagle was a problem child and was disciplined severely. In the climbing class he beat all the others to the top of the tree, but insisted on using his own way to get there.

At the end of the year, an abnormal eel that could swim exceedingly well, and also run, climb, and fly a little had the highest average and was valedictorian.

The prairie dogs stayed out of school and fought the tax levy because the administration would not add digging and burrowing to the curriculum. They apprenticed their child to a badger and later joined the groundhogs and gophers to start a successful private school.[8]

Children differ as much as do the participants in that story. One major way in which they do is in how they view the world around them.

THROUGH CHILDREN'S EYES

Sometimes we become so lost in thinking about ourselves that we forget the children, the real reason for it all. As almost any parent of a teen-ager will tell you, it's practically impossible to see things through the eyes of children. Adults and children don't share the same problems. Ours are frequently centered around money, jobs,

[8] George H. Reavis, "The Animal School," originally printed in *Better Teaching*, published by Cincinnati, Ohio, Public Schools, 1939.

sickness, or death; and theirs, just as crucial to them, are in the areas of being left out, talked about, ignored, or teased.

The solution of many of your teaching problems will be built right into the source of those problems. Being able to delve into what makes children act as they do *may* come through child-development courses and textbooks; but it can come even more readily through novels, stories, and plays that show us children as they really are. To further your understanding of how children think, and why they act as they do, try some of these other sources. You might start with the following:

Of Human Bondage by W. Somerset Maugham: episodes in the beginning of the book showing Philip as a club-footed boy with the emotional problems of a handicapped child; taunted, teased, chased, and badgered by the curious youngsters at the private school he attended

Our Miss Boo by Margaret Lee Runbeck: efforts to understand the machinations of a 5-year-old

A Handy Guide to Grownups by Jennifer Owsley

The Happy Time by Robert Fontaine: his childhood

Through Children's Eyes by Blanche Weill: an older attempt

Our Town by Thornton Wilder: the particularly touching scene where a little girl, grown up, attempts to relive her twelfth birthday; how difficult it is for her to do

One of the most creative efforts of a 4-year-old provided insights no textbook has come close to. It appeared first in the July 1, 1939, issue of *The New Yorker*.[9] The introduction said that it was sent in by a mother who called it a song or a chant or a poem. Her 4-year-old son sang it every night in the bath tub. It seemed to go on practically forever, she said, like the Old Testament. She was able to copy down only part of it. It was sung entirely on one note except that his voice dropped on the last word in every line.

BATHTUB CHANT
by Wolcott Gibbs

He will just do nothing at all,
He will just sit there in the noonday sun.
And when they speak to him, he will not answer them,
Because he does not care to.
He will stick them with spears and put them in the garbage.

[9] Reprinted by permission; Copr. © 1939 The New Yorker Magazine, Inc.

When they tell him to eat his dinner, he will just laugh at them,
And he will not take his nap, because he does not care to.
He will not talk to them, he will not say nothing,
He will just sit there in the noonday sun.
He will go away and play with the Panda.
He will not speak to nobody because he doesn't have to.
And when they come to look for him they will not find him,
Because he will not be there.
He will put spikes in their eyes and put them in the garbage,
And put the cover on.
He will not go out in the fresh air or eat his vegetables
Or make wee-wee for them, and he will get thin as a marble.
He will not do nothing at all.
He will just sit there in the noonday sun.

Little boys fall down and we tell them to forget it and "act big";
years later their wives wonder why they often act unsympathetically
and without feelings. Children sometimes pull the shutters tightly
to hide their problems. Difficulties in communication result, as in
the story of the lonely little girl who left a note hidden in a tree; it
said, "To whoever finds this—I love you."

How little understanding we have of the sensitivities of children
is apparent when we observe teachers and parents using sarcasm,
bullying, and being discourteous. Many hurts we inflict on children
can be avoided: the singling out of the shy individual for embar-
rassingly special attention; the faulty conclusions arrived at regarding the sleepy boy who delivers papers morning and night and is
embarrassed before his friends by a tactless teacher; the rudeness of
constant autocracy and bossiness from the front of the room.

Adult efforts to understand children might include looking at
areas like these as a child might view them:

Friendship patterns
Fears, normal and abnormal
Tensions that are peculiar to children
Favoritism in the family and classroom
Twins; the only boy or girl in the family; the youngest or oldest or middle
    child; the only child
Adoption
Sex attitudes
Parent-child relationships

Your responsibility was aptly stated by Jane Addams who said that "the mature of each generation run a grave risk of putting their efforts in a futile direction . . . unless they can keep in touch with the youth of their own day and know at least the trend in which eager dreams are driving them. . . ."

THE NEEDS OF CHILDREN

We can begin with food, clothing, and shelter, and move on quickly to affection, acceptance, and achievement. There is no argument up to that point. There are many lists of children's needs, and before we're through with the subject, a few of them will be cited so you don't feel cheated. But what is some of the incisive, newer type thinking on this subject? Aldous Huxley contributed to it when he admitted: "Like everyone else, I am functioning at only a fraction of my potential. How grateful I should feel if someone had taught me to be, say, thirty per cent efficient instead of fifteen or maybe twenty per cent!"[10]

Fritz Redl makes a contribution in some of his speeches when he talks about children learning to live with increased tensions and stresses, and being able to adjust to them. He points to an angry world that is racing against time, adult hostility against youth, and total impact of the setting. All of these, children and young people must be helped to endure, absorb, adjust to.

Needs for working to capacity, learning to live realistically with increasing pressures and strains and developing human sensitivities must join the usual lists that you have seen. And tomorrow's teachers are at the firing point in the battle to satisfy them. Although you are not psychiatrically prepared, you can utilize the understandings and insights of psychiatry, psychology and social work. Academic instruction is the primary function of the school; but in order to meet its goals, the obstructions to its accomplishment have to be recognized. What needs of the child must be met so that those goals can be reached?

They will, of course, differ from child to child, age to age, family

---

[10] Aldous Huxley, *Tomorrow and Tomorrow and Tomorrow*, New York, Harper & Row, Publishers, Inc., 1956, pp. 31–32.

to family, community to community; but some basic similarities exist. From your own childhood you can build up a list, consisting of items like the need for a friend on occasion, for parents who "understand," for sometimes having people say you did the right thing, for time that is occasionally free from all pressures. The list below is a composite one drawn from many sources, obviously not in order of importance. It may give you something to think about as you look toward a teaching career, for constant efforts have to be made to meet many of these needs.

Good health and physical fitness

Knowledge of rights and duties as a citizen

Skills for the world of work

Ability to establish and reach personal goals

Knowledge as a foundation and a method for maturing to one's intellectual capacity

Standards of what is good and evil, and the establishment of ideals and values to meet those standards

Encouragement to learn at one's own best rate

Freedom to think, react, and perform within the necessary limitations proposed by society

Favorable economic conditions and family life consistent with demands of physical, mental and emotional growth

Domestic unity and international peace

Dedication to one's own necessities and those of one's family—but at least *once in a while,* to people beyond one's home and even one's country

Humility, but a realistic understanding of one's abilities *and* inabilities

Understanding and appreciation of the contributions made by science, literature, communication, art, music, and nature—and a chance to develop one's capacities in these various areas

Ability to think rationally, express thoughts clearly, read and listen with understanding

Knowledge of the geographical, political, economic world around us, and the rapid changes taking place in it

If the list seems only like a lot of words with little meaning, read it again. Give it another chance. For in it are *your* basic needs as well as those of the children you will teach.

We cannot expect to be successful in meeting all of these needs, and certainly one cannot prepare with any exactness for solving problems before they arise. But we must aim to meet the needs that children have always had, and to face change in a world on wheels. Two special problems that arise out of inadequate attention to these needs are juvenile delinquency and limited opportunities for girls. They are singled out here for brief consideration.

JUVENILE DELINQUENCY

This problem of young people, which is reputed to cost $20 billion annually,[11] can be solved to some extent by prevention. We have already touched on this in earlier discussions of student dropouts and projects like Higher Horizons and Careers for Youth. Many other concrete proposals have been made to help reduce the problem, and some have been put into action in various communities. Coordinated neighborhood and community approaches have been at least partially successful in reducing delinquency and potential crime. Relationships between school failure, dropouts, and delinquency point clearly to your importance as a teacher in this disastrous chain of events.

An interesting interpretation of this problem was recently expressed by Dr. Sydney Smith, former director of the psychological clinic at Arizona State University. He has worked with more than 2500 young people with problems in the past 10 years, and points to the following as among the causes of those problems.

Parental encouragement of delinquent activity because of vicarious enjoyment of the experience

Frustration, inhibition, and lack of freedom in the parents' own childhood

Our becoming a nation of strangers—neighborhood instability, conflicts among neighbors

Feelings among institutionalized delinquents (boys, especially) that they have been abandoned by family and society

Parents feeling threatened when a child is no longer a child, no longer dependent on them

Efforts of youth to leave childhood behind, to identify as a grownup, to rebel against authority

Our false assumption that punishment solves all problems

The Phi Delta Kappa Commission on Prevention of Juvenile Delinquency has proposed a program which it feels can cut juvenile

[11] Kenyon Scudder and Kenneth Beam, *The Twenty Billion Dollar Challenge,* New York, G. P. Putnam's Sons, 1961.

delinquency in half if widely adopted.[12] It is directed toward young people who are "alienated" because they do not accept the ways of living and achieving that are standard in our society. Most of them come from low-income homes, are in the 75–90 I.Q. range, tend to come from broken or inadequate home environments. The Commission's strategy for attacking the problem consists of these phases:

1. Development of a work-study program for alienated 13- and 14-year-old boys
2. Supplementation of the work-study program by social agencies and community organizations which help create and maintain a wholesome social situation
3. Preventive programs for work with young children in the primary grades, and their families, to help them make more satisfactory progress in school

There are excellent starting points if you want to find out more about the needs of children that pertain to serious problem situations. The insightful work of Dr. William C. Kvaraceus of Boston University penetrates the problems and possible solutions of juvenile delinquency. Federal programs like the grants-in-aid and technical assistance passed by Congress are aimed at prevention and control. Exhaustive bibliographies on the subject—a 10-page list of "Juvenile Delinquency References" and a list of 477 research projects on this subject—were released by the Children's Bureau in Washington early in 1962.

LIMITED OPPORTUNITIES FOR GIRLS

Isn't it strange that even now—as advanced and broadminded as many of us think we are—the largest "minority" group against whom there are still some prejudices consists of slightly over half of our population? If you don't think this is so, do a little checking on job opportunities and salaries for women and see how they lag behind those for men. Lawrence Derthick noted that in our country only 5 percent of the physicians are women (between 60 and 70 percent in Russia), 1 percent of engineering students are women (32 percent in Russia), and only one out of 300 women capable of earn-

[12] Robert J. Havighurst and Lindley J. Stiles, "National Policy for Alienated Youth," Phi Delta Kappan, April, 1961, pp. 283–291.

ing a Ph.D. actually do so (they earn one-third of the other college and university degrees but only 10 percent of the doctorates).

Although the situation is not ideal from the distaff side's point of view, progress has certainly been made since 1867–1868 when a U.S. Office of Education report referred to areas of exceptional children and included "girls" along with "deaf mutes," "blind," "juvenile offenders," "idiots," and "orphans." That we still have a long way to go in order to satisfy feminine needs for equality of educational and occupational opportunities is evidenced by the following items. You can do something about some of them in your own professional preparation, as well as in the future teaching you do.

Although the proportion of women in the labor force has increased rapidly, their rate of entry into the professions has actually declined. Just 7 percent of those listed in the National Register of Scientific and Technical Personnel are women, mainly in biology and psychology.

Only half of our working women have finished high school; more than one-third of our total female population does not complete high school.

Our thinking still concentrates on certain areas for women, such as home economics, library work, and teaching. The assumption still remains that science, engineering, and administrative roles are somehow not ladylike. "No student of human behavior has as yet convincingly isolated any difference between the sexes that would forever preclude women from becoming competent in these fields. In the elementary schools, girls are as frequently outstanding science students as are boys."[13]

More boys than girls go on to college, mainly because parents are more inclined to help and encourage sons than daughters. Even of those in the top 10 percent of high school graduating classes, only about half go on to college. It's a simply stated problem: When funds are limited, higher education for girls frequently becomes expendable. All of this is in spite of the fact that U.S. Department of Labor predictions are that women will work outside their homes for 25 years, mainly after their children are grown. They have lots of time for a career, but sometimes have no place to go.

Women are not supposed to understand scientific concepts, so they're not taught them, can't answer their children's questions, and the circle of limitations is continued in the home and by women

[13] Harrison Brown, James Bonner, and John Weir, *The Next Hundred Years*, New York, The Viking Press, Inc., 1957, p. 135.

teachers. But slowly, things are looking up for women educationally and occupationally. Margaret Mead has been fighting the battle against whatever-is-has-to-be. The National Science Foundation in a 1961 publication (*Women in Scientific Careers*, U.S. Government Printing Office) stressed the problem and the foolishness of it. Various institutions of higher learning are in the forefront of eliminating unfair restrictions; among them are Sarah Lawrence College, which gives special consideration to undergraduate students who had to leave school and want to resume their work, and Radcliffe with its Institute for Independent Study.

The battle continues to prove the intellectual equality of women and to understand the ways in which their lives differ from the male side of family and community affairs. Their needs require more understanding and more action, a greater realization that they buy 55 percent of the goods and services in our country, that they must frequently have refresher and retraining help, that their roles in life are often of a multiple nature, that guidance is necessary to help these roles flow together smoothly as they relate to their home, community, and occupational involvements.

CREATIVITY AND CONFORMITY

Elizabeth Drews tells the story of a teacher who stormed into the office of the principal, angrily waving a paper at him. "He wants to be a surgeon, and he has the intelligence to make it, yet he writes trash like this!" "Like what?" the principal asked in a pacifying tone. "This assignment on what he'd like to be when he grows up. A beachcomber of all things!" "Well, maybe he just wanted to be creative," the principal replied.

At this the teacher pulled up to her full height and breadth, and spouted, "When I want him to be creative, I'll tell him to!"

The question to be raised is an obvious one: Must all children be filed down to the smooth surfaces of conformity? And it is rapidly joined by another: Can ideas and activities that are different, off-beat, sometimes difficult to understand be encouraged by teachers who themselves are sometimes exactly the opposite—docile, conforming, comfortable with things as they are? The pressures on the creative spirit to be like everyone else are heavy, and it's easier to go along with the crowd. Dore Schary put it this way:

> It is, of course, extremely pleasant to be popular, loved, cavity-free, and personally dainty, as the ads constantly remind us. But in our eagerness to conform to this attractive picture, the truly creative spirit is shriveling up somewhere in the background. What about our minds? If we abdicate the right of inquiry, we will offend no one, and we will remain healthy, static, and unobtrusive. Let me point out, however, that the same thing may be said of a potato.[14]

Although we often give lip service to our desire to encourage creativity, we delude ourselves by assuming that creativity and high intelligence are the same things. They *may* be, but not necessarily. Jacob W. Getzels and Philip W. Jackson in their research, their book,[15] and many articles clarify the issue, although the research picture on the whole subject is still limited. The conventional I.Q. tests, they feel, fail to identify or they actually penalize the mind that is inventive, that wants to speculate. Favored is the child who says and does what is expected of him, rather than one who thinks with originality and depth. Both creativity and conformity are found in all persons in varying proportions. Neither extreme is better or worse, more or less useful. But Getzels and Jackson quite clearly define the two processes in terms like these:

Creative: Divergent thinking; revising the known; exploring the undetermined; constructing what might be; novel and speculative; favors risk, "openness," growth, intellectual inventiveness and innovation; focuses on discovery of what is yet to be known.

Conforming: Convergent thinking; retaining the known; learning the predetermined; conserving what is; usual and expected; favors certainty, "defensiveness," "safety," intellectual conformity; focuses on knowing what is already discovered

If you happen to be the latter type of person, maybe you begin to understand the problem you face, the need for encouraging the child whose motives you may have difficulty accepting in the first place. You will have to guard against showing a preference for the youngster with a high I.Q. "who does what he is told to do" over the one

[14] Dore Schary, *NEA Journal*, May, 1960, p. 9.
[15] Jacob W. Getzels and Philip W. Jackson, *Creativity and Intelligence*, New York, John Wiley & Sons, Inc., 1962.

who may follow less acceptable routes to his goals. Your failure to be cautious in these situations may result in disillusionment, frustration, and actual school dropouts of our most creative persons. It may mean the loss of some of the brightest ideas from the literary pen, the research against disease, and the struggle to preserve a world in peace.

So-called intelligence tests, school grades, and tests of accumulation of knowledge are low predictors of creative performance. With 50 or more known factors in the intellect, the one-shot objective test and "subjective" judgment of a teacher in a single academic area fail to tell the story adequately. Although still in their infancy as far as use and effectiveness are concerned, items like these are being considered for predicting creativity: biographies, past achievements, self ratings, direct expressions of goals and aspirations, originality and personality inventories, aptitude measures, parental attitudes. Such measures may dig into characteristics not touched in I.Q. tests.

Many of the studies already conducted[16] provide you with a kind of check list of creative characteristics, but there is real danger unless you use them cautiously. Children are not test-tube chemicals, and their characteristics cannot be sorted out without the colors running together. These will give you some guidance toward creativity, but don't bet on them without reservations. Creative individuals won't have all of them, by any means, and noncreative individuals will share in many.

Solitary activities early in life
More autonomous attitudes
Striving for more distant goals
More integrative attitudes
More cautious and realistic
More consistent in desires for rewards
Perception of self as assertive and authoritative, with leadership ability
Intensity of moral and aesthetic commitment
Voluminous production
Diligence, discipline, total commitment to his work
More dominant, inhibited, emotionally sensitive, radical
Unconventional standards of success

[16] Calvin W. Taylor and John L. Holland, "Development and Application of Tests of Creativity," *Review of Educational Research*, February, 1962, pp. 91–102.

Aspirations for unconventional careers
More willingness to take the calculated risk
Openness to experience

The need persists for further exploration into the multiple criteria of creative performance. No single factor or characteristic describes the individual inclined in this direction any more than a single one tells us who is gifted. Because "too little liberty brings stagnation, and too much brings chaos,"[17] your task is to provide and stimulate "the right amount" for each child. You certainly can't achieve it by rewarding docility and crushing independence.

Although we seem to do an increasingly good job in our schools of transmitting knowledge and teaching facts and skills, we are still on the frontier when it comes to creative thinking and imagination. Whenever anyone tosses around sarcastic comments about your being in a stodgy profession, think of the challenge that frontier can provide. The trouble is that their comments may be appropriate for too many of us unless we learn what creative thought is, how it can be identified, measured, and nurtured, and profit from the research of others in this realm.

One of the most thought-provoking comments related to this subject was provided by Leonard W. Mayo when he said:

Individuals do not become civilized and mature without the opportunity for thought and reflection; they do not become great until they are first creative. A major question for all of us in these days of rapid and extensive change, therefore, is how to make it possible for young people to think in a culture where there is much to discourage thought; how we can provide an opportunity for reflection in a culture that regards action as one of the main criteria of success; how we can insure creativity in the spiritual sense in a society that places so much importance on material possessions.[18]

The challenge of cultivating individuality is one of the toughest you face. With much of our civilization resting on mass production of identical units (and people), the difficulties will remain with us in an intense way through your teaching career. Solutions must come at least partially through school organizational patterns (like the

[17] Bertrand Russell, *Authority and the Individual*, New York, Simon and Schuster, Inc., 1949, p. 25.
[18] In a presentation to the 1960 White House Conference on Children and Youth.

nongraded school and primary groups), newer techniques (like brain storming and individualized reading), and newer materials (like programmed learning). That challenge exists in the home, too.

"We'd better face it," said Rev. Donald Harrington in a sermon at the Community Church in New York. "We will either help our young people to find great dreams to work and live for, or they will give us nightmares to live with. Man must have adequate opportunities to create according to a dream. Denied them, he will destroy out of the dark, blind impulses of the nightmare of frustration."

This release of human potentialities with which you are being urged to assist, the seven-eighths of the thought "iceberg" that you are being asked to help bring to the surface was referred to by Gardner Murphy:

> . . . this great burst of fresh enthusiasm which sweeps like wildfire through the minds of those boys and girls who want to know, to control, who want to get hold of meanings, who want to grow in and through this strange, exciting, challenging environment . . . preserving primitive intensities.[19]

But, he cautions, it will take strenuous efforts to avoid over-control:

> . . . how to allow the first generous outpouring of mind and heart to have its way. We know relatively little about how to encourage but all too much about how to impede. We find a thousand devices for regularizing, stabilizing, restraining, or even for poking fun at the earliest exploratory efforts of children who are transported by a great challenge or a great discovery. Whatever stray creativeness gets through the sieve of our adult system of approvals and disapprovals of children's behavior is likely to be knocked down by classmates who, through their own earlier subjection to restraints or ridicule, have learned that to poetize, to daub, to speculate, or to dream is just a "waste of time."[20]

What kinds of homes help children think most creatively? In what home environment are they motivated to their highest achievement? One study pin-pointed the answers in some detail:

More books owned by the children
Larger family libraries

[19] Gardner Murphy, *Human Potentialities*, New York, Basic Books, Inc., Publishers, 1958, pp. 165, 166.
[20] *Ibid.*, p. 163.

More travel
More musical instruments
More music and other outside lessons
Greater communication among family members
More family or group activities in the home
More self-conscious planning for development of individual family members
Higher representation of professional and managerial parents
Higher values, shared among family members[21]

However, you must not conclude that sound thinking and high creativity and achievement come only from homes in the top socio-economic levels. With the general extension downward of opportunities for learning and for participation in talent-developing activities, the barriers are also lowered.

To distinguish between pressure and guidance, overindulgence and reasonable enrichment, lazy loafing and meditative thoughtfulness, the adults who live and work with children must be vigilant. Of course we want them to perform at the top level of which they are capable; but we don't want them to miss childhood on the way. On the school evaluation of a little boy, one teacher wrote: "Danny sometimes says he has too many things to do. He often asks for a chance to sit quietly and relax. I think that maybe we push children too hard and fast, and forget that after all they are children only once, and for such a short time."

In this era when speed, production, and mechanization are zooming upward in almost a perpendicular manner, maybe one ought to pause for a moment and listen to her. Common sense in both home and school often comes in quiet words rather than in bombastic orations. Pressures on children are excused in several ways that seem to satisfy many teachers and parents:

He's bright and capable—but lazy, so let's give him more to do.
He's bright and *not* lazy, so let's be sure he doesn't develop bad habits. Give him more to fill those free moments.
He's not very bright, so let's be sure he learns as much as possible. After all, he needs the drill now, and he'll have to earn a living later.

[21] Reported by Dr. Nicholas Hobbs of George Peabody College for Teachers, Nashville, in a speech to the annual convention of the Council for Exceptional Children, April, 1958.

The *real* reason for pushing so hard may not be easily understood, but it might be a very simple one: Many of us fear being alone, being where it is quiet, or being between activities. The bustle of our lives for the past 20 years gives us the erroneous belief that it has to be a hurried, busy existence for children, too. For aren't they also a product of this tense, swift world, we ask ourselves?

The answer, surprisingly enough, should be "No." Rather than being a product of the 1960s, they belong to Childhood, a much more changeless, eternal kind of environment than a year or even a decade is. When many of us were children we had time: time to read *Tom Swift, and the Land of Wonders* and *The Bobbsey Twins* as we leaned against a tree in the back yard; time to lick the sliver of ice snatched off the back of the ice truck; time to suck a jaw-breaker through all its layers, color by color by color.

The world has changed, we have changed, our habits and desires and fears have changed, but children have remained as they have always been. Their minds must have a chance to dwell before they can create, to meditate, be quiet, maybe even seem to do nothing. They need a vacation from excursions, piano lessons, phonics, and weight-lifting, all fine in their way and in moderation. Collectively we are developing a nation of poor little rich boys and girls who need some protection from the overanxious teachers and parents who are conscientiously trying to "do good" for them.

Although you're getting in on the ground floor of the whole subject, it's smart to respect those who have excavated and established the foundation. Their contributions are among the most fascinating in recent and current educational literature. The big push toward research in this field was provided single-handedly by J. P. Guilford of the University of Southern California when he was president of the American Psychological Association. In 1950 he told that organization that he had combed the *Psychological Abstracts* for a quarter of a century and found that only 186 out of 121,000 entries dealt in any way with subjects related to creativity. His work has been joined by the research of many others in the years since his challenge was tossed out (Getzels, Jackson, Murphy, Taylor, Torrance, and Barzun, who takes the "creative cult" to task, viewing creativity as just another opportunity to avoid discipline[22]).

[22] Jacques Barzun, "The Cults of 'Research' and 'Creativity'," *Harper's Magazine,* October, 1960, pp. 69–74.

Conformity, much more than creativity, has been our guiding light. The gray flannel suit of a few years ago (now somewhat out of date), "the organization man," motivational research, tract houses, outside cooking—the push toward similarity has dominated all of our lives. And yet, we do want the individual spirit of the dreamer— as long as he doesn't disturb our classroom or home routines. But the rewards more frequently go to the conformist who does what is expected of him and does it fairly well. Respect for the unorthodox thought and pioneering effort is still more rare than it should be, especially in classrooms.

CHILD-STUDY TECHNIQUES

Even before a teacher meets his class he may have heard that Johnny is "a little devil," Bill is "unmanageable," Sue is "a bad influence on the others," and Mary is "the sweet, shy type." The line of least resistance for the teaching novice is to follow judgments of the more experienced teachers instead of absorbing whatever test, health, and anecdotal materials might be in a child's cumulative folder. Not that the folder will always be more revealing than the "helpful hints" dropped by a former teacher; actually, it may say more about the teacher than it does about the child! A sound academic program can neither be set up nor evaluated unless one knows a great deal about the children in it. Teachers who lack the knowledge of how to get the needed information, the desire for getting it, or the awareness that it is needed can hardly do a good job in teaching. It's a case of first things first: knowing the children before actual teaching and learning take place.

Of course, some teachers start out with a handicap. Their lack of insight into the problems of others and their inability to think beyond themselves are hardly a good launching pad for understanding the difficulties of children. On the other hand, there are fortunately many thousands of persons who enter teaching with a well-established basis for seeing into and through the abilities, aptitudes, and personalities of their children, and whose own mental health is on an even enough keel so they can help straighten out the rockiness that shakes their students once in a while.

Voluminous materials are available on guidance and child

psychology. Your problem won't be in locating sources, but rather in determining *which* to use and *when* to stop, for the repetitive factor enters here just as it does in several other major fields of professional education. As you look through the writings of various persons, you may be in dependable company, but you'll rapidly become aware of the overlapping in ideas and recommendations. But then, it's the old story of every publisher wanting to have his own horses in the stable. A few of the many competent guides to child-study techniques are those of Millie Almy, W. Carson Ryan, Ruth Strang, Theodore Torgerson, DeVerl Willey, Paul A. Witty, and the old standby put out by the American Council on Education some years ago, *Helping Teachers Understand Children.*

What are the various child-study techniques? Which ones are most teachers qualified to use? Which must they generally steer clear of unless they've had special preparation? Test materials immediately step into the picture, with guidelines for their use and interpretation available in the accompanying manuals and usually in Buros, *Mental Measurement Yearbooks.* Tests are of various types: individual, group, mental ability, achievement, personality, short and long forms. The variety becomes greater each year, and each year it becomes more necessary to rely on the "test experts" in your school to help you be selective and intelligent about using them and their results.

Your own observation will be a good source of information; but its value will depend a great deal on your objectivity, insight, alertness, and how you use and report the information you obtain. The anecdotal records you will write up may help or hinder a child. *What* you select to write about may be more revealing and helpful than *how* you do it. Too many teachers select the same kind of thing to react to, for example, cleanliness, honesty, noisiness, or ability in a particular subject. The result is a limited amount of information about children but some real disclosures about the teacher's own prejudices and attitudes.

Tests and observational and anecdotal information frequently follow a child through school in a cumulative folder. And there's the rub; for why is it necessary that every teacher all the way through know (or care!) that Johnny's nose ran on January 14 in kindergarten? The sheer junk that often accumulates in these folders is a very discouraging sight for many conscientious teachers. But with careful administrative guidance and teacher cooperation, it needn't be that way. Selectively chosen materials *can* provide a story, a pattern on the background of each child.

The list of additional sources of child study is long. It includes home visitation, parent conferences, child interviews, and auto-biographies written by the child. It consists of information that fits into a total teaching guide for each child; information related to mental age, sight, hearing, speech, emotional and social development and maturity, language development, experiential background, and family background. It can give a picture of school progress, general physical health, and basic abilities and aptitudes related to each phase and level of the school program.

Caution is necessary in the use of all of these materials and information. Especially is this so in sociometry (does being left out mean passive ignoring or outright rejection?), painting as an interpretation of personality (does he use black paint because he's a morbid little character, or because it's the only color available?), and play therapy (what do pins stuck in the papa doll *really* mean?).

A teacher who works hard at teaching (defined in a narrow sense) may discover it is a waste of time unless he works almost as hard at obtaining a basic understanding of the changing, intricate personalities of those at the receiving end. One without the other brings half-way results, with both "normal" and "exceptional" children, for too many reasonably intelligent teachers.

PHYSICALLY AND MENTALLY HANDICAPPED CHILDREN: SOME GENERAL COMMENTS

. . . and it was the first time in three months that the little girl was un-chained from the bed in the dark room. In her halting speech she told the police a grim story of solitude and darkness. Her mother and father blamed that treatment on their shame related to the child's inability to walk, speak well, and play with other children.

"We had all been ridiculed so much," the mother explained, "that we didn't know which way to turn. We couldn't let her out of the house. We were ashamed . . ."

Stories still occasionally appear in the newspapers regarding abuse of children who deviate from the so-called normal. For the moment they shock the reader; but the later response often is that it concerns someone else's child. "It couldn't happen to me or mine," they insist. What are the facts on such children which every future teacher must face and understand?

Every classroom in the country randomly set up includes at least one such exceptional child, whose sight, hearing, speech, emotional adjustment, intellectual level, or physical condition deviates from the so-called normal enough to require some special educational help.

Only one-sixth of the estimated 6 million handicapped children of school age in the United States are receiving help.

Things are getting better every year, however. More than 4000 public school systems provide special educational opportunities for handicapped children. (We'll single out the gifted for consideration in another chapter.) The figure was only 1400 in the late 1940s.

Every state offers some special help, and nearly all state departments of education employ one or more specialists in a specific handicap; some have as many as 15 specialists.

More than 3000 local school systems now have programs for educating mentally retarded children in special classes in regular schools. *But,* only about one-fifth of the estimated 1.2 million or more mentally retarded children of school age in the United States are receiving special education.

Out of 35,000 deaf children 25,000 are in special classes, but only one-fourth of the 2 million speech-handicapped children are receiving speech correction.

As you would expect, parents have been the pioneers in getting proper educational opportunities for these exceptional children. One enlightened parent with a cerebral palsied youngster recently said:

We love her and want to keep her with us. It isn't ever too much for us to feed and clothe her because she can't do those things for herself. We're eager to have her become a contributing member of society as far as her limitations will permit her, but why don't people show some sense? Can't they stop looking at her as though she's a freak? They make us want to put a high wall up to protect her. They hurt her so much.

In their writings a few intelligent parents have expressed similar fears. They imply that because their families include a child who differs so could yours and everyone else's. A brilliant young lawyer,

John Frank, and his equally bright wife had a first son who was mentally limited, and they reported the sequence of events in *My Son's Story*. Pearl Buck, the widely heralded novelist, wrote about her daughter in *The Child Who Never Grew*. Dale Rogers, wife of the cowboy movie star, Roy Rogers, tried to console others through a heart-tugging little book about their baby, *Angel Unaware*.

Many teachers of so-called normal children have realized during recent years that in order to be really good teachers they have to understand the child who deviates. An obvious fact brought that thought to their attention: All children (and adults) deviate in some way from the normal; no one is average. Fortified with that idea they have read books and taken courses which help them study and understand *all* children, and these exceptional children are inevitably included. Their "free" summers have included courses that provide guidance in this area. They are learning the terminology of such exceptional children, how to identify them, what their basic characteristics generally are, their fundamental needs, the relationship of their major deviation to their mental health and that of their parents, what school curriculums meet their needs. They are learning about teacher qualifications, helpful organizations, publications, and institutions, and many, many additional factors.

Misunderstandings related to these children don't reside only with the uneducated. What about those now teaching or you who will teach who may not know which of the following are *necessarily* related to limited intelligence: cerebral palsy, epilepsy, polio, slowness in learning, brain injury, mental illness. What about those who may decide, on the basis of emotion only, that so-called normal children should be totally sheltered from the others?

In addition to more money being available for the education of such exceptional children and more knowledge of them, many trends are readily noticeable. Some of them are just beginning and need a big push forward; others are far along in their development:

More frequent consideration of the needs of these children in programs preparing people like you to teach "regular" elementary and secondary school; prevention; correction of minor problems; referral

Integrating blind children into regular classes—*your* future class—with a resource teacher to help the child, teacher and parent; more than half the blind children of school age now in regular classrooms

Speech and lip reading for the hearing handicapped, as a replacement for or in addition to "sign language"

Schooling and state and community help and encouragement for the trainable mentally retarded child (I.Q. of approximately 25 to 50)

Larger number of well-planned college and university programs to prepare teachers of such exceptional children

Regional planning for the children and for teacher preparation, especially in the South and West

Clarification and development of more acceptable terminology; the old moron, imbecile, idiot tags being replaced by educable, trainable, custodial (nontrainable) or mildly retarded, moderately retarded, severely retarded

More specialized and knowledgeable administrative personnel—federal, state, county, city, school district; strengthening of specific teacher certification requirements

Improved social attitudes toward the handicapped, through the help of the mass media especially motion pictures, popular magazines, and books, both fiction and nonfiction. Is anyone *really* to blame? Why should there be any stigma?

Emphasis on vocational preparation of those who in the past were considered economically "hopeless"; an awareness that society can save millions by spending a far smaller amount to train and educate

Great strides forward in research, especially in causes of handicaps—retrolental fibroplasia in sight and phenylketonuria in mental retardation, for example.

The changes in attitudes toward the handicapped and the trends in working with them are all part of an evolving philosophy of education related to these children. It is based on starting with the idea that all children—if at all possible—are to be educated in "regular" public school classes. But a screening should take place. Some profit more from "special" classes in public schools. Others need "special" classes in "special" public schools or private schools or institutions. The proper setting must always stem from the needs of the child and his family plus the attitudes and facilities of the community. No stock answer can be given about what is "best" for a child. *Which* child, *which* family, and *which* community all have to get into the act.

Other basic parts of the philosophy toward the education of physically or mentally limited children have matured greatly in recent years. The responsibility for educating these children has been shared by many: the community, in providing necessary educational services; the parents, in making their needs known; the school, in bringing current knowledge into action. In addition there are the contributions of the professionals: pediatricians, psychologists, psychiatrists, therapists, and people in higher education. This "team effort" has paid off for children whose neighborhoods in the past had a hidden-away, attic-and-cellar complex about the whole subject. "The sick or crippled child has offered a challenge and brought a response; he has inspired in us a mood, a spirit, an attitude. The thought of the challenged and inspired teacher has moved forward in response to him."[23] As a future teacher, you too will be faced with personal and professional demands in this area.

But, despite all the gains, unfinished business certainly remains in regard to these children who differ. It includes persistently retained misunderstandings regarding causes, prevention, and correction; size and scope of the problem; parental, school, and community attitudes; the need for early discovery followed by appropriate help; support for organizations struggling in the field; need for more and better teacher preparation programs; shaking-up the attitudes of parents of so-called normal children; more personnel and funds for research.

Recognition of the problems comes from high places. On February 6, 1962, President Kennedy presented a message to Congress that has direct and important implications for all of our children and all of us. He said:

Today, more than at any other time in our history, we need to develop our intellectual resources to the fullest. But the facts of the matter are that many thousands of our young people are not educated to their maximum capacity—and they are not, therefore, making the maximum contribution of which they are capable to themselves, their families, their communities and the Nation. Their talents lie wasted—their lives are frequently pale and blighted—and their contribution to our economy and culture are lamentably below the levels of their potential skills, knowledge, and creative ability....

Another longstanding national concern has been the provision of specially trained teachers to meet the educational needs of children afflicted

[23] Gardner Murphy, op. cit., p. 174.

with physical and mental disabilities. The existing program providing Federal assistance to higher education institutions and to State education agencies for training teachers and supervisory personnel for mentally retarded children was supplemented last year to provide temporarily for training teachers of the deaf. I recommend broadening the basic program to include assistance for the special training needed to help all our children afflicted with the entire range of physical and mental handicaps.

Argue about the *source* of support if you want to, but put off rejecting the *need* for it until you know more about it.

THE SLOW LEARNER

Among the various categories of exceptional children none is more frequently overlooked than the ones who "look so normal" but are not, mentally at least. None will demand more of your energy, time, and ingenuity when you start to teach. Because of their appearance, normal performance is often expected of them, an expectation that frequently leads to disappointment, frustration, and considerable unhappiness for both children and adults.

The expression "slow learner" can be used to describe several groups. It literally can be applied to the bright youngster who works beneath his capacity, the able and unambitious performing adequately at his grade level but capable of doing much more. It can also be used for the "pseudo slow learner" who learns more slowly only because we ignore his problems which may have no direct relationship to mentality, but are instead related to socioeconomic, cultural or language factors. However, for a consistent point of departure, the following ingredients of a definition of slow learners are proposed for your consideration here:

An intelligence range of approximately 75 to 90 (I.Q.). But keep in mind the limitations of tests and testing personnel and the variations in scores depending on what test is used, who administers it, when it is given, and other factors. Also performance may be at 75 to 90 I.Q. level despite indications of higher capabilities.

Children in a regular classroom who do not quite keep up in the early grades and lag behind even more later on.

Children who are usually slow in intellectual matters, but not necessarily slow in artistic, mechanical, or social activities.

These children constitute a major problem. When one ~bserves their attendance in nearly every classroom, and considers the frequency with which their education is the subject of conferences of teachers and administrators, the amount of concern they cause their parents, and the added price communities pay when their education is inadequate, it is easy to understand the proportions of the subject.

With our increasing school population, more children will be in this learning category, more will need parental help and understanding, school programs, teachers, and community action. And more will be able to profit from the sincere consideration of newer approaches to living and working with these children in our homes, schools, and neighborhoods.

Some writers in the field use I.Q. exclusively in describing this group; others confuse the issue because of awkward terminology; and still others contribute unclear thinking induced by vague discussions of aptitudes, talents, achievement, abilities, and intelligence. I.Q.s of 80 to 95, 85 or less, 70 to 89, and 50 to 89 are found in the literature on this subject. Terms like the following appear: *borderline, borderline retarded, low normal, dull, dull normal, mildly handicapped, dullards, backward, nonacademic.* One refers to "island children," the ones who "are surrounded and isolated in our educational hierarchy." However, agreement is fairly general that slow learners constitute 15 to 20 percent of our school population. They must not be confused with the "mentally retarded" who are generally below an I.Q. of 70 or 75.

A distinction can be made between generalized slowness and retardation in specific fields. Practically all of us may be described as a slow learner in one or more ways, failing to learn in proportion to our desires, efforts, or instruction. But our emphasis here is on the children who are scholastically below the average because of intellectual limitations. Even in recent years a number of misconceptions and misunderstandings about slow learners have persisted among parents and teachers. For example, many still believe that an I.Q. is immobile, unchangeable, set for all time, instead of recognizing the influence on intelligence of a rich or barren environment.

Common misconceptions may be comforting, but they must be replaced by facts. A child who is slow in one area is *not* necessarily superior in others. Nor is there a balance established between low verbal abilities and high nonverbal ones, or low book-mindedness and high hand-mindedness. Hand activities may provide an area of reasonable success because of their concrete, meaningful nature, rather than as a compensating factor for low academic abilities; they also may develop, of course, because more time is put into them.

Slow learners do *not* balance their lower intellectual abilities with greater height and strength. That misconception stems from the fact that they may be the tallest and huskiest in their classrooms—an easy matter to understand when one notes that they also may be the oldest because of nonpromotion.

A rather common misunderstanding is that slow learners are potential delinquents. It could be stated more accurately that *all* children are potential delinquents. Because the environment (home, school, and community) of many slow learners is conducive to delinquent behavior, it may more accurately be assumed that this environment may contribute to both delinquency and slow learning.

It is important to recognize that while backwardness in some children may be innate and permanent, in others it may be accidental, acquired *and* correctable. One would be mistaken in assuming that in the former case they are slow but will catch up in time. Equally erroneous in the latter situation would be the assumption that *all* slowness is unalterable. Predictions must be based on the individual and his own potentialities, rather than on generalizations from studies of large groups.

The causes of mental and academic slowness in children may be traced to two major areas which are usually intertwined, the innate mental capacity and the influence of environmental factors. Research in medicine and biochemistry may in time bring more understanding of the inborn limitations which must be recognized as key causes in many cases. Sociologists, educators, and parents recognize a large number of other, more likely, causes of slowness. The clear relationship between these factors and a child's slowness implies that removal or modification of them may help elevate the achievement level of the child, perhaps even bringing it up to the normal range.

The extent or degree of the problem and the length of time it has existed are items inevitably involved in possible correction. Among the various limiting factors are the following:

Socio-economic limitations
Cultural and language deprivations or differences
Physical factors, based on sight, hearing, immature development, malnutrition, or other health conditions
Family problems or tensions, anxieties, quarrels, excessive mobility, lack of acceptance of child
School-related factors, such as irregular attendance, inefficient teaching, distaste for school, poor study habits, repeated failure
Meager or barren educational resources in the home and/or community
Incongruities among factors of ability, achievement, and aspiration as they relate to each other
Accidents, infections or diseases resulting in physical or emotional problems
Inappropriate educational pressures before the child is ready
Emotional disturbances related to above or other factors
The absence of drive, inner urge, or motivation, existent but not traceable to any of the factors listed above

The problem of causation becomes more complicated if you recognize that many thousands of children who possess one or a combination of these factors are *not* slow learners. Thus, slowness does not inevitably result from a particular circumstance, but seems to be the outcome of combinations of conditions as they join and affect a child. Recognizing the causes and adapting solutions to them are basic in your approach to the slow child.

Just as with any large group of average or above-average children or adults, slow learners vary in their physical and emotional characteristics and development. No single trait describes them other than that they learn more slowly and to a lesser degree. Nor can one determine true capacity by appearance or by superficial observation of performance. (Even the teachers of Thomas Edison and Isaac Newton tried and failed.) Slowness in school as a single factor is not sufficient, for in another educational setting the child may perform on an average level. Their differences from other children are in degree rather than in kind, as variations exist among all of us.

Although some writers in the field state that slow learners are essentially normal in their emotional, social, physical, and motor development, others point out many differences. Slow learners are often characterized by the following:

Short attention and interest span

Limited imagination, creative thinking

Slow reaction time

Apathy, diffidence, dependence, placidity—but frequent presence of excitability, sensitivity

Academic retardation, especially in reading; achievement age lagging behind chronological age

Absence or easy loss of self-confidence

Gullibility, instability, shyness, submissiveness

Low power of retention, memory

Inability to do abstract thinking, to handle symbols, to evaluate results, to foresee consequences of acts

Failure to transfer ideas, to extend beyond local point of view in time or place, to retain interest if results are deferred or intangible

Limited powers of self-direction, of adapting to change in situations and people

Low levels of initiative, vocabulary, standards of workmanship, persistence, concentration, reasoning, defining, discriminating, analyzing

Ease of confusion; fears, anxieties

Laziness—but perhaps due to ill health or emotional maladjustment rather than as a constitutional factor

Action based on impulse, insistence on quick results, inclination toward jumping to conclusions

Poorer physical development: height, weight, proportion, general health; unexplained fatigue

Some of the problems of slow learners reach a climax in intensity within the home, but a whole series of long-range climaxes emerge after school entry. For the first time strangers become directly involved in the learning and adjustment problems. Thousands of schools and teachers daily exert intensive efforts to ease these difficulties, many of which have accumulated since birth. Schools are usually aware of the problems of the insecure and the isolates, of the ways in which self-respect is limited or destroyed, and of unfair competition between unequals. Their efforts are becoming more intensified every year toward solving them. And your increasing awareness can help a great deal.

You will have to make specific adjustments in subject-matter areas if there are slow learners in your classroom, despite the fact that some say there are no special methods needed for teaching slow learners. In teaching reading, for example, a more orderly, systematic approach is necessary, with special attention to (1) reading readiness, (2) building vocabulary and methods of word recognition, (3) setting up individual standards of expectancy, and (4) selection of reading materials. Meaningful use of phonics, experience charts, auditory and visual activities and games, mechanical aids, basic reading series (plus the teachers' manuals), supplementary reading materials, and workbooks (*not* used as busywork) are all important parts of the program. The teaching of reading to slow learners may begin later and last longer than it would for other children.

When they are capable of reading the primers, these beginning books may have lost their attraction for them. A similar problem follows through the grades as ability levels lag behind interests. A broad area of literature for children has developed in recent years to meet that need. A few samples of these high-interest low-ability (vocabulary) materials are listed below:

American Adventure Series, Wheeler Publishing Company
American Heritage Series, American Book Company
Childhood of Famous Americans Series, Bobbs-Merrill
Classmate Editions, Lyons and Carnahan
Cowboy Sam Series, Beckley-Cardy
First Books Series, Franklin Watts
Landmark Books, Allabout Books, Random House
Skill Builders, Readers Digest Educational Service
True Book Series, Children's Press

Although students limited in reading speed and comprehension are frequently slow learners, this is not a necessary relationship. Because reading problems stem from a variety of sources, one cannot assume that an intellectual handicap is the sole cause. A student who lags in reading skills is not always a laggard in other subject areas, although there is often a close relationship. Improved reading ability frequently brings with it a lower number of failures in other school subjects.

For slow learners as well as others, reading should be approached from various directions, for enjoyment as well as information. Discovering causes, eliminating difficulties, and providing materials from the great choice available will help answer statements like this one: "The schools are failing to provide an educational system which will encourage the dull-normal child to learn to read so that he will read to learn."[24]

As he has so many times in his *Saturday Review* editorials, Paul Woodring gets to the core of the issue. He calls for a combination of careful diagnosis, individual instruction (if the school can take care of the cost), special grouping, and other possible solutions that meet specific needs of slow learners.

. . . until recently the schools had a simple solution for dealing with them —they were allowed to "fail" in school and drop out and go to work at an early age. This solution is no longer feasible. . . . The schools must find ways of dealing with [them] effectively. . . . There is a legitimate debate as to which of these solutions is best in any particular situation, but it can be said with some assurance that any school which uses none of them . . . is not providing equality of opportunity and is not doing justice to either bright or slow children.[25]

THE MENTALLY RETARDED

When the President of the United States and his family become deeply involved in a subject, it is probably one that has vital implications for many of us—regardless of our political leanings. The President's Panel on Mental Retardation as part of a national plan to deal effectively with the problem and work of the Joseph P. Kennedy, Jr. Foundation has made strong contributions to our understanding of the causes, prevention, and advances in combatting mental retardation.

In many communities mentally retarded children (below 70 or 75 I.Q.) are in regular classrooms. Lack of information, limited funds, or inertia may result in this unhappy teaching situation for you. And the situation, in turn, may result in your doing a poor job

[24] Samuel A. Kirk, *Teaching Reading to Slow-Learning Children*, Boston, Houghton Mifflin Company, 1940, p. 178.

[25] Paul Woodring, "Slow Learners," *Saturday Review*, February 17, 1962, pp. 53–54.

with these children as well as with all the rest. It is against this possibility that you have to insulate yourself. You can do it in several ways: with knowledge of the specific needs of mentally retarded children; by tactfully (and cautiously) contributing to the understanding of your school administrator, other teachers, and the community at large; and through a refinement of your teaching techniques adapted to individual and small-group methods. Again, the fact that many of these children look normal may present a problem.

Responsibility was squarely placed on the schools by Stanley P. Davies when he said:

The public school has not a whit less responsibility for the education of mental defectives in special classes suited to their own needs than it has to children of average or higher intelligence. In serving others well, we serve ourselves. It pays to make social assets out of what would otherwise be social liabilities. To give of our strength and knowledge to those that are weak is the kind of sharing that while strengthening the weak, also makes the strong stronger.[26]

A particularly fascinating development in this area is prevention. It has been estimated that taxpayers could save $100,000 for each case of mental retardation that was prevented. That figure is arrived at by taking the cost of special education or institutional care and adding to it the taxes and other benefits to society which would accrue if the child were to grow into a normal productive adult. Educational programs will be altered considerably in both size and content by the giant steps currently taken to help *prevent* mental retardation.

To cope with the misinformation on the whole subject still rattling around in our teacher preparation programs and the gaps of knowledge still too frequent in those programs, it is necessary to make some changes. Is there a special education department in your college or university? Do the other professors in the school or college of education use their services, establish contact between you and these specialists? And what about after you enter the doors of the profession? Will there be in-service work and a professional library in your school? Will you and your school participate in organizations like the American Association on Mental Deficiency, the National

[26] Stanley P. Davies, *American Journal of Mental Deficiency*, January, 1941, pp. 472–478.

Association for Retarded Children, and the Council for Exceptional Children (including a subscription to its magazine, *Exceptional Children*)?

Knowing something about exceptional children, mentally retarded and others, is one of the few ways in professional education of cutting through the gobbledygook of generalities, of digging into the hard facts of specific meanings related to individual differences among children.

Trends in the education of mentally retarded children are encouraging. In addition to current research on prevention, there is more free discussion of the problem in our communities and schools; terminology is changing and more personnel and funds are available. We have come a long way since the Middle Ages, when children and adults like these were the court fools and were denounced as "evil spirits," and since the days when persecution and extermination were the rule.

But our public and our teachers have more miles to travel. They have to accept the fact that children limited in mentality can be educated or trained. They should be made aware that many studies conducted in institutions dealt with the more limited children, and therefore their conclusions about intelligence and capabilities are unfair. They must be told, and told again, that these children grown up *can* work, that sterilization will *not* eradicate the occurrence in later generations, that juvenile delinquency is *not* a possession solely of this group (far from it, in fact), that institutionalizing is *not* the answer in all, or even most, instances, that the life span of the mentally retarded *is* rapidly increasing, and that research on causation and prevention is current, changing, exciting.

By 1970, our population will include more than 6 million mentally retarded (just imagine how many families are directly affected!); more than half will be children under 9. In October, 1961, President Kennedy said to his newly appointed Panel on Mental Retardation: "The manner in which our nation cares for its citizens and conserves its manpower resources is more than an index to its concern for the less fortunate. It is a key to its future." No one can disagree—least of all the parents of the mentally retarded. They are in the forefront of the battle for recognition of various facets of the problem and are most eagerly seeking solutions.

THE PSEUDO MENTALLY RETARDED

Some teachers and school administrators make tragic errors of judgment. They look at the record and classify children. Both the record and the classification may be wrong, resulting in a waste of human talent that we cannot afford.

Whole groups have been penalized directly (society indirectly) because of false conclusions. These groups include children with a language, cultural, or socioeconomic obstacle for which the rigid standards of some of our testing programs do not make allowances. They include emotionally maladjusted and mentally ill youngsters who are performing at "retarded levels," and physically handicapped ones whose sight, hearing, or skills of manipulation or coordination hold them back. They may even include some who are bright and terribly bored by the routine and repetition which stifle their creativity. The educationally deprived, the migrant, and the so-called bilingual are all involved. Invalid testing, poor tests, and poor teaching may step in for their share of blame.

One of the most neglected of these pseudo groups is the bilingual, the children who may be unilingual but in a language other than English. These children ponder—but may not have the opportunity to ask—questions like these:

Why does that lady in the front of the room dress so differently from the way my mother does?
Why doesn't she know how to pronounce my name correctly?
Why does she talk so strangely? I don't understand anything she says.
What are those things she writes up there, and the marks in the books on the table, and the songs she tries to have us sing?

These and many others are the questions that cross behind the silent faces of thousands of so-called bilingual children during their first weeks in an English-speaking classroom. Their teachers may expect them to be shy, quiet, and restrained, so the silence that dominates these children is no surprise to them. They live in more parts of this country than many of us realize: the French in New England and Louisiana; Scandinavians in the upper middle states; Puerto Rican, Polish, Italian, Greek, and many others in the foreign-speaking "islands" of New York and other large cities. In a number of the cities in Texas and other parts of the southwest half or more of the population is Spanish-speaking.

Our melting pot philosophy of fitting persons into the pattern of the stronger and richer segments of our society often results in a little child's rebellion. All *he* knows is that it's all very strange to him—and he wants to go home! An awareness of the problems such children bring to school and a knowledge of the job-seeking, job-holding, feeding, and housing problems they face with their families may help us more understandingly open up the glittering world of picture books and games and fun that the teacher can introduce to them. Through laughter and exciting new experiences she can bring them learning that they may grasp eagerly once they recognize that this new environment can provide a scope and range of enjoyment they never knew existed before.

In order to help meet the needs of children, many colleges and universities are placing emphasis on a full understanding of the specific children you future teachers will teach. The preparation program attaches no *less* importance to child development, educational psychology, techniques of teaching reading, and other usual requirements. But either inserted into those courses or in a separate course or both, attention is focused directly on the child with cultural and language differences. In a few institutions of higher learning the field of special education has added this child as a new facet. The reasoning is that if the exceptional child is defined as one who differs from the so-called normal, from the larger or dominant part of our population, then isn't this child entitled to special emphasis?

In an era when the means are available for a full understanding of each child, it is important that you and others in the profession recognize realistically the value of viewing every child for what he is and can become. Such recognition demands that a constant questioning spirit be applied to the total environment of bilingual as well as other children, to the preparation of their teachers, and to new methods of child study, of teaching, and of understanding the child in his manifold circumstances.

Eli Ginzberg pin-pointed one major issue when he wrote:

. . . currently many children are not being properly educated and trained on the assumption that they are truly mentally deficient. If more specialists were available to assess and help these children, many would be found to have specific physical or emotional defects which if corrected would enable them to learn and eventually become self-supporting.[27]

CONCLUDING REMARKS

"A time for every child" means that no child is neglected—and the time is now. The most alert, democratically oriented, education-minded, and wealthiest country of all cannot consciously settle for less. *You* can't settle for less. The excuses are all gone now; you've been alerted to the needs and the human and material riches available for satisfying them.

The creative and the conforming, the mentally retarded and the gifted, the slow ones whose slowness is or is not correctable—all of these are up for more careful attention than ever before by each teacher. And there are other groups, too. For example, what about the speech-handicapped child you will have in your classroom? The best thing you can do, of course, is to help prevent the problem in the first place. There are no pat ways for doing so; but because so much of the causation factor in some instances stems from emotional disturbances, the least you can do is provide a healthful, accepting environment for learning. You're limited in what you can do about turmoil in the home, but the classroom is often your "kingdom."

Correction of the minor speech difficulties may lie within your abilities. A cautionary note, however: keep hands off the more serious involvements even though there may be no speech specialist around. There is no need to add to the child's burden. Books like *Speech Ways* and *Talking Time* by Louise Binder Scott and J. J. Thompson, and writers like Wendell Johnson and Charles Van Riper can help you provide assistance as well as recognize your limitations.

You'll teach blind and deaf children and others with a variety of physical handicaps; some will have minor emotional problems, some serious ones. How you can prepare for the tasks ahead isn't as complicated as it sounds. Having gone through this chapter and the ones that preceded it, you have at least made a start.

[27] Eli Ginzberg, *Human Resources: The Wealth of a Nation*, New York, Simon and Schuster, Inc., 1958, p. 160.

CHAPTER 9

A TIME FOR *Encouraging the Gifted*

In selected educational and home circles, the great concern for the full development of the bright child is not new. The trouble is that it is so slow in maturing, in getting past the talk stage into one of universal action. This is one of the tragedies of our generation.

Accusations are made that we are "creating an elite" or being "undemocratic" by an opposition that wants to preserve an inadequate *status quo* which can't possibly meet our national and international needs. Although it is possible to go back as far as Plato in seeing attention directed to the intellectually superior child, our more logical beginnings for the whole issue stem from Thomas Jefferson (in *Notes on the State of Virginia* and *Jefferson Speaks*):

The object (of education) is to bring into action that mass of talents which lies buried in poverty in every country for want of the means of development, and thus give activity to a mass of mind, which, in proportion to our population, shall be the double or treble of what it is in most countries. . . . we hope to avail the state of those talents which nature has sown as liberally among the poor as the rich, but which perish without use, if not sought for and cultivated.

Jefferson advocated an educational policy of eliminating the unfit gradually and opening the way widely for the bright. His terminology was particularly unfortunate when he suggested that "twenty of the best geniuses will be raked from the rubbish annually." As Jacques Barzun once said, "The rejected applicants are 'rubbish' only with reference to collegiate work, just as Jefferson was rubbish for the boxing ring."[1]

[1] Jacques Barzun, *Teacher in America*, Boston, Little, Brown and Company, 1945, p. 256.

Efforts have been spotty throughout the years to locate, motivate, and educate bright children; to evaluate their progress; and to reconcile their ability, achievement, and aspirations. Sincere, yes, but too often the activities fail to recognize the crucial elements of *need* and *cost*. The need pertains not only to the children themselves but also to the survival of our society; and the cost of doing the job to its full measure, of making the necessary changes from an assembly-line education, is high.

Two major spurts in this century have elevated gifted children into a prominent place in educational discussions. The first came during the 1920s with the work of L. M. Terman, Leta Hollingworth, Paul Witty, and a small group of advanced thinkers and research people who felt strongly that the disservice to bright children and to all of us had to be stopped. The second surged into sight just preceding and since the Russians' first Sputnik. Now the whole subject has attained a prominent place in our national planning. The report of the President's Commission on National Goals said:

Attempts to identify children of unusual potentialities should begin when schooling begins. When a child's family and neighborhood background are culturally impoverished, the school may be the only channel through which his gifts can be nourished: the sooner they are discovered the better.

Children of high academic talent, most of whom will have to devote many more years to education than the average youngster, should be given the opportunity to move more rapidly. There should be various forms of grouping by ability from the earliest years of school; and every effort should be made in and out of school to provide enrichment for the gifted student.[2]

Although such comments obviously cannot be very specific or detailed, they can contribute to a point of view which says, "Let's stop the conversation and get on with the show!"

In *The Child Buyer,* John Hersey touches on all the peculiar attitudes of a public that still neglects most of its gifted children. He pokes fun at teachers, school administrators, guidance people, parents, and the whole community. His Barry Rudd makes a statement that can startle us more than a little right now:

[2] President's Commission on National Goals, *Goals for Americans*, Englewood Cliffs, N. J., Prentice-Hall, Inc., 1960, p. 85.

It had been drummed into me—I remember Miss Songevine used to din this into me—that precocious children grow up abnormal, neurotic, headed for imbecility or insanity. Early ripe, early rot. The Bible says, "Much learning doth make thee mad." Seneca: "There is no great genius without some touch of madness." Burton, in *The Anatomy of Melancholy,* speaking of men "out of too much learning become mad." Moreau de Tours, Lombroso, Lange-Eichbaum—"scientists" who "proved" the relationship between brilliance and madness; Miss Songevine threw them at me. I felt doomed. Doomed.[3]

We have come a long way from the nineteenth-century philosophy which felt that gifted children "ripen early and rot early." Now we *know* that as a group they retain their gifted tendencies in adulthood; but the road ahead is still long and bumpy. Isn't it ironic that our "ally" in moving along is the country some of us fear obsessively, the country whose advances in science have brought a partial realization that our major hope is in our youth, the greatest natural resource of all?

Our newest frontier in the United States is not industrial, economic, or political. It is intellectual, and the more quickly we recognize it, the more we will be able to retain our superiority in a competitive world. Many of our popular magazines have tried to awaken the public to this need. So have individual articles and whole series of them in professional magazines such as the *NEA Journal* and *Educational Leadership.*

However, many of our discussions about gifted children are still where they were 10 or 15 years ago. We continue to define, identify, and list characteristics; argue about enrichment versus acceleration versus special classes; quote the Terman study; haggle over what term will best describe these children and whether they should even be included in exceptional-child categories.

Until we are able to educate *each* child up to his capacity, there will be unfinished business in the realm of the bright child. A steadily increased birth rate, potentially good teachers being attracted into other fields, the current skilled manpower shortages, our slow awakening to the fact that it costs, costs, costs to educate well—these are just a few of the contributing factors to the unfinished state of affairs regarding the gifted.

[3] John Hersey, *The Child Buyer,* New York, Alfred A. Knopf, Inc., 1960, p. 107.

We must consider many factors in this area—geographic (from one coast to another and beyond), age (infancy to old age), sources (fortunately on the increase), extremes of conformity and creativity, patterns of income, achievement, teacher ability and preparation, community and parental attitudes.

THE PRICE OF MEDIOCRITY

Watering down our expectations—whether we are talking about popular songs, awards for the motion picture industry, or classroom activities—will lead only to mass mediocrity. Words like "deadening," "destructive," and "blight" have been used to warn us about the acceptance of mediocre work in various parts of our society,[4] and to call to those in high places to help elevate our national standards. Respecting the greatest number and trying to seek the greatest good for them has led us to a point of neglecting the relatively small group of potential leaders. If we sacrifice quality for quantity, we obviously have not given sufficient thought to the subject. John W. Gardner blasted at our acceptance of inefficiency wherever it may be located when he wrote:

We must recognize that there may be excellence or shoddiness in every line of human endeavor. . . . The society which scorns excellence in plumbing because plumbing is a humble activity and tolerates shoddiness in philosophy because it is an exalted activity will have neither good plumbing nor good philosophy. Neither its pipes nor its theories will hold water.[5]

However, a more complete, total concept of the error of our ways was tackled by Claude M. Fuess:

It is significant that the number of first-rate statesmen in the United States of the post-Revolutionary period, when the country had a population of not much over three million, was greater than it is today when we have 180,000,000. One of the reasons, perhaps, is that our generation has reversed the pattern and established a cult, not of genius, but of mediocrity, by its approval of conformity and orthodoxy and the kindred color-

[4] Claude M. Fuess quoted in the *Amherst Alumni News*, Summer, 1960.
[5] John W. Gardner, "Quality in Higher Education," *NEA Journal*, September, 1958, p. 364.

less virtues which keep a social organism static. Various observers deplore the growing tendency to distrust those who are different, those who deviate in their thinking or writing or behavior from what we have been taught to consider normal. Uniformity of ideas seems to be regarded as a protection against the dangers of so-called radical thought.[6]

Perhaps we fear some things in addition to the aggressiveness of Russia. Are we afraid that we will have too many people going to college, entering professions, earning big incomes? Will we run out of jobs "at the top," disrupt society by a top-heavy, literate populace? Students of the subject like David C. McClelland, David Riesman and Dael Wolfle assure us that there is nothing to fear in the foreseeable future from these directions. Much more serious is the danger of having people working below their capabilities; here is where the seeds of frustration, anger, and distrust are liberally sown. Underprivileged minorities; women held back occupationally just because they are "the wrong sex"; persons unfortunate enough to live in economically depressed areas; older workers "put out to pasture" too early; wasted talents in large businesses and other organizations: these are some of the elements of our loss. Bright men and women may decide that loneliness, restricting normal family activities, and foregoing current pleasures for future gain are too high a price for fulfilling their capabilities.

Deeply troubled by our waste of human resources is Eli Ginzberg[7] who reminds us that we are willing to drill for oil with the odds heavily against us, write off a half-billion dollar investment in a new missile as a bad mistake, and make large grants and loans to other nations in the hope that they will be friendly and peaceful. But when we hear suggestions to invest in our brain power, we continue to look for bargains. How many bright people do we fail to educate? Here are some of the figures:

Fewer than half of the top 25 percent of our high school graduates finish college, a disturbing figure of about 250,000 or more being lost each year; only 6 out of 10 of the top 5 percent finish. And you can add to these the thousands who drop out even before they finish high school. They are

[6] Claude M. Fuess, "The Retreat from Excellence," *Saturday Review*, March 24, 1960, p. 23.

[7] Eli Ginzberg, *Human Resources: The Wealth of a Nation*, New York, Simon and Schuster, Inc., 1958.

more likely to go to college if they are from families with money, if they are urban boys, if they represent "white collar" fathers, and if their parents are well educated.

It has been estimated that children with I.Q.s of 140 waste half their time in the "average" classroom, and those at the 170 level waste practically all of their time.

Only about one in 50 who are intellectually qualified to obtain our top academic degrees actually does so.

More than half of the children with I.Q.s above 135 already mastered the school curriculum and are at least two full grades beyond the one in which they are enrolled. (Don't you think that ignoring *this* fact contributes to our dropout rate?)

In the selective Terman study,[8] 30 percent of these potentially superior college people were not graduated from college. Major causes given were finances, lack of parental encouragement, and failure of high schools to recognize potentialities.

Maybe the attitudes are changing now. Maybe the climate is encouraging an affirmative approach to the too-frequently scorned "egg-head." But we cannot yet relax in the assurance that this is so. We certainly cannot be sure, at least until we really understand what "equality of opportunity" means.

Equal opportunity for an education doesn't mean the *same* opportunity. It could not mean, for example, identical work for the borderline mentally retarded child and the very bright youngster. It was once put succinctly like this: "There is nothing so unequal as the equal treatment of unequals." This is true whether we are discussing football, art, music, the school newspaper, or academic ability. The sameness of educational programs couldn't possibly have been inherent in the democratic concept based on respecting individuals and their differences. In an age when guided missiles have taken on more importance for some people than unguided children, we are forced to cling to and increase our respect for the productive and creative person. That respect has to thrive in schools (as well as homes) in a democracy.

The bulletin of the Council for Basic Education put it this way:

Are we really to assume, then, that it would be a mortal threat to our way of life if we were to give the same kind of special attention to the gifted

---

[8] Lewis M. Terman and Melita Oden, *Genetic Studies of Genius* (five volumes), Stanford, Calif., Stanford University Press, 1959.

that we now give to the retarded? Or to the football players, baton twirlers, and school queens for a day? Are we really to continue in the name of Democracy to undermine, as we have systematically and pigheadedly undermined in the past, our best hope of the future because we think free men dare not recognize and reward talent? Are we really to deny the true democratic rights of the gifted for fear of producing tyrants instead of Jeffersons, Millikans, even John Deweys, and other uncommon men? If we answer yes, we might be wise to resign ourselves to cultural, not to mention national, suicide. And we will have earned it.[9]

A few self-evident truths begin to emerge:

Equality as human beings and before the law does not imply intellectual equality.

The great intelligence of the relatively few has been our major source of progress.

That progress can be spurred even more by recognizing and nurturing our reservoir of intelligence that is now being neglected.

Equal opportunity means *different* opportunity, and giving the *same* education to all is a perversion of the whole idea.

"Surely it is exactly as undemocratic to penalize the gifted child, simply because he is gifted, as it is to bar a citizen from a town meeting solely on grounds he belongs to a minority race or religion. It is just as undemocratic to slow the class down to the level of the dullard as it is to require all people to eat beans because not everyone can afford pheasant."[10]

Underlying all of these points is the need to recognize that bright children come from rich and poor backgrounds, that scholarship and fellowship programs are essential to help equalize opportunities. Many of us "prefer to indulge in the fantasy that the really able and deserving young people can all get an education and get ahead in the world if they will only work hard enough."[11]

Money for the intelligent as well as the retarded; excellent performance as the rule rather than the exception; and challenges for the bright as well as a preservation of the confidence, will power, and

[9] The Bulletin of the Council for Basic Education, March, 1958.

[10] John Keats, *Schools Without Scholars,* Boston, Houghton Mifflin Company, 1958, p. 100.

[11] W. Lloyd Warner, *et al., Who Shall Be Educated?* New York, Harper & Row, Publishers, Inc., 1944, p. 166.

motivation of all the rest are goals to be sought constantly in our efforts as teachers to stem the tide of mediocrity. Whether we're talking about making a fence that will withstand winter gales, teaching mathematics with ingenuity, intelligence, and enthusiasm, or encouraging children to take excellence for granted in their own performance, our goals must be high.

TERMINOLOGY AND IDENTIFICATION

A speaker on the subject of gifted children once said, "Define them in any way you want to, and I'll go along with your definition." And it's not a bad idea, when one considers how often in the education field we get bogged down in the mire of terminology. In recent years, these children have been described as *gifted, superior, talented, bright, geniuses, academically talented, able, ambitious*. Other attempts at defining them include the non-I.Q. description of Paul Witty who refers to "consistently remarkable performance in any worthwhile line of endeavor"; the cut-off score of 110 on the Army General Classification Test used as a device for selecting men for Officers' Candidate Schools; Leta Hollingworth's work with children above 180 I.Q.; the singling out of the top 15 to 20 percent of our school population in some of the work of James B. Conant; Terman's lower limit of 110 I.Q. in his early days (120 and 140 in later years); the Stanford-Binet test indicating that 1 percent of our population are above 135 I.Q. and 25 percent are above 110 I.Q.; the Cleveland Major Work Class line of 125 I.Q.

Far more important than the labels used are the ways of identifying bright children. The easiest method, of course, might be to ask any parent! However, in order for parents to do at least a partially adequate task of identifying intelligence, it's necessary for us to help them view their child in a broad framework of other children. If we are to identify these children early, even before the first year in school, our dependence on the assistance we can get from parents becomes increasingly obvious. And to identify them early *is* essential, although it may be difficult. Habits, attitudes, and expectations begin to freeze at home in the beginning months and years. To put off consideration of a child's ability and potential is doing a disservice that may be irreparable. In Hersey's book one of the characters indicates the need for early identification in this way:

At an astonishingly early age he goes through a quest for meaning, for values, for the significance of life, and this quest turns, also early, into a struggle to make a place in society and to find values in it that will meet his particular needs. I hardly have to tell you that the culture in which we live is riddled with inconsistencies, from the point of view of a child with a quick mind, who sees that he is punished more than he is rewarded for his brilliance.[12]

But parents' judgment alone is not sufficient. Added to it might be the following: group and individual mental tests; scholastic achievement as discerned by standardized achievement and aptitude tests; newly developed scales and tests of creativity; teacher judgment and the judgment of others who may have contacts with the child (boy scout leader, social worker, pediatrician, for example); community and school "talent hunts" in areas such as science, art, music, written and oral expression; school cumulative records, including anecdotal notes and grades; sociometric devices; child self-evaluation, reading or play preferences; attitudes toward school; extracurricular activities. In evaluating the gifted, Terman included one other factor: being the youngest in the class. Others have put emphasis on physical, emotional, and social traits, laying to rest the thought that a child or adult high in these is necessarily low in intelligence, or vice versa.

A check list can help in the identification of gifted children—if used carefully. The 12 "signs" given below are an effort in that direction:

1. Learns easily. Walks and talks early, perhaps learns to read before entering school. Wants to be taught to read at an early age.
2. Seeks answers. Has diverse and intense interests. When he asks questions, really wants the answers, to the point of becoming very angry if he doesn't get them.
3. Collects all kinds of things—birds, stamps, chemicals, pictures of ball-players or movie stars, rocks, marbles, insignia. Often these collections are very complicated.

12 Hersey, *op. cit.*, p. 34.

4. Is physically advanced. Usually above average in height, weight. Above average measurements of shoulders, hips. Has developed strength, co-ordination and endurance. Physical poise may be one of first indications of giftedness.
5. Enjoys complicated games. Especially those involving a system or rules. Plays easily alone. When young, often develops imaginary playmates.
6. Is highly creative. Tends to be original in all things: play, work, planning, conversation, writing, and in adjusting to new situations. May show unusual skill in art or music, have good sense of rhythm or color. States an idea in a picturesque way.
7. Has sense of humor. Makes up jokes and laughs at the humor of others on a more mature level, often on an abstract or imaginary basis.
8. Likes school. At least at first. But achievement in subjects may be lower than expected because of boredom. Participates in many extra-curricular activities.
9. Understands element of time. Studies calendars; takes clocks apart; talks about "yesterday" and "tomorrow," days of the week, "then" and "now."
10. Analyzes himself objectively. Is usually more trustworthy when tempted, is more honest, has better emotional stability.
11. Prefers older children. Even though rejected and mistreated by bigger friends.
12. May be "difficult." Passive attitude of those around him, including parents and teachers, may make a gifted child impatient and even at times rebellious.

Parents especially can be easily misled in using a list of this type. For example, a sense of humor frequently *does* accompany intelligence, but not necessarily. However, who would question the brightness of the three children cited below:

A boy was overheard carrying on a telephone conversation in a drug store. He was inquiring if the person at the other end needed someone to cut his grass. After a pause, he asked, "Well, are you satisfied with the way the work is being done?" There was another pause, and then a good-bye. A man standing nearby told the boy that *he* needed someone to cut *his* grass, and that he'd like to hire him. "I already have a job," the lad replied. "But you were just inquiring about one," was the puzzled reaction. "Oh, that! That's the job I have. I was just checking up!"

A little girl was seen leading her little brother down the street, his eyes tightly closed. When asked about it, she replied, "He closes his eyes at home and doesn't open them until we get to the movies. Then he finds seats for us."

A boy was given a message by his room teacher to deliver to the gym teacher. He knew he had to go through the gymnasium dressing room but forgot it was the girls' period. He opened the door, and amidst much shrieking, he thought fast and called out, "Shut your eyes, girls! I'm coming through!"

The time or era is important, too, in how we view children's characteristics. Pressey stated this factor most picturesquely in the following statement, which has important implications for early identification of our bright children:

Suppose Mozart had been born to a middle-class couple in present-day America! The kindergarten teacher would have shooed him away from the piano out onto the playground to get big-muscle exercise and socialize with the other children. In elementary school, the parents would have been told of the grave dangers of advancing a child beyond his age group, the unhealthiness of too much association with adults, the grave risks to health and to personality of any program of public appearances. Summers at camp would have involved little opportunity for the development of musical virtuosity; the college adviser would have urged *not* majoring in music but rather getting a broad education; and other students would have regarded piano players a bit contemptuously. Might he, at 35 have been only a bright young junior executive who could be very musically entertaining at an office party![13]

Even though most current thinkers on the subject know that identification of the gifted without appropriate programs is a barren procedure, they also know that it is an important link in reaching the goal of educating each child to his capacity. Attention has carefully been directed to the subject from many sources. Among the best is the publication of the NEA Project on the Academically Talented Student entitled *The Identification and Education of the Academically Talented Student.*

Brief consideration is necessary at this point on the whole testing and I.Q. controversy as it pertains to the identification of gifted children. If we were to have a "test tube" approach to measuring

[13] S. L. Pressey and Raymond G. Kuhlen, *Psychological Development Through the Life Span,* New York, Harper & Row, Publishers, Inc., 1957, p. 146.

intelligence, the results would be exact and predictable. Numerically, they might work out this way:

I.Q.	Percent of Total Population
130 and above	2.2
120–129	6.7
110–119	16.1
90–109	50.0
80–89	16.1
70–79	6.7
69 and below	2.2
Total	100.0

But the relationships and development of human beings are not entirely on the chemical level. Because increasingly large numbers of bright college graduates marry bright college graduates, it is to be expected that as a group their offspring will be intellectually above average, whether we attribute that quality to heredity or environment. And with the average family size on upper socioeconomic levels becoming larger, a greater proportion of births will result in brighter children. These factors pertain to *percentage,* but *numbers* of bright children will continue to reside predominantly where the larger numbers of people are—in the masses of our great middle class.

The pure chance of marriage and birth isn't the only reason for an increase in our bright population. More favorable family and total environmental circumstances in the upbringing of most of our children, and deliberate efforts to spur creative thinking and problem solving, can also contribute. In fact, one recent publication[14] maintains that a series of exercises designed to improve basic analytic abilities can raise I.Q. scores. They don't increase native intelligence, but they can release unused brain power. Argue that point if you want to; but isn't there a factor related to not working up to capacity which we should at least consider? It's one that pertains to most of us; and we are often aware of it in our daily study, reading, and decision making.

But tests to single out the highly intelligent may be limited in

[14] Albert Upton and Richard W. Samson, *Creative Analysis,* Whittier, Calif., Whittier College Press, 1962.

another direction. As Adam Yarmolinsky wrote in *Recognition of Excellence:*

This "dragnet" function of testing is almost completely ineffectual in a situation where a child's home and community background has denied him the cultural experience that the test assumes. Intelligence tests are standardized to a native white population. The discrepancy is particularly evident in testing children from disadvantaged ethnic minorities: not only Negroes but Puerto Ricans, American Indians, Japanese- and Chinese-Americans, Spanish Americans in the southwest of the United States, persons from U.S. Territories, and even Appalachian mountain whites.[15]

Additional and revised tests or other devices may be necessary in the achievement area, too. The College Entrance Examination Board reported that the tests they have used to measure mathematical and verbal skills may be obsolete because they are often too easily passed by the faster students. In other words, they fail to give an accurate picture of the ceilings of their abilities.

Refined approaches to testing of all types may help us admit and adapt to human differences and uncover them wherever they are; we may no longer be able to condone practices that result in their going unnoticed, untended throughout full lifetimes. Because of a personality pattern or depth in reasoning, a child may not provide the "right" answer on a test. His answer may be more profound and thorough; but because it isn't an acceptable one, he becomes another in the long line of neglected cogs in our cult of mediocrity.

GUIDANCE AND MOTIVATION

Just because the gifted are especially good at analyzing themselves and their problems, does that mean they don't need or want help from outside? Even the brightest political, business, and labor leaders ask for the advice, assistance, and reactions of others. The little fellows with mental gifts or special talents are no less in need. Nor are they generally smug about their ability to decide things for themselves. Although they may know very well how bright they are,

[15] Edgar Stern Family Fund, *Recognition of Excellence,* New York, The Free Press of Glencoe, 1960, p. 52.

they are subject to the same feelings of inadequacy and the same need for an occasional good listener, which all of us ought to have once in a while. And if they *are* smug about their possessions, a steady "listening post" should be nearby. While more adept than the average person in analyzing and discussing their strengths and weaknesses, even the smartest cannot be completely objective regarding their abilities, appearance, and personality.

Guidance comes from parents and teachers, starting in the home and nursery school and continuing on to the highest academic levels attained, in the classroom and in the offices of specialized counseling personnel and administrators. Each child needs it, and the presence or absence of giftedness won't dictate the amount. The difficulty in connection with bright children occurs sometimes because we forget them. "They'll get along all right; they're smart. Don't the studies show they're more stable emotionally?" Thus the usual pattern of neglect begins, and thus we slough them off to make room for others. But the gifted child might reply: "I'm a child too. I need the advantages of your maturity, your judgment. I need to have someone listen to me too." And so we may begin to understand that all require the acceptance of others.

For some very obvious reasons the gifted child may require help even *more* than others. He may have been tossed back on his own resources since early childhood. His parents may expect more of him than his considerable abilities can accomplish. He may be alone more than he wants to be. Perhaps there have been teachers in his experience who have acted as though he threatened their authority. He may be impatient, inconsiderate, overly aggressive, or demanding because of the superiority he possesses. And he may be discouraged because he recognizes his capacity but hasn't been able to work up to it.

Good teachers accept a guidance point of view based on knowing the child and doing something about his problems. Just because he is working up to his grade level does not mean that no difficulty exists; the objective should be to help him raise his sights and accomplishments right up to his *capacity*, and that capacity may be far beyond the grade where he is now enrolled. If he is underachieving, what are the reasons? Whose fault is it, and what can be done about it? Guidance and teaching are intertwined, and the competent teacher realizes that academic achievement follows closely on the heels of a stable and happy home and school environment.

If we agree that one of our objectives is to stimulate the gifted to progress academically just as far as they can go, then we must recognize the importance of studies which indicate that guidance helps encourage youngsters to stay in school longer. Guide them, help them realize what an education means, alert them to their own abilities, treat them to the pleasure of making decisions based on a sound foundation of fact and understanding. The result may be a university graduate who might otherwise have dropped by the way when he was only 16. Values and activities related to guidance need not stop at graduation on any of the educational levels. Follow-up studies will answer questions like these: Did they make good use of their abilities? Are their earnings what they should be for persons with the potentialities they showed? What ideas do they now have on the basis of their job experiences which can help us improve the school program for gifted children? One such specific value of educational guidance was shown in a report by Rothney and Roens.[16] Two groups of high school students were studied, one of which received educational guidance while the other did not. Of the first group, 53 percent went on to college; only 36 percent of the nonguided group did, even though both groups were equated on intelligence and other important variables.

Guidance is *not* telling a fellow what to do. It *is* helping him do better what he might have accomplished with some degree of success anyway. Families, teachers, other school personnel, neighbors, friends, and the folks around the neighborhood have all contributed pieces to the jigsaw that each one of us has become. Formally or informally, for good or evil, it was guidance, and we need more of it; but in expert, trained hands.

The specific area of vocational guidance also steps into the picture. A very wise man by the name of Thomas Carlyle once said: "It is the first of all problems for a man to find out what kind of work he is to do in this universe." Doesn't this problem seem important enough to be singled out from the mass of problems with which guidance deals? It is an especially tough one for bright youth, for they have

---

[16] J. W. M. Rothney and B. A. Roens, *Guidance of American Youth: An Experimental Study,* Cambridge, Harvard University Press, 1950.

so many areas to choose from, so many vocations in which they could be successful. Their situation is very different from that of the person who can barely make the grade in a simple vocation. *Here* we're talking about an individual who can contribute toward our knowledge of how cells multiply in a malignancy, how rays of various energies can be harnessed for peaceful pursuits, how bigger buildings, longer bridges, and safer stratospheric conveyances can be constructed. For the gifted group the occupational possibilities are enticingly numerous.

Competent counseling will point out new fields which the individual may never have considered, and encourage delaying a decision until the major possibilities have been thoroughly surveyed. It will help the youngster decide in a rational way and evaluate parental pressures toward or away from a particular vocation. Scholarship opportunities will be pointed out. The question of the moment may be whether to get a job or go on to advanced study, and although no one can decide for the person intimately involved, the facts now and for the future must be brought to light and considered.

The files of guidance personnel bulge with job materials, details of college and university programs, and figures on earnings and employment trends. We can expect even more data regarding skilled and professional fields during the next few years as our manpower needs become more acute. The Bureau of Labor Statistics in Washington will continue to provide the most authoritative basic information. And from the American Personnel and Guidance Association and one of its divisions, the National Vocational Guidance Association, come valuable materials in this area.

While gifted youngsters will frequently find ways to guide themselves, they should not be expected to resolve conflicts with their parents without emotion and without help. All the sources for information are at the finger tips of a guidance person who has kept on top of the latest releases available. Sometimes we face a difficulty in encouraging a young person to think about his vocational future. "Couldn't care less" is an attitude which cannot be permitted to continue unchallenged for too long a time. The admonishment of George Bernard Shaw is appropriate in that problem situation: "Take care to get what you like or you will be forced to like what you get."

Engineering, medicine, scientific research, and related fields are publicized a great deal in efforts to entice our bright youth. And they'll get many of those who advance academically to the heights of their abilities. Teachers are needed who will encourage the gifted ones to stay in school, inspire them to work to their capacities, and provide the professional understanding and guidance that is vital. Despite the earnings (which have always been too limited), the respect (which is shamefully limited), and the restricted opportunities for advancement, the profession into which we must bring a fair share of our best minds is teaching. The teacher on all levels will be the most valuable instrument to protect the future against the loss of the gifted suffered by present and past generations. Fewer mediocre and more wonderful teachers are essential.

The importance of vocational guidance in a broader sense was stressed in these remarks: "We lure far too many talented young people into advertising and far too few into city planning, far too many into car-dealing and far too few into teaching, far too many into high-priced private psychiatry and far too few into low-cost public health. The gross misuse of human resources is a situation that cries out for correction."[17]

Care must always be taken in trying to help people, especially bright ones. Sometimes the best of all approaches is to get out of their way, clear a path, let them alone. The crux of the issue is timing. And that's where your common sense and preparation step in. Luther Burbank exaggerated this factor when he said, "If we paid no more attention to our plants than we have to our children, we would now be living in a jungle of weeds." Yet if we're conscientious, we worry when a complete hands-off policy is followed.

There are currently seeds of conflict in both our homes and our schools; a basic inconsistency seeps into some of them. On the one hand we see our adult population watching television from 6 P.M. through the late late movie; edging toward shorter work days, weeks, and lives; reading comic books on trains and subways; listening to music piped in to their offices and factories; and participating in longer coffee breaks. Now turn the picture over and look at the setting we reserve for the gifted child: Longer school days, weeks,

[17] John K. Jessup et al., The National Purpose, New York, Holt, Rinehart and Winston, Inc., 1960, p. 88.

and years; less television and fewer comics; the austere study situation; and harder and more courses. In other words, long hours and hard work are fine for children but undesirable for adults.

Of course we cannot condone coddling children, especially the gifted. But it is interesting that Russian education is tending toward a lighter student load and more recreation to meet the objections of their physicians about endangering mental and physical health resulting from too much pressure. This whole idea can lead us down some fascinating conversational channels concerning our gifted children. And perhaps it can lead to a middle course in a guidance program for them in which achievement is closer to their abilities, but also related to their age and maturity.

The underachievement of many gifted children is obviously serious. Guiding these children and educating them is a detailed, difficult, costly process; but it is well worth the effort. The choice is a relatively simple one to express: Guide them, and help meet society's major ills with the skilled personnel capable of working toward those goals; ignore them, and delay solution of our medical, social and other problems, lose the major contributions of potentially qualified personnel to their nation and community, and condone the frustrations of many who for their entire lives operate on a plane below their own capabilities.

We must understand the symptoms of poor study habits, the pattern of underachievement, the reason for more boys than girls in this category, the overlapping factors of broken and disturbed homes, poor physical health, family mobility, parental rejection, immaturity and others. Following are some recommendations and ideas that dig deeply into the issue.

THE PLACE OF INSPIRATION

The child who is bright and fast, but moving at a slow pace academically, needs outside interest, enthusiasm, and support. Though some may consider this point to be naïve or unrealistic, it must be stated and recognized for its real worth: The key to unlock the achievement commensurate with a child's abilities may come from the inspiration provided by *one* adult. This one-to-one relationship, whether it comes from a teacher, guidance person, parent, school administrator, neighbor, or sibling may provide the one bit of stimulation that is missing. This may be the needed push toward helping the child realize he is important or smart or capable. Such inspiration may be expensive if provided by a professional person working with many young people. But the American dream of educating all children to their capacities is costly as well as worthy. Few thoughtful people could conclude that it is not worth the expense.

A TIME FOR AN EARTHY APPROACH

What encourages us to battle the problems of overweight, a faulty golf game, making ends meet financially, or playing bridge better than the neighbors with whom we've been competing for years? The stimulant varies from one problem to another, and from one individual to another. Although the sheer enjoyment of reading, solving problems, or performing scientific experiments may motivate some bright children to perform to their capacities, for others a more "basic" (and to some, less desirable) approach can be successful. One must decide whether the end is worth the means employed. Here are some examples:

Earnings: Figures have been given many times which indicate that the lifetime earnings of the average college graduate are $100,000 or more in excess of the average high school graduate.

Grades: It is not enough to place bright youngsters in "honors" or other special class settings and hope that such placement will be sufficient motivation for all of them. An "A" in a special class does not mean the same thing as an "A" in a regular class (unless grades have lost the meaning which has unfortunately been so strongly attached to them for many years). Successful methods have been used in numerous school systems to weight the grades so that on the transcript grades received in special classes or courses are worth more credit. Another approach has been to assure the student of a top grade as long as he performs adequately in the enriched setting. A third is to footnote the type of class on transcripts so that colleges and universities to which they are sent can recognize the distinction.

Guidance in terms of change: Although the U.S. Bureau of Labor Statistics and other public, professional, and private sources can be helpful, and despite the existence of trends expertly analyzed, no one can be sure what tomorrow will bring in occupational changes. How much did we know 20 or 25 years ago about the tremendous recent changes and demands of science, engineering, and even the field of teaching? We cannot now know with certainty that far in advance which fields will be in short supply or, in fact (on the basis of recent experiences), what new fields will exist of which we at present are unaware. One of the world's oldest religions includes the admonition to "limit not thy children to thine own ideas. They are born in a different time."

THE FACTOR OF FREEDOM

A recent educational film on gifted children arrives at the mistaken conclusions that a 10-year-old with an I.Q. of 130 "thinks and acts" like a 13-year-old, one with an I.Q. of 170 or 180 "thinks and acts" like a 17- or 18-year-old, and one with an I.Q. of 200 "thinks and acts" like a person 20 years old! Such interpretations interfere with a bright child's enjoyment of the one childhood he is entitled to. That interference can slow down the learning process for him because expectations may be all wrong and pressures may be too great. If there is any time appropriate for having fun, being different, exercising creativity, and experimenting within "reasonable limits" with knowledge and life, the childhood years are that time. To treat intellect with a heavy burden of seriousness may be to stifle or discourage its normal growth.

SEPARATE CLASSES, ACCELERATION, ENRICHMENT

Teachers, administrators, and school boards are arriving at some conclusions which pose answers just beyond their grasp: No single method of teaching is necessarily best for all gifted children. No particular school or classroom organization will meet all their needs. No clear-cut personality type makes the best teacher for the gifted. No simple solution suits all schools or communities.

At that point it is probably very easy to say, "So why talk about it anymore? Let's just curl up again in our comfortable little rut of day-to-day routinized teaching, and forget the whole thing." Fortunately for all of us it is too late to turn back the clock to teaching methods that were based exclusively on routine, the same amount of drill for all, and the same program for each new group as long as they were in the same grade. We are too well informed not to be concerned because a youngster is doing average or even better-than-average work. We now know there is such a student as an "underachiever," one who is stopping short of his capacity; we have ways to find him, and through our classroom and specialized guidance we hope to bring him closer to his potential.

It doesn't take an expert to see warning signs of danger in a child or in a classroom. If the child is bright and daydreaming to excess, pestering any child or adult around him, succumbing to truancy or petty vandalism, suffering from a short attention span or no spark of interest at all, or reading far beneath his intellectual capacity, the signs are clear. All those involved, the teachers, parents, administrators, and all the folks in his community have been given the warning. Being bright isn't enough now and it never was. It won't get a youngster into college and *keep* him there or prevent him from losing his job.

Those who favor separate classes for the gifted reason as follows: With classes so large and with such a wide range of ability some children are bound to be overlooked. Johnny, the bright one, will be among the first to be ignored. He'll get along anyway, the teacher may think. So we will group the bright ones together and give them the education they need and deserve. And we will keep these groups flexible so children can be transferred into and out of special classes as the need arises.

Before you jump to a quick decision on this controversial question, at least skim over this list of favorable and unfavorable reasons for separate classes for the gifted child. Here are the arguments as they are usually made; draw your own conclusions:

For separate classes

1. In a class on his own mental level a child is stimulated and motivated to work closer to his capacity. The competition is there, and the experiences may be more varied and suitable than in the regular classroom. The teacher is more likely to have time *for* him and the qualifications and desire to work *with* him, and the pace will more logically be swift enough. Plain talk and common sense tell us, say the proponents, that the standards are higher. Forcing everyone to get an education planned for the average is wrong.

2. He will have practice in being both a leader and follower, rather than perhaps always being a leader in a class where all the other youngsters lag behind him mentally. And we are not taking away the leaders in regular classrooms either; leadership and giftedness do not necessarily go together.

3. He is getting more practice for the adulthood he faces, where he will continue to be able to choose friends on his own intellectual level. In spite

of what some folks say, we do have a chance to choose our adult friends and occasionally co-workers, and our tendency is to select those with whom we have something in common.

4. He will be less conceited and smug than in a situation where he is the one "brain" in a class of average and below-average students. Envy really rears its head where brightness is constantly in evidence for the average child to see.

5. If we let him stay with the others he will frustrate and frighten them as they aim toward his level, a level they never will be capable of reaching. If we play tennis, do we play with those whose skills are far above ours? Not on your life! Averageness or mediocrity seeks, and is satisfied with, its own level. No one has proved that the less capable students need the brighter ones around in order to work to their capacity. And no one is suggesting that the regular classroom will have a very limited range of ability. It will have only a few skimmed off, with a wide range among those remaining. The bright one tends to segregate himself anyway whether we like it or not; as parents know so well, friendship cannot be forced.

6. More concentration can be given to abstract and creative ideas and to critical thinking materials; there can be less devotion to unnecessary drill in adapting to the special needs and abilities of a selected group.

7. In special classes a bright child can see himself more realistically in relation to those on his level, a possibility which may not exist in the regular classroom. He also sees his limitations more clearly; if he stays with others below his level his limitations may seem nonexistent.

8. He will work harder with less superficial bluffing, and he will develop fewer lazy habits when others are on his ability level. There will be less tendency to slide along and expect rewards for his natural abilities rather than for accomplishments resulting from trying hard to get a job done.

9. He will be better adjusted socially because now he won't be the "odd ball," the one who is so different, therefore peculiar and outside the realm of "us kids." He will be with those who more frequently think, do, and aspire as he does. Besides, he won't be isolated from the others; there are plenty of club, extracurricular, and playground activities during which he will not be separated.

10. Nothing at all undemocratic about it, say many writers in the field. The nub of their thinking is that "so long as the selection is based upon ability and no one is excluded because of race, social, or economic status . . . there can be no basis to the charge that selected classes are undemocratic."[18] We segregate chronological age groups now, and also socioeconomic groups by neighborhoods.

[18] D. A. Worcester, *The Education of Children of Above-Average Mentality*, Lincoln, University of Nebraska Press, 1956, p. 47.

Against separate classes

1. He will become arrogant and superior because he has been selected for a special class, and the one left behind will certainly feel the stigma. Anyone who tells you that children are not aware of which class is the "best" or "highest" just doesn't know how alert children are to such divisions and how much feeling they have about them.

2. He will have little practice for living in a democracy where each person must get along with all other kinds of persons. Are we eager to create an aristocracy of intelligence, a kind of superrace based on mentality and on people who lose the common touch?

3. Where will the leadership in the regular classroom come from if these youngsters are filtered out? Who will set the pace to which others want to aspire, stimulate them to *their* capacities?

4. Other children will become jealous, and maybe even somewhat awed, suspicious, and resentful.

5. If we pull out the bright ones for special treatment, we will have too much of a tendency to press them, push them, prod them to depths and heights that make them into little adults and use up their childhood speedily.

6. How can the gifted be selected anyway for this special treatment? Are the devices, tests, observational techniques good enough to say that this one goes on and that one stays back with the average and slow groups? And shouldn't we be concerned about the friendships already formed if we decide to pull youngsters away from the group of which they already feel a part?

7. We must not forget the small and poorer schools and districts which cannot set up special classes. In a time when money is so short for educational needs anyway, it is foolish to spend it on the few at the expense of the many who also need small classes and better teachers.

8. If the children in selected classes are on the same mental level, but vary in their actual ages, a lot of social maladjustments result. The very bright large 6-year-old girl and the almost as bright little 8-year-old boy really don't have much in common even though their I.Q.s *are* fairly close.

9. There is no such thing as a "homogeneous" group, so why kid ourselves? Children differ from each other; they are not cut from the same molds, and we may as well recognize that our classrooms will have a wide range in personality and other factors no matter how closely we try to limit the extremes in the area of mentality.

10. If we strain off the cream, who will want to teach the ones left? Most teachers will resent remaining with the rest, and their teaching plus the

mirrored resentment of their students will show up in lesser achievement and increased dropouts among the average and below-average students.

There are plenty of variations on these themes, and the arguments are just as difficult to resolve as the perennial dispute of demand versus regular feeding of babies. The evidence is just not clear enough to point toward an unchangeable answer for all time and for all children. So it becomes necessary that the decisions be based on *this* school, *these* teachers and administrators, and *these* children and parents.

All kinds of questions crop up: How do the teachers and administrators feel about separate classes? How many gifted children are there; do we have enough facilities? What will separate classes cost in this school or school system; can we afford them? Can we afford *not* to have them? What do the parents think about them? Will an orientation meeting or series of meetings be worth the trouble for both teachers and parents? What are the mechanics involved? If we go ahead with special classes, what basis will be used for selection: mental age, chronological age, achievement, social and emotional maturity, talents, interests? Should we use such classes in combination with other methods? Has there been enough research, has the method been adequately tested by others, to indicate that it is worth our while to try it out on our children?

When most of us were in elementary school, "skipping" was used as both a promise and a threat. "If you continue to do well, you'll move up to the next grade in the middle of the year" or "if you don't keep up, you'll move back again." Based on a negative kind of reward and punishment, and conjuring up ideas of a tiny child among those bigger and brawnier, the procedure fell into disrepute. There would have been nothing particularly wrong about the whole idea if it had been used carefully. But we had peculiar and usually unwarranted thoughts about what it meant.

Skipping may mean moving on without accomplishing the skills and goals of a given level; acceleration has a healthier connotation, for here the onward movement leaves no gaps behind. The basic ingredients of the course of study—whether they are fractions, percentages, square roots, geography, or science experiments—are all covered. But because this is a bright youngster who doesn't need as much time or drill as the others, the program is covered faster.

Feelings run high about this method of helping the gifted, with plenty of support and opposition. The points of view go something like this:

For acceleration

1. It is the easiest and most economical way of providing for individual differences based on mentality. The school's basic curriculum doesn't have to be changed, and it does not disrupt classes or classrooms, so there is no cost to the school system.

2. Acceleration helps provide the motivation which will keep a gifted child on his toes instead of encouraging slovenly and lazy habits by insisting that he slow down to the average. By leading him into studies that challenge he will relieve his boredom and his frustrations, both of which inevitably result to a great degree from the large classes of today. We may be able to reduce social and emotional maladjustments too.

3. Our gifted children are usually capable of going into professional careers which demand so many years of education that they may be 30 years old or more before they can begin their actual work. Why not shorten that time at the most easily consolidated part? We need their skills as fast as we can get them, as our studies of automation and manpower shortages indicate; and if we don't let these youngsters race along closer to their capacities we may never get them at all. It is from the ranks of the bored bright ones that thousands of our school dropouts come each year.

4. Promotion should not be based on sheer time spent on a subject. What is so magic about that? No correlation has been found between the time devoted to a subject and the knowledge gained; it all depends on *who* is devoting the time. Nothing is by-passed or skipped in this plan; much of the work is merely accomplished more quickly, letting the child progress at the speed at which he is capable. So why hold him back? And anyway, isn't it much *more* dangerous to do nothing at all than it is to accelerate? Our error is so often in the direction of just plain lethargy or fear of change.

Against acceleration

1. It is very important to keep the child with those of his size and social and emotional level. Moving him up to his mental level may not take these other factors into consideration and may therefore increase maladjustments.

2. As long as teachers follow a course of study and have crowded classes, the child who is accelerated will be forced to follow the curriculum of

average older children and is bound to skip some vital segments of his schooling.

3. Mental age by itself is a questionable factor to use for grade placement. Just because two youngsters have the same mental age does not mean they will learn, respond, or be interested in the same way; their chronological age difference may get in the way.

4. Since no child is accelerated to the same extent in all subjects, inequalities will result from jumping a full grade.

Many questions have to be answered before a particular school decides to adopt this method which was one of the earliest used: How are we to choose which children are to be accelerated? When is the best time to let a youngster move ahead—what grade, age, and time of the year? How can parents be brought into the plan? How can the activities in the grade the child is leaving be coordinated with those in the grade he is skipping to so the child isn't left at loose ends? What can we do to be sure that in the new room the youngster gets what he needs, and not what the average older child is getting? Are we capable of doing it in our school on the kind of individual basis it demands, taking into consideration many phases of maturity, in addition to just the mental, so that no social misfits result?

What is right for one child may not work at all for another. Donald may be bright, large, well adjusted socially, well coordinated physically; he might easily be ready to move on a year or two and occupy a secure niche in the higher grade. Ronald may have only a high mentality pushing him on, and both physically and socially he might be very much out of place among the older children. One thing is certainly true: Ability to do the work of the next grade is never enough by itself to move a child up to that level. The I.Q. gives only part of the story.

Few people advocate acceleration alone, without enrichment or other ways of working with the gifted. As a sole solution it is a thin answer to a very complicated problem. And those who suggest it insist on limited use, perhaps a year or two at most for even very bright children.

In Terman's long-range study of gifted children he concluded that acceleration worked well for that particular group; those who were moved ahead did better academically in high school, with a higher proportion graduating from college, more graduating with honors, and more going on to graduate work. He found no significant differences in social adjustments, and in adulthood they were more often occupationally successful than were nonaccelerated gifted students. With the most creative work done in nearly all areas of science, music, art, and other fields between ages 25 and 35, he pointed out the need for not delaying this productivity too long because of strung-out academic requirements. Let them enter college at 16 or 17, he insisted.

Enrichment of the academic program of the gifted is by all odds the current favorite, and while its heart is in the right place, it remains unproven and unsatisfying. And it is often misunderstood. In schools we most frequently relate enrichment to (1) keeping a child with his age group in a regular class and (2) broadening the program or content covered by him. However, enrichment can certainly be offered in separate classes, special courses, and by the use of special facilities such as laboratories and shops.

Since the regular classroom setting is the one usually associated with enrichment, let's take a peephole look and talk about what we see. Here are some of the sights we observe:

The teacher who really believes that children differ from each other and adapts the program to their abilities and needs on an individual and small-group basis. She may never use the word "enrich," but she does it just the same.

The teacher who gives all the rest of the children one assignment but gives two to a particular child because he's so smart. When he slows down to the point where she'll shake her head and wonder whatever happened to his brightness, she won't realize that it wasn't *what* but *who* happened to him. This so-called enrichment Goddard referred to in this way: "A curriculum that is not fitted to the type of mind possessed by the gifted child, we attempted to adjust to his needs by giving him twice as much of it!"[19]

The workbooks, seat work, and other varieties of busywork that are used to "kill time." Used meaningfully they can serve an excellent educational need, but as time-users they are futile replacements for activities that could be exciting and invigorating.

The overworked teacher prodding slow children up to an average they

[19] Henry H. Goddard, *School Training of Gifted Children*, New York, Harcourt, Brace & World, Inc., 1928, p. 3.

may not be able to reach while a child who no longer cares is looking out the window through glazed eyes. A clear desk, an empty sheet of paper, and immobilized thoughts represent the product of the classroom where the bright are sacrificed for the dull.

The teacher who feels insecure or pushed by bright children and who repays in terms of impatience.

Where does enrichment end, and busywork begin? Are teachers in regular classrooms capable of motivating *all* their children to capacity? Which activities are challenging for a particular child? When should we admit we have failed in our objectives of providing an enriched program? Are bright and slower children stimulated or held back by the presence of the others? How can community facilities be utilized to their maximum? How these questions are answered will determine whether this method is just so much talk or whether it actually holds promise for today's gifted children.

Ask some teachers, and they will tell you in no uncertain terms: "I can't do it, and the reasons are obvious: too many children, too few materials, too many little jobs and records piled on me to handle. Cut my student load and watch the enrichment activities flood in. Until then, just get out of my way as I try my best to meet the needs of the majority."

Others will say: "It doesn't matter what you call it. I've been doing it for years! Give it any name you want, but it still means the best teaching I can do adapted to this child, and that one, and the quiet one over there, based on what they're capable of and what problems they have here and at home. And let's not belittle it because some teachers don't know how; it's *still* the best method."

Enrichment cannot be separated from the skill of a teacher. The teacher who barely gets through the day as far as his own stamina is concerned and who forgot long ago that these are isolated as well as interrelated, different as well as similar little people in front of him obviously will not enrich the children's education. His own life is probably without brightness too, so of course we can't expect any better of him on the job. "Too low they build who build beneath the stars." Stodgy, frozen outlooks do not encourage the brightness of new ideas, the constant expansion of young minds, the searching of children who have not yet had the world of the future close in on them.

Thousands of courses of study, teachers' guides issued from reputable publishing firms, and ideas of creative teachers put the finger on the teacher who mourns over the poor child with nothing to do while he works with the others. Nothing to do? How can that be when we have the vibrant, ever-expanding curiosity of a child on one side and the whole world full of changing patterns of persons, places, and things on the other?

Childhood's world always has new horizons; and our task is, first of all, to guide and shape the child and then to get out of the way! We can help a great deal by having available the equipment and materials children need but may not *express* a need for if they don't happen to know about them: encyclopedia, tape recorder, record player, programmed books and booklets, typewriter, terrarium, flannelboards, games such as chess and anagrams, tools including hammers, saws, screw drivers, chisels, and a broad expanse of reading materials in various subjects and on different ability levels.

Enrichment at its richest must be based on real understanding and not just the barren accumulation of facts. The teacher must be willing to devote to drill only the time that is absolutely necessary, and realize that bright children get the idea fast and are ready to move on. He should be ready to step along and move fast and out of the way. Don't let anyone tell you that *no* drill is necessary; learning frequently demands repetition. But we ought not run practice into the ground with these children who catch on quickly. A little alert checking now and then can indicate to the discerning teacher whether they really did get the idea. These students will be the first to know when they fall short and need more help on fundamentals.

A recent tendency in enrichment is to broaden the program by including subjects not formerly taught. A good example is foreign-language teaching on the elementary level. The advantages are apparent: easy for young children to learn; valuable for children in areas where other languages are spoken (e.g., along the Mexican border and in foreign sections of large cities); related to cultural understandings. However, unless this teaching does more than fill a time gap it ought to be forgotten. A few hours a week in third grade, with nothing in either the previous or the next year, is a hollow approach; continuity is essential. Most regular elementary school teachers cannot handle this task, and if they can't, an additional expense is obviously necessary.

Enrichment programs need breadth and balance without exploitation of the child. Workbooks, yes—if they aren't just to fill time. Teaching other children, of course—but not a heavy load of it. Excess is a danger here and in other educational programs just as it is in business, industry, family life, and everywhere else. The program for these children can be a combination which includes regular classroom enrichment *and* segregated classes for special enrichment. Some communities have worked out what is for them the ideal compromise solution, combining the best of two major approaches to the problem.

Regardless of which approach you favor or which your school believes in, you would have a difficult time disagreeing with Elizabeth Drews' statement that "it is immoral for us to squander a child's time by asking him to learn what he already knows."[20] In addition to the approaches already discussed, there are several others which are attracting increasing attention and action, including early or flexible school entry. The "advanced placement" approach is also in greater use than ever; it offers bright students an opportunity to omit college work they covered in secondary school. In 1960–1961 more than 600 institutions of higher learning and 13,000 students were involved in this kind of program. A related but less widespread approach is that of the student who is admitted to college early, before he has officially completed all required secondary-school courses.

CONCLUDING REMARKS

Throughout this chapter are references to and implications of what some schools and communities are doing for the gifted. And all the way through there is a thread of doubt, of criticism, of awareness that there is still neglect based on oversight, ignorance, or lack of funds. All educational levels are involved, including higher education whose student body is too often "a haphazard mixture of brains

[20] Elizabeth Drews, "Quality Is Next," *Educational Leadership*, January, 1960, p. 201.

and bank accounts,"[21] too seldom a vehicle for flexible courses of study that take ability differences into consideration.

Obviously the schools cannot do the job alone. A hostile attitude toward the education of bright children can effectively stifle the creative ideas of teachers and administrators. But evidence is strong that the educators have an increasingly large army of support. The Memphis Conference on the Academically Talented (March, 1962) which seemed to mobilize the entire community was a vivid example of it. So are the community efforts exemplified by children's theaters, art centers, libraries, museums, special summer programs, and fraternal, business and labor organizations. Laymen are resources, too—retired professional people, linguists, nature lovers, and parents with skills or professional competencies.

One of the most difficult groups to win over consists of some mothers and fathers of so-called average children who may directly or indirectly hamper, ridicule, or discourage progress. They may resent any special educational provision for the gifted, failing to realize both the democratic need for it and its value for their own children. They may provide the negative end of a tug-of-war that can result only in a watered down educational program. Perhaps they were a significant part of a 1959 Gallup Poll which revealed these opinions, unfortunately not unexpected in our society: When asked whether teachers should devote extra time to bright children, only 26 percent answered "Yes"; but when asked the same question for "slow" students 86 percent answered "Yes."

A levelheaded appraisal of the issue came from John W. Gardner when he wrote:

> . . . if the measures designed to assist the gifted youngster are such as to arouse hostility in those who are not gifted (and their parents), there is certain to be a backlash. Children who are not gifted—and parents who do not have gifted children—are in the great majority.
>
> Anyone who cares about excellence in education (and someone had *better* care!) must ask himself how it is possible to cultivate it in ways that do not provoke such restraining or defeating countermoves.
>
> I believe that an answer is to be found. But it requires first that we restate the problem in somewhat more constructive terms: "How can we

[21] Barzun, *ibid.*, p. 257.

provide opportunities and rewards for individuals of every degree of ability so that individuals at every level will realize their full potentialities, perform at their best and harbor no resentment toward any other level?"

. . . When the society as a whole devises rules which are calculated to inhibit excellence or stifle the person of superior gifts, then all who pray for the continued vitality of democracy must protest.[22]

More help is available than ever before in evaluating the status and progress of gifted-child programs, including the following:

Board of Education of the City of New York, "Check List on Educating the Gifted," *Curriculum and Materials,* May–June, 1957.

Kough, Jack, and Robert F. DeHaan, *Teacher's Guidance Handbooks,* Chicago, Science Research Associates, 1957.

NEA, *Finding and Educating the Academically Talented Student in the Secondary School,* Washington, D.C., 1958.

Newland, T. Ernest, *et al., How to Conduct a Self-Survey of Special Education Needs,* Washington, D.C., Council for Exceptional Children, 1958.

Pilch, Mary M., *Criteria for an Evaluation of Programs for Gifted Students in Representative Schools,* St. Paul Public Schools (undated).

Shannon, Gail, "Principles of Program Evaluation," speech presented at the University of Oklahoma, July 19, 1958.

Talented Youth Project, *A Guide for Rating Provisions for the Gifted,* New York, Bureau of Publications, Teachers College, Columbia University, 1961.

This vital subject must not be left without providing "next steps" for those of you interested in taking them. "Where can I find out more?" you might ask. Long lists of books, articles and pamphlets have been compiled, but few school or community libraries do them justice. You may have to do some searching, requesting, perhaps even demanding to get even a glimmer of recognition that this is a field of top importance in our country today. Just a few carefully selected sources are listed here to help you get started. They can lead to many others, however.

Abraham, Willard, *Common Sense About Gifted Children,* New York, Harper & Row, Publishers, Inc., 1958.

California State Department of Education, *Educational Programs for Gifted Pupils,* Sacramento, 1961.

[22] John W. Gardner, *Excellence,* New York, Harper & Row, Publishers, Inc., 1961, pp. 115, 110.

Everett, Samuel (ed), *Programs for the Gifted,* New York, Harper & Row, Publishers, Inc., 1961.

Fliegler, Louis A. (ed.), *Curriculum Planning for the Gifted,* Englewood Cliffs, N.J., Prentice-Hall, Inc., 1961.

Gallagher, James J., *Analysis of Research on the Education of Gifted Children,* Springfield, Ill., Office of the Superintendent of Public Instruction, 1960.

Gardner, John W., *Excellence,* New York, Harper & Row, Publishers, Inc., 1961.

Henry, Nelson B., *Education for the Gifted,* 57th Yearbook of the National Society for the Study of Education, pt. II, Chicago, 1958.

Project on the Academically Talented Student, *An Annotated Bibliography on the Academically Talented Student,* Washington, D.C., NEA, 1961. Compiled by John C. Gowan, one of the most complete and inexpensive sources available to you. See also the many special publications of the Project on the Academically Talented Student.

Review of Educational Research, February, 1963, Chapter VI, "The Gifted" by Jack W. Birch and Maynard C. Reynolds.

Stern, Edgar, Family Fund, *Recognition of Excellence,* New York, The Free Press of Glencoe, 1960.

Witty, Paul A. (ed.), "Our Greatest Challenge—The Gifted and the Creative," *Education,* April, 1962, pp. 496–499 and bibliography. (See also many other publications by Witty on this subject.)

CHAPTER 10

A TIME FOR *Public Relations and Parents*

It is appropriate that the last chapter in a book prepared to introduce future teachers to their profession should discuss two topics too often ignored or skimmed over. Without active and continuous support from the public and your children's parents you can never expect to do an effective job, so it is necessary to give those overlapping groups special attention.

To ensure their support you have to understand their problems, realize that you and they share many of the same ones, see the world through their eyes. Because your youth and inexperience (factors that time has an inevitable way of managing to correct) may limit you when you start to teach, a basic approach to both subjects is attempted here.

WHAT THE PUBLIC SHOULD KNOW

"Lack of information is crippling," wrote Dr. Wayne O. Reed, Deputy U.S. Commissioner of Education. "If the public does not understand, then pupils do not do their best, teachers are less happy and effective, the administrator is hampered, and the school's resources are cramped."[1]

Despite the millions of words, thousands of newspaper columns and magazine articles, and hundreds of books, the schools and the work going on in them are still a mystery to a large part of the

[1] Wayne O. Reed, "New Horizons in Educational Information," *School Life*, September, 1960, p. 5.

public. Administrators and teachers are frequently at fault. They have not often enough told their story realistically, exactly, dramatically. They are sometimes too busy "administering the program" without realizing that the "boss" out there in the community has to be "kept posted"; too busy teaching children to realize that their parents must know what is going on in the classroom.

"Educational gobbledygook," the use of esoteric, confusing terminology instead of easily understood, simple language, is an occupational hazard. The words and phrases of some persons in your profession could provide a heyday for the "sick" nightclub comedians. This language is pompous, vague, and ignores the public who "needs to know." Lectures, textbooks, college catalogues, and professional publications provide overwhelming evidence to support this sad accusation.

Teachers are no more adept at public relations than are their administrators—frequently much less so. For example, one kindergarten teacher "told off" a pair of parents because they had read their precocious child all the stories she intended to read to them; so "what is there left for *me* to do?" A fourth-grade teacher blew off at a first-grade teacher the day after Sputnik I went into orbit because she had passed the latter's room and overheard a discussion of space, planets, and constellations when "everybody knows that such subjects are in my fourth-grade course of study!" A teacher in a home visit said, "Everybody knows mental retardation exists only in families where there is a previous trace of it," thus making two mistakes: (1) telling a lie and (2) telling it to people who had had a mentally retarded son who had died a few years before.

Honest, clear-cut efforts have, of course, been made to "tell the truth" in fully understandable terms about schools and their workers. Newspaper reporters and popular home magazines are at the task almost constantly. A few books have made valiant attempts to keep the public informed. Others have presented an antischool bias so flagrantly that they almost undermine the objective efforts of those who want to be fair in discussing school problems. Sometimes the attacks get so wild that a person might begin to wonder how the schools can continue to support the freedom of a press and publishers that occasionally become almost ridiculous in their criticism. In reference to this point Martin Mayer wrote:

The most convincing proof that the American high school has its heart in the right place is its leaders' continuing advocacy of a free press. No other American institution in the last generation has received the lambasting in print that has been absorbed by the high school. Newspaper stories, magazine articles and books have implied that the high schools are breeding grounds for crime and vice, that their teachers are ill-educated weaklings unable to cope with the students, that the kids spend their time playing skip-to-my-lou and taking driving lessons when they are not pulling switch-blade knives on the teachers or taking dope in the bathrooms.

And most of the individual stories, of course, are true. There are nearly nine million adolescents and 450,000 teachers in American high schools. It is by no means remarkable that hundreds of thousands of the children and tens of thousands of the teachers are, to coin a phrase, no good. . . . But the shocking stories are only part of it; the press has also given its headlines to strong statements by experts about the low quality of work in the high schools. The outstanding "expert" on education, inevitably, is the college president, though his actual knowledge of secondary education may not qualify him to give advice to his own admissions officer.[2]

School public relations are in a bad way on all levels. If they were not, how would you account for the strong sentiment against nursery schools, for the absence of kindergartens in many localities and states, for the generally low prestige of elementary and secondary school teachers? How would you explain the occasional attacks on universities when they try to *act* like universities by providing a free forum for different opinions on subjects like science, religion, education, politics, and literature?

It is obviously time, and past time, for letting the public know more about what schools and teachers are doing, what problems they face, and how bleak the future is for education if our lethargy continues. Right in the forefront of the necessary leadership in informing the public are the future teachers, the ones who will be new teachers in the next 3 to 5 years, at exactly the time when education in our country will take the greatest numerical surge it has ever faced and require the largest financial boost it has ever needed.

We are way past the time, for example, when school public relations should depend on pictures of kindergartners "graduating" in caps and gowns, feature stories based on "cute" sayings and doings of

[2] Martin Mayer, *The Schools*, New York, Harper & Row, Publishers, Inc., 1961, pp. 319–320.

children, and efforts of school people to "get the press on our side" and "tell off those who are criticizing us." Such superficial approaches to bringing the public into the picture were nailed for what they were by Alfred North Whitehead when he called attention to "the broken lives, the defeated hopes, the national failures, which result from the frivolous inertia." They were shown in their ineffective light by John Dewey who said that "whatever obstructs and restricts publicity, limits and distorts public opinion."

Honestly, how many people agree that "school houses are the republican line of fortifications" (Horace Mann), that "education is the cheap defense of nations" (Edmund Burke), or that educated men are superior to those uneducated "as much as the living are to the dead" (Aristotle)? Whose life is not touched every day by news of how others vote, do their work, spend their money, and rear their children? Because of its importance to all of us, education is big news, and every effort must be found to make it dramatic news, too. Emphasis on the trivial will not do it. The public must be told our accomplishments and our advances toward the goals for America in literature, science, social studies, and all the rest.

The vehicles for telling the story are available. Educational television channels are new and vital outlets. Motion pictures are a fairly recent "find" of fraternal organizations, clubs, social groups, and community agencies. Is news of our educational growth, gains, and goals any *less* worthy than the objectives which prompted repeated showings of *Operation Abolition* by such groups in the past few years? The stage is too seldom thought of for this purpose, and yet one educational segment received its greatest boost from this medium through the beautiful story of Helen Keller's education in *The Miracle Worker*. The press, radio, magazines, speeches, and personal contacts with parents and citizens in every community can round out our public relations contacts.

People won't read, listen, or watch for long if the core of what we have to tell them concentrates only on Miss Bishop's retirement or Miss Brooks' marriage, as important as those events are to the ladies involved. Education is controversial: progressive versus traditional, subversion or not, public versus parochial versus private, choices between textbooks. Education is newsworthy because people are the basis for it, especially when we know them or they are in our family or live in our neighborhood. Education is money and health and the future; is there anything more vital to each of us?

If we agree that (1) education is important and (2) the public awareness of it on an *accurate* basis is also important then we're on our way. But where to—and how to get there? Before we find out, a few points of agreement are vital. Can we agree to the following:

Education's growth and improvement require public awareness and understanding.

Public relations must not be feared, ignored, or ridiculed, for it is a tool, a friend, and a necessity.

The objectives of public relations include (1) developing an awareness of how vital education is to the future of all of us; (2) establishing a greater understanding of and confidence in the schools; (3) acquainting the public with what is new and good in education; (4) gaining support for the schools, financial and otherwise; (5) strengthening the partnership concept of parents, teachers, administrators, and community; (6) correcting misunderstandings and misconceptions.

Our skimpy approach to the whole problem indicates the basic immaturity of many school people. Business has its Madison Avenue, labor borrows pages from its book, medicine puts in millions so that its best foot is forward with the public; but teachers and administrators too often feel that all this is beneath their professional dignity. So they may be satisfied with so-called parent-teacher meetings which are attended by the father one month, the mother the next, and the teachers only when absolutely necessary. Or they may put on a big "front" for visitors, but only when the visitors are state or city education officials. Then the preparation becomes a nerve-wracking experience for all involved, based on teacher-prepared bulletin boards, teacher-centered projects and displays, and similar kinds of fakery. Or they ask, instead of tell, what and how the schools should teach, thus demonstrating a weakness that belittles their profession right out in public. Or they satisfy themselves by saying what should be done rather than explaining in 1-2-3 order exactly what they are going to *do*. Or they use emotion to answer criticism, as if the public will learn and respond in a thoroughly honest manner when facts and problems are camouflaged by verbiage.

Despite your youth or newness to teaching or both, you have the heavy responsibility of helping carry some little bit of light into the darkness of public understanding about their most costly possession and their most vital one. Sometimes you will face what may seem to be a very strange and unexpected problem. This public is really many publics, and different elements of it have different axes to grind. "This is what we need . . . ," you will begin; and before you can finish, you may receive the response, "Now *this* is what *we* would like you to do." Pressure is a problem schools have always felt. The closer the school is to the local community the more frequently it has to bend to the will of the local pressure groups. A recent year-book of the National Society for the Study of Education viewed such pressure in this way:

> Some groups, such as the American Legion and the National Association of Manufacturers, have continuous programs with large funds and professional staffs to carry their messages into the schools. Many of these programs have been extensively integrated into public school programs. Other groups are noisier; some are more sporadic. But, they all constitute demands upon the schools to affect the curriculum in a way that is sympathetic to a particular group's interest in the hope that they may be successful in their battle for the minds of children.[3]

This is public relations in reverse, sometimes with the "you *will*" approach only partially hidden. Because schools are the servants of society they would be somewhat out of their role if *they* attempted to apply pressures. Their efforts must be more along the lines of explaining, cajoling, pleading. The role requires tact, is interwoven with frustration, and is built on patience and determination. The complexity of the pressures on schools is something that the various publics may fail to recognize. It may not be a bad idea at all to make them aware of the breadth and variability of demands made on the school. Why not help clear the air sometime by bringing to their attention the vast array given below—and by the time you have taught for a while you will even be able to add others.

> Many hundreds of groups, organized, unorganized and disorganized—press on [the schools'] attention so great and bewildering a variety of view-

[3] National Society for the Study of Education, *Social Forces Influencing American Education,* 60th Yearbook, University of Chicago Press, 1961, p. 32.

points about education. All through the alphabet, from the American Legion and the Better Business Bureau to the Youth Council and the Zoological Society, these groups speak their varied opinions about what the schools should teach. Sometimes they speak temperately, sometimes indignantly, but always persistently. They sponsor pamphlets, books and films; essays and oratorical contests; drives and collections; free materials, inexpensive materials, and expensive materials.

They demand that the public schools give more attention to Little League baseball, first aid, mental hygiene, speech correction, Spanish in the first grade, military preparedness, international goodwill, modern music, world history, American history and local history, geography, homemaking, Canada, Latin America, the Far East, the Near East and the Middle East, NATO, how to detect counterfeit money, safe driving, the United Nations, Christopher Columbus and Leif Ericson, Robert E. Lee and Woodrow Wilson, fire prevention, nutrition, care of the teeth, free enterprise, labor relations, cancer prevention, human rights, atomic energy, the use of firearms, the protection of wild life, the Constitution, tobacco, temperance, kindness to animals, Esperanto, the 3R's, the 3C's, and 4 F's, use of the typewriter, legible penmanship, moral values, physical fitness, civil defense, conservation, ethical concepts, the Air Age, religious literacy, thrift, law observance, consumer education, mathematics, dramatics, narcotics, physics, ceramics, and (that latest of all educational discoveries) phonics.

Each of these groups is anxious to avoid over-loading the curriculum. All they ask is that the non-essentials be dropped in order to get their material in. Few of them want a special course—they just want their idea to permeate the entire school program. If that seems impractical, they are ready to organize special days or weeks to fill in the long hours of idle boredom from which, it must be assumed, they think the school teachers and their pupils suffer.

I have made all this sound as bad as I can in order to add that it is not so bad as it may seem. For we can, if we will, perceive in these apparently chaotic pressures a great popular vote of confidence in the power of education. The American people thus provide us with daily proof that they believe they can adapt their system of education to new circumstances.[4]

You need not be an expert to give information, show friendliness,

[4] From an address given by William G. Carr, Executive Secretary of the NEA, at the 1957 convention of the American Association of School Administrators; quoted by C. C. Trillingham, Los Angeles County Superintendent of Schools, at the annual convention of the Association for Supervision and Curriculum Development, March 1958.

demonstrate competence, and indicate that education is the most important endeavor of the country. But you do have to have a professional "feel" for the school and its vital tasks.

Educational Gobbledygook

"The whole thing just *can't* be a typographical error" said Paul Witty of Northwestern University as he discussed educational literature. But you know what he meant, because you've been exposed to the dullness and the repetitiousness that exist in some of that literature.

One contributor to educational literature who abhors platitudes is Kenneth H. Hansen, Director of the School of Education at Western State College of Colorado. In fact, he has set up a list of comments, made by those inside and outside the education profession, of which we should beware. How often have you said, read, or heard these?

We don't teach subject matter; we teach children.
We learn by doing.
Education is life itself, not preparation for life.
The aim of education is growth; the aim of growth is just more growth.
The school should be child-centered.
Students really learn only when they are interested.
The school curriculum is as broad as life itself.
Let's cut out the frills in education.
Competition is the life blood of achievement.
There's too much progressive education in the schools.
Let's go back to the three R's.
Psychologists tell us . . .
We teach them how to think, not what to think.[5]

Dr. Hansen's list is provocative; we might add others to it such as the following:

Education is free. (How about a poor family deprived of one teen-ager's income because he is attending a "free" high school or college?)
Education pays off. (Did you ever read the W. Somerset Maugham short story of the church janitor who made a fortune because he could *not* read or write?)
Teachers are born, not made. (This is an obvious effort to convince some

[5] Kenneth H. Hansen, *Public Education in American Society*, Englewood Cliffs, N.J., Prentice-Hall, Inc., 1956, pp. 391–427.

people that teaching is the only profession for which no preparation at all is necessary.)

She's sweet and means well—won't do the children any harm. (A backhanded compliment, at best, for a teacher who is incompetent and should not be permitted to teach.)

She's a first-grade teacher. (Or it may be made even worse by saying, "She's *just* a first-grade teacher." Even as it stands the question could be asked: "Is there any class of first-grade children where *all* the abilities of *all* the children are on that level?" Does your answer indicate that perhaps there is no such person, strictly speaking, as a first (or any other) grade teacher or a first (or any other) grade class?)

Incidental learning. (Or is that a cover-up for either sloppy learning or no learning at all?)

Take the child where he is; teach the whole child; meet individual differences. (So easy to say, so difficult to understand in their full meaning, and so seldom accomplished. Yet parts of the education profession roll them around like ball bearings.)

Jacques Barzun said:

As regards writing, we in the twentieth century must offset not only the constant influence of careless speech and the indifference of parents, but the tremendous output of jargon issuing from the new mechanical means at man's disposal. Worst of all, circumstances have conspired to put the most corrupting force at the very heart of the school system. It is not newspapers, radio-scripts, and movies that spoil our language so much as textbooks, official documents, commencement speeches, and learned works.[6]

Our need is to both speak and write the people's language, in the best public relations sense. Primary teachers generally do a good job; college and university professors are among the least effective. One reason, of course, is that some of them are more intent on impressing someone with their erudition rather than teaching. It takes more than the utterance of words for the spark to fly between teacher and student or between school and home or between administrator and community. Your concern in all your dealings— school, home, and community—must be for precise and effective use of language. Ponderous verbiage may enable us to communicate with each other within the profession, but that happens to be the least important of all our communication duties.

[6] Jacques Barzun, *Teacher in America*, Boston, Little, Brown and Company, 1945, p. 55.

Quoting slogans, jargon, terminology, and words or phrases without analyzing their meanings is dangerous in one's speech or writing. For teachers it is unforgiveable, whether they are communicating with each other or the public. In all their activities teachers must be on the alert lest they become slaves to cant phrases, clichés, the commonplace, the inexact, the shopworn. The public deserves better—and what is far more important, it *needs* better in order to be on our side in the struggle for good schools, competent teaching, and alert administration.

It isn't only in ideas, like those listed by Dr. Hansen, that we err on the side of gobbledygook. It is in specific words, too. Is it necessary that we deliberately turn on the learned, highbrow, scholarly bit? Or should we translate our ideas into easily and exactly understood language? No one misunderstood former President Truman when he said, "If you can't stand the heat, don't go into the kitchen." On the other hand, there may be quite a bit of misunderstanding in verbiage like the following, which Jacques Barzun referred to as "ghoulish Desperanto":

In the proposed study I wish to describe and evaluate representative programs in these fields as a means of documenting what seems to me a trend of increasing concern with the role of higher education in the improvement of interpersonal and intergroup relations and of calling attention in this way to outstanding contributions in practice.[7]

Barzun also refers to a faculty meeting where a teacher asked the Director of Admissions why more music students were applying than before, and drew this reply, "Well, I should say that the forces undergirding the process are societal." At the same meeting a committee chairman who wanted to know what to do next was told that "we should go on to institute actual implementation." "The reader must imagine not merely a paragraph taken at random," Barzun concludes, "but pages and pages of similar woolly abstractions, mimeographed at the rate of nine and one-half pounds per person per semester."

Below is a glossary of words and phrases for your careful consideration, and careful and exact use. You've heard them, maybe even used a few in a term paper now and then. There is nothing wrong with them if they are used with real meaning and understanding.

[7] *Ibid.*, p. 57.

You might try a little exercise with them: Say the same thing in deliberately clear language that the average newspaper reader (or the average fifth-grader) could easily understand. How can we get across our ideas and hopes for education unless we do so in words that leave no confusion, no doubt?

> felt needs
> meaningful, purposeful
> articulation, integration, coordination
> social milieu, environmental setting
> objective, subjective, passive, abortive, specific
> regressive, retrogressive, static
> aims, goals, objectives, purposes, emphases
> traditional, conservative, progressive
> autocratic, democratic
> intellectualized
> I.Q. (Dr. Edgar Doll refers to *four* I.Q.s)
> emotional, physical, social
> challenge, living, vital, gripping, dynamic, organic, exciting, creative, rich, significant, constructive
> child-centered, subject-centered, life-related
> in terms of, in point of fact, "irregardless," education-wise
> central focus
> evaluative criteria
> empathy
> group activity, outgoing, democracy in education, social adjustment, life adjustment, disciplines
> reading readiness

Among the fairly recent additions to educational jargon are "image," "extra sensory perception" (ESP), and "know-how." In some education courses terms like the following are tossed around, but fortunately in some places they are explained clearly:[8] "rational humanism" (Robert M. Hutchins); "education for life adjustment" (Harold C. Hand); "experimentalism" (John Dewey); "social reconstructionism" (Theodore Brameld). The *new* gobbledygook includes expressions like "excellence," "structure of the discipline," "theoretical frameworks," "cognitive learnings," and "convergent and divergent thinking." The new breed of "reformed" educationists have their own nebulous lingo.

[8] Myron Lieberman, *Education as a Profession*, Englewood Cliffs, N.J., Prentice-Hall, Inc., 1956, pp. 23–27.

It is only fair that you be cautioned about these obstacles to communication between the schools and the public. Our first step in getting respect for education and educational personnel is to speak the language of those who support us.

The Teacher in the Community

Your most constant public-relations role will be in your everyday relationships in the community: at the barber shop or beauty parlor, in the grocery store, as you talk to the newspaper boy, the man delivering your cleaning, and the lady who lives next door. All of these relationships require a classic kind of tact of the type reported in a Bennett Cerf story about Marlene Dietrich. She had her picture taken and fumed at the result. "I can't understand it," she said. "The last time I posed for you, the photographs were heavenly." "Ah, yes," sighed the camera man, "but you must remember that I was eight years younger then."

Public relations, good will, interference, and imposition have very thin lines between them, and this is especially so in the afterschool hours of the teacher. Perhaps it is unfortunate that the community will be more interested in you, just because you are a teacher, than it is in other workers who live there. On the other hand, that may be a very fortunate thing because it indicates that it is also interested in its children and its schools. When the concern over your activities stops, that may be a real danger sign. However, that concern may become "meddling" in private affairs, and at that point the thin line has been crossed. It is inevitable, though, that the taxpayer will see you as a dollar sign, the church as another member, the drug store as a new customer, the young men or women as a new prospect for dating, and the newspaper as a new subscriber.

You are a public relations person for education in general and specifically for your school. The way you talk, dress, and act will reflect on both. Although it may be unfair for a community, as some of the smaller ones do, to expect different standards for its teachers than for its other citizens, that is frequently the case and a fact to face. A lot of grief can be avoided if you know something about the community before you go into it. If a moderate amount of smoking and drinking are important to you, and the community turns thumbs down on one or both, doesn't that give you a hint about your future happiness there? If you like to dance, go to shows, visit art galleries, and the nearest opportunities are 218 miles away, what does *that* tell you? If it is a church-going community and you couldn't care less, or if your religion isn't even represented in the town, isn't that a guide toward whether or not you should sign the contract? Climate, the smile of the principal, and salary are not the only considerations. There are others, and they are important.

What you say and your activities in one town may take on great proportions although they would go unobserved elsewhere. What this means to you is that after you know what the community likes and dislikes, you should make up your mind to adjust or leave. And yet most communities do not require the kind of conforming that creates a problem. Let us just hope that those of you who like to rebel a little bit have teaching jobs in areas that encourage or at least tolerate nonconformists. However, in most places the tendency to talk too much about your children, their parents, and other teachers, to socialize indiscriminately, and to criticize without being careful who is listening may all be a mistake. You must be sensitive to the threshold of a community's tolerance and acceptance. You may feel that the community is getting entirely "too personal." But the community has great interest because it is their money, their school, and their children.

The people in it will usually help more than hinder. They want you to be part of them, join their activities, share their interests. And if you do, before long you'll no doubt find that they view you as they view the other young people of the community, as just a fellow or girl who wants to do a job, have friends, and be liked.

It is at that point—when you are liked and accepted—that your public relations value goes into high gear.

LOOKING THROUGH PARENTS' EYES

When we were children, a child always seemed to be blamed for everything. Now that we are reaching or have reached adulthood, it's the parent who is to blame—or so it appears anyway. Even President Eisenhower contributed to the burden we put on parents when he said:

We hear a lot about the deficiencies and woeful conditions of education in America, a criticism that suggests a few questions. How many parents have offered to relieve some of the routine burdens of the teachers, or invited them to a friendly supper at home? How many parents have tried to make the teacher a real partner in the responsibility—and the priceless privilege—of educating our children?[9]

It *is* true that parents may become self-appointed experts in the field of education. Sometimes their pressures may discourage teachers from doing the job for which they are prepared. Architecture, geology, medicine, and other areas are left alone to develop as fast as their qualified personnel can take them; but when it comes to those who teach our children—and those who teach the teachers—some of the barriers are down, and the least informed may become the most critical. And yet, why should we assume that fathers and mothers are invariably incompetent and teachers are unquestionably knowledgeable and skillful?

Sometimes the dissatisfaction parents encounter in their own lives, through rocky marriages, in-law troubles, or other tensions, turn them into malcontents in need of an outlet. So what is more convenient than their child's teacher or school? And, after all, don't the schools belong to the people? The danger of the off-with-their-heads approach by parents is all too common among a vocal minority whose difficulties may lie in other directions.

It is important to recognize that the concern of most parents for the education of their children is sincere and should be respected. But this concern, when it is converted into oral and verbal criticism, must be accompanied by responsibility. It should not be limited only to superficial comments like these, for example:

"I learned the alphabet and multiplication tables, and I just don't see why my children shouldn't be taught in the same way."

"When I went to school we all read when we were in the first grade. Now they talk about such things as readiness and having some children start to read when they are 7 or 8."

"We started writing in the regular way, with none of that manuscript stuff. There are some children who never do learn how to write correctly these days."

Such remarks frequently are made by persons whose knowledge of current teaching techniques may be limited and who assume that

[9] In a speech at the NEA Centennial Birthday Party, Washington, D.C., April 4, 1957.

methods today are vastly different from those used when they were in the elementary grades. It's true that some students cannot read, write, spell, and add as we would like them to; but the fault does not necessarily lie in "newer" methods. There are *always* some children who are deficient in these skills. The mistake is made in headlining those youngsters out of proportion to their numbers, and in addition, putting all of the blame on techniques which actually have never been given a fair trial in American education. While you will no doubt try new methods and materials, some of our teachers still teach as they in turn were taught. Although it is healthful to question newer methods in education, as well as in other professions, in business, and in government, it is dangerous to stop respectable experimentation. Children suffer, and so do all of us, when the activities of teachers and administrators who are trying to find better ways are restricted.

Suspicion and fear have frequently been the undergirding of home-school relationships, buttressed by the lack of insight each has regarding the objectives of the other. In one of the better education films, a teacher visits a child's home and is greeted in a rather chilly manner by the mother who asks, "What's she done wrong now?"

We realize more frequently these days that we're all in this educational endeavor together, and that if we pool our information and energy we're more certain of doing a better job of educating our children. The intimate knowledge of parents (despite its apparent bias) is as important as the technical skill of the teacher, both fitting together as closely as the pieces of a jigsaw puzzle. Parents who visit their children's school and participate in its activities know more about what it is attempting to do, see what it is up against in money problems and crowded conditions, and appreciate the accomplishments of its teachers. It works out just as well in the other direction, too, in providing teachers with the reasons why Ronnie has such a short attention span or Nancy seeks affection from the teacher. Getting acquainted, listening, and sharing problems are helpful for both sides. Details regarding early childhood diseases or operations may help the teacher; and general information regarding intelligence and achievement can help parents fulfill the function they want so much to do well.

A home visit should be preceded by an inquiry regarding the convenience as far as time is concerned; and telephone calls to your home should be scheduled so that they don't interfere with your free evenings. It's just as much a shame for you to have an "unlisted telephone" for this reason as for the parents to wish you didn't have their address because of your unannounced visits. Obviously you'll have to find time for parents, during or after school hours, at your convenience and theirs. Parent conferences, PTA meetings, and home visitations may be part of the answer. Your school may already have satisfactory arrangements, but if it doesn't, your awareness of this need will encourage it to set them up as time goes on.

There should be little disagreement about the right of parents to share whatever information we have concerning their children. Whether it relates to intelligence, physical health, academic achievement, or anything else available within the school, that availability extends to them. It should reach them promptly, understandably, and accurately. Teachers themselves are not in agreement on whether or how much information should be shared. They tend to be unduly secretive, in fact. An NEA survey of more than 1600 teachers revealed the extent to which teachers were willing to share information.

I.Q. Information	Elementary Teachers	Secondary Teachers
Routinely shared with parents	9.3%	17.4%
Shared in most cases	22.8	29.3
Shared only in unusual cases	49.7	40.1
Never shared	15.1	11.4
Undecided	3.1	1.8
	100.0%	100.0%

Achievement-Test Information	Elementary Teachers	Secondary Teachers
Routinely shared	31.7%	53.0%
Shared in most cases	41.7	36.7
Shared only in unusual cases	21.0	8.0
Never shared	4.6	1.7
Undecided	1.0	.6
	100.0%	100.0%

"Exact" scores on standardized tests should not be disclosed for a very simple reason: there are no such things. The results depend on *which* test is used, *who* administers and scores it, and *when* it is given. Parents deserve information about their children in less exact but more helpful terms.

In its relationship with parents the school should cooperate and expect cooperation in return; attempt to understand parents' problems, and hope they will understand the school's; try not to generalize about the knowledge and attitudes of all parents, and trust they will have that understanding toward all teachers. In addition the school should make at least some effort toward seeing the persistent problems of home and family through parents' eyes. The sections that follow will attempt to help you do so.

The results of some studies indicate that teachers come primarily from the "middle class" while children represent all levels of the socioeconomic ladder. If we accept these as facts, then we have to know something about the feelings, mores, and habits of the families from which the children come. If we regularly criticize a child for words, phrases, clothing, and lack of cleanliness and he comes from a home where all of these are perfectly acceptable, then we have to ask ourselves, "Is it part of our job to create cleavages and suspicions in the family? Or should we help build respect for parents and acceptance of cultural deviations and limitations?"

Problems of Parents

"I told them off, and they deserved it! Your kids are monsters, I said. They're impossible to live with and to work with. It's your fault and your problem. I have them only 5 hours a day, but you'll have them the rest of your lives!"

With pride and pleasure, an elementary school teacher of the discipline-is-everything school thus restated what she had said to a group of parents at a parents' night. She ventured further and told them collectively what they were doing wrong and what was wrong with their children. Destructively, tactlessly, unknowingly, she bolstered her own ego and sense of importance, and at the same time alienated some of the very persons who could help her with her daily problems. But she didn't need any help, she thought. "The whole bad bunch of kids in my room add up to your problem," she said to the parents.

Perhaps this episode is an extreme one. But when you are teaching it will be necessary for you to appraise more carefully than she did the situation in which most parents find themselves. You are not the only one who will have daily problems to face. Many teachers (especially the unmarried ones without dependents and the married teachers whose husbands or wives are working) are at least relieved of the major pressure facing the majority of parents—the financial burden.

What are some of the factors in the home lives of your children which you will have to consider? What in the background and future of the child, as well as in his present, is responsible for the way he thinks, acts and talks? Through answers to these questions a teacher may leave the ivory tower of his own life and be more tolerant of the problems his children bring to school. Out of such understanding may also develop a teacher with more warmth and less rigidity; a person whose dignity comes not from the authority vested in him due to his education, age, height, loudness of voice, or sternness of countenance, but rather whose dignity comes from recognizing the undermining pressures on parents which inevitably reflect themselves in their children. Many key problem situations are faced by parents and need sympathetic understanding on the part of teachers. Among them are the following, most of which will still be around in one form or another when you start to teach.

HIGH PRICES

When children's shoes, outgrown in weeks or months, cost $6 or more, when milk is far beyond $.20 cents a quart ($1 a day means a milk bill of $30 a month), when children's clothing costs more and lasts a far shorter period of time than did the adult clothing a few years ago, then serious problems are faced by the majority of parents every day. It is true that wages are higher than ever, but prices have so outrun them that the average mother is forced to consider working to augment the family income. Only one of the many current family tensions is caused by the need for cutting down on insurance and stinting on the family food budget. Most parents cannot escape the squeeze of the shrinking dollar bill. Nor can their children.

ATOM BOMB

A few short years ago it was the atom bomb, yesterday it was the hydrogen bomb and tomorrow it may be something else. Whatever it is, many children will feel threatened and insecure. Many will be crowded into corridors, and told to crouch against the walls and hide their heads. Some teachers will discuss this new experience with them, and a minority will do what they can in this difficult situation to alleviate the terror which some children may feel and comparatively few adults understand. There are youngsters who go home with their burden, about which they may or may not talk to their parents. In the night, however, the terror may reach the surface, for tears and fearful crying are not uncommon in some American homes in the 1960s. And nightmares far away from the school and much later than the 3 o'clock bell are part of the teacher's responsibility. He must know about them and do whatever he can to prevent or calm the fears.

CROWDED HOUSING

The era of two or more families in an apartment, of six or eight persons sleeping in one room, is sadly still with us. The child who has never known what it is to get into a cool clean bed alone, whose knowledge of sex relationships has always seemed a part of him, and who does not know what a 12-hour night of quiet is may not understand some of the things many teachers take for granted. "Hang your two toothbrushes in the bathroom" (18 are lying around in *his* bathroom, only one is his, and he's never absolutely sure that he uses the same one time after time). "Take a bath every day" (there wouldn't be enough hot water for all of them even if his mother had *time* to bathe all six of the young ones). "Do your home work where it's quiet" (this is a joke in his home). The teacher who does not know what goes on in the home is missing one of the main sources for understanding the child.

FAMILY CONFLICTS

There are the homes which are possessive, oversolicitous, bickering, unreliable, nagging, frigid, neglectful, or child-dictated—and in all of them the child is strongly affected. Parents may be separated, cultural conflicts of a religious, national, urban-rural or financial basis may exist, sudden wealth may appear—and again the children are caught in the middle. A child may be unwanted, may have been eagerly awaited for many years, or may be sickly—and the effect on him is apparent to any serious student of how children develop and grow. The obvious conflicts and frustrations of family life are frequently a thin disguise for the underlying causes. While teachers are limited in how far they should delve into such situations, that they exist and that they influence the attitudes and activities of children must be clearly understood.

AUTHORITATIVE CONFUSION

Never has a generation of parents been made so aware of their handling of their own children. The huge sales of books telling parents how to live with their children are testimony to the hundreds of thousands of pseudo-experts we now have as heads of families. But since child authorities are sometimes confused and fluctuate in the advice they give, the parents are even more mixed up and worried. "Shall I love—or ignore?" "Shall I feed on the clock— or by demand?" "Shall I be a pal—or a parent?" "Am I doing right —or wrong?" Many authorities speak soundly on the basis of long experience and study, using the best of the past and bringing it up to date. But for some the human quality is missing, a key factor, which makes an authority different from a parent and causes him to lack a real understanding of parents. If he has never lived with his own children 24 hours each day, walked the floor with a sick child at night, and carried the burden which only parents of young children have so thoroughly endured, then his advice and suggestions, no matter how scientifically correct and useful they are, may be limited in their value. The close relationship between experience and learning has a place here similar to the one it holds in other educational activities.

TEACHERS

Parents are worried about teachers. They worry about the teachers their children now have and will have next year. "Will she be patient?" "Will she know how far my child has progressed—and take him on from there?" "Will she try to overlook his faults and realize how precious he is to me?" Just in being a teacher, you may become a problem to conscientious parents who are entrusting a most valuable possession to you.

These factors, and many others related to them, can provide a cornerstone of understanding when you look at your children and try to accept and appreciate the difficulties of their parents. But this understanding is a two-way street, for parents certainly must also work constantly to understand the problems of teachers. They may have difficulty with 2 children, but what about the teacher with 35 or 40? They may be tempted to criticize what a particular teacher does, but do they have all the facts? They may show favoritism toward one of their own children, so can they expect teachers not even to have human preferences for one person over another? Are they as objective about the job of the teacher as they might be?

A basic understanding of home conditions, attitudes, and problems is necessary if parents and teachers are to have a realistic picture of what to expect from children. Gardner stated one aspect of the issue well when he wrote:

> We are beginning to understand that the various kinds of talents that flower in any society are the kinds that are valued in the society. On a recent visit to Holland, my wife asked a Dutchwoman why children and adults in that country showed such an extraordinarily high incidence of language skills. "We expect it of children," the woman said simply. "We think it important."
>
> More and more we are coming to see that high performance, particularly where children are concerned, takes place in a framework of expectation. If it is expected it will often occur. If there are no expectations, there will be little high performance. . . . as a society, we shall have only the kinds of talent we nourish, only the kinds of talent we want and expect. *Are we nourishing the kinds of talent that will create a great civilization or are we not?* In matters relating to talent and society that is not just another question. It is The Question.[10]

The mental health of parents sometimes takes a beating because they worry about the point Gardner makes. Am I expecting enough —or too much? Am I overlooking talent and ability that are right in my own home? Do we talk together enough in our home—or is the conversation one-sided (on mine) unless there's an argument or reprimand in the air? Do I try to answer questions—or ignore them?

You may have heard about the parent who faced the "question problem" with realism, or so he thought. His little boy asked "Daddy, what makes the grass so green?" "I don't know," his father

---

[10] John W. Gardner, *Excellence*, New York, Harper & Row, Publishers, Inc., 1961, pp. 101–102.

replied. "Well, what makes the sky blue?" the boy asked. "I don't know," was the reply. The little boy looked perturbed, but persisted in his questioning. He asked in a worried manner, "The waves, Daddy, the waves. What makes them roar and beat on the shore?" "I'm sorry, but I don't know that either." Then the child's concern turned to anger as he said, "That's the last time, Daddy! I'm not going to ask you any more questions—not forever and ever." Now it was the father's turn to be troubled: "But you've *got* to ask questions! You must! How are you going to learn anything if you don't?"

Questions that bring thoughtful answers, helpful attitudes, and guidance toward growth are the ones that count. It's the results that matter, not the mere spinning of wheels in putting words together.

In another situation a child asked, "Where did I come from?" The mother, who was brought up not to delay answers or discussions, dug right in, explaining all the specific details of pregnancy and birth. After the lengthy discourse, she asked her young child whether it was all clear. "Oh yes, Mommy," he replied, "but that wasn't what I wanted to know. Jimmy came from Boston, and I want to know where I come from."

The problems of parents, serious and humorous, permeate every hour of their lives. From whether there will even be a tomorrow to how much television watching should be permitted, from issues like war and cost-of-living to comic-book reading, these problems are an invisible cloak that accompany their children wherever they go.

In your classroom they will be a constant companion.

CONCLUDING REMARKS

You can't walk alone through the maze of problems faced by the teaching profession, and fortunately you don't have to. You need help, and so do the thousands who preceded you. Your strongest assistance will come from the public who pays the bill, owns the schools, and wants the best for its children. It was once said that "only men who do nothing are always right." So you have a choice of vegetation or contribution. If you choose the positive route, you will help bring understanding of the school's job to those who are most in need of it. Using the public relations possibilities that lie within your capacity and realizing the problems that parents face every day will enable you to plant the seed of that understanding.

Does a good teacher have to go to Japan in order to teach about it? Does a good teacher have to be a parent in order to see through parents' eyes? Of course not. Merely visiting or being doesn't give the breadth of knowledge, insight, and sensitivity that may be needed. In both travel and parenthood we may wear the blinders that deprive us of a real understanding of the route involved and of the ability to transmit ideas based on it.

"Parents are the key" proclaims the title of a pamphlet prepared by the Arizona Congress of Parents and Teachers. And yet, the full strength in bringing up and educating children falls on collective shoulders. Theirs are the primary ones, the strongest ones, the ones providing the greatest continuity, but you as a teacher bear the burden, too. All that has been said in this book has had the single objective of helping you bear it intelligently. That you will have frequent doubts and face many difficulties now and in the years ahead is expected, but the effort, the dedication, and the need are ever present.

Words like these may rub you the wrong way: "One hand washes the other," "I'll do my part, but no more," "It's every man for himself; let the best man win." They may be symptomatic of the major attitudes of people in the challenging 1960s, of *your* attitudes. But as indicated so many times, here and elsewhere, teaching requires much more.

It demands the glowing terms like "cooperation," the shining words like "achievement," the realistic ones like "hard work." It will be a constant struggle against people, time, and money to get the job done right. But there is no choice. It *must* be done for a very simple reason: The world as we know it will survive only if teachers, working closely with parents and other dedicated persons in each community, teach children to seek truth, respect honesty, and perform to the great capacities of which most of them are capable.

Epilogue

Pick up almost any newspaper or magazine, watch television, listen to the radio, and you must come to a major conclusion about this profession—it is big news in the 1960s. It has always been important, but the difference these days is that people *know* how important it is.

They may not vote affirmatively on every school-bond issue or raise teachers' salaries sufficiently; but when Conant's book *The Education of American Teachers* occupies a prominent week-after-week place on the list of national best sellers, you know the subject has arrived. When the television show about a high school teacher "Mr. Novak," warrants a weekly hour of prime evening viewing time and attracts huge audiences in all parts of the country, on all age levels, and with various educational backgrounds, it may be the good-looking young teacher who pulls them in, but it may also be the depth of a nation's interest in the education of its children. When the *Saturday Evening Post* uses a blurb about "Our Backward Schools" on its front cover to help sell magazines and feels Martin Mayer's article "Last Chance for Our Schools?" is strong enough to warrant that kind of come-on, the future of education begins to look brighter. And when enthusiasm is beginning to overtake fear in teachers' feelings about the newer developments available to them—such as the ungraded school, team teaching, educational television, programmed learning, and current approaches to teaching science, mathematics, and foreign languages—then we really are on the threshold of becoming the profession our children deserve.

Awareness of our own deficiencies and responsiveness to the demands made on us will keep us from being the "national failure" that Admiral Rickover recently said we are (*American Education—A National Failure*, New York, E. P. Dutton & Co., Inc.). Change is in the wind—from our pie-shaped schools, to individual learning cubicles, to teachers going back to school more to learn than to receive credit. If you're a betting person, put your money on change rather than on the *status quo* in this profession, for no occupation has been on such inconstant, shifty, and promising sands as this one is today and for many tomorrows.

Right from under us its total foundation of preparation is being challenged, and not by a wild-eyed dreamer either. James Bryant Conant is a respected educator, and people are listening to what he has to say. He had plenty of ideas about our high schools, junior high schools, slums, and suburbs. And now the preparation of our teachers has attracted his staff and his typewriter. The ripples of reaction have appeared, and it is no wonder when you note the areas which his recommendations touch, areas of tremendous importance to future and present teachers, parents, and the public as a whole. Here are just a few of them:

Teacher's certification requirements: based on a bachelor's degree, student teaching, and the endorsement of the college or university, removing the certification authority from state departments of education

Student teaching: close college-public school cooperation, with programs receiving state approval

Teacher assignment: only to duties for which the teacher is specifically prepared

Certification reciprocity: among all the states

Postgraduate work of teachers: summers, leaves of absence and in-service; but no encouragement toward late afternoon, evening, or extension classes

Collegiate or university responsibility: an all-institution approach

Content and methodology both to be emphasized, especially in grades 1–6

Teacher recruitment: from the upper third of high school graduating classes on a national basis

In his investigations, Dr. Conant found much to criticize strongly both in faculties of education and those of arts and sciences, so neither escapes unscathed from the scalpel he wields so deftly in this analysis. His own summary of the work he has done goes this way: "If I were to characterize in two words the conclusion of my study, these words would be 'freedom' and 'responsibility'."[1] They

[1] James Bryant Conant, *The Education of American Teachers*, New York, McGraw-Hill Book Company, Inc., 1963, p. 217.

seem eminently appropriate as we apply both of them to the experimentation in which our teacher-preparation institutions must participate in the years ahead.

Although no one has placed "Mr. Novak" in the same arena with Dr. Conant, indirectly some of their objectives are not far apart; for example, their desire to bring additional respectability to the teaching profession. Just as the American Medical Association and American Bar Association help on television shows involving doctors and lawyers, the National Education Association filled an advisory function on television's "Mr. Novak." Perhaps the most intriguing aspect of this series is that controversy is actually courted rather than avoided, in scripts that center around the dropout, blind children in regular classes, sex education, integration, and propaganda in the classroom. It makes you think that not only is education growing up—so is television.

Jefferson High is a battlefield, says the show's executive producer E. Jack Neuman. "There, Mr. Novak wages war five days a week against ignorance, intolerance, cruelty, and injustice. For this, the board of education pays him $5,842 and gets more than its money's worth."[2]

He is far from a Mr. Peepers or a Miss Brooks, and he's brought added dignity and excitement to a profession that needs more of both. He represents an occupation based on hard work, tough situations, sensitivity, and a steep road toward its full potential.

A best seller and a television show begin to make the point more effectively than the thousands of pages each month in the journals teachers read and for which they may write. It is the slightly off-beat approach to your profession that brings it more recognition and respect. It is the item that causes people to take a surprised second look which will bring increases in salaries, more men into the profession, less feeling that it is an occupation fit only for those who cannot succeed in the more "demanding" business world.

It is the feature story in a popular weekly magazine, for example, that can show just *how* demanding and exciting this profession is—or rather, can be for the kind of young person it requires to meet its increasingly high standards. "Last Chance for Our Schools?" was the

[2] E. Jack Neuman, quoted in "Meet Mr. Novak," *NEA Journal*, September, 1963, p. 32.

question asked by Martin Mayer, who became an "expert" on education because he wrote about it. Whether he is or not doesn't matter. The points he made in this article hit close to some of the problems we face.

The United States has "to yank its schools into the 20th century," he wrote. They need the help that is just beginning to trickle down from the university scholars in mathematics, science, and linguistics. We are far too glib, he believes, when we talk about a "revolution" in education, for though it really is going on, it affects only "a few hundreds out of tens of thousands of schools, a few tens of thousands out of tens of millions of students."[3] In his criticisms of schools of education and school administrators Mayer is often guilty of over-simplification for journalistic effect. But his ideas are forceful. "Our worst scandal is the failure of the new teaching ideas and materials themselves, and even the new gadgets, to reach into the backwoods areas and the urban slums where 10-15 million children now learn so little in school that they will not be able to function well as adults." He singles out New York City and St. Louis for their strong efforts to turn this tide. "We cannot afford another generation as ignorant as we are," he concludes.

And we won't have it if we select our future teachers more discriminately, prepare them more intelligently, and respect the work they are trying to do more wholeheartedly. As you know, outside groups and persons have all kinds of ideas for how the profession can reach those goals. But one of the most encouraging factors is that more efforts—bright hard-hitting ones—are being made within, too.

A few years ago the NEA set up a Project on Instruction, which has now issued a series of reports. The overview volume is called *Schools for the Sixties*. In it the NEA finally bends in its complete support for the self-contained, one-teacher classroom, recognizing that the speed and explosive qualities of our times demand a flexible kind of respect for change, innovation, experimentation. Its series of 33 recommendations for self-improvement include the following:

Faculty freedom and authority in what and how to teach

[3] Martin Mayer, "Last Chance for Our Schools?", *Saturday Evening Post*, September 14, 1963, pp. 24–37.

School-budget allocation for research and related activities
Rational discussion of controversial issues in the schools
Nongrading and multigrading as alternative possibilities to the traditional graded school
Team teaching; also educational television and programmed learning
Space flexibility to allow for individual and seminar study[4]

So the barriers toward stodginess in your profession are gradually crumbling. Its changes must be matched by yours, however. Without awareness, alertness, and knowledge you can't teach. You need eagerness to listen to and try the new, empathy to soften your words and feelings with children, and energy to make certain that you don't smother an idea by never letting it expand, whether yours or a child's in your class. Without scrutinizing and questioning the words of Bruner, Gardner, Lieberman, Neill, Trump, Woodring, and others at the cutting edge of your profession today and in your teaching tomorrows, you can't do the job you should.

If all this is too much to expect of a young person just entering, then the full-blown seriousness of our times is not recognized. In a setting which includes poverty and increasing population, automation and unemployment, materialism and waste, we cannot harbor mediocrity among those who presume to provide the inspiration our children need for their trying years ahead.

The frontier of the classroom, where both quality and equality are essential, demands creative spirits who are eager to do battle against unfairness, narrowness, and ignorance whether among these children or in the world society that keeps butting its way into our daily lives.

[4] NEA, *Schools for the Sixties,* New York, McGraw-Hill Book Company, Inc., 1963.

Selected Bibliography

The following publications represent the materials used as a "backdrop" for this book. You may find many of them informative and stimulating. You can be certain they will be helpful in filling in some of the gaps too many of our teachers have.

Abraham, Willard, *A Handbook for the New Teacher,* New York, Holt, Rinehart and Winston, Inc., 1960.

Abraham, Willard, *Common Sense About Gifted Children,* New York, Harper & Row, Publishers, Inc., 1958.

Abraham, Willard, *The Slow Learner,* Syracuse, N. Y., The Center for Applied Research in Education, Inc., 1964.

American Association of School Administrators and Research Division, National Education Association, *Teacher-Aides: Current Practices and Experiments,* Educational Research Service, Circular no. 5. Washington, D.C., American Association of School Administrators, 1960.

American Council on Education, *How Fare American Youth?* Washington, D.C., 1937.

Arizona State University, *Investigation of Mental Retardation and Pseudo-Mental Retardation in Relation to Bilingual and Sub-Cultural Factors,* Tempe, Arizona, 1960.

Ashton-Warner, Sylvia, *Teacher,* New York, Simon and Schuster, 1963.

Association for Higher Education, *Current Issues in Higher Education,* Washington, D.C., NEA, 1963.

1963 Conference theme:	"Critical Decisions in Higher Education"
1962 Conference theme:	"Higher Education in an Age of Revolutions"
1961 Conference theme:	"Goals for Higher Education in a Decade of Decision"
1960 Conference theme:	"Platform for Higher Education: Guide Lines for the 60's"
1959 Conference theme:	"The Race Against Time: New Perspectives and Imperatives in Higher Education"

Association for Supervision and Curriculum Development, *The Self-Contained Classroom.* Washington, D.C., 1960.

Austin, Mary C., and Coleman Morrison, *The First R,* New York, The Macmillan Company, 1963.

Austin, Mary C., *The Torch Lighters,* Cambridge, Harvard University Press, 1962.

Baller, Warren R., and Don C. Charles, *The Psychology of Human Growth and Development,* New York, Holt, Rinehart and Winston, Inc., 1961.

Barzun, Jacques, *Teacher in America,* Boston, Little, Brown and Company, 1945.

Barzun, Jacques, "The Cults of 'Research' and 'Creativity,' " *Harper's Magazine,* October, 1960, pp. 69–74.

Barzun, Jacques, *The House of Intellect,* New York, Harper & Row, Publishers, Inc., 1959.

Bell, Bernard Iddings, *Crisis in Education,* New York, McGraw-Hill Book Company, Inc., 1949.

Benjamin, Harold, *The Cultivation of Idiosyncrasy,* Cambridge, Harvard University Press, 1949.

Bestor, Arthur E., *Educational Wastelands,* Urbana, University of Illinois Press, 1953.

Bestor, Arthur E., *The Restoration of Learning,* New York, Alfred A. Knopf, Inc., 1955.

Black, Hillel, *They Shall Not Pass,* New York, William Morrow, 1963.

Boroff, David, *Campus U.S.A.,* New York, Harper & Row, Publishers, Inc., 1961.

Brameld, Theodore, *Cultural Foundations of Education,* New York, Harper & Row, Publishers, Inc., 1957.

Brameld, Theodore, *Education for the Emerging Age,* New York, Harper & Row, Publishers, Inc., 1961.

Brown, B. Frank, *The Nongraded High School,* Englewood Cliffs, N. J., Prentice-Hall, 1963.

Brown, Harrison, *The Challenge of Man's Future,* New York, The Viking Press, Inc., 1954.

Brown, Harrison, James Bonner, and John Weir, *The Next Hundred Years,* New York, The Viking Press, Inc., 1957.

Bruner, Jerome S., *The Process of Education,* Cambridge, Harvard University Press, 1961.

Burrup, Percy E., *The Teacher and the Public School System,* New York, Harper & Row, Publishers, Inc., 1960.

California Teachers Association, *Judging and Improving the Schools: Current Issues,* Burlingame, Calif., California Teachers Association, 1960.

Cambridge Conference on School Mathematics, *Goals for School Mathematics,* Boston, Houghton Mifflin, 1963.

Caplow, Theodore, and Reece J. McGee, *The Academic Marketplace,* New York, Basic Books, Inc., Publishers, 1958.

Carmichael, Oliver, *Graduate Education,* New York, Harper & Row, Publishers, Inc., 1961.

Catskill Area Project in Small School Design, *School Aides at Work,* Oneonta, N.Y., 1960.

Catskill Area Project in Small School Design, *Sharing Educational Services,* Oneonta, N.Y., 1960.

Chase, Stuart, *Some Things Worth Knowing,* New York, Harper & Row, Publishers, Inc., 1958.

Clift, Virgil A., Archibald W. Anderson, and H. Gordon Hullfish (eds.), *Negro Education in America,* New York, Harper & Row, Publishers, Inc., 1962.

College Entrance Examination Board, *The Behavioral Sciences and Education,* Princeton, The Board, 1963.

Commission on Education of Women of the American Council on Education, *The Education of Women,* no. 11. Washington, D.C., American Council on Education, 1960.

Committee on Utilization of College Teaching Resources, *Better Utilization of College Teaching Resources,* New York, Fund for the Advancement of Education, 1959.

Conant, James B., *Recommendations for Education in the Junior High School Years: A Memorandum to School Boards.* Princeton, N.J., Educational Testing Service, 1960.

Conant, James B., *Slums and Suburbs,* New York, McGraw-Hill Book Company, Inc., 1961.

Conant, James B., *The American High School Today,* New York, McGraw-Hill Book Company, Inc., 1959.

Conant, James B., *The Education of American Teachers,* New York, McGraw-Hill Book Company, Inc., 1963.

Cook, Walter W., "The Gifted and the Retarded in Historical Perspective," *Phi Delta Kappan,* March, 1958, pp. 249–255.

Cousins, Norman, *In Place of Folly,* New York, Harper & Row, Publishers, Inc., 1961.

Cousins, Norman, *Modern Man Is Obsolete,* New York, The Viking Press, Inc., 1945.

Cousins, Norman, "The Great Debate in American Education," *Saturday Review,* September 11, 1954.

Cousins, Norman, *Who Speaks for Man?* New York, The Macmillan Company, 1953.

Cremin, Lawrence A., *The Transformation of the School: Progressivism in American Education, 1867–1957,* New York, Alfred A. Knopf, Inc., 1961.

"Crisis in Education," *Life,* issues of March 24 to April 21, 1958.

Crow, Lester D., and Alice Crow, *Introduction to Education,* New York, American Book Company, 1960.

Department of Classroom Teachers, NEA, *Conditions of Work for Quality Teaching,* Washington, D.C., 1959.

DeYoung, Chris A., *Introduction to American Public Education,* New York, McGraw-Hill Book Company, Inc., 1955.

Edling, Jack V., *The New Media in Education,* Sacramento, Calif., Sacramento State College Foundation, 1961.

Educational Facilities Laboratories, *Design for Educational TV: Planning for Schools with Television,* New York, 1960.

Educational Facilities Laboratories, *Profiles of Significant Schools,* New York, 1960.

Educational Facilities Laboratories, *The Cost of a Schoolhouse,* New York, 1960.

Educational Policies Commission, *An Essay on Quality in Public Education,* Washington, D.C., NEA, 1959.

Educational Policies Commission, *Contemporary Issues in Elementary Education,* Washington, D.C., NEA, 1960.

Educational Policies Commission, *Education and the Disadvantaged American,* Washington, D.C., NEA, 1962.

Educational Policies Commission, *The Contemporary Challenge to American Education,* Washington, D.C., NEA, 1958.

Ehlers, Henry, and Gordon C. Lee (eds.), *Crucial Issues in Education,* New York, Holt, Rinehart and Winston, Inc., 1959.

Fadiman, Clifton, "The Mess in Education—Who Is Responsible?" *Holiday,* August, 1958.

Fattu, Nicholas, *Who's a Good Teacher?* Washington, D.C., NEA, 1961.

Filbin, Robert L., and Stefan Vogel, *So You're Going To Be a Teacher,* Great Neck, N.Y., Barron's Educational Series, Inc., 1962.

Fine, Benjamin, *Educational Publicity,* New York, Harper & Row, Publishers, Inc., 1951.

Fine, Benjamin, *Our Children Are Cheated,* New York, Holt, Rinehart and Winston, Inc., 1959.

Fine, Benjamin, *Teaching Machines,* New York, Sterling Publishing Co., 1962.

Fine, Benjamin, and Lillian Fine, *How to Get the Best Education For Your Child,* New York, G. P. Putnam's Sons, 1959.

Finn, James D., "Technology and the Instructional Process," *Phi Delta Kappan,* June, 1960, pp. 371-377.

Foff, Arthur, and Jean D. Grambs, *Readings in Education,* New York, Harper & Row, Publishers, Inc., 1956.

Ford Foundation, *The New Teacher,* New York, 1962.

Frasier, George Willard, *An Introduction to the Study of Education,* New York, Harper & Row, Publishers, Inc., 1956.

Fromm, Erich, *May Man Prevail?* Garden City, N.Y., Doubleday & Company, Inc., 1961.

Fuess, Claude M., "The Retreat from Excellence," *Saturday Review,* March 26, 1960, pp. 21-23.

Fuess, Claude M., and Emory S. Basford (eds.), *Unseen Harvests,* New York, The Macmillan Company, 1947.

Fund for the Advancement of Education, *Decade of Experiment,* New York, The Fund, 1961.

Fusco, Gene C., "Technology in the Classroom: Challenges to the School Administrator," *School Life,* May, 1960, pp. 20-25, 30.

Gage, N. L. (ed.), *Handbook of Research on Teaching,* Chicago, Rand McNally & Company, 1963.

Galanter, Eugene (ed.), *Automatic Teaching,* New York, John Wiley & Sons, Inc., 1959.

Gans, Roma, *Common Sense in Teaching Reading,* Indianapolis, Bobbs-Merrill, 1963.

Gardner, John W., *Excellence,* New York, Harper & Row, Publishers, Inc., 1961.

Gardner, John W., *Self-Renewal,* New York, Harper & Row, Publishers, Inc., 1964.

Getzels, Jacob W., and Philip W. Jackson, *Creativity and Intelligence,* New York, John Wiley & Sons, Inc., 1962.

Ginzberg, Eli, *Human Resources: The Wealth of a Nation,* New York, Simon and Schuster, Inc., 1958.

Ginzberg, Eli, and Douglas W. Bray, *The Uneducated,* New York, Columbia University Press, 1953.

Goodlad, John I., and Robert H. Anderson, *The Nongraded Elementary School,* New York, Harcourt, Brace & World, Inc., 1963.

Green, Edward J., *The Learning Process and Programmed Instruction,* New York, Holt, Rinehart and Winston, Inc., 1962.

Gross, Martin L., *The Brain Watchers,* New York, Random House, Inc., 1962.

Gruber, Howard E., Glenn Terrell, and Michael Wertheimer (eds.), *Contemporary Approaches to Creative Thinking,* New York, Atherton Press, 1963.

Hand, Harold C., "Black Horses Eat More than White Horses," *AAUP Bulletin,* June, 1957, pp. 266–279.

Hansen, Carl F., *The Amidon Elementary School,* Englewood Cliffs, N.J., Prentice-Hall, Inc., 1962.

Hansen, Kenneth H., *Philosophy for American Education,* Englewood Cliffs, N.J., Prentice-Hall, Inc., 1960.

Hansen, Kenneth H., *Public Education in American Society,* Englewood Cliffs, N.J., Prentice-Hall, Inc., 1963.

Harrington, Michael, *The Other America,* New York, The Macmillan Company, 1962.

Hart, Joseph Kinmont, *Democracy in Education,* New York, Appleton-Century-Crofts, Inc., 1918.

Haskew, Laurence D., *This Is Teaching,* Chicago, Scott, Foresman and Company, 1956.

Hatch, Winslow R., and Ann Bennet, *Effectiveness in Teaching,* New Dimensions in Higher Education, no. 2, Washington, D.C., U.S. Department of Health, Education, and Welfare, 1960.

Hechinger, Fred M., *The Big Red Schoolhouse,* Garden City, N.Y., Doubleday & Company, Inc., 1962.

Henry, David D., *What Priority for Education?* Urbana, University of Illinois Press, 1961.

Hersey, John, *The Child Buyer,* New York, Alfred A. Knopf, Inc., 1960.

Hersey, John, *Why Do Students Bog Down on First R?* Washington, D.C., National School Public Relations Association, NEA, 1954.

Hill, Henry H., "Wanted: Professional Teachers," *The Atlantic,* May, 1960, pp. 37–40.

Hodenfield, G. K., and T. M. Stinnett, *The Education of Teachers,* Englewood Cliffs, N.J., Prentice-Hall, Inc., 1961.

Hoffman, Banesh, *The Tyranny of Testing,* New York, Crowell-Collier Publishing Co., 1962.

Hofstadter, Richard, and Wilson Smith (eds.), *American Higher Education,* University of Chicago Press, 1961.

Huggett, Albert J., and T. M. Stinnett, *Professional Problems of Teachers,* New York, The Macmillan Company, 1962.

Hutchins, Robert M., *Some Observations on American Education,* Cambridge University Press, 1956.

Huxley, Aldous, *Brave New World,* New York, Random House, Inc., 1932.

Huxley, Aldous, *Brave New World Revisited,* New York, Harper & Row, Publishers, Inc., 1958.

Huxley, Aldous, *Tomorrow and Tomorrow and Tomorrow,* New York, Harper & Row, Publishers, Inc., 1956.

Jefferson, Thomas, *Notes on the State of Virginia,* Philadelphia, H. C. Carey & I. Lea, 1825.

Jessup, John K., *et al., The National Purpose,* New York, Holt, Rinehart and Winston, Inc., 1960.

Keats, John, *Schools Without Scholars,* Boston, Houghton Mifflin Company, 1958.

Kelley, Earl C., *In Defense of Youth,* Englewood Cliffs, N.J., Prentice-Hall, Inc., 1962.

Kershaw, Joseph A., and Roland N. McKean, *Teacher Shortages and Salary Schedules,* New York, McGraw-Hill Book Company, Inc., 1962.

Kirk, Samuel A., and Bluma B. Weiner (eds.), *Behavioral Research on Exceptional Children,* Washington, D.C., The Council for Exceptional Children, 1963.

Knapp, R. H., and H. B. Goodrich, *Origins of American Scientists,* Middletown, Conn., The University of Chicago Press (for Wesleyan University), 1952.

Knapp, Robert H., and Joseph J. Greenbaum, *The Younger American Scholar,* Middletown, Conn., The University of Chicago Press and The Wesleyan University Press Incorporated, 1953.

Koerner, James D. (ed.), *The Case for Basic Education,* Boston, Little, Brown and Company, 1959.

Koerner, James D., *The Miseducation of American Teachers,* Boston, Houghton Mifflin Company, 1963.

Koury, Rose, *Elementary School Organization—What Direction Shall It Take?* Washington, D.C., Office of Education, 1960.

Krug, Edward A., *The Secondary School Curriculum,* New York, Harper & Row, Publishers, Inc., 1960.

Labels & Fingerprints, joint statement by American Association of School Administration, Association for Supervision and Curriculum Development, National Association of Secondary-School Principals, NEA Department of Elementary School Principals, and NEA Department of Rural Education, 1960.

Lichter, Solomon, Elsie Rapien, Frances Seibert, and Morris Sklansky, *The Drop-outs,* New York, The Free Press of Glencoe, 1962.

Lieberman, Myron, *Education as a Profession,* Englewood Cliffs, N.J., Prentice-Hall, Inc., 1956.

Lieberman, Myron, *The Future of Public Education,* The University of Chicago Press, 1960.

Liebman, Mary Bruhnke, "A Simple Answer to the School Problem," *Woman's Day,* October, 1959, pp. 33–35, 97–100.

Lindner, Robert, *Must You Conform?* New York, Holt, Rinehart and Winston, Inc., 1956.

Lindquist, Clarence B., *College and University Faculties,* Washington, D.C., U.S. Department of Health, Education and Welfare, 1959.

Lumsdaine, A. A., and Robert Glaser (eds.), *Teaching Machines and Programmed Learning,* Washington, D.C., NEA, 1960.

Lynd, Albert, *Quackery in the Public Schools,* Boston, Little, Brown and Company, 1950.

McClelland, David C., Alfred L. Baldwin, Urie Bronfenbrenner, and Fred L. Strodtbeck, *Talent and Society,* Princeton, N.J., D. Van Nostrand Company, Inc., 1958.

McCloskey, Gordon, *Education and Public Understanding,* New York, Harper & Row, Publishers, Inc., 1959.

McCloskey, Gordon, Zeno B. Katterle, and Delmar T. Oviatt, *Introduction to Teaching in American Schools,* New York, Harcourt, Brace & World, Inc., 1954.

McConnell, T. R., *A General Pattern for American Higher Education,* New York, McGraw-Hill Book Company, Inc., 1962.

McCracken, Glenn, *The Right to Learn,* Chicago, Henry Regnery Company, 1959.

Mallery, David, *High School Students Speak Out,* New York, Harper & Row, Publishers, Inc., 1962.

Manning, Duane, *The Qualitative Elementary School,* New York, Harper & Row, Publishers, Inc., 1963.

Maritain, Jacques, *Education at the Crossroads,* New Haven, Yale University Press, 1943.

Marshall, Robert A., *The Story of Our Schools*, Washington, The National Council for the Social Studies, 1962.

Marson, Philip, *The American Tragedy—Our Schools*, Cambridge, Berkshire Publishing Company, 1958.

Mathewson, Robert Hendry, *A Strategy for American Education*, New York, Harper & Row, Publishers, Inc., 1957.

Mayer, Martin, *The Schools*, New York, Harper & Row, Publishers, Inc., 1961.

Mayer, Martin, *Where, When and Why*, New York, Harper & Row, Publishers, Inc., 1963.

Millard, C. V., and Albert J. Huggett, *An Introduction to Elementary Education*, New York, McGraw-Hill Book Company, Inc., 1953.

Morrill, J. L., *et al.*, *The University and World Affairs*, New York, Ford Foundation, 1960.

Morris, VanCleve, *et al.*, *Becoming an Educator*, Boston, Houghton Mifflin, 1963.

Morse, Arthur D., *Schools of Tomorrow—Today*, Garden City, N.Y., Doubleday & Company, Inc., 1960.

Murphy, Gardner, *Human Potentialities*, New York, Basic Books, Inc., 1958.

National Association of Secondary-School Principals, *Junior High-School Development, Practices, and Research*, Washington, D.C., 1962.

National Association of Secondary-School Principals, *Locus of Change: Staff Utilization Studies*, Washington, D.C., 1962.

National Commission on Teacher Education and Professional Standards, *New Horizons For The Teaching Profession*, Washington, D.C., NEA, 1961.

National Council for the Social Studies and American Council of Learned Societies, *The Social Studies and the Social Sciences*, New York, Harcourt, Brace & World, Inc., 1962.

National Society for the Study of Education, *Social Forces Influencing American Education*, 60th Yearbook, pt. II, Chicago, 1961.

National Society for the Study of Education, *The Impact and Improvement of School Testing Programs*, 62nd Yearbook, pt. II, 1963.

NEA, Department of Classroom Teachers, Official Report, 1959–1960, Washington, D.C., 1960.

NEA, Research Division, *Communities with Ungraded Primary Programs*, Research Memo 1959-R7, Washington, D.C., 1959.

NEA, Research Division, *Rankings of the States, 1963*, Washington, D.C., 1963.

NEA, Research Division, *Teacher Supply and Demand in Public Schools,* Washington, D.C., 1963.

NEA, *Schools for the Sixties,* New York, McGraw-Hill Book Company, Inc., 1963.

NEA, *The Scholars Look at the Schools,* Washington, D.C., 1962.

NEA, *Will Your Child Get a Quality Education?* Washington, D.C., 1960.

Neill, A. S., *Summerhill,* New York, Hart Publishing Co., 1960.

Newson, Carroll, *A University President Speaks Out,* New York, Harper & Row, Publishers, Inc., 1962.

Packard, Vance, *The Hidden Persuaders,* New York, David McKay Company, Inc., 1957.

Packard, Vance, *The Status Seekers,* New York, David McKay Company, Inc., 1959.

Packard, Vance, *The Waste Makers,* New York, David McKay Company, Inc., 1960.

Passow, A. Harry (ed.), *Education in Depressed Areas,* New York, Teachers College, Columbia University, 1963.

President's Commission on National Goals, *Goals for Americans,* Englewood Cliffs, N.J., Prentice-Hall, Inc., 1960.

President's Committee on Education Beyond the High School, *Education Beyond the High School,* Government Printing Office, 1957.

Quattlebaum, Charles A., *Federal Educational Policies, Programs and Proposals,* pts. I, II, and III, Government Printing Office, 1960.

Ramsbusch, Nancy McCormick, *Learning How to Learn—An American Approach to Montessori,* Baltimore, Helicon Press, 1962.

Raywid, Mary Anne, *The Ax-Grinders,* New York, The Macmillan Company, 1962.

Read, Herbert, *Education through Art,* New York, Random House, Inc., 1945.

Reeder, Ward G., *A First Course in Education,* New York, The Macmillan Company, 1950.

Reinhardt, Emma, *American Education,* New York, Harper & Row, Publishers, Inc., 1954, 1960.

Rickover, H. G., *American Education—A National Failure,* New York, E. P. Dutton & Co., Inc., 1963.

Rickover, H. G., *Education and Freedom,* New York, E. P. Dutton & Co., Inc., 1959.

Rickover, H. G., *Swiss Schools and Ours*, Boston, Little, Brown and Company, 1962.

Riessman, Frank, *The Culturally Deprived Child*, New York, Harper & Row, Publishers, Inc., 1962.

Rinker, Floyd, *Council for a Television Course in the Humanities: Its Concept and Development*, Boston, 1960.

Rockefeller Brothers Fund, *The Pursuit of Excellence*, Garden City, N.Y., Doubleday & Company, Inc., 1958.

Roper, Elmo, and Associates, *Parents' College Plans Study*, 1959.

Russell, Bertrand, *Authority and the Individual*, New York, Simon and Schuster, Inc., 1949.

Sanford, Nevitt (ed.), *The American College*, New York, John Wiley & Sons, Inc., 1961.

Sarason, Seymour, Kenneth Davidson, and Burton Blatt, *The Preparation of Teachers*, New York, John Wiley & Sons, Inc., 1962.

Scott, C. Winfield, Clyde M. Hill, and Robert W. Burns (eds.), *The Great Debate: Our Schools in Crisis*, Englewood Cliffs, N.J., Prentice-Hall, Inc., 1959.

Shaplin, Judson T., and Olds, Henry F. Jr. (eds.), *Team Teaching*, Harper & Row, Publishers, Inc., 1963.

Shipley, Ferne, and Ethelouise Carpenter, *Freedom to Move*, Washington, D.C., Department of Elementary-Kindergarten-Nursery Education, NEA, 1962.

Silberman, Charles E., "The Remaking of American Education," *Fortune*, April, 1961.

Smiley, Marjorie B., and John S. Diekhoff, *Prologue to Teaching*, Fair Lawn, N.J., Oxford University Press, 1959.

Smith, Elmer R. (ed.), *Teacher Education*, New York, Harper & Row, Publishers, Inc., 1962.

Smith, Mortimer, *A Citizens Manual for Public Schools*, Washington, D.C., Council for Basic Education, 1959.

Smith, Mortimer, *And Madly Teach*, Chicago, Henry Regnery Company, 1949.

Smith, Mortimer (ed.), *The Public Schools in Crisis*, Chicago, Henry Regnery Company, 1956.

Snitzer, Herb, *A Loving World*, New York, The Macmillan Company, 1963.

Standing, E. M., *The Montessori Method: A Revolution in Education*, Fresno, Calif., Academy Library Guild, 1962.

Stern, Edgar, Family Fund, *Recognition of Excellence*, New York, The Free Press of Glencoe, 1960.

Stiles, Lindley J. (ed.), *The Teacher's Role in American Society*, New York, Harper & Row, Publishers, Inc., 1957.

Stinnett, T. M., and L. D. Haskew, *Teaching in American Schools*, New York, Harcourt, Brace & World, Inc., 1962.

Stocking, Fred H., "The Important Balance," *Harvard Graduate School of Education Association Bulletin*, Special Edition 1959, vol. IV, no. 3, pp. 10–16.

Stoddard, George D., *The Dual Progress Plan*, New York, Harper & Row, Publishers, Inc., 1961.

Tead, Ordway, *The Climate of Learning*, New York, Harper & Row, Publishers, Inc., 1958.

Terman, Lewis M. (ed.), *The Gifted Group at Mid-life*, Stanford, Calif., Stanford University Press, 1959.

Thayer, V. T., *The Role of the School in American Society*, New York, Dodd, Mead & Company, Inc., 1960.

Thelan, Herbert A., *Education and the Human Quest*, New York, Harper & Row, Publishers, Inc., 1960.

Thomas, Maurice J., *The Concern of All*, Pittsburgh, The Tri-State Area School Study Council, 1960.

Torrance, E. Paul, *Education and the Creative Potential*, St. Paul, University of Minnesota Press, 1963.

Torrance, E. Paul, *Guiding Creative Talent*, Englewood Cliffs, N. J., Prentice-Hall, Inc., 1962.

Trace, Arther S., Jr., *What Ivan Knows That Johnny Doesn't*, New York, Random House, Inc., 1961.

Trump, J. Lloyd, *Images of the Future*, Washington, D.C., The National Association of Secondary-School Principals, 1959.

Trump, J. Lloyd, *New Directions to Quality Education*, Washington, D.C., The National Association of Secondary-School Principals, 1960.

Trump, J. Lloyd, and Dorsey Baynham, *Focus on Change—Guide to Better Schools*, Chicago, Rand McNally & Company, 1961.

U.S. Department of Health, Education, and Welfare, *College and University Faculties: Recent Personnel and Instructional Practices*, Bulletin 1959, no. 27, Washington, D.C., Office of Education, 1959.

U.S. Department of Health, Education, and Welfare, *Programs '63*, Washington, D.C., Office of Education, 1963.

U.S. Department of Health, Education, and Welfare, *Progress of Public*

Education in the United States of America, 1959-60, Washington, D.C., Office of Education, 1960.

U.S. Department of Health, Education, and Welfare, *Soviet Commitment to Education,* Bulletin 1959, no. 16, Washington, D.C., Office of Education, 1959.

U.S. Department of Health, Education, and Welfare, *Teaching as a Career,* Washington, D.C., Office of Education, 1959.

U.S. Department of Health, Education, and Welfare, *Teaching Opportunities,* Washington, D.C., Office of Education. (See current or latest edition available.)

U.S. Department of Health, Education, and Welfare, *The Needs of Education for Television Channel Allocations,* Washington, D.C., Office of Education, 1962.

U.S. Department of Health, Education, and Welfare, *What High School Pupils Study,* Washington, D.C., Office of Education, 1962.

U.S. Department of Labor, *Manpower, Challenge of the 1960's,* Washington, D.C., Government Printing Office, 1960.

U.S. Department of Labor, *State Child-Labor Standards,* Bulletin 158, Washington, D.C., Bureau of Labor Standards, Department of Labor, 1960.

Walcutt, Charles C. (ed.), *Tomorrow's Illiterates,* Boston, Little, Brown and Company, 1961.

Warner, W. Lloyd, Robert J. Havighurst, and Martin B. Loeb, *Who Shall Be Educated?* New York, Harper & Row, Publishers, Inc., 1944.

White House Conference on Children and Youth, *Children in a Changing World,* Washington, D.C., 1960.

White House Conference on Children and Youth, *Conference Proceedings,* Washington, D.C., 1960.

Whyte, William, *The Organization Man,* New York, Simon and Schuster, Inc., 1956.

Williams, George, *Some of My Best Friends Are Professors,* New York, Abelard-Schuman, Limited, 1958.

Williams, Roger J., *Biochemical Individuality,* New York, John Wiley & Sons, Inc., 1956.

Williams, Roger J., *Free and Unequal,* Austin, University of Texas Press, 1953.

Willing, M. H., *et al., Schools and Our Democratic Society,* New York, Harper & Row, Publishers, Inc., 1951.

Wilson, James W., and Edward H. Lyons, *Work-Study College Programs,* New York, Harper & Row, Publishers, Inc., 1961.

Wolfle, Dael, *America's Resources of Specialized Talent*, New York, Harper & Row, Publishers, Inc., 1954.

Woodring, Paul, *A Fourth of a Nation*, New York, McGraw-Hill Book Company, Inc., 1957.

Woodring, Paul, *Let's Talk Sense About Our Schools*, New York, McGraw-Hill Book Company, Inc., 1953.

Woodring, Paul, *New Directions in Teacher Education*, New York, The Fund for the Advancement of Education, 1957.

Woodring, Paul, and John Scanlon (eds.), *American Education Today*, New York, McGraw-Hill Book Company, Inc., 1963.

Woods, Margaret S., *Thinking, Feeling, Experiencing: Toward Realization of Full Potential*, Washington, D.C., NEA, 1962.

Also, selected articles, features, and data from the following publications:

AAUP Bulletin, American Association of University Professors.

CBE Bulletin, Council for Basic Education.

Children, U.S. Department of Health, Education, and Welfare.

College and University Bulletin, Association for Higher Education, NEA.

Education Digest.

Educational Leadership, Association for Supervision and Curriculum Development.

Exceptional Children, Council for Exceptional Children.

Health, Education, and Welfare Indicators, U.S. Department of Health, Education, and Welfare.

Higher Education, U.S. Department of Health, Education, and Welfare.

Higher Education and National Affairs, American Council on Education.

NEA Journal.

New York Times, The, Sunday, education feature page.

Phi Delta Kappan, Phi Delta Kappa.

Research Relating to Children, U.S. Department of Health, Education, and Welfare.

Saturday Review, monthly education supplement.

School Life, U.S. Department of Health, Education, and Welfare.

Index